HEGEL AND CANADA

Unity of Opposites?

Hegel and Canada

Unity of Opposites?

EDITED BY SUSAN M. DODD AND
NEIL G. ROBERTSON

UNIVERSITY OF TORONTO PRESS
Toronto Buffalo London

Toronto Buffalo London
www.utorontopress.com

ISBN 978-1-4426-4447-2

Library and Archives Canada Cataloguing in Publication

Hegel and Canada : unity of opposites? / edited by Susan M. Dodd and Neil G. Robertson.

Includes bibliographical references and index.
ISBN 978-1-4426-4447-2 (cloth)

1. Hegel, Georg Wilhelm Friedrich, 1770–1831 – Influence. 2. Philosophy, Canadian – History – 20th century. 3. Political science – Canada – Philosophy – History – 20th century. 4. Canada – Intellectual life – 20th century. I. Dodd, Susan, 1966–, editor II. Robertson, Neil G., author, editor

B981.H44 2018 191 C2017-900086-1

This book has been published with the help of a grant from the Federation for the Humanities and Social Sciences, through the Awards to Scholarly Publications Program, using funds provided by the Social Sciences and Humanities Research Council of Canada.

University of Toronto Press acknowledges the financial assistance to its publishing program of the Canada Council for the Arts and the Ontario Arts Council, an agency of the Government of Ontario.

Funded by the Government of Canada
Financé par le gouvernement du Canada

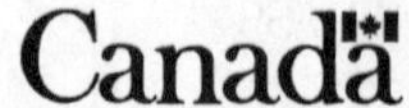

In memory of Professor Angus Johnston, the very spirit of the Foundation Year Programme, and to all our teachers and students on this, FYP's forty-fifth anniversary.

"… its own time raised to the level of thought."

Hegel, *The Philosophy of Right*

Contents

Acknowledgments

Thank you to:

Len Husband and the manuscript appraisers from the University of Toronto Press.

John Hartman for his permission to use "The Narrows" as our cover art.

The Owl of Minerva, especially Ardis Collins, for permission to reprint articles by George di Giovanni and John Burbidge.

Charles Taylor and the Cambridge University Press for permission to reprint "Hegel's Philosophy of Mind."

Our remarkable student assistants through the University of King's College Student Assistant Programme: Torin Vigerstad, Aaron Shenkman, Rachel Glickman Klein, Nick Stark, Eleanor Hornbeck, and Rachel O'Brien.

Patricia Robertson and Henry Roper for careful critical readings and discussions.

Angus Johnston for constant discussion, criticism, and insight.

HEGEL AND CANADA

Unity of Opposites?

1 Introduction: Unity of Opposites? Hegel and Canada

SUSAN M. DODD[1]

Why a book about Canada's relation to G.W.F. Hegel – the maddeningly difficult and controversial nineteenth-century German philosopher? Firstly, Hegel has been a striking presence in Canadian political philosophy especially since the Second World War,[2] as is evident in the works of James Doull (Dalhousie), Emil Fackenheim (University of Toronto), George Grant (Dalhousie and McMaster), Henry S. Harris (York), and Charles Taylor (McGill). Writing and teaching in Canadian universities, these philosophers won international respect for their careful and passionate interpretations of Hegel's work.[3] Secondly, the debates among these thinkers and their students about Hegel's vision of modern freedom – especially the mutual interdependency of individual and collective goods – expressed the philosophical aspect of Canada's nation-building ethos in the second half of the twentieth century. Finally, in a critical return to these post-war debates, scholars from philosophy, political science, and sociology ask, Does Hegel offer anything to Canada *today*? Can Hegel help us to affirm Canada as a self-conscious, historically aware, self-governing nation in a rapidly changing global scene? More particularly, in this time of uncertainty about the viability and legitimacy of a single Canadian nation, as such, can Hegel help us to rethink nationhood, to face our colonial inheritances (the positive and the negative), and to affirm our distinction from our gargantuan, fractured neighbour to the south?

The post-war Hegelians and the authors included in this collection agree that Hegel has much to offer us, though they disagree about what that offer entails. Despite their deep differences, Doull, Fackenheim, Grant, Harris, and Taylor each argued for community-based politics as a counter to the liberal-capitalism of the postcolonial, globalizing world.

For Hegel-influenced political philosophers, achieving modern freedom is not a matter of tweaking current socio-political forms. Modern freedom requires a thorough revision of politics that begins by unveiling ancient goods that are already at work in existing practices and their attendant modes of selfhood. The goal of political philosophy as Hegel and his Canadian interpreters see it is thus to reconcile modern self-governance with ancient forms of community in self-conscious institutions.

This introduction begins with a consideration of recent shifts in what we might call Canada's self-image, starting with the nation-building ethos of the post-war era, and opening into a new self-questioning, exemplified in the 2015 Truth and Reconciliation Commission report on the residential schools for Aboriginal children. With this shifting self-image in mind, I review Hegel's political philosophy. Then, I explore how Doull, Fackenheim, Grant, Harris, and Taylor each presents a distinctive argument about the post-war prospects for a politics that, being grounded in communities, opposes the homogenizing forces of global liberal capitalism while affirming modern aspirations to rational freedom. My approach to introducing these five diverse thinkers and their relations to one another is to recall their reflections on whether even Hegel could hold to Hegelian political philosophy in view of the technocratic condition of Western culture, revealed in its murderous fullness in the "great" nationalistic wars of the twentieth century, and especially the Holocaust. The post-war Hegelians differ on this, and their reflections on the question of whether Hegel could be Hegelian today offers us a way of drawing out their various positions before we turn to consider the ways contemporary Canadian scholars envision Hegel's relevance for current political perplexities.

Canada: From Nation-Building to Nation-Questioning

Between the nation-building confidence of the 1950s and today's nation-questioning stance, as exemplified in the report of Canada's Truth and Reconciliation Commission (2015), Canada's self-understanding shifted dramatically. Reviewing these shifts will prepare us for the generational differences between the ways Hegel spoke to the post-war generation and the ways he might speak to us today. At root is the question of how we characterize the contemporary world: selves, communities, our political situation, their ailments, and emerging possibilities.

Nation-Building

Immediately following the wars, Canada set off on a path away from British colonial control with Lester Pearson's diplomatic work during the 1956 Suez Crisis, for which he received the Nobel Peace Prize. Pearson positioned Canada internationally as a "moderate, mediatory, middle power"[4] that held international influence far surpassing its military and economic force. As globalization intensified, many feared that Canada was being reduced to a mere "branch-plant" of corporate America. Canadians responded with what now appears to us as a remarkable period of nation-building: *public Canada* took institutional form in public health care, public broadcasting, public universities, and public pensions. Meanwhile, Canadians puzzled over whether a national identity could reconcile the "two solitudes" of the "founding nations" of English Canada and Quebec. Canadian national identity was a puzzle for theorists, writers, and artists, and government responded with the notorious "Canadian content" regulations and other policies to nurture a distinct and somewhat unified national culture amid the U.S. mass market. The question of Canadian identity was posed expressly in a decades-long debate over Quebec sovereignty/separation that ended with a minuscule win for those who argued to keep Quebec within Canada in the 1995 Quebec referendum.

All of this took place in the context of debates over what kind of constitution was appropriate for Canada. The British North America Act, with precedents set in English courts, was stale; Canada was no longer the federation envisioned by the self-proclaimed "Hegelian" jurist and "wicked stepfather" of Canada's constitution, the Viscount Haldane in the early post–First World War years.[5] Haldane's controversial rulings gave Canadian federalism its distinctive shape by restricting the powers the federal government could exercise over provincial matters in the name of "peace, order, and good government." In 1982, after decades of debate, the country "repatriated" its constitution from England, and Canada became a self-created nation with a rational, liberal, constitution of its own making.

The confidence of Canadian institutions in the post-war decades – in themselves and in the unifying power of the Canadian nation – may be exemplified in the Canadian Anglican Church's commissioning Pierre Berton, a diehard Canadian nationalist and a liberal, progressive popular historian, to write a review of the state of the church in society in 1963.[6] Berton's *Comfortable Pew* called out the church establishment for turning their religion into a "sugar-coated pill" that appeased the middle class by making a soporific of the gospel's call to charity. For Berton, the betrayal in making worship comfortable was that it offended liberal demands for a generic culture; what other objection could a liberal moralist like Berton raise? Berton called upon the church to abandon traditional modes of worship, to adopt modern communications techniques, and to update its symbols (specifically, to replace the cross with more relevant imagery).[7]

Emil Fackenheim – the Hegel scholar and conservative rabbi – responded to Berton's call for the church to secularize with a reminder that secularity itself was the outcome of the Judeo-Christian culture, and he marvelled that the church had exposed itself to Berton's ahistorical, secular judgment in the first place. By hiring Berton, the Anglican Church opened itself to the liberal ideology of the age, and so – ironically – entertained the possibility that to be true to its mission it should overcome its particular tradition in the name of a secular or at least radically multi-faith approach. In his landmark *The Religious Dimension in Hegel's Thought* (1967), Fackenheim identified the same irony in Hegel; for Fackenheim, Hegel's Protestantism, rationalized in modernity, demanded a radical religious pluralism that entailed cutting itself off from the historical and cultural roots that grounded and nourished it. The question of the best path to forms of life more adequate to human flourishing than the dominant liberal capitalism remains one of the most urgent debates among Hegel-influenced political thinkers, as many chapters in this collection show.

The confident Canadian nation-building of the 1950s and 1960s carried on into the 1970s, when the sexual revolution and language debates[8] gave way to the multiculturalism, religious pluralism, neoconservatism, and postcolonialism of the 1980s and 1990s. This in turn ushered in the heightened attentiveness to race, class, gender, sexual orientation, and increasingly diagnosed mental illness of the 2000s. Victims gained symbolic importance, and calls for the judiciary to protect victims' rights placed new pressures on the "presumption of innocence" of the accused, and on the corresponding burden of proof for admissible evidence in criminal trials. The social-democratic presuppositions of welfare state supports were challenged by utilitarian and free-market approaches – especially during the decade of neoconservative Conservative Party rule (2006–15) when, for many, the economy came to stand for the nation itself. At the same time, "social conservatives" became radicalized and hoped to use national policies to reinforce what they claimed were "traditional" Euro-Christian values. Across the political spectrum, campaigning parties addressed the public more and more as economic family units, motivated almost exclusively by "pocketbook issues" and fear for personal, household security. For Hegel, particular self-interest and fear is anti-political until it has been transformed by participation in deliberating over collective goods within institutional life. Intensified reduction of political debate to pocketbook issues contributed to breaking "public" Canada into ever-smaller neighbourhoods of self-interests. Increasingly, activists organized sporadically in projects, such as Idle No More, Occupy, and the outpouring of support for Syrian refugees. Lacking institutional stability, these shaped public discussion for a time and then seemed to disappear. That said, the full effects of such movements remain to be seen. One possibility is that they, along with intensifying concerns about climate change and sustainability, are the new focal questions in an era of Canadian nation-questioning.[9]

Nation-Questioning

"There is nothing about being Canadian that we can be proud of," a student declared recently in one of my classes. During the passionate discussion that ensued, the students agreed that our colonial history, capitalistic destruction of the natural environment, and military involvement in the Middle East implicates Canada in a world-wide crisis. The students felt both guilty and threatened by widening income gaps, religious extremism, intolerance of diversity, and forms of technology that were corrosive to natural and human flourishing. For the students, Canada's validity as a nation was in doubt, and this doubt was exemplified in the shame of cultural domination detailed in the report of Canada's Truth and Reconciliation Commission. Between 1883 and 1980, the Canadian government conducted an assimilation program that processed at least 150,000 First Nations, Metis, and Inuit children. The five-year Truth and Reconciliation Commission was conducted by the Canadian government as one of the terms of a legal settlement with Aboriginal victims. The commission reports that the church-run residential schools were "created for the purpose of separating Aboriginal children from their families in order to minimize and weaken family ties and cultural linkages, and to indoctrinate children into a new culture – a culture of the legally dominant Euro-Christian Canadian society, led by Canada's first prime minister, Sir John A. Macdonald."[10]

This removal of Aboriginal children from their homes and culture, first into church-run residential schools, and later into secular institutions and adoptions by non-Aboriginal families, was an attempted "cultural genocide" by the Canadian state.[11] In this, the report retells Canadian national history, this time from the view of victims. What began under Prime Minister Macdonald as a program to coerce/convert Aboriginal children into the dominant Christian culture became, at its height in the 1950s to 1970s, a program to assimilate Aboriginal peoples into liberal capitalism.[12] In the secularizing spirit of the early post-war decades, assimilation was thought to liberate the Aboriginal people into an emerging rational culture of self-making individuals.[13]

Detailing Canada's efforts to impose colonist, Eurocentric, "Christian" culture by extinguishing Aboriginal "savage" culture, the Truth and Reconciliation Commission articulates a new moment in Canada's cultural history: the privileged subject position here is that of excluded, marginalized people. This corrective against the millennia-long privileging of the European male perspective rejects any validity in the formerly authoritative stance and is deeply sceptical about claims that any aspect of the "cultural genocide" was the unintended consequence of good intention.[14]

We begin this collection with a reminder of this challenge to heroic Canadian nationalist myths, in part in response to the urgent attention of our students, but also because it is a meeting place between the current spirit of nation-questioning and the post-war generation of Hegel scholars who had sought a thorough overturning of twentieth-century liberal capitalism, rather than the moderations provided by welfare state policies. It offers also an opportunity to begin to dispel some prejudices about the Hegelian insistence that for freedom to become actualized it must take concrete form in institutions. The 2015 Truth and Reconciliation report condemns the perpetrators of the attempted cultural genocide because they sought to deprive Aboriginal peoples of their traditions and embodied cultural practices, that is, of what Hegel calls "ethical life" (*Sittlichkeit*). The report argues that vibrant community life is integral to freedom; each stands or falls with the other. Furthermore, the Truth and Reconciliation Commission sees the practice of writing history as essential to our capacity to turn from the violence of the past to any hope for the future; as the subtitle to the report puts it, "Honouring the Truth, Reconciling for the Future." The report uses terms that Hegel uses in roughly related ways when it argues that Canada must bring the diverse cultures into relation with one another, in *recognition*, *reconciliation*, and *mutual respect*.[15]

The report's account of the brutality of the attempted cultural genocide is so convincing that it reminds us to be wary of our current cultural confidences. As we read, we can only marvel at the historical blindness of those times and ask, were *all of* the policy's designers intentionally genocidal? Is there any credence whatsoever in the claim of the express goal of the programs, and that is to include Aboriginal peoples in the general community, in keeping with the liberal goal of "liberating" everyone, including religious adherents of European descent, from tradition, superstition, and the weight of history? Why is the violence of those mid-twentieth-century social reforms *so* obvious to us now? The answers to these questions are far too complex for this introduction, but they pose precisely the same questions as those raised by Hegel: how can we become self-conscious about the cultural presuppositions that guide our daily lives, and how do we reconcile our needs for freedom with our situation in a community that precedes us and is not entirely subject to our control?

As understood in the post-war period, Hegel offered a model of the modern state where the individual was reconciled to institutional constraints because he or she was part of that body. Some contemporary thinkers are much more suspicious of Hegel's vision of reconciling diverse individuals in a stable, self-conscious corporate body, as we will see.

Hegel's Political Thought[16]

Hegel's account of modern freedom depends on his claim that when we engage in the decision-making of collective life our wills are transformed. In all of Hegel's work, but most widely read in *The Phenomenology of Spirit* and *The Philosophy of Right,* freedom is the telos – the end, purpose, and goal – of human life. Freedom is accomplished fully only once humanity knows itself as historical, and its institutions as rational, i.e., created and sustained by humans who know themselves to be free in the practice of politics. It is only when we raise our minds to goods that exceed but also ground our self-interests, that is, when we think beyond our pocketbooks and personal fears, to the good of an organization, that we become capable of self-government.

Freedom reaches a kind of maturity in the modern state because modernity fosters both community and self-government and recognizes them as interdependent cultural achievements. The partial freedoms that Hegel sees as realized in various "earlier" stages of history contribute to the historical development of humanity's understanding of itself and the diverse needs of each person. For example, in the ancient Greek polis some segments of the population were free, but only at the expense of a class of slaves. The modern state is possible only as the result – and recollection – of a long history of cycles of alienation, conflict, and reconciliation.

Freedom and the Will

For Hegel, freedom is a condition and activity of the human will. The desire for universal freedom is inherent in human nature and appears in history as the dissatisfactions and ambitions that drive people to develop new kinds of politics (sometimes by revolution, but also by incremental modifications of given practices). Hence, autonomy is not "natural" as presupposed by contract theorists like Hobbes and liberals like Mill, it is not "rational" in the sense presupposed by formal ethicists like Kant, and it is not a God-given "right" as presupposed by French and American revolutionaries.[17] Neither is community "natural" as it is in the "veritable youth of the world" stage of Rousseau's hypothetical human history in the *Discourse on the Origin of Inequality*, or "rational" as in contract theory, or even in avowed responsibilities as in medieval institutions (i.e., feudal estates, monasteries, guilds). Hegel says, "The basis of right is, in general, mind [*Geist*]; its precise place and point of origin in the will. The will is free, so that freedom is both the substance of right and its goal, while the system of right is the realm of freedom made actual, the world of mind bought forth out of itself like a second nature."[18] The "second nature" of life in the modern state is not simply an addition to a collection of individual people; the practice of freedom in the state transforms the will: in subjecting the particular will to rational law, the modern citizen becomes free.

To actualize free will in all its aspects, the modern state fosters and expresses three "spheres" of human activity: the family, civil society, and the government (in Hegel's terms, the "state proper"). It is crucial to Hegel's account of freedom that we understand the citizen to be *always already situated* in collective life. The most fundamental form of this is the family: no one is born an independent, autonomous being.[19] In Hegel's civil society, citizens are free as producers and competitors within a regulatory structure (what Hegel calls the "external state").[20] In the work of government, men transform their particular wills by participating in universal reason as they make the very laws that govern them (through participating in the constitutional order). Individual and collective freedoms are interdependent: "The state is the actuality of concrete freedom. But concrete freedom consists in this, that personal individuality and its particular interests not only achieve their complete development and gain explicit recognition for their right (as they do in the sphere of the family and civil society) but, for one thing, they also pass over of their own accord into the interest of the universal, and, for another thing, they know and will the universal; they even recognize it as their own substantive mind; they take it as their end and aim and are active in its pursuit."[21] Freedom is made concrete by the individual's situation within family and civil society, and also in the individual's participating in decision-making, that is, in knowing and willing the universal.

The "second nature" of Hegel's freedom is expressed in the practical judgment each person exercizes in his or her participation in the institutions that make up the state. Hegel's answer to the age-old problem, inherited from Plato's *Republic*, of how to determine the proper place of any individual within a society of differentiated activities is a kind of practical education. It is only when individuals engage in the decision-making of an intermediary institution[22] that they overcome the "abstraction" of sheer membership in the state by filling their judgment with the "determinacy" of the particular; "the single person attains his actual and living destiny for universality only when he becomes a member of a Corporation, a society, etc."[23] Community is essential to individuality and freedom.

Community and Conscience

According to Hegel, the modern state overcomes the opposition of community and conscience that has recurred in various forms over the course of human history. From Socrates's decision to accept death from Athens, through Hellenistic forms of seeking *ataraxia*, the individual finds a kind of freedom from external contingency by retreating to the inner citadel of the self, or fleeing towards an utterly transcendent Good/One. This private conscience is then literally externalized in the Christian Middle Ages; that is, conscience is placed in sacred objects, rituals, and priestly authority. That externality is overcome in a personal mysticism, in the direct heart-to-heart relationship between the individual and Christ of the Protestant Reformation. Ultimately, conscience finds its most rational, Enlightenment expression in the categorical imperative that Immanuel Kant declares to be: "Act in such a way that you treat humanity, whether in your own person or in the person of another, always at the same time as an end and never simply as a means."[24] This sketch of a very complicated historical development is intended to remind readers that Hegel's famous criticism of Kant's "empty formalism" by no means rejects the rational content of moral law, but instead shifts it into the rational knowledge of the ethical standards already at work in embodied community life. Hegel sees the modern state as recovering, in rational form, the positive contents of ancient public debate and integrated community, united now with true self-consciousness.

For Hegel, freedom in community is humankind's destiny, the home for which we have been striving from the moment that consciousness broke from intuitive immersion in nature: "For it is the nature of humanity to press onward to agreement with others; human nature only really exists in an achieved community of minds. The anti-human, the merely animal, consists in staying within the sphere of feeling and being able to communicate only at that level."[25] The "free" atomistic individual of classical liberalism is a dangerous fiction, "empty self-activity" as Hegel says of the abstract agent of Kant's categorical imperative.[26] It is empty because it bases action on context-free principles, and it is self-activity because it does not reach beyond itself (beyond phenomena as held in Kant's unity of apperception) to concrete otherness (noumena). In the modern state, the situation of the citizen in family, competition in the civil society, and participation in political life gives content to the principled judgment of each individual.

Recognition

The modern state is the stable actualization of the relations of mutual recognition that Hegel sees as the intersubjective ground of self-consciousness. Hegel famously details the interdependency of self-consciousnesses in the "Master/Slave" (or "Lordship and Bondage") section of *The Phenomenology of Spirit*. This is "the process of Recognition" where Hegel shows that "self-consciousness exists in and for itself when, and by the fact that, it so exists for another; that is, it exists only in being acknowledged."[27] The dialectic begins with two less-than-self-conscious beings, each struggling to express its particular will in the world. (Hegel translators use the pronoun *it*, which conveys the proto-human character of the agent from whom the self-conscious self emerges.) The conflict is a struggle to the death. "And it is only through staking one's life that freedom is won,"[28] Hegel says. The victor's triumph is empty, however, because in killing the other, the victor is left alone, with no one to offer acknowledgment. Eventually, one combatant submits to slavery, choosing a life of bondage over death.[29] Ironically, the time of slavery gradually inverts the master–slave relationship because slaves cultivate their relationship with nature through the work of transforming matter into useful objects. At the same time, slaves expand their capacity for thinking because, in anticipating their master's desires, they think through another, from another perspective.[30] The slaves' expanded empathetic capacity becomes a "desire for desire" – aiming to please, they want to be desired by the other.[31]

While slaves learn discipline and expand their thinking through their service, the masters lose touch with nature, themselves, and others. A crucial aspect of self-retrieval for slaves is their realization that the other for whom they have been performing is their own projection. They thought they were oppressed and judged by the standards of an alien force, but in fact, they provided the content for that judgment. Hegel says, "Self-consciousness is faced by another self-consciousness; it has come out of itself. This has a twofold significance: first, it has lost itself, for it finds itself as an other being; secondly, in doing so it has superseded the other, for it does not see the other as an essential being, but in the other sees its own self."[32] This dialectic is taken up and transformed by Marx, Kojève, de Beauvoir, Fanon, and every major revolutionary thinker after Hegel. While subordinated, the self is a kind of object – in itself but not yet for itself. Overcoming the separation between appearance and essence is a first step on the path to becoming self-governing participants in a common world.

Philosophical History

When Hegel declares, "The owl of Minerva spreads its wings only with the falling of the dusk,"[33] he cautions against philosophical didacticism that aims to "give instruction as to what the world ought to be."[34] Teaching us to be who we are and how that is appropriate to our time is "history's inescapable lesson."[35] It is only with the passing of time that we can understand ourselves. To know, or even to be able to clearly see the logic that underlies a particular cultural moment, so as to become self-conscious and rational in the practices of our ethical life we need a "science" of human history. Hegel's science is the bringing to consciousness of the grounds of our presuppositions and ways of knowing. In *The Philosophy of Right*, this is the science of "right," i.e., the human will as actualized in the free activity of the modern state.

According to Hegel, the affirmations, negations, and developments of human collective life can be discerned by modern philosophers who discover in them an analogy between the structure of all being and the unfolding of history.[36] In *Geist* (translated variously as "Spirit" or "Mind"), transcendent principle and immanent particulars are reconciled not (or not only) religiously through Christ's life, death, and resurrection, but in the patterns of history.[37] Human history, then, *is* the Incarnation, and thus it is the creator's reconciliation with an originally alienated creation, and we, God's only rational creatures, realize the creator's full reunion with this world only once philosophy sees and affirms every glorious – and bloody – turn of history as a necessary moment of progress.[38]

In the *Philosophy of Right*, Hegel says, "To comprehend what is, this is the task of philosophy, because what is, is reason. Whatever happens, every individual is a child of his time; so philosophy too is its own time apprehended in thoughts."[39] Some see this as theodicy – a justification of the ways of the Judeo-Christian God to humankind – through the dialectic of history. Others see it as a progressive, secularizing enlightenment, and so a kind of theodicy of the God of Reason.

Either way, the modern state is not simply a mechanism that coordinates the particular interests of an aggregation of autonomous atomic individuals. Instead, the modern state is a body of interrelated institutions within which divers particular/individual aspects of people's wills are universalized and concretely integrated.[40] In this, the modern state reconciles conflicts between the particular, practices of ethical life and the abstract principles of reason. The performance of duty within the state, even when a citizen experiences this as an imposition of an "external" limitation or demand, is, in fact, a protection of the particular individual and "the satisfaction of the depths of his being, the consciousness and feeling of himself as a member of the whole."[41] The modern state combines private spheres of personal intimacy with public spaces of competition and appearance so that the human exchange of recognition is provided stable institutional form.

Hegel Today?

Does Hegel offer anything to Canada today? Could even Hegel hope for a "philosophical science" that brings to light the logic at work in who we are already, as "Canadians," and so brings our ethical life into rationally affirmed self-consciousness? At stake in this question is the possibility of freedom itself, because for Hegel, the will is transformed in the modern state by rational decision-making aimed at self-interest in and through the actualization of collective good. Hegel's salience for Canadian politics depends on whether reconciliation between community and rational self-government is even desirable, let alone possible.

If reconciliation is desirable and possible, how might it be realized? If it is not, what then?

Emil Fackenheim (1916–2003)[42]

In his landmark study, *The Religious Dimension in Hegel's Thought* (1967), Fackenheim started the argument about whether even Hegel could hold to his nineteenth-century political vision. Fackenheim claimed that had Hegel lived to see the Holocaust he would have had to acknowledge that the fundaments of his philosophical history were broken, especially the aspiration to reconcile divers wills in a community of free people through the modern rational state.[43] For Fackenheim, the Holocaust manifests an irrevocable collapse of the possibility of mediation, in human history, of transcendent meaning and immanent experience – what Fackenheim calls the "Hegelian middle" – that is essential to Hegel's project. For Fackenheim, the Holocaust marks a change in the very duty of Jews; as Fackenheim puts it in his "614th Commandment," Jews must not permit Hitler any posthumous victories, and that is to say, their imperative is to survive and to remember qua Jews.[44]

The problem of modernity then is not only that Hegel's progressive model of history is broken by the horror of Auschwitz – Hegel had seen the revolutionary Terror in France, after all – but also that the kind of evil at work at Auschwitz is new; it is a technocratic modernity that expresses itself in purposeless mastery, negation for its own sake. Instead of the disordered love of the Platonic-Augustinian tradition, the extermination camps expressed a positive enthusiasm for evil (to use Schelling's phrase). Thus, the demonic personal evil of the Nazis was an "evil which had become the universal, the 'rational,' the 'laws,' the 'determinations of spirit,' and when the second world war ended, Hegel's 'true modern state' was all-but-replaced by quite another state – the Nazi murder camp."[45] Hegel *could* not be a Hegelian now, because, as Fackenheim sees it, the Nazi program to exterminate the Jews is a negation without a dialectical counter, and as such, it defies mediation.[46] There can be no reconciliation of differences, and therefore the human world is irredeemably fragmented.

In *The Religious Dimension in Hegel's Thought,* Fackenheim identifies Hegel's existentialist and Marxist followers as immanentist, and his conservative, religious, traditionalist followers as transcendent-metaphysical. He calls the purported unification of transcendence and immanence "the Hegelian middle" and sees it as the now-cracked heart of Hegel's ontology: "Hegel's thought dwells in the middle between these extremes, and how it can dwell there is its innermost secret."[47] Not only do one-sided accounts misread Hegel, they mask what Fackenheim sees as a fundamental problem internal to Hegel's system: the reconciliation between the transcendent and the immanent depends on Christianity and Hegel's reading of the Incarnation as a working out of the problem of mediation through human history. The mysterious Hegelian "middle" is precisely the "religious dimension" of Fackenheim's title.

Hegel's "science of the experience of consciousness" in *The Phenomenology of Spirit* claims to "introduce" us to philosophical history; that is, it is the first moment of critical self-awareness, analogous to the violent moment in Plato's *Republic* when the ignorant cave dweller is wrenched from fascination with the fleeting images on the cave wall. Hegel's claim is that true self-knowledge always already contains this critical beginning. According to Fackenheim, Hegel's phenomenology does not eliminate the need for the philosopher king to educate us into self-knowledge; it rather displaces this need. Hegel *achieves* the standpoint of absolute knowledge – through modern bourgeois Protestantism – before he can hand us the ladder that mediates the transcendent and immanent.[48] For Fackenheim, such a reconciliation in human history cannot be thought: the God of Abraham must remain transcendent, self-making, and known through generosity, that is, by revelation.

When Fackenheim claims that if Hegel had lived to see the twentieth century, Hegel himself "would not be a Hegelian," Fackenheim might have said that Hegel *could not* be a Hegelian today. In Fackenheim's view, to enter into Hegel's "rationality" is to accept a secularized version of modern Protestant Christianity that is built into the system's supposed universality.[49] The unity of opposites that Hegel wanted his philosophy to demonstrate as active in modern freedom is a fundamentally Christian mediation: "What, we might ask, would happen to the unity of the Hegelian system, if its religious-existential basis is not one of absolute religion but rather a radical and unsurmountable religious plurality?"[50] Fackenheim concludes that Hegel's system demands a religious pluralism that makes impossible the unity of that very system.[51]

Fackenheim left Canada for Israel in 1967, the same year he published both *The Religious Dimension in Hegel's Thought* and a collection of essays on theology, the need for a Jewish state in Israel, and the relations between Christianity and secular liberalism (including his response to Pierre Berton's liberal advice to the Anglican Church).

James Doull (1918–2001)[52]

James Doull disagrees with Fackenheim's claims that Hegel could not be Hegelian today and that Hegel's philosophy is rendered unsustainable in the face of the reduction of bourgeois Protestantism to "sugar-coated pills" for the comfort of the bourgeoisie.[53] For Doull, Hegel's system is adequate to the oppositions of the technological age, even as expressed in the Nazi death camps and the Manhattan Project / bombing of Hiroshima and Nagasaki. Doull writes that the Nazi state "sought to unite interest again through the natural solidarity of the 'Volk.' In the Nazi state abstract democratic freedom and 'race' coalesced and in this unity set themselves against liberal democracy and communism alike. There was no primary reduction of national sentiment to universal humanity such as was present alike in the traditional state and in Hegel's ideal."[54] That evil was retrograde rather than unprecedented; Europe "had fallen back to forms of thought long superseded."[55] In particular, the Nazis perverted the lesson that Hegel takes from Rousseau, that the true will is rationally subjected to laws of its own making. In unifying particular wills under the false "universality" of the will of the führer, Nazis sought an intuitive, natural unity, whereas the modern age demands a "primary reduction of national sentiment to universal humanity."[56] Nazis sought to unify the wills of individual people directly, in the sentimental nationalism of the volk, based in the "natural" unity of racial purity, and thereby to eliminate the transformation of the individual in the course of deliberating over collective goods.

Doull aims to take Hegel at his word, and so the task of contemporary philosophy is to look to past ages, not in nostalgic desire but "as that through which what we are directly liberated from took shape."[57] Doull describes us as orienting ourselves in the present with "bat-like vision," looking to the past for what it has given, and for what it lacked, for the injustices it was blind to, which are now so obvious to us.[58] To know ourselves as Canadians we need to understand two things: we are less European than we think, because we are part of the American revolutionary experiment, and our identity as an independent people (however defined) depends on our making this history conscious rather than intuitive.

The cost of being part of the revolutionary age without ever being active revolutionaries ourselves is that we Canadians have a vague sense that we are free, but we are not sufficiently self-conscious about it.[59] The divided identities, even of Canadian colonial nationalisms, contribute also to a distinctive predisposition towards liberalism that fends off the kinds of totalizing collectivism that end in European fascism and Soviet communism, where the individual is seen as a collection of energies that must be freed as far as possible from material necessity but also directed to common ends by external authority. The absence of European-style national myths based upon language groups in North America mediates the linguistic communities, universal human rights, and economy in ways the European nation states cannot. For Doull, Hegel's account of the modern state in *The Philosophy of Right* speaks directly to Canada, particularly in its unification of the ancient presupposition that humans are situated in a given ethical community with the modern demand for rational self-governance, but, at the same time, Hegel's account of the state must be modified in the light of post-national federal states, such as Canada, found in the new world.

George Grant (1918–1988)

Grant's first book, *Philosophy in the Mass Age*, was written under the express influence of Hegel (and Doull), and it forecast the dawning of a new age of reason in North America. Later, under the influence of Leo Strauss, Grant came to believe that the Enlightenment project was the outcome of a wrong turn in Western culture. For Grant, then, no one should be Hegelian today, because Hegel's aspiration to unite enlightenment rationality with ancient community is yet another step towards tyrannical technocracy. The technocratic utilitarianism of the nineteenth century has its roots in the West's embrace of an active model of the human will. Hegel's account of the will as participating in *Geist*'s manifestation is, for Grant, the ground for the technological world view wherein to know anything – or anyone – is to make it conform to our purpose: knowing *is* making. Grant's central preoccupation is the question of whether freedom is possible in the technological age: he deplores equally the fiction that technology is a collection of tools that human societies use to liberate ourselves, and progressivist accounts of history that valorize the technological world view as more advanced than premodern ways of life. More than any other Canadian writer, Grant embraced Heidegger's view of technology as an "enframing."[60] For Grant, technology is a way of being, an attitude towards nature, work, and the future that follows Robert Oppenheimer's claim that "if an experiment is sweet, one must go ahead with it."[61] A brilliant polemicist, Grant argued that as a satellite to the technocratic empire of the United States, "the primary purpose of Canadian society is to keep technology dynamic within the context of the continental state capitalist structure. By technology I mean 'the totality of methods rationally arrived at and having absolute efficiency (for a given stage of development) in every field of human activity.'"[62] Technology is moved by mastery – no other purpose, not even human betterment – but mastery as "an autonomous quest."[63]

In "Tyranny and Wisdom," Grant revisits the debate between Alexandre Kojève and Leo Strauss. Kojève interprets Hegel to be proclaiming the "universal and homogeneous state," i.e., a global, liberal, atheist state around the world. In Kojève's reading, Hegel is anti-theist and, as such, he ushered in a new era of human radical self-making. Grant takes Kojève to task for replacing the Bible with Hegel's philosophy, so that the globalism of the century after Hegel's writings was seen to fulfil a Hegelian prophecy of a "universal and homogeneous state."[64]

For Grant, "liberalism" is the ideology of technology; the "free" self-creating individual is a fiction that masks intricate forms of social, ideological and economic domination towards efficiency – efficiency for its own sake. The "universal and homogeneous state" that Kojève develops out of Hegel would be a tyranny.[65]

Charles Taylor (1931–)[66]

In "Hegel Today," the concluding chapter of *Hegel* (1975) Charles Taylor writes, "No one actually believes his central ontological thesis, that the universe is posited by a Spirit whose essence is rational necessity."[67] For Hegel, the modern state expresses "the ontological structure of things,"[68] so to be at home in political life is to be free in the sense of being in tune with the cosmos. The rational state will recover the community identity of the ancient Greek polis, "but on a higher level. For the fully developed state will incorporate the principle of the individual rational will judging by universal criteria."[69] The modern state can be fully rational because it expresses citizens' own ideas and norms in its institutions and practices. We know and recognize ourselves in and through our collective life.

Taylor emphasizes the importance of alienation in Hegel's philosophical history, but he argues that Hegel underestimated the extent to which industrial society undermined distinctions between the spheres of activity, and estranged individuals from community membership.[70] Taylor argues, "The aspiration to expressive unity between man and the natural and social world on which he depends can only be fulfilled by his freely reshaping nature and society. In this kind of vision expressive unity is combined, as in Hegel's philosophy, with a radical notion of freedom, but in a fundamentally different way. Hegel's synthesis has been, as it were, anthropologized – transferred from *Geist* onto man."[71] Rather than a metaphysical principle that is realizing itself in the historical development of human culture and self-understanding, *Geist* (as Mind, more than Spirit) is the gradual realization that human freedom is a cultural achievement.

The anthropologized Hegelian synthesis is a kind of communicative ethic, wherein metaphysics is replaced with grammar – the rules always already at work, pragmatically, in communication – as the unification of opposites.[72] Thus, Taylor's Hegel offers grounds for a multiculturalism that is situated, liberal, and transformative: modern freedom is realized in mutual recognition that reconciles individuals and diverse cultures through a "fusion of horizons."[73] For Taylor, though Hegel's *Geist* is no longer tenable as a totality of human history and nature, situated freedom is already built into the ways we talk about ourselves, others, and collective goods. Social life always already expresses qualitative distinctions, such as in judgments of better and worse courses of action. The interpretive quality of human action per se is inalienable but prone to forgetfulness and must be awakened through philosophical history on one hand, and the presentation of self in a community of recognition and respect on the other. In presenting our actions for judgment and remembrance among others, we also expand the horizons of our individual perspectives.

Taylor sees Canada as a precarious possibility of something even better than what it has been. For him, the 1982 adoption of a formal Charter of Rights and Freedoms is a move towards U.S.-style individualism, but this is mitigated by the assertion of "collective rights," particularly language rights in Quebec, and Aboriginal rights. Taylor argues that the Canadian "social imaginary" or national myth is continually disrupted by disputes over demands for recognition. Taylor proposes that we reconsider the modes of citizenship that led to Quebec separatism and conflicts over the designation of "distinct society," regionalism, and individual rights.

Henry S. Harris (1927–1996)[74]

In a speech to open the Annual Meeting of the Hegel Society of America in 1980, Henry S. Harris argues that those who deny that Hegel would be Hegelian today contradict themselves.[75] For Harris, Hegel is able to bring to consciousness the logic of history, even from within his historical moment, despite what critics claim: "They all agree with Hegel's definition of philosophy as 'its own time grasped in thoughts.' What they cannot see is how the 'comprehension of one's time' can possibly produce a philosophy that is out of time and somehow final."[76] Harris targets Fackenheim and Taylor – Fackenheim for his religious conservatism, and Taylor for his rejection of Hegel's ontology. Harris is "content to proclaim" both himself and Hegel as "Hegelian today"[77] and dismisses Fackenheim as being theologically wedded to revealed truth, and Taylor as being unable to see the pragmatic underpinning of Hegel's method.

Instead of accepting that Hegel's ontology is still open to the contradictions of the technocratic age, as Doull does, or rejecting the Hegelian *Geist* as the logical unity of all things, as postmodernists do, Harris rethinks Hegel's system. He argues that *Geist* is a secularized form of the Christian Incarnation realized in the self-knowledge of a free, rational, secular humanity. For Harris, then, *The Phenomenology of Spirit* is a philosophical "science of experience" that is concerned with what we can mean by "God." Harris says, "The Phenomenology should be thought of as the logical theory of finite experience. In its 'introductory' aspect, it has the task of overcoming the temporal 'standpoint of consciousness' and replacing it with the eternal standpoint of speculative logic, while in its systematic aspect, it is a 'Science of experience' that provides the comprehensive understanding of historical time … The Phenomenology is the conceptual comprehension of time and systematic philosophy is the exhibition of the 'true infinite' circularity of the temporal and eternal standpoints."[78]

In this, Harris's Hegel falls on the secular, socialist, and naturalist side of Canadian political thought, emphasizing phenomenology as an ethical and political activity.[79] Harris reads Hegel in relation to Hume and holds that this transforms our understanding of both thinkers, turning us to seek a logic underlying the practices of ordinary life.[80] Thus, Harris emphasizes that Hegel wants to study experience itself and to take us with him on a journey to rational self-consciousness, starting from phenomena. We move through the world to self-knowledge: "The final object of our knowledge is not 'God,' but ourselves as knowers," Harris argues. "Ours is not a 'journey of the mind to God,' but a transformation of philosophy (the love of wisdom) into a logical science of our own being in the world."[81] Harris is adamant that Hegel sees world history as the movement of "Providence"; that is, events of human life unfold in a maturation that manifests God's presence in the world: "What is rational is actual and what is actual is rational."[82] Harris finds in the development of medieval and then Protestant Christianity the emergence of both "the central place of the human individual in the universe and also a 'personal, demonic evil.'"[83] For Harris, every way in which Hegel's philosophy presents history as Divine Providence is "superstitious and reactionary."[84] Harris explains,

> To believe that ought implies can here is to admit the saving capacity of reason, to recognize the positive presence of the Spirit, its existence as moral necessity, i.e., as freedom and as charity. It is not a very comfortable home that we have made for ourselves in this world. But the absolute philosophy is the one that shows us that it is our home, and that we are the ones who have built it. The only comfort that philosophy can add to its amenities must come from our understanding why it is idle to look for comfort in it. That insight is, indeed, as cold as any comfort Job was offered. But it remains nonetheless the absolute truth that "Ich ist in der Welt zu Hause; wenn es sie kennt, noch mehr wenn es sie begriffen hat" ["I am at home in the world when I know it, still more so when I have understood it"; Hegel, *Philosophy of Right*, 4A].[85]

For Harris's Hegel, it is reason, not faith that calls us to recognize the positive presence of *Geist* in history, and thus to know ourselves to be responsible for seeking universal social justice.[86]

A Unity of Opposites?

In *Hegel and Canada: A Unity of Opposites?* a new generation of scholars considers Hegel's political philosophy as passed to us by the scholars of the post–Second World War nation-building chapter of Canadian history. Instead of self-assuredly asserting the triumph of the modern state, contemporary Hegel scholars raise questions about whether and how it might be possible to have institutions adequate to our aspirations. In the first section of our collection, "Hegel and Canadian Political Philosophy," scholars consider the possibility of a reconciliation between liberty and community through theoretical tensions in the interrelated writings of Doull, Fackenheim, Grant, Harris, and Taylor. In the second section, "Hegel in Canadian Politics," scholars explore what a Hegel-influenced contemporary state might look like.

Hegel and Canadian Political Philosophy

John Burbidge, the past president of the Hegel Society of America and author of numerous works on Hegel's ontology, argues that while there is no single "school" of Hegelian thought in Canada, there is a Canadian ideal that has Hegelian form: "We have the ideal of a total, coherent integration of reason and experience, of individual freedom and community, of the finite and the divine, of thought and reality."[87] For Burbidge, this ideal is not a school, it does not fall under a single brand of Hegelianism, but is "an ongoing dynamic, open toward the future."[88] Burbidge explains that Hegel scholars like himself and Harris "read that open-ended dialectic into Hegel's own systematic pronouncements," while others, like Taylor and Fackenheim, "adopt the dialectic while rejecting Hegel's claim to an achieved reconciliation."[89] Burbidge includes our next author, di Giovanni, also with him and Harris. Doull offers yet another reading of the open-ended dialectic: he sees the integration of opposites as continuing to unfold in further realizations of self-conscious modern freedom; for Doull, even the most profound contradictions of our age retain dialectical unity. Grant, as we have noted, has no place in this list, because he sees the whole project of reading a "total, coherent integration of reason and experience" into human history as a profound mistake. In Burbidge's view, Canada's unusually strong interest in Hegel is directly related to a "vision of an integrated society" that expresses itself in a social concern for a just society and a religious concern "for what is genuinely ultimate." These concerns manifest in Canadian politics in social policies that include universal health care, unemployment insurance, and old age pensions.

George di Giovanni concludes his chapter, "Jewish and Post-Christian Interpretations of Hegel: Emil Fackenheim and Henry S. Harris," with a tribute: *Laudemus viros gloriosos.* Di Giovanni contrasts Fackenheim and

Harris by asking the classic question of the relation of the reason of Socrates to the revealed truth of religion: *What does Athens have to do with Jerusalem?* For di Giovanni, the fundamental difference between Fackenheim's and Harris's readings of Hegel hangs on the character of the Incarnation and the nature of evil, especially post-Auschwitz. Harris and Fackenheim had radically different motives, and yet each seeks reconciliation.[90] For both Fackenheim and Harris, the "middle" connecting the transcendent and the immanent is a kind of remembering. "Reconciliation" is the rational gathering of history, beginning with the (impossible) bringing to consciousness of the presuppositions that make consciousness possible in the first place. The crucial difference between Harris and Fackenheim is, as di Giovanni explains, that the origin of thought for Harris is the God of Reason, and for Fackenheim, the God of Abraham.[91] For Harris, God is "just the name for the categorical structure of self-consciousness that is communally recognized to be necessary." In contrast, Fackenheim sees in Hegel's formula of union of union and non-union a possible mediation between revelation and reason, because the Christian doctrine of the Trinity "contributes a perfectly rational and perfectly intelligible *a priori* reconstruction of experience that nonetheless saves the immediacy of religion." One of the wonders of Canadian Hegel scholarship is that the most ardent student of the meaning of the Christian Trinity is a Jewish philosopher/theologian who ends his life as a devout Zionist.

In "Fackenheim on Self-Making, Divine and Human," Daniel Brandes asks of Fackenheim's remarkable *To Mend the World*, "Why should the fate of Hegelianism, or indeed of any philosophical system, occupy such pride of place in a work taken up with the concrete suffering and near-extinction of a people?" For Brandes, Fackenheim's attachment to Hegel ties him to an active will that, in seeking to find itself, always cancels the difference of the other. Instead of a Hegelian unity of opposites, Brandes would have identity reconsidered in the light of Schelling's understanding of a "Godself" that entails difference. Identity, for Brandes, "is the product, not the condition, of free action," because "freedom precedes identity and is irreducible to it." Divine self-making ex nihilo is exemplary for "man's historical project of self-making."[92] "The danger," according to Brandes, in Fackenheim's attachment to a Hegelian striving for reconciliation between the transcendent and the immanent is "that it grasps human historicity itself in terms of reduction and excision (we make our situating past our own by cancelling its difference, discovering ourselves) rather than in terms of an orienting affirmation and exposition of difference (we have been acted upon by what must be affirmed in its otherness to ourselves)."[93] The problem is that when we find ourselves in the metanarrative of philosophical history, we simply transform otherness into a mirror of ourselves.

For John Russon in "Conscience, Religion, and Multiculturalism," the phenomenological attitude is an ethical posture that can, indeed, make something new in the postmodern embrace of multiculturalism. Russon argues that Hegel's *Phenomenology of Spirit* is the most influential of his works in Canadian political thought. Harris' demystification of Hegel's concept of religion opens the way for a secular conscience, grounded in community life where we are affirmed in our particularity in the activity of being with others; we transcend our particularity in active mutual recognition. Selfhood is a cultural achievement that is possible only in conditions of mutual recognition.

In "Conquering Finitude: Towards a Renewed Hegelian Middle," Jim Vernon reminds us that many, if not all, Hegelian*isms* betray Hegel's promise of a politics that reconciles transcendence with immanence, instead of collapsing one into the other. Vernon argues that Taylor, Harris, and Russon emphasize the embodied, situated freedom at work in ethical life when we recognize and affirm in action the norms of our culture. In all these, Vernon argues, the transcendent is reduced to a socially constructed anthropological structure. Such leftist philosophies of immanence limit political thought to observation and description: they have so stripped Hegelian political thought of transcendence that there are no grounds to make moral or political judgments. Vernon turns to Doull's "centrist" account to argue for the renewal of "the 'Hegelian middle' which unites the account of human finitude with the infinite, self-actualizing Idea," and thus to provide "a compelling case for once again reviving a universalist, prescriptive conception of politics in our fragmented social alignment."[94] Vernon appeals for a renewed "Hegelian middle," founded on the aspiration to recover both Hegel's universalist and his emancipatory demands.[95]

In "Hegel's Philosophy of Mind," Charles Taylor presents Hegel's account of human action as the *achievement* of self-conscious volition: "Action is not essentially or originally conscious. To make it so is an achievement, and this achievement transforms it."[96] For Taylor, Hegel's philosophy of mind answers the modern split of subject and object; the achievement of human freedom is possible only through a coming-to-consciousness of the relations between our intentions, decisions, and situation. He says, "Our self-understanding is conceived as the inner self-reflection of a life process that at the outset fails to grasp what it is about." We know moral precepts because the interactions of daily life perform belief in freedom, God, and immortality. "If we ask what makes these starting points allegedly undeniable, I think the answer can only be that we can be sure of them because they are what we are doing when we perceive the world or determine our action on moral grounds."[97] Our deep existential dependence on others entails a mutual recognition driven by our fundamentally human "desire for desire,"[98] that is our need to be seen, known, respected – recognized – within a community.

In "Negativity: Charles Taylor, Hegel, and the Problem of Modern Freedom," Kenneth Kierans argues that Taylor finds the union of opposites always already at work in languages of signification.[99] Kierans argues that the historical development of the West's passage through Neoplatonism raises the problem of the reciprocal movements of the Universal or divine will towards humanity, and human will's movement towards the divine. For Hegel, the relationship must be mutual, which means that the human will must find reconciliation with the divine will in earthly activity. Kierans argues that Taylor inherits from Hegel the belief that modern subjective freedom is necessarily in tension with community goods, but that whereas Hegel sees a resolution emerging only once this tension reaches crisis, Taylor modifies Hegel's position by seeking a moderation instead of a crisis. Instead of looking to an eternal, Taylor looks to *Sittlichkeit*, the real, existing social life.

Hegel in Canadian Politics

The chapters in this section treat Canadian politics in practice through the interpretive lenses of our five focal Hegel scholars. A key question here is what the implications might be for Canadian foreign policy in accepting the rereading of Hegel given in Kojève's influential 1933–9 lectures on *The Phenomenology of Spirit*, where Hegel's "end of history" is taken as a call to expand a liberal state around the globe (i.e., a Universal and Homogeneous State). Authors also consider questions of the relations between cultural identity and autonomous action, and related tensions between the practices of ethical life and the rule of law.

Canada's relation with Hegel began with Professor John Watson, who headed the Philosophy Department at Queen's for fifty-two years (1872–1924), and with the rulings of the self-proclaimed "Hegelian" British jurist Viscount Haldane in the early twentieth century.[100] In "Early Canadian Political Culture: Hegelian Adaptations in John Watson,"

Elizabeth Trott gives an intellectual portrait of Watson, building on her work with Leslie Armour in *Faces of Reason: An Essay on Philosophy and Culture in English Canada*. Trott shows how Watson brought the Scottish Hegelianism of Edward Caird to Canada, where he then transformed it into a liberal openness grounded in a robust ethical culture committed to "peace, order and good government." Trott provides a helpful overview of some of Robert Meynell's main points from *Canadian Idealism and the Philosophy of Freedom* (2011), particularly where he counters Robert Sibley's view that Canadian Hegelianism lends itself to new forms of cultural imperialism. Trott counters Sibley's sense that Watson's imperialism is necessary to his vision of the nation state, seeing it rather as a defence against being subsumed into the United States. She quotes Watson: "The glorification of war as the nursery of manly virtues and the contempt for the weak states that cannot defend themselves ... is a palpable distortion of the doctrine of Hegel, that the state rests upon Will, not upon Force." Watson drew on Hegel to inculcate virtues of toleration and intellectual courage in his student, and Trott argues that these civic virtues have shaped Canadian politics as a result.

Robert Sibley continues this argument with Trott, drawing the question of imperialism from Watson's British Empire to the one-time Canadian Liberal Party leader's adoption of Kojève's Universal and Homogeneous State in "Idealism and Empire: John Watson, Michael Ignatieff, and the Moral Warrant for 'Liberal Imperialism.'" Sibley finds in Watson's nineteenth-century Hegelian "hopes for the British Empire" the philosophical rationality for a contemporary, liberal imperialist "war on terror." He draws a direct line between Watson and some writings by Michael Ignatieff, Harvard professor and one-time leader of Canada's Liberal Party. Sibley asserts that when arguing in favour of military intervention during the Libyan civil war, "Ignatieff ... sounded like old-style imperialists who argued that empire could bring order out of disorder. 'We need to be part of an international community action that isolates this regime, says Paul Martin to Gaddafi: "Turn back before you precipitate civil war, understand that the international community will not tolerate this behaviour."'"[101] Sibley tracks Ignatieff's interventionist stance to Watson, arguing that they share an idea of empire that commits the powerful to spread liberalism both as a shared international good and as a defensive strategy.

In "Beyond 'Hegel's Time': Made in the USA, Not Available in Canada," David MacGregor constructs a vision of the United States and the importance of the American Revolution from Hegel's perspective, despite the absence of direct references from Hegel himself.[102] MacGregor recounts the friendship between Hegel and the political economist Frederick List, and shows the parallels between their writings. List was exiled to the United States for writing texts that were critical of the German government. MacGregor argues that Hegel's America, his "land of the future," lies outside his dialectical science precisely because the future is not accessible to history. MacGregor paints a vivid picture of the reach of the British Empire in Hegel's time, details Hegel's reflections on the limits of freedom in England, and argues that Hegel could not but have been intrigued by the developing United States, as what Doull calls "the first post-national state."

In "Freedom and the Tradition: George Grant, James Doull, and the Character of Modernity," Neil Robertson reprises the disagreement between the friends and sometime-colleagues Grant and Doull, particularly about the fate of Canada in the face of its vulnerability to absorption into the technocratic empire of the United States. Absorption for both Doull and Grant meant the transformation from an aspiring modern state into a branch of the mass culture of world technocracy. Robertson shows how this disagreement is grounded in divergent foundational conceptions of the state, technology, God, and history, which come into clear focus in Grant and Doull's disagreement over the question: What is Canada? Whereas Grant sees technology as an all-absorbing destiny that Canada embraced, Doull sees technology as one aspect in the ongoing dialectics of modernity and postmodernity. Grant agrees with Kojève-Hegel that the "end of history" is the triumph of the Universal and Homogeneous State, and that this "state" is the expression of the technological imperative to assert the active will over nature so that technology "enfolds the very fundamental ways of our thinking and being." Robertson argues that Grant points to two ways "out" of the technological imperative: a retrieval of practices that retain contact with premodern goods (Grant's conservatism), and the acceleration of technological civilization to the point of collapse when humanity can then take up a "receptive relation to the divine" (Grant's radicalism). Hence, Grant turned back to Plato and forward to Heidegger to lament the absorption of modern aspirations to freedom in technocratic webs of control.[103] For Doull, in contrast, Canada retains "communitarian" aspects, which "preserve a realm of being from the technological reduction." Doull holds that the opposition between technology and community, self-making and situation, reason and various forms of faith, continue to point dialectically to a standpoint beyond their opposition, one that can be objective. Robertson argues that we experience this live ambiguity in Canadian political life when we struggle to understand how one group can be so confident of the country's conservatism, while another attests to its liberalism. "Canada is substantial or real in its history and institutions and so is capable of relating and integrating seemingly opposed qualitatively distinctive distinctions. On Doull's account, then, Canada is not – or at least, need not be – a confusion or mixture of technology and tradition, but rather a certain form of the unity of the two."[104] The very contradictions of Canadian politics are a positive corrective to the totalizing ideologies at work elsewhere.

In "Grant, Hegel, and the 'Impossibility of Canada,'" Robert Sibley argues that Grant's "lament" for Canada is his despair over technocratic modernity: we are now simply a satellite of the technological-liberal empire of the United States. Responding to Robert Meynell,[105] Sibley argues that the implications of Hegel's politics are that the world is moving towards the Universal and Homogeneous State that Kojève described. Sibley's Kojève-informed Hegel sees modern human will as necessarily active and future-directed. For Sibley, liberal imperialism is realizing Hegel's concept of "progress" as an actualization of "a theology of glory that exalts human will and makes the realm of necessity or history, and not the Good or eternity (or nature) the arena for redemption." Sibley sees the ultimate elimination of particular cultures as inevitable.

In "Hegel and Canada's Constitution," Graeme Nicholson disagrees with the doctrine of the Universal and Homogeneous State as taken up here in the chapters by Sibley and Cooper. For Nicholson, Hegel's account of the modern state "provides the best optic for understanding Canada," because it invites us to examine the existing, ongoing interplay between *Sittlichkeit* and law. Nicholson emphasizes that Doull's contemporary political thought always orients back to ancient aspirations to freedom within close communities, universalized by the rationalist aspirations of the Enlightenment. From Doull's account of the will in *The Philosophy of Right*, and particularly the distinction between externally imposed duties (*Moralität*) and civilization (*Sittlichkeit*), Nicholson draws a method of analysing crucial constitutional debates and court rulings as expressions of the habits and presuppositions of Canadian life made rational in formal law, particularly the Constitution. Following an exposition of Doull's Hegel in relation to the Canadian Constitution, Nicholson considers the 1998 Supreme Court Reference to the Succession of Quebec. He finds here an implicitly Hegelian understanding of the Canadian *Sittlichkeit*: four interwoven "norms of civilization or *Sittlichkeit* … have been at work, and are at work, not only in legal interpretation but also in concrete political life."[106] These are federalism, democracy, rule of law, and protection of minorities. For Nicholson, the purpose of the state is the life of the state itself, that is, the life of the state is the interrelations between mechanisms of government and the laws and policies they express and embody.

In "Hegel's Laurentian Fragments," Barry Cooper adopts Kojève's Universal and Homogeneous State and contrasts it with the valorization of situated cultures found in Grant and Taylor. Cooper rejects Grant's and Taylor's views as myopically "Laurentian" – i.e., Ontario- and Quebec-centric[107] – and so their "discovery" of Hegelian reconciliation in Canada (or even the potential for it) is a "survivalist political myth" that suppresses the tensions and resentments of non-Laurentian regions of Canada, especially the West. Cooper retrieves Prime Minister Diefenbaker's Western identity from what he sees as Grant's misrepresentation of Diefenbaker as an aspiring Laurentian in *Lament for a Nation*. He objects to Taylor's emphasis on the politics of recognition as a "politicization of culture." "Laurentian" thinkers such as Taylor and Grant provide only "fragments" masquerading as system. Cooper dismisses the politics of collective or community recognition as ineffectual and fanciful, especially when it lays its claim to particularity on the basis of culture or language.

In "Hegel and the Possibility of Intercultural Criticism," Shannon Hoff argues that contemporary tensions between personal identity as formed in communities (*Sittlichkeit*) and self-making (conscience) provide a ground for feminist analyses of culturally based practices. Hoff's nuanced feminism responds to the kind of liberal imperialism advocated in some versions of the Universal and Homogeneous State. Feminist action and judgment is possible "across socio-cultural borders and between worlds" through a practical fusion of horizons (Gadamer's approach as adapted for the qualitative social inquiry by Charles Taylor in "Understanding and Ethnocentricity").[108] For Hoff, in contrast with Cooper, culture is always already politicized, and so a political agent encountering a pre-existing culture is inevitably met with the dilemma of how to respect the particularity of the culture but also to retain the possibility of judging cultural practices as more or less adequate to its citizens' full humanity. Hoff considers examples from Canadian law to show the tensions at work. First, Hoff presents a case where a Muslim woman brought an accusation of child abuse against her uncle and cousin, and was called upon to testify without her habitual hijab because of the accuseds' rights to "demeanour evidence." This case exemplifies the call on liberal law to uphold the interrelation between cultural practice and identity. Second, Hoff presents the case where the Islamic Institute of Civil Justice announced that it would begin to offer private arbitration in family and business disputes, just as Jewish and Christian communities had done as an alternative dispute resolution process under Ontario's Arbitrations Act. The Liberal government of Dalton McGuinty pre-empted this use of Muslim customary dispute resolution, announcing the Act's replacement on 11 September 2006. Hoff emphasizes the enervating contradiction in failing to enact critical perspectives on socio-cultural worlds beyond our own ethnic community, arguing that this is fundamentally disrespect masked as non-intervention.

Neil Robertson concludes by returning to the titular question of this collection: "Canada and the Unity of Opposites?" Robertson argues that Hegel's salience for/in Canada does point, however cryptically, to Canada's distinctive version of the broader liberal-communitarian debate. For Robertson, the opposition of universal revolutionary freedom and situated finite freedom provides a basis for recovering unity through the "principle of constitutional liberty." Robertson draws this term from Charles Inglis, the founder of the University of King's College, who wrote in opposition to Thomas Paine's *Common Sense*. It is *through* opposition, not by suppressing conflict, that custom and formal law, tradition and science, situated and unsituated freedoms, can be reconciled.

Canadian Freedom?

As we look back on the liberal capitalists and the Hegelian social democrats of the post-war era, we do so with critical eyes, alert now to questions of cultural situation, to the "self" as a perplexity as much as a presupposition, and to violence, exclusions, and micro-divisions formerly masked by the heroic tale of a Canada born from the conflict between the two "founding nations" of English Canada and Quebec. According to Taylor, Doull, and Harris, we can revise current practices by showing continuities between our thoughts, aspirations, and alienations, and those of the ancients, especially the Greeks. For Fackenheim, the Hegelian promise of a reconciliation between Hellenic forms of community and modern rationality is most enticing and troubling. Fackenheim highlights for us the question of whether philosophical history can reveal our own selves and thoughts to us in rational form, or whether that is, in itself, a kind of idolatry: when we claim to do philosophical history, do we not simply project ourselves onto the past, and thus efface the radical otherness of earlier modes of being? Fackenheim immigrated to Israel in 1967, where he dedicated himself to the perpetuation of the Jewish people, and to a rethinking of Jewish-Christian relations through a common attentiveness to the "commanding voice of Auschwitz."[109] Grant is an outlier here, because he concludes that we retain fragments from the past that are active in us as unrealizable yearnings, and to strive to revive them within modern ways of life is a spider's web – the more we struggle, the more we increase our bondage. The task set for us, in Grant's view, is to show the thorough brokenness of modern Western culture and to seek a way back to premodern forms of life. Hence, each thinker had his own view of the extent to which Hegel's philosophy can guide us, and especially whether or not anything like Hegel's account of human history as the unfolding of a universal, transcendent principle in the particularity of the immanent world has any relevance in the contemporary age. Fackenheim embraced Zionism in a sense because he saw the possibility of a reconciliation between transcendent and immanent through reason as necessarily excluding Jews (i.e., those whose mediation must always be paradoxically glimpsed in its absence). Thus, Fackenheim moved towards Grant's late position, and that is the belief that the only reconciliation is through revelation. For Fackenheim, though, it is a revelation to the people of Israel (both in direct messages and in the history of the people), whereas for Grant it is a revelation directly from Christ to each individual. Taylor, Harris, and Doull each believes that reconciliation is possible, though, as Jim Vernon argues below, Taylor and Harris privilege the immanent at the expense of the transcendent, while Doull sees reconciliation as there already at work in the life of Canadian institutions, though not fully self-aware.

The question of what freedom is and how it might be actualized in contemporary institutions presses ever more urgently, as we saw with the Truth and Reconciliation Commission's assertion of the interdependency of community and identity. Freedom cannot consist in a false choice of community over self, or tradition over change: for it to be true freedom, in the full sense that Hegel saw as the emerging possibility of the modern state, both the practices of ethical life that are always already at work, and the particular choices of individuals must be brought to light, reconsidered, affirmed, and/or modified. What this means for now and in the future will depend on Canada's capacity to recollect its history in ways that can affirm the manifold cultural experiences of a diverse people – as we have begun with the work of the Truth and Reconciliation Commission, and in more general ways in rethinking curricula, commemorations, and museum exhibits. This cannot be the stripping away of particular tradition – the adoption of modern communication techniques and the abandonment of meaningful symbols in the restless pursuit of "relevance." Contemporary freedom will depend instead on the depth and breadth of people's ability to know their best selves as actualized in mutual recognition among diverse communities. This calls for symbolic gestures, certainly, but also for the valorization of manifold cultural traditions – including Euro-Judeo-Christian traditions – without the conceits of the atomistic liberalism of the twentieth century. That said, we must resist the fantasy that social activist movements, as in spontaneous reactions of individuals to particular events (even when they exemplify entrenched conditions), are adequate responses to liberal-capitalism in its current form: we must seek ways of realizing our intuitions of freedom concretely in institutions.

If Hegel teaches us anything, it is that human beings are meant to be free, and that freedom can be fully expressed only in institutions that bring our particular interests into relation with universal goods. Freedom needs stability, memory, and self-discipline that are possible only within decision-making about common goods, taken over time.

NOTES

1 Thank you to Angus Johnston, Patricia Robertson, Henry Roper, Neil Robertson, Victoria Goddard, and the anonymous reviewers for the University of Toronto Press for comments. As well, thank you to my colleagues in the Foundation Year Programme for years of collegial debates about curriculum and pedagogy.

2 See John Burbidge in this collection, and David MacGregor, "Hegel's Canada," *Literary Review of Canada*, February 1994, http://reviewcanada.ca/magazine/1994/02/canadas-hegel/.

3 Harris, Fackenheim, and Taylor each wrote classics in international Hegel scholarship. Fackenheim's 1967 *The Religious Dimension in Hegel's Thought* is perhaps the most influential exploration of the dialectical reconciliation

of transcendent, meta-historical standpoint with historically situated immanence in what Fackenheim calls "the Hegelian middle." Taylor's 1975 *Hegel* reintroduced the German thinker into English-language philosophy, as an inheritor of the Romantic and Kantian traditions, and while Taylor considers Hegel's metaphysical ontology carefully, Taylor himself strives, in later writings such as *Sources of the Self*, to present a secular, Hegel-inspired, practical, communicative ground for contemporary ethics. Harris's monumental 1997 *Hegel's Ladder* details the cultural, literary, and philosophical contexts and allusions of the *Phenomenology of Spirit* and presents Hegel's account of history as a "pilgrimage of reason" wherein the religious dimension of Western culture is secularized and transformed into a self-conscious, rational, ethical community. Doull's influence is more localized; he was primarily a teacher devoted to the exposition of Hegel's work and to the recollection of classical goods that he saw as enduringly present in modern, rational institutions, and also in scholarly discussions about the Canadian constitution. Key writings and commentaries by Doull's students were gathered posthumously in the 2003 *Philosophy and Freedom: The Legacy of James Doull*. We include George Grant somewhat problematically, because, while Grant has sometimes been called a "Hegelian," his relationship with Hegel was complex and varied. In fact, while Grant's earliest book *Philosophy and the Mass Age* (1955) is written under Hegel's (and Doull's) influence, he broke with Hegel expressly in *Lament for a Nation* (1965) and *Technology and Justice* (1986), because he thought that Western history was driven by an ever more active will to dominate nature and expel chance from human affairs. For the gifted polemicist, the Hegelian promise of an institutional mediation between individual self and cosmic other invited ever more enthusiastic participation in the technological imperative, and the devastating alienation of modern life from Truth. For the later Grant, as a Christian Platonist, the only possible mediation between self and cosmic other was a mystical, personal union.

4 John Holms, in Alistair D. Edgar, "Canada's Changing Participation in International Peacekeeping and Peace Enforcement: What, If Anything, Does It Mean?," *Canadian Foreign Policy Journal* 10, no. 1 (2002): 107–17, DOI: 10.1080/11926422.2002.9673309.

5 Frederick Vaughan, *Viscount Haldane: "The Wicked Step-father of the Canadian Constitution"* (Toronto: University of Toronto Press, 2010).

6 See also Pierre Trudeau's writings on federalism and Quebec, where he argues for breaking with the authorities of the past, but is wary about replacing old institutional power with ethnic nationalism. For Trudeau in this period, the ethical aspects of nationhood were residues from the past

that would eventually give way to the rational society that was emerging through progress. Trudeau writes, "The nation is, in fact, the guardian of certain very positive qualities: a cultural heritage, common traditions, a community awareness, historical continuity, a set of mores; all of which, at this juncture in history, go to make a man what he is. Certainly, these qualities are more private than public, more introverted than extroverted, more instinctive and primitive than intelligent and civilized, more self-centred and impulsive than generous and reasonable. They belong to a transitional period in world history. But they are a reality of our time, probably useful, and in any event considered indispensable by all national communities." Pierre Trudeau, "New Treason of the Intellectuals," in *Federalism and the French Canadians* (Toronto: Macmillan, 1968), 177.

7 Pierre Berton, *The Comfortable Pew* (Toronto: McClelland and Stewart, 1965), 104.

8 Pierre Trudeau wrote, in 1964,

> During several generations, the stability of the Canadian consensus was due to Quebec's inability to do anything about it. Ottawa took advantage of Quebec's backwardness to centralize; and because of its backwardness that province was unable to participate adequately in the benefits of centralization. The vicious circle could only be broken if Quebec managed to become a modern society. But how could this be done? The very ideology which was marshalled to preserve Quebec's integrity, French-Canadian nationalism, was setting up defence mechanisms the effect of which was to turn Quebec resolutely inward and backwards. It befell the generation of French Canadians who came of age during the Second World War to break out of the dilemma; instead of bucking the rising tides of industrialization and modernization in a vain effort to preserve traditional values, they threw the flood-gates open to the force of change. And if ever proof be required that nationalism is a sterile force, let it be considered that fifteen years of systematic non-nationalism and sometimes ruthless anti-nationalism at a few key points of the society were enough to help Quebec to pass from a feudal into a modern era.

Pierre Trudeau, "Federalism, Nationalism, and Reason," in *Federalism and the French Canadians*, 201.

9 Thanks to Mary Campbell of the *Cape Breton Spectator* for pressing this point.

10 Truth and Reconciliation Commission of Canada, *Honouring the Truth, Reconciling for the Future: Summary of the Final Report of the Truth and Reconciliation Commission of Canada* (hereafter TRC *Summary*) (2015), v.

11 The report distinguishes "cultural" from "physical" and "biological" genocide: "*Physical genocide* is the mass killing of the members of a targeted group, and *biological genocide* is the destruction of the group's reproductive capacity. *Cultural genocide* is the destruction of those structures and practices that allow the group to continue as a group" (TRC *Summary*, 1).

12 It is worth quoting at length:

> From the 1940s onwards, residential schools increasingly served as orphanages and child-welfare facilities. By 1960, the federal government estimated that 50% of the children in residential schools were there for child-welfare reasons. What has come to be referred to as the "Sixties Scoop" – the dramatic increase in the apprehension of Aboriginal children from the 1960s onwards – was in some measure simply a transferring of children from one form of institution, the residential school, to another, the child-welfare agency ... The closure of residential schools, which commenced in earnest in 1970, was accompanied by a significant increase in the number of children being taken into care by child-welfare agencies. (TRC *Summary*, 68–9)

13 The residential schools were part of a broad program of assimilation, by control of land use, religious and language practices, and education: "The long-term goal should be to instruct 'our Indian and half-breed populations' in farming, raising cattle, and the mechanical trades, rendering them self-sufficient. This would pave the way 'for their emancipation from tribal government, and for their final absorption into the general community'" (TRC *Summary*, 59).

14 The report explains, "In 1957, the principal of the Gordon's Reserve school in Saskatchewan, Albert Southard, wrote that he believed that the goal of residential schooling was to 'change the philosophy of the Indian child.' In other words since they must work and live with 'whites' then they must begin to think as 'whites'" (TRC *Summary*, 6). As well, the report details the ways that the schools sought to "turn the children into farmers and farmers' wives," that is, into utilitarian contributors to Canada's economy who were unimpeded by their particular identities as Aboriginal people. In the earliest days, the adoption of "Christianity" was seen to be essential to full assimilation (TRC *Summary*, 47).

15 "The Truth and Reconciliation Commission has a robust sense of the interrelationship between individual and community as being necessarily historical, particularly in the hope that both aboriginal and non-aboriginal

youths will come to understand Canada's past, present, and future, in the light of this legacy of attempted 'cultural genocide.' As the TRC describes the future of ongoing reconciliation, it is the work of building a community around the study and retelling of our history as 'Canadians' through questions. Aboriginal children and youth need to know, 'Who are my people? What is our history? How are we unique? Where do I belong? Where is my homeland? What is my language and how does it connect me to my nation's spiritual beliefs, cultural practices, and ways of being in the world? They also need to know why things are the way they are today.' Non-Aboriginal children and youth need to know 'how their own identities and family histories have been shaped by a version of Canadian history that has marginalized Aboriginal peoples' history and experience. They need to know how notions of European superiority and Aboriginal inferiority have tainted mainstream society's ideas about, and attitudes towards, Aboriginal peoples in ways that have been profoundly disrespectful and damaging. They too need to understand Canada's history as a settler society and how assimilation policies have affected Aboriginal peoples. In short, a national engagement with the history of communities is essential to the reconciliation of peoples with peoples, and individuals with their own pasts and with each other" (TRC *Summary*, 235).

16 The immense difficulty of Hegel's writings and the interminable debates about their meaning makes Hegel perhaps the most controversial and contested political thinker in the Western tradition. Hegel is revered and reviled across the political spectrum by Marxists, existentialists, and constitutional monarchists. He is revered as *the* philosopher of freedom, culture, rationality, and history, and of personal and collective transformation through conflict and resolution. He is reviled as at best a step on the path to fascism, relativistic historicism, technocracy, and Western triumphalism. For postmoderns such as Lyotard and Foucault, Hegel *is* the metanarrative against which we are called to make war. No one who spends any serious time struggling through any part of Hegel's thought emerges unchanged. Hegel is enigmatic, shattering, and hope-inspiring, especially when we look to him for hints about how to overcome our own alienation and exploitation, as well as our guilt for benefiting from the alienation and exploitation of others.

17 G.W.F. Hegel, *The Philosophy of Right*, trans. T.M. Knox (Oxford: Oxford University Press, 1952), ¶166. See also Hegel, *The Phenomenology of Spirit*, trans. A.V. Miller (Oxford: Oxford University Press, 1977), ¶457; and "Womankind – the everlasting irony [in the life] of the community – changes by intrigue the universal end of the government into a private

end, transforms its universal activity into the work of some particular individual, and perverts the universal property of the state into a possession and ornament for the Family. Woman in this way turns to ridicule the earnest wisdom of mature age" (¶475).

18 Hegel, *Philosophy of Right*, ¶4.

19 See David Ciavatta, *Spirit, the Family, and the Unconscious in Hegel's Philosophy* (Albany, NY: State University of New York Press, 2009), for an account of Hegel's presentations of the family as the foundational site of relations of mutual recognition.

20 Hegel says, "Individuals can attain their ends only insofar as they themselves determine their knowing, willing and acting in a universal way and make themselves links in this chain of social connections" (*Philosophy of Right*, ¶187); see also ¶184 and ¶188. In *The Phenomenology of Spirit* Hegel emphasizes that the individual possession of property depends on the social (¶431).

21 Hegel continues,

> The result is that the universal does not prevail or achieve completion except along with particular interests and through the co-operation of particular knowing and willing; and individuals likewise do not live as private persons for their own ends alone, but in the very act of willing these they will the universal in the light of the universal, and their activity is consciously aimed at none but the universal end. The principle of modern states has prodigious strength and depth because it allows the principle of subjectivity to progress to its culmination in the extreme of self-subsistent personal particularity, and yet at the same time brings it back to the substantive unity and so maintains this unity in the principle of subjectivity itself. (*Philosophy of Right*, ¶260)

22 Hegel considers at length the role of "the Estates," a "middle term" that prevents the isolation of the sovereign on one hand and on the other, "they prevent individuals from having the appearance of a mass or an aggregate and so from acquiring an unorganized opinion and volition and from crystallizing into a powerful *bloc* in opposition to the organized state" (ibid., ¶302).

23 Ibid., ¶308.

24 Kant, *Grounding for the Metaphysics of Morals*, trans. James Ellington (Indianapolis: Hackett, 1993), 36.

25 Hegel, *Phenomenology of Spirit*, ¶69.

26 Hegel, *Philosophy of Right*, ¶15R. Hegel says earlier,

> What is fundamental, substantive and primary is supposed to be the will of a single person in his own private self-will, not the absolute or rational will, and mind as a particular individual, not mind as it is in its truth. Once this principle is adopted, of course the rational can come on the scene only as a restriction on the type of freedom which this principle involves, and so also not as something immanently rational but only as an external abstract universal. This view is devoid of any speculative thinking and is repudiated by the philosophic concept. And the phenomena which it has produced both in men's heads and in the world are of a frightfulness parallel only to the superficiality of the thoughts on which they are based. (¶29R)

27 Hegel, *Phenomenology of Spirit*, ¶ en.
28 Ibid.
29 "One is the independent consciousness whose essential nature is to be for itself, the other is the dependent consciousness whose essential nature is simply to live or to be for another. The former is lord, the other is bondsman" (ibid., ¶188).
30 "Although the fear of the lord is indeed the beginning of wisdom, consciousness is not therein aware that it is a being-for-self. Through work, however, the bondsman becomes conscious of what he truly is … Through his rediscovery of himself by himself, the bondsman realizes that it is precisely in his work wherein he seemed to have only an alienated existence that he acquires a mind of his own" (ibid., ¶195).
31 Taylor, in this collection.
32 Hegel, *Phenomenology of Spirit*, ¶¶178–96.
33 Hegel, *Philosophy of Right*, Preface, 13.
34 Ibid.
35 Ibid.
36 As Burbidge puts this,

> Creation and fall reproduce the structures of judging: quality, quantity, relation, and modality … To be sure, Christian doctrine is not expressed in such logical terms. It needs to be conceived philosophically before the inherent pattern is visible. But the relation is not one-sided. For philosophy also benefits from this encounter. Were it not for the fact that Christian doctrine represents as true of the cosmic order the same pattern that emerged in the processes of pure thought, Hegel could not have assumed that what is rational is actual and what is actual is rational … Only with the affirmation that ultimate reality involves the pattern of creator and creation, fall and reconciliation, can Hegel establish his claim

that reason and actuality are one. He must believe Christian doctrine; else his philosophy becomes illusion – nothing but a Kantian categorical framework which says nothing about the world in itself.

John Burbidge, *Hegel on Logic and Religion: The Reasonableness of Christianity* (New York: SUNY Press, 1992), 149.

37 Verene explains that *Geist* is "breath," and further,

> Geist for Hegel expresses the interconnection between the mental, spiritual, and willful properties of the human individual and the collective activities that make up human culture – art, religion, theoretical thought, and so forth. And it also includes what the French is called moeurs (as, for example, in Rousseau's Discourses) – "manners, habits, customs, ways, morals." These realities – individual, social, cultural – which exist as Geist "show" themselves as phenomena. They are "appearances" that can be described in language and conceptually formed as parts of a total process, developmentally and dialectically comprehended.

Donald Verne, *Hegel's Absolute: An Introduction to Reading the "Phenomenology of Spirit"* (Albany, NY: SUNY Press, 2007), 109.

38 Hegel is most vivid in this point when he spoke of "the slaughter bench of history," where multitudes bled out their lives in the anonymous service of the epoch-defining "world historical individuals" such as Alexander, Julius Cesar, and Napoleon Bonaparte. G.W.H. Hegel, *Introduction to the Philosophy of History*, trans. Leo Rauch (Cambridge: Hackett, 1988), 24.

39 Hegel, *Philosophy of Right*, Preface, 11.

40 This point is crucial in Doull's response to Fackenheim's claim that the Nazi program to systematically murder Jews demonstrates the emptiness of the modern state. For Doull, the Nazi period was retrograde; that is, it asserted a "natural" national collectivity ("race") instead of subjecting particular wills to universals.

41 Paragraph 262, Hegel, *Philosophy of Right*, 162.

42 Emil Fackenheim was born in Germany. Imprisoned in Nazi Germany on Kristallnacht in 1938, Fackenheim escaped to Canada via Scotland with the help of diplomatic interventions by friends. Initially held in a refugee camp in northern Quebec, young Fackenheim made his way to the University of Toronto where, with only a rabbinical certificate from Berlin, he was admitted to doctoral studies in philosophy and ultimately awarded a faculty position where he specialized in German idealism. He taught philosophy at the University of Toronto (1948–84).

43 Emil L. Fackenheim, *The Religious Dimension in Hegel's Thought* (Bloomington: Indiana University Press, 1967), 224; Fackenheim repeats this in an exchange with Doull that is reprinted in "The Doull Fackenheim Debate: Would Hegel Today Be a Hegelian?," *Philosophy and Freedom*, ed. David G. Peddle and Neil G. Robertson, 330–42 (Toronto: University of Toronto Press, 2003).

44 When Fackenheim first declared the impossibility of Hegelianism in the post-war age, he was a professor at the University of Toronto, publishing one of the most important works of Hegel scholarship of the twentieth century, and on the verge of embracing Zionism. From 1967, when he tells us that he "opened [his] mind" to the Holocaust, Fackenheim moves ever further into abiding by what he calls the "614th Commandment," that "Jews are forbidden to give Hitler posthumous victories." In *To Mend the World: Foundations of Future Jewish Thought* (Bloomington: Indiana University Press, 1982), Fackenheim explains that this includes recalling Jewish thought, remembering the Holocaust and its victims, testifying to miraculous acts of transcendence from within the death camps, and setting the ground in every possible way for a Jewish future. Fackenheim moves from a Jewish philosophy about the relation of God to the world to the question of what is possible/demanded of Jews – and the human world – after the Holocaust. For Fackenheim, as for Primo Levi and Hannah Arendt, the most diabolical creation of the Nazis was the "muselmann," the undead of the camps in whom "the spark of transcendence was extinguished." In contrast with the victims in the camps, Fackenheim insists that the evil perpetrated by the Nazis is chosen and so in no way "banal": the Holocaust was committed by morally responsible agents, agents who *chose* irrational destruction and dehumanization as their purpose. He reminds us that in 1921 the Nazi party threatened to fracture between Nationalist and Socialist factions but that Hitler unified them in a raging anti-Semitic speech, securing their unified purpose in an Anti-Jew Revolution (10). Part of Fackenheim's own resistance is to retell the stories of those who resisted Nazism, particularly moments of impossible, miraculous transcendence within the camps – girls marking Yom Kippur, men defiantly singing songs of a Jewish future, women concealing newborns in the face of a sadistic program of murdering babies in front of their mothers. Fackenheim pointedly contrasts the acts of resistance committed by non-Jews outside the camps with the almost global silence about the Nazi extermination program. He notes, particularly, Kurt Huber, the philosophy professor who distributed leaflets with the White Rose movement (in contrast with Heidegger), and the priest who prayed publicly in Berlin for the Jews every

day for almost three years, from Kristallnacht to the day he was arrested (in contrast with the pope and Christians around the world).

45 Fackenehim continues, "The enthusiasm Schelling speaks of embraced Hitler's ideology. It showed a terrifying power when the murder camps began to run themselves – an 'objective spirit' which might well have conquered Europe. And it was supremely manifest in the 'absolute' anti-spirit displayed by Eichmann, who diverted trains desperately needed for military purposes in order to dispatch men, women, and children to their death at Auschwitz" ("Doull Fackenheim Debate," 333).

46 Hegel says,

> The life of Spirit is not the life that shrinks from death and keeps itself untouched by devastation, but rather the life that endures it and maintains itself in it. It wins its truth only when, in utter dismemberment, it finds itself. It is this power, not as something positive, which closes its eyes to the negative, as when we say of something that it is nothing or is false, and then, having done with it, turn away and pass on to something else; on the contrary, Spirit is this power only by looking the negative in the face, and tarrying with it. This tarrying with the negative is the magical power that converts into being. (*Phenomenology of Spirit*, ¶32)

47 Fackenheim, *Religious Dimension in Hegel's Thought*, 77.

48 Fackenheim argues that the problem of the "Hegelian middle" is fundamentally a problem of the relation between religious practice and philosophy. He points to what he sees as an insurmountable contradiction in Hegel: that overcoming the separation of transcendent principle and immanent cultural practice is possible only in the rationalization of the Christian doctrine of the Incarnation through human history. Fackenheim argues, "Hegelian thought can be a middle overreaching the actual world only on the assumption that it has overreaching power. Hegel's 'appearing science' and his 'science proper' must both fail to demonstrate their crucial assumption unless the final dualism can be disposed of between the totality of nonphilosophic life and the philosophic thought which is to comprehend it. Hegel asserts, with unwavering insistence, that Christianity is the absolutely true content, and that his philosophy both can and must give that content its absolutely true form" (*Religious Dimension in Hegel's Thought*, 111–12).

49 Fackenheim insists, "My grasping of Hegel's ladder requires of me a leap of faith quite unHegelian in nature – a faith in Hegel's premise that philosophical science will 'do justice' to all religions (and hence to my

own) such as, according to Hegel, no religion, the Christian included, can do no other" (Fackenheim, "Doull Fackenheim Debate," 331).

50 Ibid., 332.

51 Ibid.

52 James Doull was born in Nova Scotia and educated at Dalhousie, University of Toronto, Harvard, and Oxford. He taught at Dalhousie University in the Classics Department from the late 1940s until the mid 1980s. A collection of his writings was compiled and combined with commentaries in *Philosophy and Freedom.*

53 Doull tempered an otherwise positive review of Fackenheim's book with the counter-claim that Hegel's system can, indeed, stand up to the horrors of the twentieth century, and what is more, that Hegel alone can tell us who we are, as moderns, and who we might best be as citizens in an increasingly globalized world.

54 Doull, *Philosophy and Freedom*, 340.

55 Doull continues, "But then this was because the problems of the revolutionary wars were again with us and demanded a more thorough solution than Europe had lived with in the nineteenth century" (340). And "the evil is not in the system and a self-confidence which can act but exactly in the absence of them" (341).

56 Ibid., 340.

57 Ibid., 7.

58 Ibid.

59 Ibid., 501.

60 Martin Heidegger, trans. William Lovitt, "The Question Concerning Technology," in *The Question Concerning Technology and Other Essays*, 3–35 (New York: Harper Torchbooks, 1977).

61 In Grant, "The University Curriculum," in *Technology and Empire: Perspectives on North America*, 111–34 (Toronto: House of Anansi, 1969).

62 J. Ellul, *The Technological Society* (London: Knopf, 1965), xxxiii.

63 This fragmentation is the failure of what Fackenheim calls Hegel's "experiment," and that is the ambition of showing the transcendent creativity of human actors as reconciled with their immanent situation in particular times, places, and natures over the course of human history. The failure of Hegel's experiment means that the transcendent and immanent remain divorced, and for both Fackenheim and Grant this means that revelation and reason can face and even complement each other but they cannot unify as Hegel thought they could. "Only slowly and often almost imperceptibly do curricula respond to the powers and purposes of society" (Grant, "University Curriculum," 115). Even university-based

scientific researchers are being subsumed into "pragmatic processes" in a "growing victory of power over wonder" (116). As Grant predicted, "The 'value-free' social sciences not only provide the means of control, but also provide a large percentage of the preachers who proclaim the dogmas which legitimize modern liberalism within the university" (119).

64 Grant, "Tyranny and Wisdom," 91.

65 *George Grant Reader*, 273–4.

66 Born in Montreal to a francophone mother and an anglophone father, Taylor studied at McGill and Oxford. He has taught at Oxford and Northwestern, and is professor emeritus at McGill University. In 2007, he served with Gérard Bouchard on a one-year commission of inquiry into "reasonable accommodation" for minority cultures. A prolific writer, his books include *Hegel* (1975), *Hegel and Modern Society* (1979), *Philosophical Papers 1 and 2* (1985), *Sources of the Self* (1989), *Multiculturalism: Examining the Politics of Multiculturalism* (1994), *A Catholic Modernity?* (1999), *A Secular Age* (2007), and *Dilemmas and Connections: Selected Essays* (2014).

67 Taylor, *Hegel* (Cambridge: Cambridge University Press, 1975), 538.

68 Ibid., 386.

69 Ibid., 388.

70 "If the goal of a return to unity with the great current of life is no longer plausible, even combined with the spiral vision of history where the restored unity incorporates subjective freedom; if the historical experience of objectifying and transforming nature in theory and practice is too powerful for it to survive as an interlocutor" (ibid., 546).

71 Ibid.

72 "Hegel laid bare the emptiness of the free self and the pure rational will, in his critique of Kant's morality and the politics of absolute freedom. And he hoped to overcome this emptiness, to give man a situation, without abandoning the notion of a rational will. This was to be done by showing man to be the vehicle of a cosmic reason, which generated its articulations out of itself.

"But once this solution in terms of cosmic spirit became untenable … the dilemma recurs, and indeed all the more pressingly in that the notion of freedom has been intensified, made at once more urgent and more all-embracing in its passage through German Idealism and its materialist transposition in Marx" (ibid., 562).

73 Gadamer's concept of a "fusion of horizons" is crucial for Taylor. For example, in "On Recognition," Taylor responds to calls to expand the canon and so to have university curricula "recognize" the diversity of its students by speaking to them, showing their kind as worthy of attention

and study. Taylor dismisses any demand for "preemptory demands for favourable judgments" as hypocritical and condescending. He calls instead for a true engagement – grounded in one's tradition and able to encounter another as a contrast that could result in a "fusion of horizons."

74 Henry S. Harris was born in England and educated at Oxford and the University of Illinois. He taught for ten years at the University of Illinois and Ohio State University, and then at York University's Glendon College in the Philosophy Department from 1962 to 1994. His major publications include *Hegel's Development I: Toward the Sunlight (1770–1801)* (1972), *Hegel's Development II: Night Thoughts (Jena 1801–1806)* (1983), and *Hegel's Ladder: A Draft of a Commentary on Hegel's Phenomenology of Spirit* (1985). Harris also translated Hegel's "First Philosophy of Spirit" (1979), "Lectures on the Philosophy of Religion" (1984), and "Encyclopedia of Logic with the Zusatze" (1991).

75 Harris's *Hegel's Ladder* (1995) is a monumental line-by-line analysis of *The Phenomenology of Spirit*, while his concise *Hegel: Phenomenology and System* (Indianapolis: Hackett, 1995) is deceptively simple. Harris was central to the international scholarly community. His graduate seminar on *The Phenomenology* for York and University of Toronto students, combined with his international involvement in the translation of Hegel's writings into English, mean that Harris's students now populate philosophy departments around the world.

76 H.S. Harris, "Would Hegel Be a 'Hegelian' Today?," *Cosmos and History: The Journal of Natural and Social Philosophy* 3, nos 2–3 (July 2007): 7.

77 Ibid., 37.

78 Harris, *Hegel: Phenomenology and System*, viii–ix.

79 Harris says, "Only the human community, as sharing the common duty and delight of knowing the world as its home, and exploring and forever extending its free range of self-expression in that home, can be the subject for which the 'order' of nature, and the dialectical disorder of history exists. Thus 'philosophy is the thinking spirit in world-history'; and the self-formative or phenomenological problem of the philosopher is to raise himself to the standpoint of this real transcendental subjectivity" ("Would Hegel Be a 'Hegelian' Today?," 10). Harris also says, "Hegel knew that, far from being spiritually 'perfect,' the bourgeois world is utterly 'without wisdom' in its worship of Mammon, and more than forty years before Marx, he saw and said both that the 'Wealth of Nations' is the angel of death for the nations, and that the abstract rationalization of labour (with an apparently consequent lightening of the burdens) destroys the concrete rationality of life as human work" (17).

80 Burbidge explains that, for Harris (via Hegel and Hume), custom entails "the whole wealth of Western tradition, reaching back over the centuries to the arcadia of ancient Greece and the excitement of Renaissance Italy." He continues, "Imagination is not simply an artificial construct of retained impressions; it is the integrative vision of the artist, the fit that sets details into a more comprehensive whole. Sentiment is not just a motive for human action; it is a sense of fulfilment, of feeling life as integrated, not only internally within the individual person, but also within the whole realm of social interaction" (*Hegel on Logic and Religion*, x).

Burbidge says further, "While human rationality is a communal consciousness, it does not require consensus or agreement. It respects and thrives on diversity and difference. And that difference is acknowledged in the moment of subjection" (*Hegel on Logic*, xiii).

81 Harris *Phenomenology and System*, 14.

82 Hegel, *The Philosophy of Right*, Preface 10

83 Elsewhere in this collection, di Giovanni explains that, for Harris, "in the *Phenomenology of Spirit* we are ready for the demythologization in chapter 7 ["Religion"] of the story of the Fall, of the Incarnation, Redemption, and Reconciliation, only when the conceptual means are at hand for interpreting these myths in social terms – that is, as the story of a society that is communally cognizant of the evil of its members and has learned how to contain it."

84 Harris, *Phenomenology and System*, 5.

85 Harris, "Would Hegel Be a 'Hegelian' Today?," 23.

86 Harris finds that "every rational person today is fully conscious of the negative presence of [the self-positing Spirit whose essence is rational necessity]. Few of us have much confidence in its saving power, when we contemplate the appalling problems (and costs) of establishing any charitably endurable measure of social justice in the world community as a whole" ("Would Hegel Be a 'Hegelian' Today?," 22).

87 Burbidge, in this collection.

88 Ibid.

89 Ibid.

90 Di Giovanni, in this collection.

91 Ibid.

92 Brandes, in this collection.

93 Ibid.

94 Vernon, in this collection.

95 Vernon argues, "Freedom arises not from embracing our situated finitude, nor from seeking to transcend it into a mystical beyond, but in the concrete,

progressive, incessant conquering of the given situation through the transcendental infinity of universal freedom. Thus, Hegel's politics is universalist (applies to all subjects and social alignments at all times) and emancipatory (elucidates our essential duty to emancipate humanity from given social restrictions)."

96 Taylor, in this collection.

97 Ibid.

98 Taylor, in this collection.

99 "Taylor does not deny that there is reason in history, but for him it is discernible only from our immediate social experience as interpreted by language and symbols. This is a more cautious and modest standpoint, to be sure, and yet Taylor does have a vision of history in which the world and the self come together as one. He does not contradict, but rather complements, Hegel: both offer us inspiring, affirmative visions of modern freedom and of the history which gave rise to it" (Kierans in this collection).

100 See Elizabeth Trott, in this collection.

101 Sibley, in this collection.

102 Rupert H. Gordon, "Hegel's Patriotism," *Review of Politics* 26, no. 2 (Spring 2000): 295–325. Gordon argues that Hegel's opinion of the United States as problematically "instrumental" is very clear in *The Philosophy of Right*.

103 "Western peoples (and perhaps soon all peoples) take themselves as subjects confronting otherness as objects – objects lying as raw material at the disposal of knowing and making subjects" (Robertson, in this collection).

104 Ibid., in this collection.

105 Robert Meynell, *Canadian Idealism and the Philosophy of Freedom* (Montreal and Kingston, McGill-Queen's University Press, 2011), 217–23.

106 Nicholson, in this collection.

107 Cooper classes Doull as a "Laurentian," despite his Nova Scotia roots and adult life, which may protect Doull from participation in what Cooper sees at the Maritime tradition of being "capitulationist" "pensioners and placemen."

108 In *Philosophy and the Human Sciences: Philosophical Papers 2* (Cambridge: Cambridge University Press, 1985), 116–33.

109 Emil Fackenheim, *God's Presence in History* (New York: New York University Press, 1970).

PART ONE

Hegel and Canadian Political Philosophy

2 Hegel in Canada

JOHN BURBIDGE

Over the years, in various journals, I have seen lengthy articles about Hegelianism in Poland, in Japan, or in Holland. Never, however, have I seen anything about Hegel studies in Canada. In Europe, for example, Anglophone Canadians are simply identified with Americans.[1] On the other hand, in the membership list of the Hegel Society of America, Canadians are lumped together with all the others "outside the USA" – this despite the fact that three times over the past thirteen biennials Canadians have been elected president of the HSA, and three Canadians vice-president.[2]

Yet for over a hundred years there has been a consistent interest in Hegel in Canada. In the recent past, one thinks of Emil Fackenheim's *The Religious Dimension in Hegel's Thought*, H.S. Harris's *Hegel's Development*, Charles Taylor's *Hegel*, and John Burbidge's *On Hegel's Logic*.[3] Significant contributions by way of articles have been made by Theodore Geraets, George di Giovanni, James Doull, and Kenneth Schmitz.[4] One can even find the Hegelian logic, filtered by way of Collingwood and W.H. Walsh, in W.H. Dray's analytic philosophy of history. In addition, Fackenheim, Harris, and Schmitz have made Toronto a significant centre for graduate studies in Hegel for over three decades.

It is tempting to think of this as a recent phenomenon, but the tradition goes back well into the nineteenth century. Unlike the United States, where most of the early Hegelians were immigrants from Germany, Canada's Hegelianism came by way of Scotland. In 1862, John Clark Murray arrived at Queen's University, Kingston – the centre for training clergy for the Church of Scotland in Canada – from Edinburgh by way of Heidelberg and Göttingen. While Murray does not explicitly discuss Hegel, he advocates what he calls a speculative ideal: "The labours of science aim at discovering to consciousness this reciprocal connection of different truths; and the intellectual ideal is thus a system of thought, in which all cognitions, that is, all truths, all objective connections, are conceived as component factors of one self-consciousness. Such a system is absolute truth."[5]

When Murray moved on to McGill University in 1872, he was succeeded at Queen's by John Watson, a student of Edward Caird, who continued to teach there until well after the First World War. Watson not only wrote studies on Schelling and Kant, but also confessed in the Preface to his Gifford Lectures of 1910–1912: "It will of course be evident to anyone familiar with the subject that in the constructive part of the undertaking I have found in Hegel, and in his English exponents, the most suggestive ideas for my purpose."[6]

From Queen's, Presbyterian clergy spread across the country preaching a vision of "seeing life clearly and seeing it whole" – words which I recall hearing more than once in my youth – which moulded several generations of Protestant thought and contributed to the intellectual foundations of the United Church of Canada.

There is some evidence, indeed, that this Canadian tradition spilled over into the United States. Jacob Gould Schurman, born in Prince Edward Island and educated in Nova Scotia and London, England, was offered the chair of philosophy at the recently founded Cornell University in 1885 on the strength of his *Kantian Ethics and the Ethics of Evaluation: A Critical Study*.[7] A comment in his *Belief in God: Its Origin, Nature, and Basis* noted that Hegel was right to insist "that identity and difference are both necessary to the being of the infinite spirit."[8] In 1892 Schurman became president of Cornell, and, in due course, American ambassador to Greece, Macedonia, China, and Germany. One of his graduate students, James Edwin Creighton from Nova Scotia, became first co-editor with him, and then editor of the *Philosophical Review*, which provided a forum for a number of Canadian authors. It was also in this Cornell department that Gustavus Watts Cunningham wrote his dissertation, "Thought and Reality in Hegel's System."[9]

Apart from this connection between Canada and Cornell, the Canadian tradition appears to have followed its own path. H.S. Harris finished his studies in the United States, and both he and Schmitz taught there before settling in Toronto. Taylor was for a time professor at Oxford, but all have devoted the bulk of their teaching years to Canada, and some have resisted attempts to entice them elsewhere.

Yet there is no single "Canadian school." Though both Burbidge and di Giovanni wrote their dissertations under Fackenheim's direction, they have developed their Hegelian studies in independent ways. For a time, Harris, Schmitz, di Giovanni, and Burbidge, with many others, collaborated in translating Hegelian texts,[10] but those discussions were enlivened by a diversity of approach rather than by a single interpretative schema. Geraets and Schmitz both come from a Catholic background. Harris and Burbidge are touched by Peirce and American pragmatism (though Harris started his venture into idealism with a study of Gentile). Taylor was inspired (as were many others) by Isaiah Berlin, who, like Fackenheim, came from a German Jewish background. Few, if any, of the more recent Hegelians were influenced by the tradition of Caird, Bradley, and Bosanquet that inspired Watson. (Despite the fact that G.R.G. Mure was still at Merton when Harris studied at Oxford, there was no direct contact.[11])

Missing from this account of influences are such names as Werkmeister and Loewenberg, Findlay and Lauer, W.T. and E.E. Harris, Mueller and Kaufmann: the names that would surface from a comparable American story. In fact, one has the sense that each of the Canadian Hegelians has worked out his interpretation through a personal and disciplined struggle with the texts.

There are nonetheless common themes that weave their way through the various writings. One involves the dynamic character of society. "The freedom of the individual is an empty abstraction apart from the social order by which it is maintained, and the social order is properly the realization of individual freedom," Murray wrote.[12] In a similar vein Watson wrote: "Liberty is the essence of opportunity, for self-development is the creation of law, and not something which could exist apart from the action of the State."[13]

This early vision finds an echo in Taylor: "We have to combine this recovered sense of a relation to nature which is not purely exploitative with the free, equal individual of modern society. We need at once freedom and a post-industrial *Sittlichkeit*";[14] and in Harris: "Human rationality as communal consciousness – that and nothing else – is the *Gegenwart* that philosophy of its charity gives to the faith and hope of religion."[15]

Unlike in America, where the early colonists banded together to defend individual liberty against the demands of a distant state, Canadians have had to build a consensus within a widely divergent constituency, and to find a community that respects differences: differences of French and English; among English, Scots, and Irish; between settlers and new immigrants from Eastern Europe or the Far East; between the native and the dominant cultures; and among Baptist, Methodist, Catholic, Anglican, and Presbyterian. So Hegelian thought has been mined for its ability to show how a community can be created that integrates yet respects cultural differences and individual freedom.

Murray challenged, in addition, the sharp division between the wealthy, propertied classes and the labouring class, urging a system of "copartnership" that anticipated the Cooperative Commonwealth of J.S. Woodsworth and the social democratic movement in Canada. Many years later, Taylor was mentioned as a possible leader for the New Democratic Party when it succeeded the Co-operative Commonwealth Federation. The vision of an integrated society, appropriated from Hegel, has contributed to a Canadian political order in which all parties support the institution of universal health care, unemployment insurance, and old age pensions.

The ideal of an all-encompassing community became, in both Watson and Harris, a definition of absolute spirit, though Watson identified it directly with the God of the Christian tradition, while Harris seeks to broaden the perspective to incorporate the modern secular world. The social concern for a just society (which found expression in left-wing Hegelianism) has thereby been integrated with the right-wing religious concern for what is genuinely ultimate.

Despite the fact that Fackenheim has challenged the religious dimension which committed Hegel to a Christian reconciliation because it could not do justice to the horror of Auschwitz, he is still prepared to appropriate it as a model for modern Judaism, struggling to make sense of a fragmented world. "With the Notion vanished," he writes, "a Hegelian way of philosophical thought supplies the means … of doing conceptual justice to the inner logic of Judaism."[16]

Similarly, Schmitz explored Hegelian themes as he developed a Catholic philosophy of religion, and Burbidge, in *Being and Will*, brought out an apologetics based on his reading of Hegel as distinctively Christian.[17]

Di Giovanni, Geraets, and Burbidge have all devoted considerable attention to Hegel's logic. They do so, however, not as if it were the total explanation of all reality, but rather as a logical framework which one then uses to comprehend an alien nature and a human society bedevilled by contingency. On this reading, one cannot assume that the logic defines the complete structure of Hegel's philosophy, but rather that the necessity and completeness of pure thought must cope, in some way, with a recalcitrant and contingent reality.

What is interesting is that the Canadian Hegelian tradition does not focus overly much on using *absolute* as a noun. (The one major exception appears to have been George John Blewett in *The Study of Nature and the Vision of God* and *The Christian View of the World*.[18]) We have the ideal of a total, coherent integration of reason and experience, of individual freedom and community, of the finite and the divine, of thought and reality. But that ideal is not an entity with a distinctive name. It is an ongoing dynamic, open towards the future. Some, like Harris and Burbidge, read that open-ended dialectic into Hegel's own systematic pronouncements. Others, like Taylor, Fackenheim, and di Giovanni, adopt the dialectic while rejecting Hegel's claim to an achieved reconciliation.

So Canadian Hegelians, for nearly a hundred and fifty years, have found in Hegel's thought a basis for understanding society and religion, thought and reality. Perhaps they have domesticated him, in that they have not been as inclined as others to dismiss his claims to absolute knowledge in preference for the discontinuities of a Kierkegaard or a Heidegger, for the revolutionary disruption of a Marx, or for the liberal atomism of a John Stuart Mill. Perhaps as well, they have made him more human, for there is little trace of Findlay's Neoplatonism, Errol E. Harris's Spinozism, or Bradley's atemporal Absolute. A comprehensive integration has yet to be achieved; it is not already present.

In a way Watson sums up what is essential about Canadian Hegelianism when he wrote:

> What Speculative Idealism maintains is that, while the "world" is a "cosmos of experience," and therefore exists for each thinking subject only in experience, it is a "cosmos" just because the thinking subject is capable of grasping the permanent or essential nature of reality. There is no object apart from a subject, and yet it is only as the subject is capable of grasping the universal or necessary constitution of reality that there is for him "a world of things." This implies that, while in each subject there is a process of intelligent activity, through which alone his experience of a world of things originates, he yet is able to comprehend the true nature of the world because there is in him the principle which is involved in the actual nature of reality. The supposition that a world assumed to lie beyond intelligent experience is identical with what it is within intelligent experience is manifestly absurd, since it implies that the whole process in which the "cosmos of experience" is gradually formed through the exercise of intelligence is superfluous.[19]

Or, as Harris wrote: "Hegel's philosophy is a four-part fugue, because the three parts of the 'system' lead back to what is outwardly present as a 'prelude.' It does this because its goal is to bring the kingdom of the spirit down to earth, to bring philosophy down out of the clouds, and raise the quest itself into wisdom, by making it terminate in knowledge (Spirit's knowledge of itself) rather than in faith."[20]

NOTES

Reprinted by permission from *Owl of Minerva* 25, no. 2 (Spring 1994): 215–19.

1 [This article was written for the 25th anniversary edition of the *Owl of Minerva* in 1994, and constraints of space prevented it from being exhaustive. In addition, much work has been published by Canadians since that time. Mention needs to be made of Jonathan Robinson, Barry Cooper, David MacGregor, Dale Schlitt, John Russon, Peter Simpson, Peter Merklinger, Jay Lampert, Jeffrey Reid, David Morris, Jim Vernon, David Ciavatta, Bruce Gilbert, Jennifer Bates, and others.] In this paper I shall not discuss the Canadian francophone Hegelian tradition other than the works of Theo Geraets, who teaches at the bilingual University of Ottawa and who translated the *Encyclopedia Logic* into English with W.A. Suchting and H.S. Harris.

2 Presidents were Kenneth Schmitz, H.S. Harris, and John Burbidge; vice-presidents were H.S. Harris, John Burbidge, and George di Giovanni.

3 Emil Fackenheim, *The Religious Dimension in Hegel's Thought* (Bloomington: Indiana University Press, 1967); H.S. Harris, *Hegel's Development*, vol. 1, *Toward the Sunlight*, and vol. 2, *Night Thoughts* (Oxford: Clarendon, 1972–83); Charles Taylor, *Hegel* (Cambridge: Cambridge University Press, 1975); John Burbidge, *On Hegel's Logic: Fragments of a Commentary* (Atlantic Highlands, NJ: Humanities, 1981).

4 Theodore F. Geraets, "Les trios lectures philosophiques de l'Encyclopédie ou la réalisation du concept de la philosophie chez Hegel," *Hegel-Studien* 10 (1975): 231–54; George di Giovanni, "Reflection and Contradiction: A Commentary on Some Passages of Hegel's Science of Logic," *Hegel-Studien* 8 (1973): 131–62; di Giovanni, "The Category of Contingency in Hegelian Logic," in *Art and Logic in Hegel's Philosophy*, ed. Warren E. Steinkraus and Kenneth L. Schmitz, 179–200 (Atlantic Highlands, NJ: Humanities, 1980); James A. Doull, "Would Hegel Today Be a Hegelian?," *Dialogue* 9 (1970): 226–35; Doull, "Hegel's Philosophy of Nature," *Dialogue* 11 (1972): 379–99; Kenneth L. Schmitz, "Hegel's Philosophy of Religion," *Review of*

Metaphysics 23 (1970): 717–36; Schmitz, "Hegel's Attempt to Forge a Logic of Spirit," *Dialogue* 10 (1971): 653–72; Schmitz, "The Conceptualization of Religious Mystery," in *The Legacy of Hegel*, ed. J.J. O'Malley et al., 108–36 (Hague: Nijhoff, 1973).

5 John C. Murray, *A Handbook of Psychology* (London: Gardner, 1885), 223. Cited by Leslie Armour and Elizabeth Trott, *The Faces of Reason: An Essay on Philosophy and Culture in English Canada, 1850–1950* (Waterloo, ON: Wilfrid Laurier University Press, 1981), 144.

6 John Watson, *The Interpretation of Religious Experience* (Glasgow: J. Maclehose and Sons, 1912), vi.

7 Jacob G. Schurman, *Kantian Ethics and the Ethics of Evaluation: A Critical Study* (London: Williams, 1881).

8 Jacob G. Schurman, *Belief in God: Its Origin, Nature, and Basis* (New York: Scribner's, 1890), 227. Cited in Armour and Trott, *Faces of Reason*, 205–6.

9 Jacob G. Schurman, *Thought and Reality in Hegel's System* (New York: Longmans, 1910).

10 G.W.F. Hegel, *The Jena System, 1804–5: Logic and Metaphysics*, trans. and ed. John W. Burbidge and George di Giovanni, intro. H.S. Harris (Montreal and Kingston: McGill-Queen's University Press, 1986).

11 But cf. Harris, "The Hegel Renaissance in the Anglo-Saxon World since 1945," *Owl of Minerva* 15, no. 1 (Fall 1983): 77–8, 92.

12 John Clark Murray, *An Introduction to Ethics* (Boston: DeWolfe, Fiske, 1891), 262. Cited in Armour and Trott, *Faces of Reason*, 124.

13 John Watson, *The State in Peace and War* (Glasgow: Maclehose, 1919), 232. Cited in Armour and Trott, *Faces of Reason*, 248–9.

14 Taylor, *Hegel*, 461.

15 Harris, *Night Thoughts*, 522.

16 Emil Fackenheim, *Encounters between Judaism and Modern Philosophy* (New York: Schocken Books, 1973), 162.

17 John Burbidge, *Being and Will: An Essay in Philosophical Theology* (New York: Paulist, 1977).

18 George J. Blewett, *The Study of Nature and the Vision of God: With Other Essays in Philosophy* (Toronto: W. Briggs, 1907); Blewett, *The Christian View of the World* (New Haven, CT: Yale University Press, 1912).

19 John Watson, *An Outline of Philosophy: With Notes, Historical and Critical*, 4th ed. (Glasgow: J. Maclehose, 1908), 439. First published as *Comte, Mill, and Spencer: An Outline of Philosophy* (Glasgow: J. Maclehose, 1895). Cited in Armour and Trott, *Faces of Reason*, 285.

20 Harris, *Night Thoughts*, 569.

3 Jewish and Post-Christian Interpretations of Hegel: Emil Fackenheim and Henry S. Harris

GEORGE DI GIOVANNI

"What does Athens have to do with Jerusalem?" This is the question Tertullian asked in the third century. The philosopher could, of course, counter with his own question (though I cannot think of anyone who actually did in these precise words), "And what does Jerusalem have to do with Athens?" It is tempting, when reflecting on the work of Emil Fackenheim and Henry Harris,[1] to set up the contrast between the two men on the basis of these two questions, with Fackenheim representing Jerusalem and Harris standing for Athens. But the strategy would lead nowhere. True, Emil Fackenheim's mentors, even before Fackenheim himself turned his attention exclusively to the foundations of a future Jewish thought, were Franz Rosenzweig and Leo Strauss. Rosenzweig was already engaged in his day in laying the foundation for a new Jewish thought, and in recent times Leo Strauss has decried more loudly than most the constant attempt by philosophers to undermine the place that Jerusalem in fact has in Western culture. Jerusalem, not Athens, has been from the beginning Fackenheim's motivating interest. True also: Henry Harris, more forcefully perhaps than any other commentator on the *Phenomenology of Spirit*, has argued that the *Sitzt im Leben* of the birth of Christianity, that is, the culture that provided the existential conditions for the belief in the incarnation of God, was the pagan world of the Roman Empire. So far as I know, he is the only commentator who has argued for the substantial continuity between Augustan Rome and Napoleonic Europe. In this respect, Harris belongs squarely to the pagan tradition of Athens. All this is true, and one can therefore appreciate the temptation to set up the Fackenheim/Harris contrast as one between Jerusalem and Athens.

However, other considerations immediately interfere with any such simple contrast. The difference between Fackenheim and Harris is too profound, and their commonality (which makes the difference all the more significant) much too complex, to be captured by any simple formula, or, for that matter, for me to anticipate it with any simple statement. This much, however, I might hazard at the moment. Any difference will come to a head on the issue of evil. The question is whether Hegel's reason, as understood by Harris, can comprehend the evil of the Holocaust, which, as Fackenheim sees it, is demonically personal and therefore constitutes a *novum* in history.[2] Fackenheim's simple answer seems to be that it cannot, and this alone would suffice to open up an immense gap between him and Harris. But the gap cannot be the whole story. On the one side, Fackenheim never relinquishes his belief that life ought to be comprehended by reason. The scandal that is the Holocaust is due precisely to the fact that it defies this need for comprehension. And, on the other side, whatever the pagan *Sitzt im Leben* of the origin of Christianity, Harris would have to agree that, with the advent of Christian consciousness characteristic of the latter, the possibility was established for a personal evil that would have totally escaped the limits of pagan experience. Christ according to Hegel is the beautiful soul par excellence, and the beautiful soul is intrinsically evil. In a sense that is totally heterodox, it is indeed the case that for Hegel, Christ took upon himself the sins of all humankind.

This, Fackenheim's and Harris's positions on evil, is the theme I want to explore, and I ask your patience while I seem to divagate in many directions. I shall come to the point. I must stress that I am not concerned in this paper with Hegel per se. I am concerned with Fackenheim's and Harris's respective readings of him. I intend this study as a tribute to these two men, both of whom I was fortunate to have had, in different ways, as teachers.

1. Harris on the Incarnation

I begin with a theme as old as Western philosophy and that is, as we shall see, common to both Harris and Fackenheim. For the moment, it will allow me to broach Harris's position directly. The theme is that of recollection. *Mnemosyne* is the mother of all the muses because it is by re-enacting internally, in the medium of the mind's images, what would otherwise be just a naturally given content of experience, that this content is transformed into the objects of the arts, and nature itself, accordingly, into a typically human world. However, the transformation of nature thus attained by recollection would not be possible unless the latter were performed with intent – I mean to say, unless it were not just a merely passive internalization of natural occurrences but provided, rather, a transcendent context for them. It is a creative internalization, and it is in virtue of this internalization that the natural occurrences assume a specifically human significance. In other words, recollection is interpretation; or again, in recollecting nature, more than nature must be recollected. But what is this "more than nature," this "extra," so to speak, that constitutes the tacit theme underlying and motivating all experience? And how is the recollection of it existentially successful? As to the first question, Harris is quite clear regarding Hegel's answer to it. What is being recollected in experience over and above nature is precisely the presence in experience of Reason. This is a theme Hegel inherited from Kant, a theme common to all German Idealism. The interests of Reason, its totalizing tendencies, are the fundamental factors that motivate and structure experience.

But how is this presence to be conceptualized? Kant simply assumed it as a fact of reason (as Reinhold would later call it), concentrating on its structural implications so far as the unfolding of experience is concerned, and relegating any question about its origin to the realm of the noumenal. Fichte took the decisive step of conceiving it as an "event," a self-generating event that could best be defined as simply an act of freedom. But *whose* freedom it might be remains unclarified by Fichte. For Fichte, too, the origin of reason and rationality is an issue that therefore ultimately falls within the province of faith. Although the Hegel of the *Phenomenology of Spirit* is greatly indebted to Fichte – as Harris shows, in some ways even more indebted to him than to Schelling – it is to Schelling, the Schelling of 1800, that Hegel owes his understanding of the event that marks the beginning of the presence of reason in nature. This event is itself a product of nature, the final stage in a process by which nature acquires ever more complex organic shapes and hence ever greater interiority and self-control, to the point that, in a new space that reflective conceptualization (itself an organic structure) provides, nature takes hold of itself as a whole and begins to recreate itself deliberately. This space is the space of reason, the place where nature transcends itself and acquires freedom with respect to itself. It is where Spirit is born. However, so long as one stays, as one does in the formulation just used, with such abstractions as Nature in general, and Freedom in general, one still runs the risk that Fichte and Schelling both incurred, in their different ways of lapsing into myth-making. The question remains, exactly *whose* freedom is it by which nature is to be reborn as a world of experience? Hegel's answer is unambiguous. That freedom is of individual human beings, those rational animals whose otherwise organic connections with nature in general have been disturbed by this power they have of conceptualizing, a power that has had its effects even before they are conscious of having it. For these human beings, therefore, nature even as they first experience it appears problematic, as if it no longer were as it once was, as indeed it is not, for the concept has already invested it with a meaning that it does not have on its own.

To recollect the presence of reason in experience thus means to recollect the work that reason has effected, so far as any individual is concerned, even before time began (please keep this point in mind, for it will be my entry point for Fackenheim). To recollect, then, means to recover nature as it "once" was, and the natural mistake to which the individual inevitably falls prey is to believe that such a recovering requires recapturing a pristine nature physically, whereas the only recovery possible requires a new intervention of reason. This recovery requires recreating nature in such a way that the individual can be at peace with it, by substituting for what once might have been a natural harmony a new spiritual harmony that is the product of reconciliation. One must reconcile oneself with one's physical finitude, in effect with one's mortality, for it was, after all, the intervention of reason that did violence to nature, turning it in the first instance into a source of finitude and mortality for the individual.

In principle, therefore, we have already answered the second question that we just posed, regarding how the process of recollection is to be existentially successful. Recollection, in order to be a real recollection, requires that what is recollected is an historically ascertainable event. It is this requirement that distinguishes memory from mere imagination. The problem, of course, is that the event that disrupts the harmony of mere nature and sets up the need for reconciliation, namely the emergence of reason, does not itself fall within the grasp of experience, for it is constitutive of the latter. It belongs to the prehistory of anyone's self-consciousness. The temptation, therefore, is to interpret the event mythologically (as indeed both Fichte and Schelling do, not to speak of Kant), to substitute imagining for remembering. The net result is that nature itself is absorbed into unreal time, and since it is nature that individualizes the human being, the actual existence of the latter is devalued accordingly. I do not mean to say that the sufferings, or for that matter the joys, of the individual are not felt with the sharpness of immediate singularity. I mean to say that in the wider scheme of things, in the world as envisaged by the individual, such experiences have no significance as the singular events that they in fact are, but are interpreted only as re-enactments of some original story that itself escapes time. For this reason, the Christian belief in the Incarnation marks a turning point in this process of recollection. For God took up human nature, thus reconciling the infinitude of reason with the finitude of nature, in an individual human being for whom, unlike the semi-gods of pagan mythology, a definite location can be found, or is at least expected to be found, in the temporal and spatial sequence of actual human events. Christians might have indeed fallen into the illusion of projecting the final realization of this reconciliation, which the God-man has already accomplished in principle, at the end of history, when the Kingdom of God is to be revealed on earth. But whatever the fancies of the imagination at work in this belief, the important point is that this final moment is believed to be continuous with present history, and that one must work for its realization in the "here and now," each singular human action thus assuming decisive significance precisely as singular event. "Are not five sparrows sold for two farthings," the Gospel asks, "and not one of them is forgotten before God?" (Luke 12:6). It is with the belief in the Incarnation, in other words, that recollection is set on the sure footing of historical memory and not just mythological imagining.

How, according to Harris's reading of Hegel, this final reconciliation is to be conceived, free of all residue of imaginative representation, is indeed a long story. The crucial point now is that, according to Harris, the essential factor in this mental change that occurred in the Western world at the beginning of what we now call the Christian era is the *belief* in the historical reality of the Incarnation, not the supposed truth of the story itself of God becoming man, or of the other stories, such as that of the virgin conception, that are associated with it. Such stories are instances of the many gnostic myths common at the time. Again, that *that* belief should have arisen at that particular time was, according to Harris, due to social and cultural circumstances for which the whole of classical antiquity, and most proximately the Augustan Roman Empire, had prepared.[3] Few scholars now doubt the historical reality of a man called Jesus of Nazareth whose life and death were somehow instrumental to the birth and the spread of Christianity. But that he should have come out of the land of Judea, and that he (rather than somebody else) should have been associated with the birth of the new shape of consciousness heralded by Christianity, *that* is strictly an accident of history. It all could have happened otherwise. Hegel, according to Harris, is the great demythologizer: he had to be such precisely in order to bring reason to actual history. As Harris says, "God, or the Divine, is [for Hegel] just the name for the categorical structure of self-consciousness that is *communally recognized* to be necessary" (my italics).[4]

I have just said that Hegel's story of humankind's reconciliation with nature is a long one. But here is another point in this story that is immediately called to mind by the phrase "communally recognized" in the quotation from Harris. The only nature that can be party to this process of reconciliation is, of course, one that has already been spiritualized. In effect, however, this means a nature that is problematic for the human individual because, on the one hand, his singular identity depends on it, and on the other, because the individual is no longer just a natural entity, he must invest that singularity with infinite value precisely in order to safeguard his spirituality as individual. But to claim infinite value for what is essentially finite, especially when done in the face of other individuals claiming the same for their singularity (as one must indeed if the claim has to have existential grip) – to do *that* is self-conceit. It is pride, in other words, and pride is *evil – irreducible evil*, because, unlike the sufferings that are part and parcel of being flesh and bone, it is personal and demonic, the result of a decision.[5] One can see, therefore, why Hegel should look at the Christ as the prototypical figure of the beautiful soul.[6] The beautiful soul, as such, would claim absolute truth for the voice of its admittedly private conscience, and would do this in innocence. And Jesus is the one who, as innocent sacrificial lamb, would nonetheless raise his singular humanity to divinity. He is the God-man. The Incarnation is the second irruption of the Divine into history, the first irruption being creation itself, which was the beginning of history. But creation, this attempt to manifest infinite power in the finitude of nature, was "God's own pride,"[7] and so was the new creation of the Incarnation. The historical significance of the myth is that it manifests a new awareness, not only of the central place of the human individual in the universe, but of the kind of personal, demonic evil that this centrality makes possible. Now, a possibility that defines the human situation as such will be actual in real life. Evil will be. In the *Phenomenology of Spirit*, we are ready for the demythologization in chapter 7 of the story of the Fall, of the Incarnation, Redemption, and Reconciliation, only when the conceptual means are at hand for interpreting these myths in social terms – that is, as the story of a society that is *communally cognizant* of the evil of its members and has learned how to contain it. This happens at the conclusion of chapter 6 with the well-known dialectic of confession, forgiveness, and reconciliation to which the phenomenon of the beautiful soul gives rise.

2. Fackenheim on the Fragmented Hegelian Middle

I shall return to this dialectic, but I am ready at the moment to consider Emil Fackenheim. The starting point of Fackenheim's approach to Hegel is that, for Hegel, life must necessarily precede the reflection of thought.[8] This must, of course, be the case for Hegel because, as we said, the event that inaugurates experience is necessarily preconscious, and therefore the subject of experience *finds* itself always already engaged in a situation which it then has to justify by recovering (remembering) its origin. Immediate belief precedes reflection; religious faith precedes philosophy.[9] Philosophy is passionate precisely because at issue in philosophy, just as in religion and politics, is *who* we are.[10] On this, Harris and Fackenheim are, of course, at one. The difference, however, is that according to Fackenheim, what is remembered in the Hegelian reflection is first and foremost not the God of Reason as per Harris, but the God of Abraham. The *Sitzt im Leben* of Hegel's philosophy is not Athens but Jerusalem, the Jerusalem of which Christianity is an offspring.

I must stress right away that Fackenheim's is not the naive and self-serving position of, say, a Hans Küng, according to whom faith in Christ is presupposed in order to understand Hegel.[11] Fackenheim makes no claim that reason is dependent on faith for its rationality. His thought is from the start located within the tradition of Franz Rosenzweig who, in his *The Star of Redemption,* used Schelling to mediate the distance between Spinoza and the pious believer. Fackenheim's point is that Hegel's philosophy, rather than Schelling's, is the one more apt for performing the required mediation. This is precisely because of the autonomy that Hegel's reason claims for itself. The shibboleth that separates Spinoza and the pious Jew – in a dialogue internal to Judaism itself – is Revelation.[12] On the one side, there is Spinoza, who denies Revelation because of its historical particularity and, for the sake of universality, replaces the personal God of Revelation with the impersonal Substance of reason. On the other side, there is the pious Jew who stubbornly insists on the truth of his belief in God precisely because it is based on a Revelation historically made to him as a member of a very particular people. Spinoza stands as witness to the universal, and the pious Jew as witness to particularity. But by insisting on the universal, Spinoza ends up denying individuality, in effect denying human agency and its concomitant evil, and thereby reducing the whole human race to the passivity for which he blames and condemns the people of Israel. The pious Jew, for his part, by insisting on his particularity, which he will not give up even before God, surrenders the attitude of passive acceptance that God's transcendence demands and thus risks the sin of pride.[13] How to overcome the distance? The problem is to bring together the two opposite sides while respecting the intellectual imperatives of the one and the existential situatedness of the other. Here is where Hegel's formula of "union of union [i.e., Spinoza's standpoint in this case] and non-union [i.e., the religious standpoint]" comes into play as the mediating factor. However, the formula is no more than an empty conceptual recipe unless two conditions are met. On the one hand, there must be an actual experience of the presence of a transcendent God, an immediate experience that only religious imagery is in a position to capture and convey. On the other, reason (I mean, reason acting autonomously) must be able to overreach (*übergreifen*) the finite standpoint of the believer and comprehend the possibility of that presence from the standpoint of God himself, whose transcendent presence is being experienced.[14] This is the comprehension the doctrine of the Trinity provides, the Trinity understood both as the internal life of God and as that same life manifested in the work of creation. This doctrine is bound up with historical circumstances and replete with historically conditioned imagery. However, according to Fackenheim, the doctrine as conceptually distilled by Hegel constitutes a perfectly rational and perfectly intelligible a priori reconstruction of experience that nonetheless saves the immediacy of religion by reinstituting it on its own.[15] If it were not such, the "union" clause of the "union of union and non-union" formula would not be satisfied, just as the "non-union" clause would not be satisfied if the transcendence of God's presence to the individual Jew were not a reality.[16]

It is not for the comprehension of experience, therefore, that this reconstruction of the latter needs faith, but for its existential confirmation, in order that it not remain an empty conceptual edifice. Perhaps surprisingly, both Fackenheim's and Harris's understanding of Hegel's concept of "faith" turns out to be, albeit in different ways, deeply Catholic. There is nothing of the *credo quia absurdum* in this faith; also nothing of Kant's and Fichte's pragmatism. Faith is knowledge, though still as if "through a glass darkly." It is a *fides quaerens intellectum*. Now,

Fackenheim cannot accept the Christian belief either in the Trinity or in the Incarnation, but he can accept the Christian experience of an incursion of the Divine in history because it is continuous with the Jewish experience of the same incursion and equally sets up the paradox of the universal being at one with the particular. It is for this reason that Hegel can be called upon to mediate between Spinoza and the pious Jew.

However, there is a problem with this mediation, one that Fackenheim confronted from the beginning but which, as we shall see, eventually totally overtook his reflections on Hegel. The fact is that Hegel's mediation was existentially in crisis from the beginning, because, as Hegel himself admitted at the end of his *Philosophy of History,* faith was in a state of decay. This was so because religious unity had vanished from modern life, as much as it had "vanished in Imperial Rome when the Divine was profaned." Thus, "Spirit, reconciled with the actual world" was "reconciled with it only in thought – not in life."[17] It was not the logic of the mediation, but its existential basis, that was shattered even as Hegel formulated it. The history of nineteenth- and twentieth-century thought has in fact been the history of the fragmentation of the Hegelian "middle." While many have drawn fragments from this "middle," no one has been willing to respect the complexities of the union that originally animated these appropriated individual fragments. Fackenheim documents the history of this fragmentation in several places, with sadness because, in his opinion, no non-Jewish philosopher had ever been able both to recognize and respect the special historical vocation of the people of Israel as well as Hegel did.[18] It was, however, precisely in the context of this fragmentation, and of the search for a new "middle" that would replace Hegel's, that, according to Fackenheim, the uniqueness of that vocation as Hegel himself had superbly described it could "appear in its own right."[19] The vocation of the children of Israel is to give witness to "the incommensurability … of a divine Presence that is and remains infinite and universal to a humanity that remains unyieldingly finite and particular."[20] It is to give witness to a togetherness that can only be one of "contrast," and the "harshest" and an infinitely paradoxical "contrast" at that. There cannot be any talk within Judaism of a complete mediation of extremes, but only of a *movement* towards a unifying "middle" that must remain paradoxical. Hegel's mediation encompassed this "middle" only *in thought* – never as experienced in real life from within Judaism itself.

As of the 1960s, when Fackenheim was teaching in Toronto, he took this fragmentation also as opening up the space for a true dialogue between different faiths and different traditions, all united – despite their radical differences – by the existentially shared desire for reconciliation. This is a position that would have made sense in the context of the Toronto campus, where Fackenheim was in dialogue with the Catholic philosophers Etienne Gilson and Jacques Maritain, and in contact with vibrant faculties of Protestant theology. Soon, however, Fackenheim's whole attitude towards Hegel was to undergo radical change. Events into which I need not go[21] forced him to retrieve, just like Rosenzweig had done a half century earlier, his Judaic past, and in this retrieval he had to come face to face with the Holocaust. This is an event he came to consider as a *novum* in history because, unlike anything humankind had witnessed before, it was a rationally deliberate, methodical, even perversely religious outpouring of evil for its own sake, with not even a shred of pragmatic motivation behind it to redeem it in the slightest.[22] It was a *novum* that disrupted history, its occurrence putting an end to the experience of the presence of a transcendent God. The new experience is instead that of the absence of God. God is no longer a God-with-us but a *Deus absconditus*. This makes a difference to the Hegelian system. Life has literally outrun it, in an even more radical way than life had outrun it in Hegel's own time, for it is clear now that there are wounds of the spirit that cannot be healed. Of course, the idea of reconciliation by way of mediation, of redemption of evil by the grace of God, is still valid, but only in an abstract, purely speculative sense. Events have denied to it its existential traction. Therefore Fackenheim turns to the task of rediscovering even the possibility of "making sense," and for this he digs deeply into his own Judaic past, recollecting it in view of a now hidden God, retrieving in the process even the mystical tradition of the Cabbala, which earlier would have had little appeal to him. History has been disrupted and the world is broken. But, if the world cannot be healed, like a broken vessel (to use an image from the Cabbala) it can be mended. Or at least one should try to mend it.[23] This is a work that requires an intellectual effort, a new attempt at conceptual "overreaching." Fackenheim might be confronted by the absurd, but he is no philosopher of the absurd, and that is true even at a time when metaphysics (in the words of Adorno) is no longer possible. But Fackenheim did not need metaphysics for his attempt at mending, for life precedes thought, and his task, as he took it to be now that metaphysics has at least for the moment been muted, was to steep himself in the present, very particular Jewish experience, personally working for what he took to be yet another *novum* in history, the existential response to the *novum* of the Holocaust. This is the return into history of the people of Israel with the creation of the state of Israel, an event that would have forced Spinoza to revise his judgment of his own people.

3. Rethinking the Problem of Evil

I said at the beginning that the temptation is to set up the contrast between Fackenheim and Harris as one between Jerusalem and Athens. But this would be false, for metaphysics (even when muted) is never very distant from Fackenheim's mind, and his Jerusalem is no longer Tertullian's. It is an empirical Jerusalem. Another temptation now might be to think that the Fackenheim of the 1960s, the Fackenheim in dialogue with different religious traditions on the campus of Toronto, is the one intellectually closer to Harris, that the difference between the two might ultimately boil down to a difference in approach to Hegel. Fackenheim's Hegel is the Berlin Hegel, the Hegel of the lectures on the philosophy of religion, whereas Harris's is the Hegel of the *Phenomenology of Spirit*. Of course, it is true that Hegel's lectures on religion are the text on which Fackenheim substantially bases his interpretation. But this other temptation also ought to be resisted. If there is a point at which the two men might meet, it is precisely on the issue of "evil," and it is Harris's Hegel, I believe, who best provides the conceptual framework for the experience of evil that haunts the later Fackenheim.

For this, I must make a short excursus into the late Schelling. Fackenheim always had the greatest respect for this Schelling, and in the 1960s decried (as he could no longer do now) the dearth of scholarship on the subject. But this is not the main reason for bringing him into the picture. The reason, rather, is that the older Schelling was very much dependent for his theories of religion on the heterodox element in the Christian tradition of theology, and according to Harris's reading of Hegel, this same heterodoxy conditions Hegel's reconstruction of Christian dogma in the *Phenomenology*, especially when one comes to the issue of evil. If the pagan world of Augustan Rome is for Harris the *Sitzt im Leben* of the birth of Christianity, it is the heterodox element within the latter, shunning as it does the fine conceptual compromises of the schools, that finally forces into the open the atheism that is in fact present from the beginning in the belief that God has become man. From Harris's point of view, Fackenheim's reading in Hegel of the doctrine of the Trinity would be much too orthodox, even Thomist in tone, and his ecumenism of the 1960s, based as it was on the belief that there is a spark of Divinity in every religion, strangely reminiscent of the universalism of the Enlightenment. What gets lost in this reading is the scandal of the particular, the evil that religions necessarily bring on other religions because of their necessary particularity. The pride of God is forgotten. As Harris says in a comment on ecumenism which I count among his most precious, the Christian is indeed obliged to forgive the non-Christian for being non-Christian. But he must equally ask forgiveness for being Christian.[24]

The older Schelling had been forced to amend his own early idealism, and to inveigh bitterly against Hegel's, by the phenomenon of evil, the irreducibility of which, he believed, no form of idealism can ultimately maintain. Precisely in order to save this irreducibility, Schelling was forced to say that evil, no less than the good, is in God himself. This is not to say that for Schelling one should therefore take God as the malign agent behind any irruption of evil. That was not his intention. His position, rather, is that there is within God the potential for both good and evil. But it is only when he lets go of his inner life and, in creation, lets this world of ours come into being – it is only in the fragmented existence of the latter – that evil is actualized, itself a fragment among other fragments, its immediate cause also one of these fragments. God is not to be held responsible, therefore, for any single irruption of evil. To the question, however, of why God ever resolved to create, consequently letting evil come into existence – to this question, Schelling had no answer. This is where his philosophy, as he himself acknowledged, reaches its limit of comprehension.

This is a very brief account of the late Schelling, which for my present purposes I have drawn from Fackenheim's own reading of the texts.[25] My point is that Schelling could not answer the question that he himself had posed because he was deliberately confining himself to the language of myth. As a matter of fact, Hegel (if Schelling had just bothered to understand him) had already posed the question and had also been able to answer it because, rather than falling back on the mythology of heterodox Christianity, he used such a mythology in order to demythologize the orthodox. Hegel, at least as read by Harris, translated both question and answer into social terms. I am back to all that is implied in the claim that for Hegel, "God ... is just the name for the categorical structure of self-consciousness that is *communally recognized* to be necessary."[26] The possibility of evil lies in the very structure of human individuality that wants to be universal while being bound to the particularity of existence. That possibility is necessarily actualized in action, where individuality establishes its identity. We are all born already in sin. The significance in Hegel of the "beautiful soul," the Romantic figure of the individual who takes the particular voice of his conscience as the norm of universal truth and necessarily runs into conflict with other like-minded individuals, is that this fact, that violence is endemic to the human situation, is explicitly recognized. Such individuals can therefore consciously undertake (east of Eden) the task of creating a society based, not on any utopian ideal of perfect harmony, but on the reconciliation that comes from confession and forgiveness.

I am reminded here of the concluding lines of Steinbeck's great novel, which I cite from distant memory: "'I am the daughter of a thief,' says she; and 'I am the son of a whore,' says he. And they walked away from the shade of the tree under which they had been sitting, together to create a new family." In Hegel's fictional – mind you, not *mythical* – reconstruction of this human situation, the two "beautiful souls" enacting it represent, respectively, one dedicated to action and the other to judgment. It is the final confrontation of the speculative and practical standpoint, of theory and praxis. It is also comparable to the confrontation of Spinoza and the pious Jew – with the big difference, which only affects Spinoza, that the latter has acquired a new subjective dimension. What makes for the "hardness of heart" of the two characters, that is, the conceit of their particularity, is not just that each is *de facto* bound to a naturally limited situation, yet the one will take his deeds to have absolute value and the other will pass his judgments with categorical universality. That's all part of being rational. The "hardness" lies rather in the fact that the man of action will not acknowledge the truth of the theoretical judgment exposing the de facto particularity of his deeds, and the man of judgment will not recognize that it is indeed impossible to act morally without presuming that one's actions set up a universal norm of conduct. The beginning of reconciliation, the "melting of the hard heart," occurs only when the one recognizes the truth of the theoretical judgment and, while continuing to act, asks forgiveness for the violence that inevitably attaches to his deeds, and the other recognizes the constraints of actions and, without abdicating the privilege of theoretical judgment, reserves any moral indictment to the judgment of history. When I say "history" here, I do not mean the object of any grand theory – "History" capitalized, so to speak – but the concrete situation that given actions will immediately create. And, as Harris remarks echoing the Gospel, *there will be sins against the Spirit that cannot be forgiven* (Mark 3:29).[27]

Schelling's question, "Why did God do it?" thus gets translated by Hegel into the historical question, "Why do individuals do what they do?" The only possible answer to this is the same as the one to which Fackenheim himself was forced when he asked, "Why did they perpetrate the evil of the Holocaust?" *They did it because they decided to do it.* It is because of this commonality of answer that I hazarded above the prospect of a meeting point between the late Fackenheim and Harris.[28] I only "hazarded" it because whether there is in fact any meeting point at all depends on many questions to which I have no answer. Would Fackenheim accept that Hegel's logical reconciliation (as understood by Harris) still has existential relevance? Most of all, would he acknowledge that, while perfectly justified in resolutely assuming the standpoint of particularity, this posture necessarily bears violence and consequences for which one eventually will have to answer? For his part, Harris does acknowledge that he is the inauthentic professor enjoying the rest of Resurrection Sunday. But would he also confess that, while the experience that he has recollected does indeed display in full the logic of the human situation (and this logic has absolute validity), this experience is of Hegel's particular world, that history has in many ways long since outrun it, that many are the Golgothas that our world has since experienced, that a new recollection is therefore necessary, and for such a recollection to have existential traction it will first require immersion in the particular? Of course, I have no answer to these questions. Therefore, the contrast that I have been trying to sketch will have to remain inconclusive. But I would not be able to raise such questions were it not for the fact that both Fackenheim and Harris did their Hegel with passion. And that has been enough for me to relieve the monotony of painting grey on grey that is the work of scholarship. *Laudemus viros gloriosos.*

NOTES

Reprinted by permission from *Owl of Minerva* 40, no. 2 (Spring/Summer 2009): 223–39.

This paper was first read on 29 December 2007, at the Baltimore meeting of the American Philosophical Association, as a contribution to the session on H.S. Harris and Hegel's *Phenomenology of Spirit* sponsored by the Hegel Society of America. I must stress that the paper is a reflection of Fackenheim's and Harris's thought, and only indirectly refers to Hegel's.

1 My treatment of Harris's thought is based on his magnum opus, *Hegel's Ladder*, vol. 1, *The Pilgrimage of Reason*; and vol. 2, *The Odyssey of Spirit* (Indianapolis: Hackett, 1997), cited as Harris 1 and Harris 2.

2 For Fackenheim, I am basing my reflections on the following works, which I list chronologically: *The Religious Dimension in Hegel's Thought* (Bloomington: Indiana University Press, 1967); *Encounters between Judaism and Modern Philosophy* (New York: Schocken Books, 1971); *The Jewish Return into History: Reflections in the Age of Auschwitz and a New Jerusalem* (New York: Schocken Books, 1978); *To Mend the World* (New York: Schocken Books, 1982); *The God Within: Kant, Schelling, and Historicity*, ed. John Burbidge (Toronto: University of Toronto Press, 1996). For the Holocaust as a *novum* in history, see, among many other places, *To Mend the World*, 133, 248.

3 "The crucial point is that to 'remember' something is different from the conscious knowledge that you are imagining it. What is remembered now is that God was sensibly present with us and died among us. It is remembered (rather than dreamed) because the world has come to the point where the memory is necessary. We do not know what happened historically, but our faith tells us that we are remembering a 'Gospel.' The necessity of this Gospel is what we have already comprehended; and it has nothing to do with empirical truth, because no empirical truth could be 'necessary' in this conceptual way. In a world full of saving fantasies [i.e., such as the world of Augustan Rome was] a story that is reported as history emerges; and the world must believe it, because its truth is what is logically needed" (Harris 2:663).

The whole section on the "Incarnation" (658–66), is relevant. Cf. also 583: "Paul did not 'choose' Jesus, any more than Jesus chose himself. It was the 'inhabited world' of the Roman Imperium which 'chose' the story that Paul helped to make."

4 Harris 2:681. The community expresses in the medium of its representation of God its own interpretation of life and the world. The myth of creation is a "mythical" way of expressing the freedom that we have in this interpretation of the world (682).

5 Cf. Harris 2:682–4. It is the Christian preacher who created the spirit of evil by polarizing Being and Thought, or in more concrete terms, the natural and the transcendent. This was a novum in history. There were indeed inimical forces in other religions and morally flawed gods, but none of them was essentially malevolent, i.e., evil in this demonic sense. Cf. 684.

6 Harris 2:671.

7 Harris 2:685–97. See Hegel's text, *Phänomenologie des Geistes*, in *Gesammelte Werke* (Hamburg: Meiner, 1980), 9:413 (line 37)–414 (line 15); and Harris's commentary on 685.

8 Cf. *Religious Dimension*, 8–9.
9 Harris 2:731: "So the historic evolution of religion comes first."
10 Cf. Fichte (who echoed Jacobi): "[First] Introduction to the Wissenschaftslehre," in J.G. Fichte: *Introductions to the Wissenschaftslehre and Other Writings*, trans. Daniel Breazeale (Indianapolis: Hackett, 1994), 19–20: "His belief in himself is immediate. This interest also permits us to understand why the defense of a philosophical system is customarily accompanied by a certain amount of passion ... The kind of philosophy one chooses ... depends on the kind of person one is."
11 Hans Küng, *The Incarnation of God*, trans. J.R. Stephenson (New York: Crossroads, 1987), 227.
12 Fackenheim, *To Mend the World*, 110–11. It is also the shibboleth in Jewish modernity, 136–8.
13 Cf.: "For such as Abraham, Moses, or Job, the One remains Other; however, these biblical figures compensate for this lack by 'renouncing renunciation' even while practicing renunciation: thus they regain the world even as they serve its Lord" (ibid., 118).
14 For one summary of Hegel's position, see ibid., 116–17.
15 Fackenheim is aware that his interpretation of Hegel diverts from the conventional. See Fackenheim, *The Religious Dimension in Hegel's Thought*, 206ff., 218–19 (Appendix 3).
16 Cf. ibid., chap. 6, "The Transfiguration of Faith into Philosophy," especially 201–6.
17 Ibid., 234.
18 Cf. the concluding chapter of Fackenheim, *The Religious Dimension in Hegel's Thought*. Also, Fackenheim, *To Mend the World*, 119–27, 139; Fackenheim, *Encounters between Judaism and Modern Philosophy*, 86, 89ff. I remember Fackenheim condemning Hermann Glockner's Jubiläumsausgabe of Hegel's works because, quite apart from the fact that it did not have any scholarly value, it expunged Hegel's every positive statement about the Jewish nation.
19 Fackenheim, *To Mend the World*, 138.
20 Ibid., 139. In this and in the preceding note, I use Fackenheim's own words because the moves that he makes in these passages are not altogether transparent. Taken in the wider context of *The Jewish Return into History*, this appearance "in its own right" of the Jewish vocation can mean only – as far as I can understand – the secular remythologizing of the Jewish experience in the shape of Zionism – a development that would have been possible at no other time except in the nineteenth century. Fackenheim adds, "The Jewish religion, unlike the Christian, cannot

accept the identity of the human nature and the Divine" (*To Mend the World*, 138). But neither can orthodox Christians accept any such identity. Fackenheim apparently has assumed this identity on Hegel's authority, not on the authority of the Councils, which have more than once declared as dogma that the two natures remain irreducibly distinct within the one exclusively divine person of the Christ. This union of two distinct natures in one person constitutes as much of a paradox as the one that is, according to Fackenheim, embedded in the Jewish experience of the Divine. This leads to a twofold consideration. (1) There is nothing orthodox about Hegel's interpretation of the Christian experience. This interpretation is itself already as "post-Christian" as is Harris's reading of it. (2) There is no doubt that for Hegel, religion is an ineliminable dimension of human existence. Once Christianity has been demythologized, however, the only religion possible in a post-Christian society would have to be secular in form. Now, we find among Fackenheim's reflections texts such as the following: "At Auschwitz every Jew represented all humanity when for reasons of birth alone he was denied life; after Auschwitz every Jew represents all humanity when he commits himself to Jewish survival. For this commitment is ipso facto testimony that there can be, must be, shall be, no second Auschwitz anywhere; on this testimony and this faith the secular no less than the religious Jew stakes his own life, the lives of his children, and the lives of his children's children. A secular holiness, side by side with religious, is becoming manifest in contemporary Jewish existence" (Fackenheim, *The Jewish Return into History*, 54). A "secular holiness," however, is all that would be possible in a Hegelian post-Christian world. Fackenheim is perhaps even more of a Hegelian when he distances himself from Hegel than when he is commenting on him. By implication, there might well be more of a commonality between him and Harris than the one I point to at the end of this essay. This novel secular religiosity of Israel, which no longer suffers from the political passivity of the Jewish people decried by Spinoza, would require a restatement of the confrontation that Hegel mediated between Spinoza and the pious Jew. I relegate this suggestion to a footnote because it requires further investigation.

21 *The Jewish Return into History* documents this change. See 55.

22 See, among many other texts, ibid., 257–8.

23 Fackenheim, *To Mend the World*, 253, 256, 262.

24 Harris 2:690.

25 Fackenheim's three essays on Schelling collected in *The God Within* ("Schelling's Philosophy of the Literary Arts," "Schelling's Philosophy

of Religion," and "Schelling's Conception of Positive Philosophy") are my sources. These essays do not represent the latest in scholarship on the subject, but I have yet to find anything that equals them in philosophical depth.

26 Harris 2:681. For Hegel's immanentism, see 732.

27 Cf. Harris 2:739.

28 See also note 21 above.

4 Fackenheim on Self-Making, Divine and Human

DANIEL BRANDES

In the Introduction to his 1982 opus *To Mend the World,* Emil Fackenheim observed that the crucial third chapter of the work, which contains its most extensive encounter with Hegel's thought, "begins with the breakdown of Hegelianism – in search, not of Hegel, but of what may be called a post-Hegelian, religiosecular truth."[1] It may seem odd that Fackenheim's great work of constructive post-Holocaust thought places at its centre a meditation on the collapse of Hegel's philosophy. Why should the fate of Hegelianism, or indeed of any philosophical system, occupy such pride of place in a work taken up with the concrete suffering and near-extinction of a people? The answer, as Fackenheim had earlier indicated in his 1968 book *The Religious Dimension in Hegel's Thought,* is that Hegel's philosophy is not simply one philosophical system among others, and the consequences of its breakdown extend well beyond Hegelianism.

In an illuminating essay on Fackenheim's intellectual career,[2] Michael Morgan has shown how Fackenheim's gradual thematizing of the Holocaust and of the absolute rupture it effected in Western (and not merely Jewish) life and thought coincided with his increasingly critical attitude towards Hegel's thought. In his early philosophical writings, Fackenheim had reflected broadly on questions concerning the relation of faith and reason in the writings of German thinkers from Kant to Kierkegaard, but by the mid-1960s he had come to focus on Hegel's philosophy, and specifically, on its claim to register the (metaphysical) truth of concrete historical events. Fackenheim found in Hegel's thought an exemplary instance of "thought going to school with life," and in the aforementioned 1968 work he sought to articulate the virtues of a life lived in the "Hegelian middle," between comprehensive conceptuality and embodied existence. Indeed, Fackenheim never abandoned his commitment to this Hegelian ideal or to the dialectical method that underpinned it. He never abandoned the ideal of a mediating reason that would do full justice to the historical situatedness of humankind without thereby forfeiting the possibility of metaphysical or trans-historical truths. But already in 1968, Fackenheim had begun to doubt whether Hegel's systematic aspirations, his claim for the absoluteness of reason's mediating power, could stand up to the unprecedented historical experiences of the recent past. Without yet entering into "the scandal of the particularity of Auschwitz," Fackenheim suggested – and repeated, in a contemporaneous essay entitled "Would Hegel Today Be a Hegelian?" – that what had appeared here was an unprecedented form of evil, an evil that must defy Hegelian synthesis (indeed, it defied all thought, philosophical or otherwise), and that Hegel, were he alive to bear witness, would himself have acknowledged it. According to Fackenheim, Hegel's own philosophical scruples would require him to admit that history had revealed the failure of the Hegelian dialectic. But, importantly, this failure itself, insofar as it has dialectical results (giving rise to "a new religiosecular truth"), remains part of the dialectic of history. It is this claim for the dialectical effects of the failure of (Hegel's) dialectic – evidenced in those pages of *To Mend the World* devoted to the "Commanding Voice" issuing even from the furnaces of Auschwitz and the imperative to which it gives rise – and not any renewed faith in reason's encompassing power, that prompts Fackenheim to describe himself as a "Hegelian-after-Hegel."

In what follows, I will not pretend to provide a comprehensive overview of Fackenheim's complex inheritance from Hegel, nor will I attempt to show through a survey of Fackenheim's work how the early appropriation and defence of Hegel's dialectical method remains operative in the later explicitly "post-Hegelian" and post-Holocaust writings. Instead, I will focus on a single, often overlooked early text, the 1961 essay *Metaphysics and Historicity*, and on a single (albeit indispensable) term from that work: *self-making*. It is here, in his early determination of humankind as a "self-making process," that Fackenheim makes a crucial interpretive decision that has been almost wholly neglected in the secondary literature but remained effective in his thinking up to the end of his life. It is a decision, as I shall suggest, for a certain *kind* of self-making, a certain way of being-in-history, and it not only informs Fackenheim's express understanding of human historicity in the 1961 essay but it continues to inform his best-known contribution to contemporary (and especially Jewish) thought: his articulation of a "614th Commandment" enjoining the survivors of the Holocaust "not to give Hitler any posthumous victories." Since the 614th Commandment is rarely thought in connection with Fackenheim's lingering Hegelianism, it will be worth seeing how the latter continues to operate there – and how a differently inflected conception of self-making, the resources of which were also available to Fackenheim, might have altered and enriched this existential and political imperative.

In the first half of *Metaphysics and Historicity* Fackenheim is concerned to establish two assumptions, both of which are essential for our understanding of human historicity (or for what Fackenheim describes as the *essentially historical* character of human being). First, following Collingwood, he draws a sharp distinction between the orders of nature and history: "History consists of actions performed by man, not of natural events which happen to him; and the latter are historical only by virtue of their relation – potential or actual – to the former."[3] It is important to note that Fackenheim is not positing a strict opposition between nature as a realm of necessity and history as a sphere of freedom. On the contrary, he shows that it is precisely by virtue of natural (biological or psychological) processes that we are able to transcend the essential passivity of nature, in which we are acted upon by forces external to us, and insert ourselves into the historical order. Instead of the Kantian language of necessity and freedom, Fackenheim follows Collingwood and speaks of an "outside" and "inside": "A natural event has an 'outside' only. An historical action has an 'inside' as well as an outside. The outside consists of physical bodies and their movement. The inside consists of human thoughts – aims, plans, and decisions." The *assumption* we must make, Fackenheim explains, is not that certain individuals believe themselves to be aiming, planning, and deciding. This is an indisputable fact. What is assumed is that they are, at least occasionally, correct in this belief – that "men are not invariably subject to compulsive urges when they believe themselves to be making free decisions ... In short, there is free action, not merely the appearance of free action."[4]

According to Fackenheim, most people do indeed assume that there is a distinction between natural events and historical actions, but this does not yet commit them to an acknowledgment of humankind's radical historicity. "For it is one thing to admit that men are capable of free action, and hence of a history. It is another thing altogether to assert that man – the being capable of a history – is himself the product of history."[5] Even granting to man the capacity for free action – and so granting that he is capable of a history – one might nevertheless suppose that this capacity itself is not historical, that it belongs to man's nature as a fixed and unchanging endowment. If this were the case, Fackenheim claims, then, the doctrine of historicity would be false. This doctrine, to repeat, claims that man is essentially (and not accidentally) historical; it is an expressly metaphysical doctrine, concerned "with human being *qua* being and *qua* human," and it requires that "there are no permanent natures, distinct from the processes in which they are involved, or at any rate, there is no permanent human nature."[6] To say that there is no permanent human nature is to say that the distinction between human being and human acting cannot finally be maintained; or, in positive terms, that it is in acting that man makes or constitutes himself. Of course, the claim that man makes himself through his actions, and that there is no independent identity prior to, or outside of, the historical sphere, is hardly original. Fackenheim acknowledges that in making this point, he is simply making explicit the basic Hegelian premise that the ontological study of man cannot be divorced from the study of history. But the question remains: if we grant, first, that there is a qualitative difference between natural events and human actions; and second, that human actions are not the product, but rather the condition, of human nature, then how shall we understand this priority and generative power of the deed? If, as Fackenheim now concludes, "human being is a self-making or self-constituting process," how shall we understand this process?

It is in his response to this question that Fackenheim makes the unheralded but far-reaching decision hinted at above. Seeking to ground his account of human self-making in an account of the divine – and specifically, *an account of God himself understood not as a Being, but as self-making, as process* – he looks beyond traditional ontological options and invokes a "rival tradition" he describes as "meontology." Given its importance, I cite the relevant passage at length:

> The concept of self-making occurs not only in a relatively brief period of modern metaphysics. It is basic to a whole metaphysical tradition which rivals the major Western tradition in metaphysics. The major tradition asserts that *operatio sequitur esse.* But there is also a minor tradition which asserts that, at least in the case of God, *esse sequitur operationem.* This tradition harks back possibly as far as to John Scotus Eriugena and, passing through such thinkers as Jacob Boehme and Schelling, finds a

> contemporary representative in Nicolas Berdyaev. In the major tradition, God is understood as Pure Being, and in substantial strains of that tradition, as creating the world *ex nihilo*. In the minor tradition, God is understood as Pure Freedom who, in creating *ex nihilo*, Himself passes *ex nihilo in aliquid*. The major tradition is ontological, in the strictest sense. The minor tradition would strictly have to be called meontological.[7]

As this passage makes clear, Fackenheim will seek to ground his account of human self-making in the process of divine self-making, a process rooted in the "pure freedom" of a God beyond Being. He explains, "The God of meontological metaphysics would have to be described as a process which (a) because it is pure *making* proceeds from the indifference of sheer possibility of nothingness into the differentiation of actuality – *ex nihilo in aliquid*; (b) because it is *self*-making establishes its own identity throughout this process by returning upon itself; or, otherwise put, proceeds into otherness, yet cancels this otherness and in so doing establishes itself; (c) because it is *absolute* self-making, actualizes *ex nihilo* the totality of possibilities."[8]

Here we find Fackenheim's argument coming into focus. Having invoked the meontological God – the God beyond Being, in whom the reality of divine freedom exceeds the necessity and eternity of the divine nature – he immediately grasps this divine freedom in terms of the act of self-making. He does this, as we have suggested, in order to discover in the divine activity a speculative expression of the same process of self-making at issue in human historicity. Indeed, looking ahead, Fackenheim will go on to distinguish the "quasi-historical" character of divine self-making (in which the process in question, *ex nihilo in aliquid*, marks a movement that nevertheless "wholly transcends temporality") from the radical historicity of human self-making, and to establish the dialectical relation between the two processes. But we cannot be too hasty here. Before turning to Fackenheim's dialectical move, we must consider how things stand with the "minor" meontological tradition whose authority he invokes. Does Fackenheim's reference to meontology help to illuminate his position? Does his recourse to this "rival tradition" register the full weight of its difference from traditional ontology? More specifically, does his description of the God of meontology capture the force of a divine freedom that precedes and exceeds divine nature? Or on the contrary, does the immediate resolution of God's Freedom beyond Being, his *actus purus*, into the act of self-making described above risk dissolving the very difference that distinguishes meontology? Suspicions regarding this latter possibility are only heightened when one reads in a footnote that "the greatest attempt to explicate this kind of [meontological] logic is beyond all doubt Hegel's work by that name."[9] The same Hegel who is commonly read as the consummate thinker of the ontological tradition is here taken as the exemplary representative of the counter-tradition. Although Fackenheim does not pause to justify this extraordinary suggestion, it obviously informs his subsequent description of human self-making in its dialectical interplay with divine self-making. Let me draw this claim out by contrasting the above description of divine self-making with the well-known meontological account presented in Schelling's *Weltalter*.

In epistemological terms, Schelling's account begins with the fact that there is something rather than nothing – that is, with the recognition of the existence of the world, and the problem of its creation. The sheer reality of this world, Schelling argues, poses a serious problem for the traditional post-Aristotelian understanding of God as perfect, eternal, and unchanging (the "ontological" portrait of God as Pure Being). On this traditional understanding, Schelling suggests, God is not "free" to act beyond his own essence – since this latter would imply a divine will distinct from divine wisdom, violating the essential unity of God – and thus the creation of the world is either denied altogether or else reduced to a necessary effect of the divine nature. The possibility of a *creatio ex nihilo*, or of the world grasped as the gracious gift of a free God, is here rendered unthinkable. "For how ... what is first purely and fully wrapped up in itself can, in a subsequent moment or act (for it cannot be thought otherwise), emerge out of itself without ground or occasioning cause, or how it could by itself sublimate or interrupt its eternal unity and stillness: this simply cannot be rendered intelligible with any kind of thought."[10] In order to account for the creation of the world, Schelling argues, we must allow that God's essential being is *not* a unity. We must allow for the possibility of a difference within God (or, as Schelling says, within Godself), the possibility of something more or other within God that could, qua extra-divine being, account for the existence of a reality other than that of divine nature. This something other "within" God but other than God (and so irreducible to the nature or essence of God) is the event of divine freedom or revelation. It is through this event that God (beyond Being) acts upon God (as Being), and thereby actualizes or externalizes God's own nature or essence – hitherto only an essence, an idea – into a stable reality. As Randi Rashkover has nicely put this point, "Revelation is the event or happening through which

God qua nature is acted upon by God qua Other. Through this event, God achieves life or comes into existence from the seclusion of his restless eternity. God's life is a result of an internal event of self-relationality or self-othering … This coming into life or existence is what Schelling also refers to as creation. The distinction, in other words, between God and the created order derives from the very difference between God's being and God's act within God-self."[11]

For our purposes here, what matters is not Schelling's doctrine of revelation or his characteristic notion that existence, both divine and human, derives from an event or act of transcendent non-Being upon Being. What is of interest here is the creative power of divine freedom – i.e., its externalization of the divine nature – and whether this freedom is properly understood as a divine "self-making" in the specific sense proposed by Fackenheim. We recall that Fackenheim distinguished ontological and meontological conceptions of divinity – the former identifying God as pure being and the latter as pure freedom – and then sought to dialectically reconcile the two conceptions in the concrete act of divine self-making. In particular, he claimed that the God of creation "proceeds into otherness, yet cancels this otherness and in so doing establishes itself." We can see that the freedom beyond being that characterizes divine freedom is here made to serve divine identity (the "self" in "self-making" absorbs the original creative activity) – an absorption that is prepared for by Fackenheim's determination of the divine activity as "quasi-historical" and so susceptible to such transformations[12] – and it is the establishment of this divine selfhood that requires the "cancellation" of the otherness of divine freedom. But – and this is the crucial point – it is precisely the *absence* of any such negation or cancellation that characterizes Schelling's account.

For Schelling, it is true that all existence, including God's own existence, requires the impact of an exterior power; and in the case of divine life, it is God who provides this act himself, acting outside his own being with a freedom that both distinguishes itself from this being *and affirms it*. This affirmative character of divine freedom is essential to Schelling's entire position. Yes, divine freedom has priority – God's existence is itself founded in the order of God's freedom – but Schelling insists repeatedly that the God of the pure free act cannot be *separated* from divine nature.[13] As he puts it, "Without a nature, the freedom in God could not be separated from the deed and hence, would not be actual freedom."[14] If God were only free act and not also nature – that is, if he were simply beyond being and not also being – then freedom would constitute his nature or necessity; that is, his freedom would no longer be freedom. Schelling's constant emphasis is on this relational character of divine freedom, its affirmation of the divine nature. But importantly, if divine existence is realized or externalized in the affirming order of God's freedom, this existence cannot be characterized by the negation or cancellation of the freedom by which it came to be. (At issue here is not only the theological question of God's affirmation of Godself in the free act of self-othering. On the contrary, since Fackenheim wishes to understand the divine self-relation as exemplary for the historical project of the self-making of humankind, its articulation has concrete and practical implications for our own action.) God's "self-making" does not, in Schelling's meontological account, imply the strict negation of the original act of freedom beyond being in the form of a retroactive assimilation of divine freedom by divine nature. Rather, inasmuch as divine freedom is essentially relational, ordering and affirming what is other than it in its very difference, its "experience" by the affirmed divine nature is not one of negation and cancellation but simply the revelation or exposition of this having-been-acted-upon. In her illuminating treatment of the Schellingian source of Franz Rosenzweig's *Star of Redemption* – a text whose importance for Fackenheim has been well documented – Rashkover provides a helpful description of the difference between Hegel's dialectical conception and Schelling's "lawful" (or difference-affirming) conception:

> If a dialectical logic presupposes that movement or change involves excision or reduction according to the drive and will of an essence that perdures over and against all else, lawful action or freedom effects change without reduction. Lawful action exposes elements as they exist within an order of other elements. Revelation is orientation. In this particular case, originary freedom is no longer independent or disordered from divine nature. As such, it is delimited or restricted, and ordered in and by its exposure as an attribute of God as creator. To be ordered and exposed as divine power, originary freedom remains – now named, now identified, and now "revealed."[15]

Again, it is not my intention (nor is it remotely possible in this space) to provide an extended engagement with Schelling's meontology. The object of this brief review is simply to raise the question concerning Fackenheim's own appeal to this concept and its implications for his account of human self-making. The danger, in my view, of reading meontology through a Hegelian lens – or as a resource for a dialectical rather than "lawful" account of the freedom beyond being – is that it grasps human historicity itself in terms of reduction and excision (we make our situating past our own by cancelling its difference, discovering ourselves) rather than in terms of an orienting affirmation and exposition of difference (we have been acted upon by what must be affirmed in its otherness to ourselves).[16]

These theological reflections may seem hopelessly abstract and removed from the concrete historical, if not political, questions that concern Fackenheim in *Metaphysics and Historicity*. However, as I suggested in the introduction, this early interpretive decision remains effective in Fackenheim's mature work, up to and including his opus *To Mend the World*, and it bears at least indirectly on the existential and political insights of that text. I want to conclude these remarks by considering in this connection one of the best known doctrinal points from Fackenheim's late work, his postulation of a "614th Commandment: not to give Hitler any posthumous victories."

The genesis of this oft-misunderstood postulate was Fackenheim's search, in the late 1960s, for what he called a "genuine response" to Auschwitz. From his earliest reflections on the "scandal of the particularity of Auschwitz," Fackenheim argued that no "philosophical" response to the event was possible. As we have seen, it was the very failure of the Hegelian resource to comprehend the calamity that underpinned Fackenheim's situation of his own thinking as explicitly "post-Hegelian," and he sought to expose philosophy to the radical challenge posed by Auschwitz to all philosophy, indeed, to all thinking as such. But if philosophy had been fatally wounded by the unprecedented evil that came to light in the camps – indeed, if no work of thought could be supposed to provide a response (Auschwitz being "the rock on which throughout eternity all rational explanations will crash and break apart"), all hope was not yet lost. A response to the event was, despite everything, possible. Not only was it possible, but it was actual – it was already taking place, in countless acts of continued faith and resistance on the part of surviving Jews everywhere. Fackenheim describes this simple but "momentous discovery: that while religious thinkers were vainly struggling for a response to Auschwitz, Jews throughout the world … had to some degree been responding all along."[17] The argument moves here from actuality to possibility – from the innumerable concrete acts of resistance (accessed by Fackenheim through documentary narratives, memoirs, and post-Holocaust diaries, and examined at great length in *To Mend the World*) to the possibility of resistance thereby proved. Moreover, given the availability of concrete acts of resistance, it should be possible to "read off of these existing responses" norms or imperatives for future authentic responses. It is just such an imperative that finds expression in what Fackenheim introduced at this time as the 614th Commandment.

The clearest account of the commandment – which occasioned a great deal of misunderstanding upon its initial publication and continues to do so – can be found in Fackenheim's late essay, "These Twenty Years," where it is expanded into four distinct imperatives of genuine response. He writes:

> I believe that whereas no redeeming voice is heard at Auschwitz a commanding voice is heard, and that it is being heard with increasing clarity. *Jews are not permitted to hand Hitler posthumous victories.* Jews are commanded to survive as Jews, lest their people perish. They are commanded to remember the victims of Auschwitz, lest their memory perish. They are forbidden to despair of God, lest Judaism perish. They are forbidden to despair of the world as the domain of God, lest the world be handed over to the forces of Auschwitz. For a Jew to break this commandment would be to do the unthinkable – to respond to Hitler by doing his work.[18]

Leaving aside the many questions and concerns that might arise from this clarification – questions, for instance, concerning the obligatory force of the imperative for secular and religious Jews; concerning the possible tensions that might arise in the fulfilment of the distinct commandments; concerning the psychological conditions supposed by the final two commandments in the aftermath of the disaster – let us focus solely on the first commandment: to survive as Jews, lest the Jewish people perish. It is this commandment that has received the lion's share of attention and that has aroused the most suspicion. What concrete acts might be mandated by this imperative? What sort of politics might be justified by it?

Are Fackenheim's own political commitments, his well-known and passionate Zionism, relevant to these questions? Is this the necessary implication of the 614th Commandment? And how does the interpretive decision highlighted above – for a dialectical rather than a "lawful" conception of meontology – inform these questions? It seems to me that had Fackenheim been guided by Schelling, by the Schellingian treatment of divine freedom (the otherness of which is not negated or cancelled in the achievement of identity but affirmed and preserved), his corresponding understanding of human freedom, and of human self-making, might have been marked by a different practical posture. In this case, the survival of Jews as Jews, the continued *identification* of Jews as Jews, would already imply an affirmation of the meontological conditions of identity: an affirmation that identity is the product, not the condition, of free action; that since freedom precedes identity and is irreducible to it, the "making" in "self-making" can never be reducible to the "self" (or to say the same thing, we can never be sovereign over our actions, insulating ourselves from their unforeseeable consequences or from the new chain of actions and reactions they may provoke in others). By reading the imperative of survival through the lens of a corrected meontology – a meontology in which the originary act of freedom beyond being, the originary being-acted-upon by what is other, is not forgotten with the establishment of identity, but continues to orient by exposing and affirming the claims of the other – we may arrive at a theologico-political standpoint that more fully accords with the 614th Commandment.

NOTES

1 Emil Fackenheim, *To Mend the World* (Bloomington: Indiana University Press, 1982). Hereafter cited as *TMW*.
2 Michael L. Morgan, "Emil Fackenheim, the Holocaust, and Philosophy," in *The Cambridge Companion to Modern Jewish Philosophy*, ed. P. Gordon and M. Morgan, 256–77 (Cambridge: Cambridge University Press, 2007).
3 Emil Fackenheim, *Metaphysics and Historicity* (Milwaukee: Marquette University Press, 1961), 17. Hereafter cited as *MH*.
4 Ibid., 19.
5 Ibid., 23.
6 Ibid., 23–4.
7 Ibid., 29–30.
8 Ibid., 31–2.
9 Ibid., 34n22.
10 F.W.J. Schelling, *The Ages of the World*, trans. J. Wirth (Albany: SUNY Press, 2000), 39.
11 Randi Rashkover, *Freedom and Law: A Jewish-Christian Apologetics* (New York: Fordham University Press, 2011), 35.
12 Fackenheim introduces a careful distinction between the temporality (or sheer passage) of natural life, the singular historicity of human beings, and the quasi-historicity of the divine being. See *MH*, 34–43.

13 Thus, for Schelling, God is both Being and beyond Being. Fackenheim's programmatic distinction between ontology and meontology, with the accompanying distinctions between a God of "pure Being" and a God of "pure freedom," is already inadequate to Schelling's account, in which the distinction between God's being and God's act is internal to the divine being.

14 Schelling, *Ages of the World*, 81.

15 Rashkover, *Freedom and Law*, 161.

16 In his illuminating chapter "Jewish and Post-Christian Interpretations of Hegel: Emil Fackenheim and Henry S. Harris" (included in this volume), George di Giovanni considers Fackenheim's respective debts to Schelling and Hegel, and he concludes that while the Schellingian resource (as mediated by Rosenzweig) informs Fackenheim's early notion of revelation, it is finally a dialectical logic that best captures the sense of human freedom under God. "Fackenheim's point," he explains, "is that Hegel's philosophy, rather than Schelling's is the one more apt for performing the required mediation [between the universalist aspirations of human reason and the historical particularity of divine revelation] ... and this is precisely because of the autonomy that Hegel's reason claims for itself." Whether we accept di Giovanni's own further reading of Fackenheim on Hegel – a critical account that hinges on Fackenheim's supposed failure to appreciate the heterodox character of Hegel's reading of the Incarnation – his emphasis on Fackenheim's distinctive Hegelianism, and on the "autonomy" of reason that underpins it, is surely correct. The autonomy at issue here names reason's putative power to synthesize and appropriate the dispensation that has given rise to it. But the question remains whether this familiar dialectical operation does not forfeit the very freedom claimed by the meontological counter-tradition – that is, a freedom that consists not in the simultaneous production and discovery of the rational self (as the ontological tradition has it) but rather in the unending exposition of this self to the (divine) freedom that has always preceded and situated its own rational exertions.

17 Fackenheim, "Jewish Faith and the Holocaust," in *The Jewish Thought of Emil Fackenheim*, ed. M. Morgan (Detroit: Wayne State University Press, 1987), 163–4.

18 Fackenheim, "These Twenty Years: A Reappraisal," in *Quest for Past and Future* (Boston: Beacon, 1968), 20. Italics are Fackenheim's.

5 Conscience, Religion, and Multiculturalism: A Canadian Hegel

JOHN RUSSON

In the two centuries since G.W.F. Hegel taught and wrote philosophy in Germany, a wide range of positions have been attributed to him by admirers and critics both. No doubt any philosopher suffers from caricature, misunderstanding, and misrepresentation, but the tradition of Hegel "interpretation" is an egregious case of this.[1] Much of the reason for this is surely to be found in the nature of Hegel's writing, and, indeed, the nature of his philosophy: both are very difficult. Hegel writes like a man in a race, scrambling to get to the finish with little room to attend to the niceties of style: his books race through ideas, containing in a single paragraph the content to which another writer might devote a chapter, and his language draws heavily on an abstract, technical vocabulary largely invented (and only minimally explained) by himself. This density and opacity in his writing is made even more challenging by the fact that the ideas he is articulating with this language are almost as novel now as they were when he first gave voice to them in the early 1800s: Hegel describes a dynamic, self-transforming reality, and he requires that the philosopher undertake this description without relying on any presumptions – there could surely be no more demanding a philosophical project. There certainly are important cases of interpreters throughout the entire history of Hegel interpretation who understood Hegel well, but, overall, the reception of Hegel has been the gradual process of deciphering his texts, with subsequent generations improving substantially upon the flawed interpretations of their teachers.[2]

It is mostly since the 1960s that scholarship on Hegel developed to a level of technical and conceptual precision that allowed it to be authoritative, through the work of a broad body of scholars, much of whose work was presented in the pages of *Hegel-Studien*. One of the most prominent and significant scholars to emerge in this environment was the Canadian Hegelian H.S. Harris. Initially through *Hegel's Development*, his two mammoth studies of Hegel's early texts, and subsequently through *Hegel's Ladder*, his massive and ground-breaking, two-volume study of Hegel's *Phenomenology of Spirit*, Harris marked himself out as the most distinguished Hegel scholar in the English-speaking world, and, perhaps, anywhere.[3] Through this work, Harris established an approach to the interpretation of Hegel that is simultaneously authoritative and distinctly Canadian: distinctly Canadian both in the sense that it is a perspective on Hegel that has been most prominently advanced by Canadian scholars, and distinctly Canadian in that it resonates powerfully with one of the most remarked aspects of Canadian political self-identity, namely, the theme of multiculturalism.[4] In what follows, I will outline the general and distinctive parameters of this interpretation of Hegel by focusing on three themes: recognition, religion, and conscience.

Recognition

The work of Hegel that has most importantly shaped this Canadian tradition of Hegel interpretation is his *Phenomenology of Spirit* of 1807.[5] In this work, Hegel endeavours to describe the immediate form of experience. The initial attempt to describe experience brings to light further aspects of experience not initially acknowledged, and the book's project of description is a progressive acknowledgment of more and more inalienable dimensions of experience.[6] The inalienable aspect of experience that is most distinctively formative for Hegel's philosophy is intersubjectivity: Hegel demonstrates that we always experience ourselves as belonging to a world in which there are perspectives other than our own, and that it is integral to our very sense of self that we seek the recognition and confirmation of these other perspectives.[7] In his study of the "dialectic of recognition [*Anerkennung*]," Hegel demonstrates the way in which our experience is formed by the ways we try to cope with our experience of being answerable to the perspective of another: specifically, he distinguishes between behavioural strategies that are rooted in a denial of the weight of the other – situations of unequal recognition – and behavioural strategies rooted in an acceptance of the equality of the worth of others' perspectives with the worth of our own.[8] It is this imperative to equality of recognition that is intrinsic to our self-consciousness experience that, Hegel shows, primarily undergirds our epistemological, political, and moral norms of truth, justice, and duty. It is this theme from the *Phenomenology of Spirit* that most informs what I understand to be the distinctive orientation of Canadian Hegel interpretation.

This basic idea behind the "dialectic of recognition" is fairly easy to grasp intuitively. The central insight behind Kant's *Critique of Pure Reason* is that we experience the world as a place that has a reality beyond our own perception and thus as inherently "public." Hegel adds that our perception of the world, then, and our actions in the world, are subject to the judgment of others, that is, our own "say so" about the meanings of our own words and deeds is not the only or the last word on our true nature, but is instead an interpretation in dialogue with interpretations of others. Our subjection to the perspectives of others, further, is not simply a matter of the evaluation of our "external" appearance, but in fact touches us at our most intimate and emotional levels as we grapple with our basic sense of self-esteem. The fact that we feel embarrassed or proud in front of others reminds us how dependent we are upon the approbation of others for our sense of self-worth. It is intrinsic to our self-experience to feel ourselves subject to the perspectives of others, and to desire their endorsement. And yet, precisely because this is such an intimate and important matter, it is also a site of great vulnerability, and can thus be quite a troubling site. For that reason, we often seek to evade acknowledging or engaging directly with this sphere, pretending to be indifferent to it; or, again, we try by implicit, manipulative means to control the perspectives of others and force their acceptance of us. These familiar psychological "defence mechanisms" are the subject of such classic studies as Eric Berne's *Games People Play* or Everett Shostrom's *Man the Manipulator*, and it is just such strategies that Hegel identifies in his study of unequal recognition.[9] What is most potent in Hegel's analysis is the demonstration that these matters of negotiating interpersonal power are not simply strategies employed by a fully developed individual in his or her dealings with other fully developed individuals, but are the very process through which our individual identities are formed in the first place.

Coherent self-identity is not an intrinsic possession, as we might imagine a property of a thing to be. Coherent self-identity, rather, is something accomplished: rather than *being* such selves by nature, we *become* individual selves through a process of interpersonal navigation and negotiation. Our sense of self is the way we have been *able* to maintain a self-interpretation in coordination with the interpretations of ourselves projected by others. In our most immediate interpersonal relations, we establish ourselves as "trusted companion," "boss," "idol," "loser," etc., that is, in the "*entre deux*" of interpersonal life we establish ourselves largely in terms of how we handle the power-plays of mutual estimation;[10] this interpersonal interaction, though, is typically situated in a broader social context, and the very terms in which we conduct our interpersonal lives are "mediated" – informed and shaped – by the shared terms of our cultural life. Our interpersonal life may be a matter of equality of recognition or inequality of recognition, but these intimate dealings typically rest more basically on an embrace of the shared terms for interaction that are the traditions and especially the language of our social culture. Our cooperative, collective embrace of these terms – the equality of our mutual recognition in the carrying on of these cultural forms, which Hegel calls "spirit" (*Geist*) – is the more basic presupposition of our more personal interactions. We adopt a "social" sense of ourselves – we embrace the forms of behaviour that make ourselves legitimate, recognizable members of "our" society – in the very process of developing an interpersonal sense of self-identity.[11]

At both the interpersonal level, then, and at the broader social level, self-identity is a collective accomplishment. Our coherent sense of self-identity is ultimately rooted in the equality of recognition that is implied in the shared terms that make cultural life possible. The terms of any given culture, however, are contingent, that is, the determinate history that led to the forms of social life that define one culture differs from the determinate history that led to the forms of social life that define other cultures. Our coherent self-identity, then, is inherently rooted in embracing the norm of equal recognition, but that "root" itself takes a contingent, historically determined form. The coherence of our self-identity simultaneously rests on a universal norm – the universal equality of recognition – and a determinate form – the distinctive cultural terms in and through which we are prepared to recognize and be recognized. It is this tension, intrinsic to the dialectic of recognition, between universality and determinacy – our non-universal particularity – that lies behind the centrality of the theme of multiculturalism in the work of Canadian scholars of Hegel.

Multiculturalism

In a corrective to early attempts to assimilate Hegel's philosophy to Christian theism, an earlier generation of Hegel scholars felt it necessary to prove that Hegel's philosophy is a kind of empiricism (which it is), and were either embarrassed by Hegel's central interest in religion or sought to show him to be reducing religion to an inessential, metaphorical covering for the truths of reason. In fact, though, Hegel is no more a reductive empiricist or a rationalist than he is a Christian theist, and one of the central emphases in Harris's study of Hegel is the autonomy of religious experience. Religion is not an optional form of "picture thinking" (a poor translation of Hegel's term *Vorstellung*, which has clouded the thinking of a few generations of students of Hegel who rely on Miller's English rendition for their study of Hegel) that intellectually weak or dishonest people rely upon instead of thinking rationally. (This attitude towards religion, in fact, is the attitude that figures of "Enlightenment" take towards what they interpret at "Superstition" – a view Hegel criticizes.[12]) Religion, rather, is the way a community establishes for itself terms through which it can embrace and articulate what is ultimate – the "absolute."[13] Philosophical thinking may well develop a purely conceptual articulation of this absolute, but that practice is itself a development of this more basic, communal grasp of reality and not the prior or separate accomplishment of a self-possessed rational mind.

Because it is possible, however, to develop such a philosophical, conceptual articulation of what is grasped religiously, and because philosophical conceptuality intrinsically and necessarily speaks to all rational individuals, the philosophical appropriation of religion must necessarily transform that original, communal grasp of reality, for that original grasp is always and necessarily particular, always a grasp inherently shaped in a determinate form inseparable from the historicality of a culture.[14] Hegel's philosophy, Harris has shown, points to the necessary multiplicity of religions and the necessary unity of "philosophical theology," so to speak.[15]

It is this understanding of the relation between philosophy and religion that lies behind what I and some others have called Hegel's "multiculturalism."[16] The multiculturalism of Hegel's philosophy is not the reflection of a "taste" for cultural variety, but is the recognition of a deep experiential pluralism – a recognition, that is, that our identities are formed by participation in determinate cultures whose particular forms permanently shape our capacities for engaging meaningfully with the world. It is our formative cultural participation that supplies us with the terms – the means – for our own growth and development, and, inasmuch as we come from different cultures, we come at experience on different terms. Whatever universality there is in human experience is something that must be accomplished and realized on the basis of these non-universal terms. Indeed, this view that universality must emerge as the "self-transcendence" of particularity is what is perhaps most distinctive of Hegel's philosophical position in general: the notion of *Aufhebung*.[17]

This notion that the norm of universality is intrinsic to our cultural particularity is similarly the basis of Charles Taylor's Hegel-inspired challenge to the idea of an irremediable ethnocentricity in experience. In "Understanding and Ethnocentricity," Taylor argues that, though we are essentially embedded in our cultural particularities, it is nonetheless in the very nature of our rational self-consciousness that we inhabit these particularities *as* answerable to a norm of universality.[18] We should not assume that our inherent, cultural embeddedness entails ethnocentricity, because it is integral to the very notion of culture that it propels us behind its limited terms. This is indeed the central idea behind a Hegelian multiculturalism, and it has its roots in the dialectic of recognition discussed above.

It is through our shared ways of articulating experience that we establish a mutuality of recognition: when we share terms, my way of expressing myself is simultaneously my endorsement of your way of expressing yourself, and vice versa. This is what is accomplished "literally" in our adopting a shared language, and, as David Ciavatta shows powerfully in his study of what Hegel calls "ethical life," it is also accomplished in all the forms of cultural life through which we behaviourally enact a shared inhabitation of the world.[19] It is precisely our need to establish a sharedness of experience that is the motivation for our commitment to determinate forms of cultural life. For this reason, then, those determinate forms have the accomplishing of community as their intrinsic norm. The "truth" of our exclusive cultural forms is thus that they are precisely *for* overcoming exclusivity: our cultural particularity, that is, is precisely *for* establishing a human universality. As I have argued in "Heidegger, Hegel, and Ethnicity," and Réal Fillion has further developed in his *Multicultural Dynamics and the Ends of History*, it is thus the demands of the dialectic of recognition that provide the reason for the imperative to universality that Taylor recognizes as overruling the ultimate exclusivity and "ethnocentricity" of our cultural forms.[20]

This idea that we live our cultural particularity "authentically," so to speak, when we live it as the imperative to universality, the imperative to communication with others, has a correlate in individual experience: as Hegel emphasizes in his description of the experience of morality, in conscience we experience personally the imperative to "live" our particularity as the site for the realizing of universality.[21] The emphasis on the ultimacy of the experience of conscience has been the other definitive theme in the Canadian tradition of Hegel interpretation.

Conscience

It is H.S. Harris, again, who has most definitively articulated the importance of the experience of conscience. In his discussion in *Hegel's Ladder* of Hegel's description of the experience of conscience, Harris identifies conscientious action as the ultimate form of human experience, that is, there is no form of living that more fully answers to the inherent demands of individual experience than the attitude of conscience, an attitude that itself has its culminating form in the practice of forgiveness.[22] In advancing this interpretation Harris is (and acknowledges himself to be) continuing in the tradition of Jean Hyppolite, the greatest of the French interpreters of Hegel. Other Hegel scholars, such as Ludwig Siep and Jay Bernstein, are also noteworthy for advancing this theme of conscience, but it is a theme that has especially defined the work of Canadian Hegel scholars: Harris, of course, and also John Burbidge, Shannon Hoff, and myself.[23]

I have argued above that the intrinsic norm of our cultural particularity is the imperative to accomplish a universality of equal recognition. But though this imperative is the very *raison d'être* of our establishing of shared cultural life, we do not typically recognize this about our cultural particularity. On the contrary, we typically live our cultural identities as closed systems for differentiating "us" from "them": though ethnocentricity is not the necessary form of our cultural existence, it is its normal form. We typically experience the terms of our familiar world as "right," as "the way things are supposed to be," and we are critical of others who fail to recognize these terms. What is distinctive of the experience of conscience is that it is the experience in which we experience the particularities of our situation as "not right" and as calling upon us – I experience myself as called upon in my most intimate singularity – to *transform these particularities into* the site for the realization of the good. In conscience I experience the singularity and the particularity of my situation as answerable to what is absolute.

Hegel's notion of *Aufhebung*, I noted above, is the idea that things in their particularity are impelled to transcend themselves and realize a higher norm. The stance of conscience is the ultimate stance of experience because it is the experience that lives itself on precisely these Hegelian terms: reality "in itself," Hegel maintains, is intrinsically impelled to transcend itself towards the absolute; conscience is this reality "for itself," that is, it is experience *experiencing itself as* thus impelled to self-transcendence.

In conscience, then, what reality is in itself becomes *self-conscious*. Further, this coming to self-consciousness is also itself the final development in the dialectic of recognition that has been guiding our interpretation all along. The notion of recognition is the notion that I cannot be myself on my own, but that instead I depend for my sense of self on the confirmation from the other. This need for recognition by the others is precisely what is recognized in the fully developed stance of conscience. My stance as an agent of conscience is that the terms of my individuality are insufficient on their own, and that I must enact the imperatives of the absolute. In endeavouring to thus transcend my own singularity in favour of what is "good in itself," however, I have only my own singularity to guide me. My effort to enact *the absolute* will, precisely, always and only be *my* effort to enact the absolute. For that reason, I am insufficient on my own to confirm my sense that I am doing what it right. This has two implications, both of which draw us back to the dialectic of recognition.

First, since I cannot determine on my own whether my action is an enactment of the good or simply an enactment of my own self-centred values, living from an attitude of conscience requires my acknowledging that I am insufficient on my own to determine my own significance, and that I will need to find from outside – from others – who I really am. Second, since I thus recognize in my own case that it is the very nature of acting in good conscience that I cannot but act in a limited, perspectival way that is necessarily subject to the criticism of self-centredness, the stance of conscience enjoins me to recognize that no one can be exempt from such criticism: the experience of conscience reveals, in other words, that we are all necessarily embedded in an irremovable particularity of perspective, with the result that we must forgive others their transgressive particularity, just as we ourselves need such forgiveness. In short, then, the stance of conscience has its culmination in the recognition that we reach the ultimate form of our self-consciousness in seeing ourselves as necessarily engaged in a dialogue of mutual recognition, a practice of forgivingly recognizing each other in our perspectival particularities. As self-conscious beings, we are always "in ourselves" answerable to the dialectic of recognition; in the fully developed stance of conscience, we are thus answerable "for ourselves."

Conclusion: Canadian Hegel

We have seen, then, that both religious experience and individual experience have their completion in the recognition of the need to experience our particularities as sites for reconciliation with others: as, that is, the medium within which to accomplish a situation of mutual recognition. This interpretation of Hegel is central to Harris's study, but it is also the primary thrust of John Burbidge's interpretation of the dialectic of religion, it has been the core of my own studies of personal and political experience, and it is the basic understanding that shapes Shannon Hoff's studies of Hegel's philosophy of law and her uses of Hegel to study cultural identity, liberalism, and prospects for contemporary feminism.[24] This interpretation is also paralleled in Charles Taylor's philosophical analyses of recognition and multiculturalism (more so than in his formal interpretations of Hegel), and is highly resonant with the specialized studies of other Canadian Hegel scholars such as Jay Lampert, David Ciavatta, and Jennifer Bates.[25] It is interesting that this distinctively multicultural, Canadian interpretation of Hegel has developed in a country that is itself typically recognized as distinctively multicultural in its political and cultural make-up.

NOTES

1 Indeed, significant enough to inspire a book: Jon Stewart, *The Hegel Myths and Legends* (Evanston, IL: Northwestern University Press, 1996).
2 I have written in some detail about the highly influential history of the reception and interpretation of Hegel in France in the twentieth century in John Russon, "Dialectic, Difference, and the Other: The Hegelianizing of French Philosophy," in *The History of Continental Philosophy*, ed. Leonard Lawlor, vol. 4, *Phenomenology: Responses and Developments*, 17–42 (Chicago: University of Chicago Press, 2010); please note that on 34, lines 18–19, the words "from Hegel's philosophy" are an accidental (and highly misleading!) editorial insertion and should be deleted. This corrected essay is also reprinted as an appendix to John Russon, *Infinite Phenomenology: The Lessons of Hegel's Science of Experience* (Evanston, IL: Northwestern University Press, 2015).

3 H.S. Harris, *Hegel's Development*, vol. 1, *Toward the Sunlight (1770–1801)* (Oxford: Clarendon, 1972); Harris, *Hegel's Development*, vol. 2, *Night Thoughts (Jena 1801–1806)* (Oxford: Clarendon, 1983); Harris, *Hegel's Ladder*, 2 vols. (Indianapolis: Hackett, 1998). For a discussion of Harris's contribution, see John W. Burbidge, "Forward: Hume, Hegel, and Harris," in *Hegel and the Tradition: Essays in Honour of H.S. Harris*, ed. Michael Baur and John Russon, ix–xv (Toronto: University of Toronto Press, 1997).

4 In a 2002 interview, the Aga Khan described Canada as "the most successful pluralist society on the face of our globe" (John Stackhouse and Patrick Martin, "Canada: A Model for the World," *Globe and Mail*, 2 February 2002); again, "Canada has for many years been a beacon to the rest of the world for its commitment to pluralism and for the support for its multicultural richness and diversity of its peoples" (news release, Aga Khan Development Network, 18 April 2005). See also Charles Taylor, "Building the Future: A Time for Reconciliation" (Quebec: Commission de consultation sur les pratiques d'accommodement reliées aux différences culturelles, 2008), for complexities in the use of this notion for the interpretation of Canadian society.

5 G.W.F. Hegel, *The Phenomenology of Spirit*, trans. A.V. Miller (Oxford: Oxford University Press, 1977). In emphasizing the importance of this work, I by no means intend to denigrate the outstanding work of Canadian Hegel scholars focused on other texts of Hegel. John Burbidge and Kenneth L. Schmitz, for example, have both done ground-breaking work on the interpretation of Hegel's *Science of Logic*, as has George di Giovanni, who has also been one of the world's leading scholars in investigating in detail the works of philosophers from the period between Kant and Hegel (which is the title of a book he co-edited with H.S. Harris, *Between Kant and Hegel: Texts in the Development of Post-Kantian Idealism*, rev. ed. [Indianapolis: Hackett Publishing, 2000]). Though I do not discuss her work in this chapter, Rebecca Comay's work on Hegel, particularly her recent study of Hegel's analysis of the French Revolution, *Mourning Sickness: Hegel and the French Revolution* (Stanford: Stanford University Press, 2010), should be recognized as a major Canadian contribution to Hegel scholarship. Jim Vernon, the author of *Hegel's Philosophy of Language* (London: Continuum, 2007), Jennifer Bates, author of *Hegel's Theory of Imagination* (Albany: State University of New York Press, 2004) and *Hegel and Shakespeare on Moral Imagination* (Albany: State University of New York Press, 2010), and Timothy Brownlee, who has done significant work on Hegel's *Philosophy of Right*, are younger Canadian scholars doing important work in Hegel interpretation.

6 I have discussed this more fully in "The Project of Hegel's Phenomenology," in *A Companion to Hegel*, ed. Stephen Houlgate and Michael Baur, 47–67 (Chester, West Sussex: Wiley-Blackwell, 2011), reprinted as the prologue to Russon, *Infinite Phenomenology*.
7 Hegel, *Phenomenology of Spirit*, paras 175–84.
8 These topics from Hegel's study of self-consciousness (*Phenomenology of Spirit*, "Independence and Dependence of Self-Consciousness: Lordship and Bondage," chap. 4, part A, paras 178–96), have been the subject of a vast body of scholarly literature. I discuss this material in greater detail in John Russon, *Reading Hegel's Phenomenology* (Bloomington: Indiana University Press, 2004), chaps 5–7, 10, and 12.
9 Eric Berne, *Games People Play: The Basic Handbook of Transactional Analysis* (New York: Ballantine Books, 1996); Everett Shostrom, *Man the Manipulator: The Inner Journey from Manipulation to Actualization* (New York: Bantam, 1968). See Hegel, *Phenomenology of Spirit*, paras 178–96.
10 Kym Maclaren has focused substantially on the "*entre deux*." Though much of her work draws more explicitly upon the philosophy of Maurice Merleau-Ponty, her thought is deeply rooted in Hegel's analysis of the dialectic of recognition; see "The Role of Emotion in Existential Education: Insights from Hegel and Plato," *International Philosophical Quarterly* 48 (2008): 471–92.
11 See John Russon, "Vision and Image in Hegel's System," in *Reading Hegel's Phenomenology*, especially 193–204.
12 Hegel, "The Struggle of Enlightenment with Superstition," *Phenomenology of Spirit*, paras 541–73. Compare also ibid., para. 528.
13 Ibid., para. 677.
14 See ibid., para. 678.
15 This is the way Harris once formulated his view to me, in the context of a discussion of Vincent McCarthy's *Quest for a Philosophical Jesus: Christianity and Philosophy in Rousseau, Kant, Hegel, and Schelling* (Macon, GA: Mercer University Press, 1986).
16 John Russon, "Heidegger, Hegel and Ethnicity: The Ritual Basis of Self-Identity," *Southern Journal of Philosophy* 33 (1995): 509–32; Réal Fillion, *Multicultural Dynamics and the Ends of History: Explorations in Kant, Hegel, and Marx* (Ottawa: University of Ottawa Press, 2008); Jay Lampert, "Hegel in the Future" (unpublished manuscript).
17 This theme and this term pervade Hegel's writing. He discusses the term explicitly at *Phenomenology of Spirit*, para. 113.
18 Charles Taylor, "Understanding and Ethnocentricity," in *Philosophy and the Human Sciences: The Collected Papers of Charles Taylor*, 116–33 (Cambridge: Cambridge University Press, 1985).

19 David Ciavatta, *Spirit, the Family and the Unconscious in Hegel's Philosophy* (Albany: State University of New York Press, 2009), esp. pt 4, "Family Property as the Materiality of Recognition."

20 See especially Réal Fillion, *Multicultural Dynamics*, chap. 3.

21 Hegel, *Phenomenology of Spirit*, paras 633–4.

22 Harris, *Hegel's Ladder*, vol. 2, *The Odyssey of Spirit*, chap. 9.

23 See, for example, John W. Burbidge, "Hegel's Absolutes," *Owl of Minerva* 29 (1997): 23–37; John Russon, "Selfhood, Conscience, and Dialectic in Hegel's Phenomenology of Spirit," *Southern Journal of Philosophy* 29 (1991): 533–50; Shannon Hoff, "Law, Love, and Life: Forgiveness and the Transformation of Politics," *Philosophy Today* 54 (2010): 163–8; and Hoff, *The Laws of the Spirit: A Hegelian Theory of Justice* (Albany: State University of New York Press, 2014), especially the conclusion. I have discussed Wahl and Hyppolite in "Dialectic, Difference, and the Other."

24 See John W. Burbidge, *Hegel on Logic and Religion* (Albany: State University of New York Press, 1992); Russon, *Infinite Phenomenology*, esp. chap. 12; Shannon Hoff, "On Law, Transgression, and Forgiveness: Hegel and the Politics of Liberalism," *Philosophical Forum* 42 (2011): 187–210.

25 See Jay Lampert, "Gadamer and Cross-cultural Hermeneutics," *Philosophical Forum* 29 (1997): 351–68; Ciavatta, *Spirit, the Family and the Unconscious*; Bates, *Hegel and Shakespeare on Moral Imagination.*

6 Conquering Finitude: Towards a Renewed Hegelian Middle

JIM VERNON

Introduction

As David MacGregor notes,[1] Canadians proportionately produce a surprisingly large amount of original work on Hegel, particularly compared with philosophers in America and Great Britain. MacGregor offers several possible explanations: a positive account of the state such as Hegel's is no doubt more alluring to those who prefer "peace, order, and good government" to "life, liberty, and the pursuit of happiness." His purported account of mutual recognition[2] speaks to a nation long-defined by the negotiations between First Nations and their colonizers, the "two solitudes" of our linguistic communities, and a growing number of immigrant groups; as well as our proximity, yet distance, from a dominant superpower – much like that of Hegel's to then-ascendant Britain – grants us both a unique vantage point and compelling need to observe the "land of the future" with both admiration and critique. My interest here, however, is less in what draws Canadians to study Hegel than in the interpretation of his work primarily and prominently defended and taught by Canadian philosophers. That is, in what follows, I assume, as Robert C. Sibley has argued, that there is "a distinction between the American and the Canadian Hegelians" in their dominant understandings of Hegel's thought.[3] I seek, here, to both explicate and problematize the mainstream, Canadian "Hegel."

In the first part of the chapter, using the commentaries of Emil Fackenheim, Charles Taylor, H.S. Harris, and John Russon, I argue that Canadian Hegelians have primarily and increasingly worked to ground Hegel's thought in the immanent, embodied finitude of human situatedness. While this has no doubt aided in maintaining a role for

Hegel in the ethical and political discourse of postmodern Canada, in my view it presents a one-sided reading of his thought. In the second half, taking up an insight of James Doull's, I offer one avenue to revive the "Hegelian Middle," which unites the account of human finitude with the infinite, self-actualizing Idea. This centrist reading, I argue, is not only more truthful to Hegel's text, it also provides a compelling case for once again reviving a universalist conception of politics in our fragmented social alignment.

I

Tracing "Canadian Hegelianism" back to John Watson, Sibley argues that its advocates hold that "community, or unity, emerges from a plurality of perspectives."[4] That is, unlike their American and British counterparts,[5] who generally defend a more abstract, self-sufficient, absolutized thought under which differences must be subsumed (undoubtedly contributing to a lesser interest in Hegel among Anglo-American philosophers), the dominant voices in Canadian Hegelianism have in the main held that unity arises from concrete differences, as their fulfilment. Rather than presupposing a transcendent Idea that must be articulated through differences, Canadian readers of Hegel, in the main, describe the immanent process through which differences come to express their rational unity. In short, most Canadian Hegelians have been of the Left.

I am referring, of course, to Emil Fackenheim's famous diagnosis of a "crisis of the Hegelian Middle." In *The Religious Dimension in Hegel's Thought*,[6] Fackenheim identified the two dominant, alternative interpretations of Hegel's work, under the traditional headings of "Right" and "Left" Hegelianism. Right-wing Hegelianism, for Fackenheim, is marked by a focus on the "transcendent" aspects of Hegel's system, and thus focused primarily on his *Logic* and the Idea.[7] Rising above the merely given finitude of human experience, Hegel's philosophies of nature and society are grounded in an Idea that is infinite and universal. Given Hegel's drive to lift thought beyond mere finitude, many Hegelians – not implausibly – came to see this self-determining Idea as all-encompassing in itself. Self-identical and self-sufficient, the Idea comprehends all, and as such, according to the Hegelian Right, need not pass through the variety of finite experiences and perspectives for its elucidation, thus relegating the "contingent and fragmented world of human experience" to philosophical irrelevance.[8] The cost of such a reading, however, is to cut Hegel's philosophy off from worldly application, rendering it at best an incomplete abstraction and at worst an illusory mysticism of pure thought.

In response and by contrast, Left-wing Hegelians eschew the transcendental aspirations of the system for "an 'immanentism' which would confine the scope of Hegel's thought to the ... world as it is *humanly* experienced."[9] On this reading, philosophy has no pretensions to infinite universality, for all aspects of the world as experienced "are shot through with contingency, externality, factual givenness."[10] Here our embodied nature and historical spirit – and thus the *Phenomenology* – take centre stage, as philosophy is limited within the bounds of our experiences of them. While perhaps saving Hegel's philosophy from illusory flights of abstract fancy, this interpretation is no less problematic in that it reduces Hegel's thought to merely "stat[ing] and justif[ying] the categories in which Nature and Spirit are experienced," thus making it a mere variant on Kantianism.[11]

Right-wing Hegelianism, then, defines Hegel's thought solely through abstract, transcendent, universal, infinite thought, while the Left-wing reading remains bound to concrete, immanent, particular, finite experience. Both, Fackenheim correctly notes, are one-sided versions of Hegel's thought which seeks both to "*rise to* [the] infinity" of the genuinely universal and trans-historical, as well as to achieve infinity's "reimmersion in the finite above which [it] has risen."[12] This return, of course, is not the simple submission of the finite to infinitude, nor is it a mere redescription of the given as universal; it is the alteration of the given as given, in the light of and through, the transcendent as transcendent. Hegel's thought seeks to preserve the contingency of the given while simultaneously transforming it such that it actualizes the truly universal. Because neither infinite thought nor given finitude can ultimately eliminate each other, this transformed unity must be continually reconstructed through what Fackenheim calls the "perpetually reenacted 'process' of conquering" the given.[13] Thus, the "Hegelian Middle" is marked by the affirmation of the eternal process through which mere finitude is raised to an infinite universality whose actualization transforms, without eliminating, the given.

For Fackenheim, however, this Middle could be affirmed only through "a reality already *present in life* before philosophy comes upon the scene," which raised finitude to infinity.[14] In particular, Fackenheim claims, "*the actual existence of one specific historical world is the cardinal condition without which ... the Hegelian philosophy cannot reach its ultimate goal.*

This specific world may be called … the modern bourgeois Protestant world."[15] Fackenheim's version of the Hegelian Middle, then, rests upon the historically achieved unity of universality and particularity found in modern social life, both religious (community of believers bearing witness to an eternal Kingdom of God) and secular (actualizations of free rationality ranging from the physical sciences to moral conscience to state institutions). Modern faith and science must no longer clash; rather each must affirm a trans-historical universal to be actualized in finite particularity through individual action (e.g., endeavouring to build God's kingdom on earth, striving to achieve a "God's-eye view" of the universe, etc.). The modern Protestant states have, in principle, overcome the conflict between the infinity of the universal with the particularity of the finite, and it is only through this achieved unity, claims Fackenheim, that Hegel's thought has any plausibility. It is precisely the subsequent developments within these states, according to Fackenheim, that have thrown the Hegelian Middle into "crisis."

Unlike the nineteenth-century Hegel, Fackenheim argues, we can no longer embrace the modern world as rationally unified. On the one hand, multiculturalism has revealed the faith community to be split beyond repair, making our world post-Christian; on the other, Auschwitz and Hiroshima have revealed the terrorizing power of the moral, political, and physical sciences. Modernity, Fackenheim claims, is now ineluctably fragmented and, because the Hegelian Middle rests upon the presence of a historically unified world, so is Hegelianism. Postmodern fragmentation has eliminated the universalist politics that extends from Hegel's system, and thus "were he alive today," Fackenheim famously suggests, Hegel would no longer espouse his own systematic views, i.e., "would not be a Hegelian."[16] Those who seek to find continuing relevance in his thought have been forced to either flee from the fragmented world into the eternity of abstract thought or, conversely, to hold that "the goal of philosophic thought is to stay with the world [i.e.,] that every philosophic flight from the world is the mark of … failure."[17] That is, the historical developments of the twentieth century fragmented the Hegelian Middle, seemingly permanently, into the opposing camps of Right-wing transcendence and Left-wing immanence.

While there are assuredly readers of Hegel representing both sides in all nations, including our own,[18] in the main Canadian philosophers who continue to find value in Hegel's thought have followed the Left-wing path. In fact, Fackenheim's analysis of the forced return to the

Hegelian Left is, perhaps, most accurately descriptive of arguably our most internationally influential Hegelian, Charles Taylor, who holds that, while "Hegel's [transcendent] ontology is near incredible [nevertheless] his philosophy is very relevant to our age."[19] For Taylor, Hegel's ontology demands the achieved synthesis of an eternal, universal, self-actualizing "cosmic spirit,"[20] with the historical and natural reality of experience through which humanity is revealed to be "the vehicle of a cosmic reason, which generated its articulations out of itself."[21] Given that human history and nature actualize this universal rationality, "Hegel thought that the forces of dissolution and homogenization of civil society would be contained because men would come to recognize themselves in the [state] structures which embodied the Idea."[22] Grounded in the universal Idea, the historical development of human finitude was for Hegel a synthesis with universal infinitude, a fact we could come to know simply by "recogniz[ing our]selves in the structures of the rational state."[23] Hegel's politics requires a firm sense of common project and duty, but, like Fackenheim, Taylor claims that the "upheavals" since 1914 have destroyed the confidence we had in state institutions, simultaneously increasing social atomism and transforming individuals into mere utilitarian tools for productive efficiency.[24] For Taylor, the undeniable and increasing social fragmentation of the twentieth century – or the advent of the "society which has become a 'heap'"[25] – demonstrates beyond doubt that "Hegel's synthesis cannot command adherents today"[26] and thus that his "conclusions are dead."[27]

This does not imply, however, that Hegel's thought lacks continuing value. To the contrary, the Hegelian problem – how to reconcile universal thought and particular givenness – remains ours, if only because of the drastic consequences of the collapse of his solution. Even in the fragmentary and stifling structures of the post-industrial, postmodern, post-Hegelian landscape, Taylor holds, we still overwhelmingly see ourselves as implicitly free, and thus, at least in part, not defined by our particular situation but by an infinity distinct from it. Conceiving ourselves as infinitely free in a world dominated by material necessity, economic efficiency, and base interest, we inevitably feel "hemmed in by modern conformity, stamped out by the great machine of Utility, [and] repressed by the 'system.'"[28] Rather than embracing the world as our rational home, we find ourselves alienated from a fragmented world increasingly distinct from our unified self-conception. Consequently, many have "envisaged an active reshaping of human life and its natural basis" through a universal freedom distinct from it.[29] On both the political Left (Bolshevism, anarchism, situationism) and Right (Fascism), the "idea of overcoming the injustice and expressive deadness of our world at one stroke by ... radically reshaping it according to a freely chosen design exercises a profound attraction."[30] While these various movements espouse distinct definitions of human freedom, all such conceptions "see it as something men win through to by setting aside obstacles or breaking loose from external impediments, ties or entanglements."[31] Taylor calls such freedom "self-dependence," in contrast to earlier views that envisioned freedom "in terms of order or right relation."[32] The consequences of conceiving freedom as self-dependence, as history has shown, vary between catastrophic destruction and repression, to petulant escapism that seeks "to think away the entire human situation."[33] According to Taylor, self-dependent freedom – freedom separable from, and therefore driven to overcome, the existent social alignment – grounds at best a goalless subject, and at worst a destructively irrational one, leaving humanity in perpetual alienation.

It is the need to overcome this alienation that draws Taylor back to Hegel. Modern alienation rests on the opposition of freedom and nature, infinity and finitude, thought and givenness, and thus the modern malaise can be overcome only by reconciling them. If Hegel fails to provide an enduringly compelling solution to the problem, he both poses the correct problem and details the required synthesis. On Taylor's reading, however, this failure of Hegel's transcendent ontology, as well as the dangers of self-dependent freedom, reveals that the synthesis must be performed on the side of finitude. That is, free subjectivity and thought can no longer be grounded in a genuine infinity or universality; rather we must "situate [free] subjectivity by relating it to our life as embodied and social beings, without [thereby] reducing it to a function of objectified nature."[34] Thus, for Taylor, while we moderns may have irrevocably rejected the theological, "cosmic" ground of Hegel's philosophy, we must, no less than Hegel, grasp how human freedom can be synthesized with the contingent finitude of nature. This means, however, eschewing transcendent conceptions of universal thought, and envisioning "thought and freedom [as] emerging from the stream of life, finding expression in the forms of social existence, and discovering themselves in relation to nature and history."[35] The infinity and universality of Hegelian freedom, present now only as alienated self-dependence, must be replaced by the immanent, but nonetheless active and expressive, conception of *situated* freedom. Situated freedom is rooted not in a transcendent spirit, concept, or capacity, but in our contingently developed nature and, in particular, our social institutions and practices. Situated freedom is not alienated from the given, but an immanent "response to what we are" as natural, socially contextualized beings.[36] As such, any and every conception of situated freedom views "free activity as grounded in the *acceptance* of our defining situation."[37] Freedom is not actualized in conquering the given that determines us, but through an "affirmation of this defining situation as ours."[38]

Once we set aside his transcendental ontology, Taylor claims, it is just such a situated conception of freedom that we find in Hegel, in particular in his conception of *Sittlichkeit*. On Taylor's reading, "*Sittlichkeit* refers to the moral obligations I have to an ongoing community of which I am a part."[39] *Sittlichkeit*, then, marks neither an abstract freedom that must be placed into a world distinct from or opposed to it, nor our merely given nature or habits; it denotes norms that are given to us in our situation, that we nevertheless must recognize as ours to carry forward, simply because they are given in our situation. The institutions and practices of social life exist only insofar as we actualize them through our actions, but it is only insofar as there are such institutions and practices that we have rational actions to undertake. Such situated freedom is a response to the given from out of the given, "free" action undertaken on the basis of social structures and norms already in place. Situated freedom seeks neither to transform the world nor to escape it, but to identify itself with what is given to it as its situation, from the resources presented to it in the situation. Situated freedom, then, seeks to conserve the resources that make it possible by sustaining them through its actions and expressions. It grasps its obligations through its situation, and thus finds "no gap between what ought to be and what is."[40] In short, the "crucial characteristic of *Sittlichkeit* is that it enjoins us to bring about what already is."[41]

Of course, Taylor's reading acknowledges that not all social alignments can sustain public identification over time, and finds in Hegel a potent resource for diagnosing the inherently unstable aspects of contemporary life that lead to the aforementioned alienation. However, his reading of freedom after Hegel as essentially immanent and situationally determined places him staunchly on the Left. It is because we find ourselves in irrational social structures that we find ourselves alienated, but it is only insofar as the resources for developing more rational ones are already implicitly present in those structures that we can hope to find ourselves at home again. Taylor's Hegelianism certainly rejects mere acquiescence to any given order, but nevertheless can bring only situationally developed resources to respond to the destructive forces that fragment society. It is only by identifying with, and sustaining, the implicitly rational assets already available in our defining situation that we can once again actualize ourselves as free.

Given the resources Taylor finds in Hegel's text for supporting a situational account of rational freedom, it is perhaps unsurprising that other Canadian Hegelians have found them to form the essential core of Hegel's account, despite its transcendent gestures. On this reading, Hegel offers a thoroughly immanent philosophy that grounds thought and freedom in our natural and historical experience, and strays from this view only on peripheral matters, as the result of personal bias, cultural prejudice, or other irrelevant reasons. The claims of universality and necessity, then, are themselves grounded in the human situation and remain valid, while the seemingly transcendental extensions of them, while certainly present, are merely peripheral and must be subordinated to his immanent account of human experience. Undoubtedly the most influential expositor of this view has been H.S. Harris.

As with Fackenheim and Taylor, Harris finds that the "world of Hegel's Philosophy of Spirit perished between 1914 and 1945."[42] Hegel, he acknowledges, was resolutely confident that modern Europe would and should continue its path of rational, emancipatory progress, and thus would never return to revolutionary upheaval or barbaric despotism after 1789, but "the experience of this century has shown how badly mistaken he was."[43] However, Harris argues, "His mistake was essentially *empirical*," rather than philosophical, and reflects the tenor of his times, rather than his systematic thought.[44] As such (and *pace* Taylor), even in the face of the horrors of the past century, his philosophical position can be essentially maintained "without change."[45] Hegel's error, in brief, lies in the contingently specific developments of the modern bourgeois state that he seems to defend as universal (i.e., as the proof of "the 'march' of a transcendent Spirit around the world with the Sun – and logically *forwards* in history");[46] for Harris, it is rather the case that, in general, "the rational structure of selfhood, the paradoxical union of singularity and universality in community membership, the identity of the 'I that is We and the We that is I' is … what is 'logically necessary.'"[47]

The grasping of these structures, or the achievement of this identity, what we can call the "passage from the [contingent, particular] natural 'body' to the [necessary, universal] spiritual one" is ensured not by the actualization of their synthesis in a cosmic order, or by the conquering of the given by free, abstract thought, but by our "own embodiment" itself, precisely "because the structure of our embodied life-experience will not change."[48] We are ineluctably embodied, situated beings, and thus our embodiment and situatedness admit of generally valid description. It is thus Hegel's *Phenomenology*, rather than his *Encyclopedia* or *Logic*, that provides the key to his system, for there we find an account of situated, embodied subjectivity from the "standpoint of ordinary human life."[49] While our empirical science, religious context, and political reality may shift throughout history, "no matter what may happen ... we must continue to live in the world of Sense-Certainty and Perception, the world of common sense and real life, in which we struggle to assert ourselves, are disciplined by our elders, and finally collaborate in a system of ... 'equal recognition.'"[50] For Harris, it is these structures of selfhood and community that form the "heart and centre of philosophical logic [that is] safe from the continual change and transformation that must be dominant" in history.[51] Even the purportedly universal thought of the *Logic*, then, is immanent to the particularity of the human situation, such that when the "philosopher moves on from being [a phenomenological] 'observer' to the pure thinking of the Logic ... it is the structure of her scientific community's life in the world that she is articulating."[52] Philosophy neither presupposes nor affirms anything beyond the finite human situation, and even in its most abstract, universal, necessary, and free thought, articulates nothing more than "the structure of the community of which [the philosopher] is already a rational member."[53] As such, it is "the *Phenomenology* [that] provides the most reliable criterion of what belongs properly to the *Logic* and ... to the Real Philosophy," for the "reliable permanence of philosophical logic depends upon the necessary primacy of 'real life.'"[54] Even if Hegel's personal "religion" suggests a transcendent ground to human life, the core of his philosophy neither depends upon, nor leads to, anything more than the immanently experienced human situation.[55] For Harris, then, Hegel is resolutely a philosopher of the embodied and the situated, and his transcendent aspirations must be subordinated to what is immanently experienced.

As with Taylor, Harris reads the political consequences of this view as broadly affirmative of the given as given. While we may often find ourselves alienated from the structures of natural, intersubjective, and institutional life, they nevertheless determine the situation from which we develop the sense of selfhood, reason, and freedom through which we can feel so estranged. Because nothing transcends our immanent experience, and because our experience is shaped by the *sittlich* structures of our time and place, "we must contribute to, and reliably maintain, the structures of Objective Spirit which the good life (shockingly *bad*, perhaps, in our own eyes) has been shown to require."[56] Again, nothing in this view requires us to affirm patently irrational structures; however, the criteria for judging the validity of our practices and institutions are themselves situational, and thus can be internally critiqued and corrected only from immanently valid reasons and methods. In short, because free, rational selfhood depends upon the given structures of our situation, we are enjoined to bring about what already is by preserving and strengthening the aspects of our situation that makes free, rational selfhood possible.

This Leftist or immanent reading of Hegel continues to dominate Canadian Hegelianism, and has, if anything, simply worked to eradicate all traces of transcendence from his thought. Influenced by a host of recent Continental philosophers of immanence, subsequent generations of Canadian Hegelians have argued that there is little "significant difference between the philosophical methods, goals, or results of Hegel's philosophy and the philosophies of such figures as Heidegger, Merleau-Ponty and Derrida."[57] As a final case, then, let me briefly turn to John Russon's account of the relationship between the *Phenomenology* and the *Logic* as perhaps the most influential example of contemporary Canadian scholarship on Hegel.

Like Harris, Russon focuses on the *Phenomenology* and holds that its arguments are "rooted in familiar phenomena of everyday life," and thus that each of its movements presents an "interpretation of an aspect of human experience."[58] The *Phenomenology* presents the structures of subjectivity and sociality, and these structures cannot be deduced from mere concepts, nor can they be transcended for some superhuman beyond; they can be only immanently observed and described. Beyond phenomenology, though, he claims that ontology itself, for Hegel, can concern being only *as experienced*, i.e., that "any claim that might be made about the nature of being is always bound by a correlative mode of experiencing."[59] Because there is nothing that transcends human situatedness, "metaphysical claims are always necessarily descriptions of the ways that being *appears*" to subjects.[60] All metaphysical objects, including the "Being" explicated in the *Logic*, are not only grounded in, but identical to, phenomenal experiences. As such, there is "no legitimacy to the claim that Hegel's *Logic* as a project can be severed from the *Phenomenology*, for they are *the same project*."[61] Logic is not simply grounded in experience, or the elucidation of it, but what experience reveals itself to immanently demand and push towards. Thus, Hegel proposes no claim about being that transcends experience, and the "conclusions of [his major] two books ... amount to the same reality."[62] Even beyond Harris, Russon completely removes transcendence from the Hegelian scheme, reducing thought to immanence, and confirms that philosophy must remain "within the parameters of its given situation, not because it is wrong to go outside, but because it is impossible."[63]

Since all philosophy is an interpretation of phenomena, all arguments amount to claims about what is experienced. However, our experience takes place only in the context of other experiencers, who equally claim to know what is. That is, any interpretation of being takes place only in the context of other interpretations of being, and "the experiences of others – like our own experiences – are ... essentially presentations of reality, presentations of what is."[64] Thus, all claims about being, just because they are claims about experience, are essentially open to the perspectives and judgments of others. As such, all genuine "efforts to know what is [seek to] reconcile our own experience with the experience of others."[65] All knowledge claims make an assertion about what others do (or should) experience, but from one situated perspective; absolute knowledge can thus be won only if we all seek to "accommodate ourselves to the experiences of others" by being "open to the way that reality shows itself as other subjects."[66] Since nothing in being transcends immanent experience, and since experience is always situated and particular, absolute knowing arises only in the reconciling dialogue between situated experiencers. In short, "being is communication."[67]

The political extensions drawn by Russon are arguably less culturally or temporally specific than those of Harris or Taylor; however, they are equally guided by, and bound to, the human situation as given. This given is not a particular set of bourgeois, *sittlich* structures but human situatedness itself, in all of its presented forms. All experiencers approach what is from specific habitual, social, and cultural contexts that inform the knowledge claims they make, or a set of "determinate practices that constitute a specific historically embodied community's efforts to say its own identity."[68] Because it affirms that all such contexts and practices offer a perspective on being, Hegel's philosophy articulates the need to comprehend all such contexts in one discourse on being, or the "conscientious commitment to a single, human, rational discourse of mutually established" perspectives.[69] For Russon, Hegel's thought reveals the implicit rationality of all perspectives, which must be brought to light through reciprocal dialogue, respect, and understanding. As such, it "demands a political commitment to the rationality of that which appears alien" on all sides.[70] There is no situated perspective that uniquely grasps what is, but neither are there any that do not shed light upon it. An immanent, embodied Hegelian politics demands the achieved unity of all given perspectives through an open dialogue of mutual understanding. This clearly applies to new perspectives as they develop from intersubjective communication; however, it leaves no room for a principled or axiomatic extra-situational judgment upon any perspectives as irrational. As such, this is not a return to a universalist political project, but a recognition that there are no such projects; the only legitimate demand one can make upon others is that they grasp the already existent intersubjective situation through which they experience being by opening their own perspectives to mutual dialogue with any and all others, not that they actualize thereby any genuinely universal Idea. Because all perspectives are both already situated in their contexts and implicitly related to the equally one-sided contexts of others, Hegel's "political vision ... can endorse *only* a cross-cultural communication that seeks not only to enlighten but to be educated by the other ... within the context of a mutual pursuit of free rationality."[71] Thus, Russon defends a Left-Hegelian politics that affirms and calls upon us to grasp and conserve the immanently given intersubjective structures that make experience and action possible.

The above should be sufficient to demonstrate the nature, strength, and continuity of the Left-wing strain of Hegelianism that dominates Canadian scholarship. While there is surely great debate at the level of detail, the overall trend in Canadian Hegelianism is towards extricating all claims of transcendence from Hegel's philosophy and rooting his thought more firmly in the immanently given, embodied human situation. In the main, Canadian Hegelians either separate the transcendent aspects of Hegel's system from the immanent ones (Taylor), subordinate the former to the latter (Harris), or identify them, on the side of finitude, as essentially the same (Russon). The result is a politics that rejects universalist visions of the emancipatory transformation of the given, for one both constrained by and conserving the contingencies of given cultural and personal perspectives (either within a single culture, or cross-culturally), albeit one directed towards the increasing, but still immanent, rationality of those perspectives. As Shannon Hoff argues in her contribution to this volume, we must replace the drive to "impos[e] a purportedly universal framework" on the situation in any form, with "two different kinds of practices: the practice of being attentive to the fact of our own particularity and to the particular shape that our intervention in the lives of others takes, and the practice of justly perceiving the particularity of others" in structures of mutual recognition. Thus, the effort to overcome the fragmentation of the post-Hegelian world must be made by better grasping the human situation as it is given, rather than acting to transform the world to actualize a universal Idea not strictly reducible to it.

Canadian, Left-wing Hegelianism, then, is marked by the thoroughly immanent description of the structures of the human situation as experienced. As such, it seems Fackenheim was basically correct in claiming that such a reading sees either the essence or enduring value of Hegel's work as lying in how well it "states and justifies" the categories of experience, rather than transforming the given through a transcendent Idea. As I have indicated above, however, I think Fackenheim is also correct in finding this reading to be one-sided. By reducing philosophy to the structures of human finitude, it undercuts many of Hegel's core commitments, for the Leftist reading can at best indicate generality, not true universality. As Russon tellingly claims in this volume, "Whatever universality there is in human experience is something that must be accomplished and realized on the basis of ... non-universal terms" immanent to the human situation. However, throughout his works, Hegel both defends the trans-historical infinity and universality of the Idea, and appears to judge the given perspectives or actions of particular individuals and cultures through its lens. This is what gives the Right-wing reading its strength, and such claims cannot be simply dismissed.

The Leftists are certainly correct, however, in abandoning the modern Protestant state as the "final" actualization of Hegelian thought, for this unifying conception of social life has long since been dismantled by historical developments. However, it also seems to contradict the Hegelian Middle to require, as Fackenheim does, any particular social alignment to actualize the Idea. Fackenheim holds that "for Hegel Christianity – and Christianity alone – is 'the absolute religion,'" and as such the actualization of his thought rests upon the specific "religious-existential basis" of bourgeois Protestant society.[72] This, however, weds universality to one finite particularity, rather than conquering finitude through infinity which, as we have noted, is for Fackenheim an essentially *perpetual* endeavour rather than a static social achievement. A true Hegelian Middle, then, cannot rest upon the presence or dominance of any particular social alignment or religious representation; to the contrary it must continually affirm the genuinely infinite and universal, while nevertheless revealing its capacity to actualize itself through the particularity and finitude of the given. That is, it must posit an Idea that transcends human finitude, but that nevertheless is *progressively actualized* through it.

In the second part of this chapter, I follow James Doull in arguing that the Hegelian Middle can, even in the face of postmodern fragmentation, still be affirmed if we move "the argument from religion to secular freedom."[73] In explicating Doull's centrist reading of Hegel, F.L. Jackson rightly reminds us that Hegel's philosophy, in all of its aspects, is essentially grounded on "the idea of *freedom*" and thus, at bottom, that his "philosophy is nothing other than the will to bring this idea to light."[74] Thus, in the next section, I aim to briefly demonstrate this, as well as how the Hegelian Middle can be reaffirmed without recourse to outmoded metaphysical concepts of God or cosmic reason, or defunct social forms like the bourgeois Protestant state, by re-examining Hegel's central, self-determining Idea – human freedom. While the "Hegelian Middle" I propose is certainly distinct from, and perhaps even at odds with, the one proposed by Doull, it is inspired in part by his efforts to make a centrist reading of Hegel's universalist thought viable in the postmodern world.

II

Hegel begins his *Philosophy of Right*[75] by claiming that the "subject matter of *the philosophical science of right* is the *Idea of right* [i.e.,] the concept of right and its actualization."[76] That is, political philosophy treats neither the institutions of right as they exist or have existed, nor merely abstract conceptualizations of right in itself; rather, it explicates the concept of right to be actualized, and the existence of right insofar as it actualizes the concept. The Idea of right is both abstract and concrete, thought and reality, universal and situated, and thus is not reducible to either. According to Hegel, this Idea has its basis in "the *realm of spirit* in general" and more precisely in the free will.[77] Thus, the two-sided Idea of right has its ground, not in the cosmic reason of a transcendent being or the historical development of Christian states, but in the essence of the human will as genuinely free. Right is a matter of secular freedom, not theological metaphysics or historical alignment, and thus Hegel's political philosophy rests entirely on correctly grasping human freedom.

Predictably, Hegel's account of freedom affirms the will's "*positing* of a determinacy as a content and object."[78] The very idea of "willing" clearly implies the capacity to act in and on one's situation, rather than being passively determined by it, and thus a will can reveal itself as free only in the "positing of itself as something *determinate*" through situated action, which Hegel calls the "absolute moment of the *finitude* or *particularization* of the 'I.'"[79] Such actions arise within human finitude and thus concern contents – external objects or internal desires – that are not willed, but are "given by nature," including the second nature of habit or culture.[80] Particular actions are immanently performed within a given situation, out of given resources, as Left Hegelians uniformly affirm.

However, such action alone is insufficient to demonstrate the existence of the will's *freedom*. Situational responses emerge from such unfree causes as biological drive, physical forces, emotional dispositions, ingrained habits, social pressure, or contingent character. So long as one's actions proceed solely from the given (embodied finitude with its particular habits and desires) to the given (contingencies of one's natural and social situation), they cannot be called free, for they are determined by pre-existent forces. Freedom, Hegel thus argues, necessarily presupposes the "*absolute possibility* of *abstracting* from every determination in which I find myself or which I have posited in myself."[81] The will is free only if it can, in principle, extricate itself from the determination of its situated embodiment into the "element of *pure indeterminacy* or of the 'I's' pure reflections into itself, in which every limitation, every content, whether present immediately through nature, through needs, desires, and drives, or given and determined in some other way, is dissolved."[82] Without this capacity to transcend particular finitude, the will would be constrained by forces that are merely given; a free will, by contrast, is defined by "the limitless infinity of *absolute abstraction* or *universality*."[83]

Freedom thus presupposes a universality abstractable in principle from the situated finitude of our embodied particularity, i.e., from every particular action, and by extension from every particular willing subject. As such, it is not the freedom of any particular situated will. To the contrary, freedom is universal because it is the abstract ground of willing in general, and thus every willing subject can be said to possess the same infinite freedom as any other subject and in equal share. Freedom – more in line with the transcendent claims of the Hegelian Right – demands a universal, impersonal ground of willing in any and every possible political subject.

Freedom presupposes the trans-historical, infinite essence of willing in general.

Of course, a freedom that remained within the abstract purity of its own universal infinity would be no more than a merely implicit, unactualized potency. Moreover, it would be conditioned by an outside that limits it, in that it would remain only free insofar as it was not affected by given finitude. As such, a free will that existed only in abstraction would be neither willing (i.e., not actualized) nor free (i.e., conditioned by something external to it). This is why the free will also presupposes a finite, situated agent. Thus, on the one hand, the free will is infinite, universal, and indifferent to all determinations and alignments, while on the other hand it must be actualized by particular subjects through specific, historical willed contents. In short, "the will is [thus] the unity of both these moments"[84] and exists neither strictly in pure abstraction nor solely in determinately willed actions; it is only in their dialectical unity, or "Idea," i.e., the identity of pure, universal concept and concrete, particular actualization, that the free will is both willing and free.

Hegel takes great pains, however, to distinguish this actualized idea of freedom from the mere "*arbitrariness*" of the will,[85] or our capacity to contingently select determinations from a given slate of options. Merely affirming a pre-existent determination of any kind (external demand, internal desire, acquired habits, etc.) maintains the will's "dependence on an inwardly or externally given content,"[86] rather than actualizing its freedom. There is, put simply, no discernible difference between a willed "arbitrary choice" and an unwilled one, for both simply affirm a content that exists prior to the wilful act. The arbitrary will is thus not free, because it posits no determinations of its own, and as such remains bound to merely given forces.

As such, the truly free will requires determinations that are objective actualizations of itself, i.e., "its object [must be] itself, and therefore not something it sees as *other* or as a *limitation*."[87] Such determinations must (1) not pre-exist the willing actualized through them (thus being grounded in the transcendent will), but (2) nonetheless exist as objective determinations independent of that willing (thus being actualizations of freedom in, and through, finitude). In other words, the determinations that actualize the free will must both arise from it as universal, and be separable from it as particular. This is why Hegel argues that the will is essentially actualized through the institutions of right, for "right is any existence in general which is the *existence* of the *free will*."[88] Specifically, it is the institutions of *Sittlichkeit* – i.e., family, civil society, and the state – that actualize the will, for they objectively exist independently of the subjects who fill them as the determinate structures that form custom and law, but also exist only in and through the willed actions and attitudes of free individuals. For example, marriage arises from the "free consent of the persons concerned ... to *constitute a single person*" in union, but such unions require each partner to take up, and place on each other, binding familial and legal duties, and as such "their union is a self-limitation" through concrete structures.[89] Marriage, like all the institutions of right identified by Hegel, is both a freely willed action and an objectively determinate social institution binding on those who will it.

This actualization of freedom, however, should not be confused with the merely situated choice to affirm social alignments as they exist, no matter how broadly construed (i.e., the current laws and mores of one's state, or even those that would result from cross-cultural negotiation between extant traditions). Adopting a slate of pre-existent institutional determinations (i.e., "bringing about what is") would clearly be an act of the merely arbitrary will, and thus the external determination, rather than actualization, of the free will. Freedom requires objective social institutions in order to be actualized, but it cannot arbitrarily preserve the "prevailing *circumstances* and *existing* ... institutions" already given.[90] This is no doubt one reason Hegel claims ordinary thinking "always describes [the will's actualization] as incomprehensible,"[91] and his own account of the process is admittedly far from clear. There is, however, only one solution that remains consistent with his core account. Freedom can only be actualized by determinate social institutions insofar as they do not externally determine the will through their given nature. As such, the will can actualize itself as free only if (at least some of) the determinations of the core institutions of right are altered through the free willing of agents. This is how, I think, we are to understand Hegel's admittedly enigmatic phrase, "The will is the unity of both of these moments – *particularity* reflected *into itself* and thereby restored to *universality*."[92] Altering the pre-existent institutions of right actualizes freedom through objectively determinate forms of custom and law, while simultaneously mitigating the limiting effect of such institutions, thereby restoring the will to universality in and through particular institutional changes, and thus actualizing human freedom.

Because these changes are required in order to limit the external determination of existent institutions on human freedom, an institutional alteration actualizes the free will only if it decreases institutional restrictions on freedom by increasing our ability to alter the essential institutions of right. In other words, if the Idea of freedom is to be actualized, the determinations of the institutions of *Sittlichkeit* must be altered to concretely increase our possibility for freely altering them, without thereby destroying them. In the example of marriage, Hegel identifies the positing of legal divorce as an emancipatory addition to inherited marriage structures,[93] in that it allows one to exit an unloving relationship, to build a loving one with another, while decrying the modern romantic conception of coupling for rendering loving relationships a "total *contingency*" achievable only by particular, lucky individuals, rather than a right and duty for all.[94] The social institutions essential for freedom can neither be accepted as they are nor altered or rejected arbitrarily; rather, their determinations must be specifically reformed to increase humanity's free self-determination. Only in this way can free agents recognize their willing in the institutions of right, and thus find themselves "at home" in the modern world.

Thus, it is not through the institutions of right themselves, but through the progressive, emancipatory supersession of their limiting determinations through the process of reform that freedom is actualized. Freedom demands the transformation of the given into the actualization of the universal, or the synthesis of the sides of the will's Idea. Of course, because such alterations produce institutions that then (by virtue of the very situational "givenness" they subsequently come to be for succeeding generations) become limitations to freedom, this process is essentially perpetual. Freedom, in short, is the incessant "activity" [*Tätigkeit*] of liberating itself from what determines it, or of "making itself" actually what it is now only "potentially."[95] Freedom arises neither from embracing our situated finitude nor from seeking to transcend it into, or subsume it under, a mystical or absolute beyond, but in the concrete, progressive, perpetual conquering of the given situation through the transcendental universality of human freedom. Thus, Hegel's politics is universalist (applies to all subjects and social alignments at all times) and emancipatory (elucidates our essential duty to liberate free humanity from given social restrictions), but also particular and situational (concerns the existent institutions of right as specifically given to free subjects in a state at some time, and targeted reforms to their restrictions on free willing). Rather than embracing our alienating situation as implicitly or already rational, or fleeing outside it to pure thought, Hegel articulates our duty to progressively conquer finitude through infinity, or to continually build a willed "home" for ourselves, in and through a truly universal politics of human emancipation.

In sum: Hegel's core Idea – human freedom – is not actualized merely through the immanent finitude of the Hegelian Left, but neither does it merely rest on the self-sufficient thought isolated in Hegel's work by the Right; it rather charts a Middle path that encompasses the essential aspects of both in the genuinely universal, concretely emancipatory political project of progressively conquering our finitude to increasingly actualize human freedom.

Conclusion

As we have seen, Canadian Hegelians have focused primarily on the finite, situated aspects of Hegel's system, thereby extricating it from the caricatures that painted it as a Panglossian, or even totalitarian, justification of the modern state as God's presence on earth. The cost, however, has been to deprive Hegel's core Idea of all transcendence, divesting his political philosophy of its ground in infinite freedom, thus foreclosing the possibility of a universalist political project through it. The result has been an overly immanentized, embodied, naturalized Hegel, perhaps made more compelling to the philosophical and political discourse of our fragmented situation, but lacking the universal dimension, and corresponding emancipatory politics, that make his ambitious thought among the most captivating and politically potent in the canon. As Fackenheim argued, "Philosophic thought, however rooted in existential commitments, craves a comprehensiveness which transcends them."[96] While Fackenheim doubted that Hegelian philosophy could be revived in our post-Christian world, the above reading of the *Philosophy of Right* reveals one path Hegelians might take to reaffirm the transcendent aspects of his thought *within finitude*, thus revitalizing their capacity to unify our alienated age. Canadian Hegelians have succeeded grandly in continuing to make Hegel's thought compelling to immanent, naturalized philosophical discourse of postmodernity; succeeding generations, however, both to remain truer to Hegel's text and to answer our craving for infinity and comprehensiveness, should reaffirm the transcendent aspects of human freedom, thereby reviving the possibility of a universal, progressive, emancipatory politics.

NOTES

1 David MacGregor, "Canada's Hegel," *Literary Review of Canada*, February 1994, 18–19.
2 I contest the dominant understanding of both the nature and importance of mutual recognition in Hegel's philosophy in "Why We Fight: Hegel's 'Struggle for Recognition' Revisited," *Cosmos and History: The Journal of Natural and Social Philosophy* 9, no. 2 (2013): 178–97.
3 Robert C. Sibley, *Northern Spirits: John Watson, George Grant, and Charles Taylor – Appropriations of Hegelian Thought* (Montreal and Kingston: McGill-Queen's University Press, 2008), 99.
4 Ibid.
5 Few Hegelians openly embrace the "Right" label, arguably as the result of its association with religious and political conservatism, but the emphasis on the self-sufficiency of philosophical thought above its various contingent expressions is not uncommon in Anglo-American literature. Sibley refers to Absolute Idealists like Josiah Royce and Bernard Bosanquet, but one might also (perhaps with some qualifications) include more recent Hegelians like Richard Dean Winfield and Stephen Houlgate. It must be recalled throughout that the Left/Right split in Hegel studies is independent of the political use of those terms. In fact, many Hegelian "Leftists" strike me as politically conservative, while the "Middle" that I propose is highly amenable to some of the "Leftist" political movements that peaked in the 1960s. See "'I am We': Dialectics of Political Will in Huey P. Newton and the Black Panther Party," *Theory and Event* 17, no. 4 (December 2014); "Liberation Theology: Hegel on Why Philosophy Takes Sides in Religious Conflict," *Canadian Journal of Continental Philosophy* 17, no. 2 (Fall 2013): 141–57; and "Hegel, Edward Sanders and Emancipatory History," *Clio: A Journal of Literature, History and the Philosophy of History* 42, no. 1 (2013): 27–52.
6 Emil L. Fackenheim, *The Religious Dimension in Hegel's Thought* (Bloomington: Indiana University Press, 1967).
7 Ibid., 77.
8 Ibid., 76.
9 Ibid., 81.
10 Ibid., 82.
11 Ibid., 83.
12 Ibid., 107.
13 Ibid.
14 Ibid., 110–11.
15 Ibid., 232.

16 Ibid., 224.
17 Ibid., 238.
18 Right-readings of Hegel (albeit with distinct critical takes on the merit of his work) are represented below in Barry Cooper (for whom Hegel's "universal historical state," the "most resolutely modern and comprehensive account of the present or actual world [yet] known," implies a "regime where natural or quasi-natural factors, that is, inherited status, religious belief, cultural tradition, gender, ethnicity, etc., play no role in the conduct of public affairs") in this volume.
19 Charles Taylor, *Hegel and Modern Society* (New York: Cambridge University Press, 1979), 135.
20 Ibid., 167.
21 Ibid., 158.
22 Ibid., 136.
23 Ibid.
24 Ibid., 138.
25 Ibid., 136.
26 Ibid., 139.
27 Ibid., 167. Thus, in this volume, Kenneth Kierans suggests that "Taylor can in no way be called a 'Hegelian,'" although, given how much Taylor draws from Hegel, this claim is perhaps a bit too strong.
28 Taylor, *Hegel and Modern Society*, 140.
29 Ibid., 141. As I shall argue below, this actually gets closer to the Hegelian, Middle position than his claims about "cosmic reason."
30 Ibid., 154.
31 Ibid., 155.
32 Ibid., 156.
33 Ibid., 155.
34 Ibid., 167.
35 Ibid., 168.
36 Ibid., 169.
37 Ibid., 160.
38 Ibid.
39 Ibid., 83.
40 Ibid.
41 Ibid.
42 H.S. Harris, *Hegel: Phenomenology and System* (Indianapolis: Hackett Publishing, 1995), 101.
43 Ibid., 107.
44 Ibid.

45 Ibid.
46 Ibid.
47 Ibid., 103–4.
48 Ibid.
49 Ibid., 104.
50 Ibid.
51 Ibid.
52 Ibid., 103.
53 Ibid.
54 Ibid., 104.
55 Ibid., 107.
56 Ibid., 104.
57 John Russon, *Reading Hegel's Phenomenology* (Indianapolis: Indiana University Press, 2004), 3. Other scholars working in Canada who argue for strong continuities between Hegel and various twentieth-century Continental philosophers of immanence would include Jay Lampert, David Morris, Rebecca Comay, and David Ciavatta.
58 Ibid., 2.
59 Ibid., 222.
60 Ibid.
61 Ibid., 225, my emphasis.
62 Ibid., 228.
63 Ibid., 163–4.
64 Ibid., 227.
65 Ibid.
66 Ibid.
67 Ibid.
68 Ibid., 208.
69 Ibid.
70 Ibid.
71 Ibid., 209, my emphasis.
72 "The Doull-Fackenheim Debate: Would Hegel be a Hegelian Today?," in *Philosophy and Freedom: The Legacy of James Doull*, ed. David G. Peddle and Neil G. Robertson (Toronto: University of Toronto Press, 2003), 332.
73 Peddle and Robertson, "Doull-Fackenheim Debate," 335. Drawing on other sources, Graeme Nicholson's contribution to this volume identifies the Hegelian Middle with a kind of liberalism (which he also identifies with mainstream Hegelianism). In what follows I seek to use Doull's insight to develop a Hegelian Middle that hews more closely to Fackenheim's specific claims regarding the perpetual conquering of finitude.

74 F.L. Jackson, "Commentary: The Hegelian Idea," in Peddle and Robertson, *Philosophy and Freedom*, 306.
75 G.W.F. Hegel, *Elements of the Philosophy of Right*, ed. Allen W. Wood, trans. H.B. Nisbet (New York: Cambridge, 1991). Citations will be to numbered paragraph in the form §23, and Hegel's own remarks will be denoted by an R, in the form §24R. In order to avoid controversies surrounding their authenticity, I refrain from citing the student lecture notes. What follows is a synopsis of an argument that I develop in more detail in "Siding with Freedom: Towards a Prescriptive Hegelianism," *Critical Horizons* 12, no. 1 (2011): 49–69.
76 Ibid., §1.
77 Ibid., §4.
78 Ibid., §6.
79 Ibid.
80 Ibid.
81 Ibid., §5R.
82 Ibid., §5.
83 Ibid.
84 Ibid., §7.
85 Ibid., §15.
86 Ibid.
87 Ibid., §22.
88 Ibid., §29.
89 Ibid., §162. For a more substantial discussion of marriage as an actualization of freedom, see my "'Free Love': A Hegelian Defense of Same-Sex Marriage Rights," *Southern Journal of Philosophy* 47, no. 1 (Spring 2009): 69–89.
90 Hegel, *Philosophy of Right*, §3R.
91 Ibid., §7R.
92 Ibid., §7.
93 Cf. ibid., §176.
94 Ibid., §162R.
95 G.W.F. Hegel, *Werke*, Bd. 12, ed. Eva Moldenhauer and Karl Markus (Frankfurt: Suhrkamp, 1970), 31; Hegel, *The Philosophy of History*, trans. J. Sibree (New York: Dover, 1956), 17 (translation modified).
96 Fackenheim, 242.

7 Hegel's Philosophy of Mind

CHARLES TAYLOR

As with any highly systematic body of thought, Hegel's philosophy of mind can be reconstructed from many perspectives. Each one gives us something, though some are more illuminating than others. But I believe that it is particularly illuminating to see Hegel's philosophy of mind through the perspective of his philosophy of action. This is, of course, hardly a surprising doctrine. Mind (*Geist*) for Hegel is thoroughgoing activity (*Tätigkeit*). But I think the insights from this perspective can be enlivened and made more penetrating if we relate Hegel's thought to a set of perennial issues that have been central to the philosophy of action in modern times. This is what I want to attempt in this paper.

At the same time, a study of this kind can be interesting in another way. Understanding Hegel's contribution to the developing modern debate on the nature of action helps us to understand the historical development of this debate. And this, I would like to argue, is important for understanding the debate itself.

I

We can perhaps identify one fundamental issue which has been left open in the philosophy of action in modern times. To do so, of course, requires some interpretation of the history of modern philosophy, and this as always can be subject to controversy. The precise question which defines this issue was not asked in the seventeenth or eighteenth century, and is rather one which is central to our twentieth-century debate. But I want to claim nevertheless that different answers to this question were espoused earlier, as one can see from a number of related philosophical doctrines which *were* expressly propounded, and which depend on these answers. I hope the plausibility of this reading will emerge in the course of the whole argument.

This being said, I will baldy identify my central issue in unashamedly contemporary terms: what is the nature of action? Or otherwise put, what distinguishes (human) action from other kinds of events? What are the peculiar features of action?

One family of views distinguishes actions by the kind of cause which brings them about. Actions are events which are peculiar in that they are brought about by desires, or intentions, or combinations of desires and beliefs. As events, actions may be described among other ways as physical movements. (Although one would have to be generous with the term "physical movements," so as to include cases of non-movement, as for example with the action we would describe as "He stood still.") In this, they resemble a host of other events which are not actions. What distinguishes them is a peculiar type of psychological cause: that they are brought on by desires or intentions. Of course, to hold this is not necessarily to hold that psychological explanations are ultimate. One can also look forward to their reduction to some neurophysiological or physical theory. But in that case, the burden of distinguishing action from non-action would be taken over by antecedents differently described: perhaps some peculiar kind of firing in the cortex, which was found to be the basis for what we identify psychologically as desire.

A view of this kind seems to have been implicit in much of Donald Davidson's work.[1] But the basic conception goes back, I believe, at least to the seventeenth century. A conception of this kind was, in a sense, even more clearly at home in the basically dualist outlook common both to Cartesian and empiricist philosophies. *Qua* bodily movements, actions resembled all other events. What distinguished them was their inner "mental" background. Within the bounds of this outlook, there was a clear ontological separation between outer event and inner background.

Against this, there is another family of views which sees action as qualitatively different from non-action, in that actions are what we might call intrinsically directed. Actions are in a sense inhabited by the purposes which direct them, so that action and purpose are ontologically inseparable. The basic intuition here is not hard to grasp, but it is difficult to articulate it very clearly. What is in any case clear is that this view involves a clear negation of the first: we cannot understand action in terms of the notions of undiscriminated event and a particular kind of cause; this is to explain it in terms of other primitive concepts. But for the second view, action is itself a primitive: there is a basic qualitative distinction between action and non-action. To the extent that action can be further explicated in terms of a concept like "purpose," this turns out not to be independently understandable. For the purpose is not ontologically separable from the action, and this means something like: it can only exist in animating this action; or its only articulation as a purpose is in animating this action; or its only articulation as a purpose is in animating the action; or perhaps a fundamental articulation of this purpose, on which all others depend, lies in the action.

The second view thus resists the basic approach of the first. We cannot understand action by first identifying it as an undifferentiated event (because it is qualitatively distinct), and then distinguishing it by some separably identifiable cause (because the only thing which could fill this function, the purpose, is not separably identifiable). One of the roots of this doctrine is plainly Aristotle's thesis of the inseparability of form and matter, and we can see that in contrast to Cartesianism and empiricism, it is plainly anti-dualist. This is not to say that the proponents of the first view are necessarily dualist – at least not simply so; just that their conception permits of dualism, whereas the qualitative distinction thesis does not.

One of the issues which is thus bound up with that of the nature of action is the question of dualism. Another which I want briefly to mention here, is the place of the subject. It is clear that the distinction between action and non-action is one that occurs to us as agents. Indeed, one can argue plausibly that a basic, not further reducible distinction between action and what just happens is indispensable and ineradicable from our self-understanding as agents.[2] That is, it is impossible to function as an agent at all unless one marks a distinction of this kind.

In this context, we can understand part of the motivation for the first, or causal, theory of action as lying in the aspiration to go beyond the subjective standpoint of the agent, and come to an understanding of things, which is objective. An objective understanding in this sense would be one which was no longer tied to a particular viewpoint, imprisoned in the categories which a certain viewpoint imposes. If agency seems to impose the qualitative conception of action, then the causal one can appear as a superior analysis, an objective portrayal of the way things really stand, of the real components of actions *an sich*. This drive for objectivity, or what Bernard Williams has called "absolute" descriptions,[3] was one of the animating motives of both Cartesianism and empiricism.

Now Hegel is clearly a proponent of the second, qualitative conception of action. And indeed, he emerges out of a climate in which this conception was staging a comeback after the ascendancy of Cartesian and empiricist views. In one sense, the comeback can be seen to start with Leibniz, but the tenor of much late-eighteenth-century thought in Germany was of this stamp. The reaction against dualism, the recovery of the subject, the rehabilitation of Aristotle-type inseparability doctrines – notably in the conception of the aesthetic object in Kant's *Third Critique* – all pushed towards, and indeed, articulated themselves through this understanding of action. I now want to develop its ramifications to show how central it is to Hegel's thought, and in particular his theory of mind.

II

The first important ramification of the qualitative theory is that it allows what I shall call agent's knowledge. The notion is that we are capable of grasping our own action in a way that we cannot come to know external objects and events. In other words, there is a knowledge we are capable of concerning our own action which we can attain as the doers of this action; and this is different from the knowledge we may gain of objects we observe or scrutinize.

This qualitative distinction in kinds of knowledge is grounded on the qualitative view of action. Action is distinct in that it is directed, aimed to encompass ends or purposes. And this notion of directedness is part of our conception of agency: the agent is the being responsible for the direction of action, the being for whom and through whom action is directed as it is. The notion of action is normally correlative to that of an agent.

Now if we think of this agent as identical with the subject of knowledge, then we can see how there can be different kinds of knowledge. One kind is gained by making articulate what we are doing, the direction we are already imprinting on events in our action. As agents, we will already have some sense, however dim, inarticulate or subliminal, of what we are doing; otherwise, we could not speak of directing at all. So agent's knowledge is a matter of bringing this sense to formulation, articulation, or full consciousness. It is a matter of making articulate something we already have an inarticulate sense of.

This evidently contrasts with knowledge of other objects, the things we observe and deal with in the world. Here we are learning about things external to our action, which we may indeed act with or on, but which stand over against action.

Now the first, or causal, view cannot draw this contrast. To begin with, we can see why it was not concerned to: because the contrast is one which is evident from the agent's standpoint; agent's knowledge is available to the knower only *qua* agent, and thus from his standpoint. It cannot be recognized as knowledge from the absolute standpoint. Thus for the causal view, my action is an external event like any other, only distinct in having a certain kind of cause. I cannot claim to know it in some special way.

Of course, what I can claim "privileged access" to is my desire, or intention – the cause of my action. And here we come closer to an analogous distinction within the causal view to that between agent's and observer's knowledge. In the original formulations of Cartesianism and empiricism, I am transparently or immediately aware of the contents of my mind. It may be accorded that I am immediately, even incorrigibly aware that I want to eat an apple, or that I intend to eat this apple. But of the consequences of this desire or intention, viz., my consuming the apple, I have knowledge like that of any other external event: I observe it.

We might then contrast the two views by noting that the causal view too recognizes two kinds of knowledge, but it draws the boundaries quite differently, between "inner" and "outer" reality. But we would have to add that this difference of location of the boundary goes along with a quite different view of what the knowledge consists of. The notion of immediate or incorrigible knowledge makes sense in the context of dualism, of a separate domain of inner, mental space, of which we can say at least that its *esse* entails its *percipi*. The contrast will be something like that between immediate and inferential knowledge, or the incorrigible and the revisable.

Once we draw the boundary in the way the qualitative theory does, there is no question of incorrigibility. We may never be without some sense of what we are doing, but coming to have knowledge is coming to formulate that correctly, and we may only do this in a partial or distorted fashion. Nor is this knowledge ever immediate; it is, on the contrary, mediated by our efforts at formulation. We have indeed a different mode of access to what we are doing, but it is questionable whether we should dub this access "privileged." Neither immediacy nor incorrigibility is a mark of agent's knowledge.

In a sense this idea of agent's knowledge originates in modern thought with Vico. But since his work did not have the influence it deserved in the eighteenth century, we should perhaps see Kant as the important seminal figure. Not that Kant allowed a full-blooded notion of agent's knowledge. Indeed, he shied away from using the word "knowledge" in this context. But he made the crucial distinction between our empirical knowledge of objects on one hand and the synthetic *a priori* truths which we can establish on the other about the mathematical and physical structure of things. In Kant's mind it is clear that we can only establish the latter with certainty because they are in an important sense our own doing.

Perceiving the world involves not just the reception of information, but crucially also our own conceptual activity, and we can know for certain the framework of empirical reality, because we ourselves provide it.

Moreover, in Kant's procedure of proof of these synthetic *a priori* truths, he shows them to be essential conditions of undeniable features of experience, such as that we mark a distinction between the objective and subjective in experience, or that the "I think" must be able to accompany all our representations. Later he will show the postulates of freedom, God, and immortality as essential conditions of the practice of determining our action by moral precepts. If we ask what makes these starting points allegedly undeniable, I think the answer can only be that we can be sure of them because they are what we are *doing*, when we perceive the world, or determine our action on moral grounds.[4]

Kant thus brings back into the centre of modern epistemological debate the notion of activity and hence of agent's knowledge. Cartesian incorrigibility, the immediate knowledge I have of myself as a thinking substance, is set aside. In its place come the certainties which we do not have immediately, but can gain, concerning not some substance, or any object of knowledge whatever, but the structures of our own activity. What we learn by this route is only accessible by this route. It is something quite different from the knowledge of objects.

This has been an immensely influential idea in modern philosophy. One line of development from Kant lies through Schopenhauer, who distinguished our grasp of ourselves as representation and as will, and from this through Wittgenstein into modern British analytical philosophy, for example in Miss Anscombe's notion of "non-observational knowledge."[5]

But the line which interests us here passes through Fichte. Fichte's attempt to define subject–object identity is grounded on the view that agent's knowledge is the only genuine form of knowledge. Both Fichte and Schelling take up Kant's notion of an "intellectual intuition," which for Kant was the kind of agent's knowledge which could only be attributed to God, one through which the existence of the object itself was given (B72), or one in which the manifold is given by the activity of the self (*selbsttätig*, B68). But they make this the basis of genuine self-knowledge of the ego; and then of all the genuine knowledge insofar as object and subject are shown to be identical.

The category of agent's knowledge has obviously taken on a central role, has exploded beyond the limits that Kant set for it; and is, indeed, the principal instrument by which these limits are breached and the realm of inaccessible noumena denied. But the extension of agent's knowledge obviously goes along with a redefinition of the subject. He is no longer simply the finite subject in general that figures in the *Critiques*, but is related in some way to a single infinite or cosmic subject.

Hegel is obviously the heir to this development. He takes up the task of demonstrating subject–object identity, and believes himself alone to be capable of demonstrating this properly. What is first seen as "other" is shown to be identical with the self. It is crucial to this demonstration that the self ceases to understand itself as merely finite, but see itself as part of spirit.

But the recognition of identity takes the form of grasping that everything emanates from spirit's activity. To understand reality aright is to understand it as actuality (translating *Wirklichkeit*), that is, as what has been actualized. This is a crucial prerequisite of the final stage, which comes when we see that the agent of this activity is not foreign to us, but that we are identical to (in our non-identity with) spirit. The highest categories of the Logic, those which provide the entry into the absolute Idea, are thus those linked with agency and activity. We move from teleology into the categories of life, and then from knowledge to the good.

The recognition thus requires that we understand reality as activity, but it requires as well that we come to understand in a fuller way what we are doing up to the point of seeing what spirit is doing through us. Coming to this point, we see the identity of the world-activity with ours.

Thought thus culminates in a form of agent's knowledge. But this is not just a department of what we know alongside observer's knowledge, as it is for our ordinary understanding. Rather observer's knowledge is ultimately superseded. But the distinction is none the less essential to the system, since its crucial claim is that we only rise to the higher kind of knowledge through a supersession of the lower kind.

And this higher knowledge is far from immediate. On the contrary, it is only possible as mediated through forms of expression, among which the only adequate medium is conceptual thought. And this brings us to another ramification of the qualitative view, which is also of central importance for Hegel. On the qualitative view, action may be totally unreflecting; it may be something we carry out without awareness. We may then become aware of what we are doing, formulate our ends. So following on a conscious desire or intention is not an inescapable feature of action. On the contrary, this degree of awareness in our action is something we come to achieve.

In achieving this, we also transform our activity. The quality of consciously directed activity is different from that of our unreflected semiconscious performance. This flows naturally from the second view on action: if action is qualitatively different from non-action, and this difference consists in the fact that action is directed, then action is also different when this direction takes on a crucially different character. And this it does when we move from unreflecting response, where we act in much the same manner as animals do, to conscious formulation of our purposes. Our action becomes directed in a different and stronger sense. To become conscious is to be able to act in a new way.

The causal theory does not allow for this kind of qualitative shift. Indeed in its original, dualist variant, it could even allow for unreflecting action. Action is essentially caused by desire or intention, and on the original Cartesian-empiricist model, our desires were essentially features of inner experience. To have a desire was to feel a desire. Hence, on this view, action was essentially preceded by a cause of which the agent was aware. This amounted in fact to making conscious action, where we are aware of our ends, the only kind of action. It left no place at all for totally unmonitored, unconscious activity, the kind of action animals engage in all the time, and we do much of the time.

And even when the causal theory is disengaged from its dualist or mentalist formulation, where the causes of action are seen as material, and hence quite conceivably largely unconscious, the theory still has no place for the notion that action is qualitatively transformed in becoming conscious. Awareness may allow us to intervene more effectively to control what comes about, but action remains essentially an undifferentiated external event with a certain kind of cause.

Now this offshoot of the qualitative view – that action is not essentially or originally conscious, that to make it so is an achievement, and that this achievement transforms it – is also crucial to the central doctrines of Hegel. I want to look at two of the here.

1

The first is what I have called elsewhere the "principle of embodiment."[6] This is the principle that the subject and all his functions, however "spiritual" they may appear, are inescapably embodied. The embodiment is in two related dimensions: first, as a "rational animal," that is, as a living being who thinks; and second, as an expressive being, that is, a being whose thinking is always and necessarily in a medium.

The basic notion here is that what passes in modern philosophy for the "mental" is the inward reflection of what was originally external activity. Self-conscious understanding is the fruit of an interiorization of what was originally external. The seeming self-coincidence of thought where I am apparently immediately aware of my desires, aims, and ideas, which is foundational to Cartesianism, is understood rather as an achievement, the overcoming of the externality of an unconscious, merely instinctive life. It is the fruit of a negation of what negates thought, not itself a positive datum. This understanding of conscious self-possession as the negation of the negation is grounded on the conception of action I have just been outlining. In effect, it involves seeing our mental life fundamentally in the category of action. If we think of the constituents of mental life, our desires, feelings, ideas, as merely given, as the objects which surround us in the world are given, then it is plausible to think of our knowledge of them as privileged. They appear to be objects which we cannot but be aware of, if we are aware at all. Our awareness of them is something basic, assured from the start, since it is essentially involved in our being aware at all.

In order to understand mental life as something we have to achieve understanding of, so that self-transparency is a goal we must work towards, we have to abandon the view of it as constituted of data. We have to understand it as action, on at least one of two levels, if not both.

On one level, we have to see self-perception as something we do, something we can bring off, or fail to bring off, rather than a feature of our basic predicament. This means that we see it as the fruit of an activity of formulating how things are with us, what we desire, feel, think, and so on. In this way, grasping what we desire or feel is something we can altogether fail to do, or do in a distorting or partial or censored fashion. If we think through the consequences of this, I believe we see that it requires that we conceive self-understanding as something that is brought off in a medium, through symbols or concepts, and formulating things in this medium as one of our fundamental activities.

We can see this if we leap out of the Hegelian context and look at the quite different case of Freud. Here we have the most notorious doctrine of the non-self-transparency of the human psyche. But this is mediated through a doctrine of self-understanding through symbols, and of our (more of less distorted and screened) formulation of our desires, fears, and soon as something we do. For although these formulations occur without our willful and conscious intent, they are nevertheless motivated. Displacements, condensations, and so on occur where we are strongly motivated to bring them off.

But on a second level, we may also see the features of ourselves that self-perception grasps not simply as given but as themselves bound up with activity. Thus desires, feelings may not be understood just as mental givens, but as the inner reflection of the life-process that we are. Our ideas may not be conceived as simple mental contents, but as the precipitates of thinking. And so on.

Hegel understands mental life as activity on both these levels. In a sense, the first can be thought to represent the influence of Kant. It was Kant who defended the principle that there is no perception of any kind which is not constituted by our conceptual activity. Thus there is no self-awareness, as there is no awareness of anything else, without the active contribution of the "I think." It was the contribution of the new richer theory of meaning that arose in the wake of Romanticism to see that this constitutive thought required an expressive medium. Freud is, of course, via Schopenhauer, the inheritor both of this Kantian doctrine and of the expressivist climate of thought, and hence also through Schopenhauer of the idea that our self-understanding can be very different in different media, as well as distorted in the interest of deeper impulses that we barely comprehend.

The making activity central on the second level is also the fruit of what I want to call the expressivist climate of thought, which refused the distinctions between mind and body, reason and instinct, intellect and feeling, which earlier Enlightenment thought had made central. Thought and reason were to be understood as having their seat in the single life-process from which feelings also arose. Hence the new vogue for Aristotelian inseparability doctrines, of form and matter, of thought and expression, of soul and body.

Hegel's theory of mind is built on both these streams. Our self-understanding is conceived as the inner self-reflection of a life-process, which at the outset fails to grasp what it is about. We learn through a painful and slow process to formulate ourselves less and less inadequately. At the beginning, desire is unreflected, and in that condition aims simply for the incorporation of the desired object. But this is inherently unsatisfactory, because the aims of spirit are to recognize the self in the other, and not simply to abolish otherness. And so we proceed to a higher form of desire, the desire for desire, the demand for recognition. This too starts off in a barely self-conscious form, which needs to be further transformed. And so on.

In this theory, activity is made central on both levels: (a) on the second, more fundamental level, what is to be understood here, the desire, is not seen as a mere psychic given, a datum of mental life. On the contrary, it is a reflection (and at first an inadequate one) of the goals of a life-process which is now embodied and in train in the world. Properly understood, this is the life-process of spirit, but we are at the outset far from seeing that. So the active life-process is primary, even in defining the object of knowledge.

Then (b) on the first level, the achievement of more and more adequate understanding is something that comes about through our activity of formulating. This takes place for Hegel, as we shall see later, not only in concepts and symbols, but also in common institution of the master–slave relationship is one "formulation" (and still an inadequate one) of the search for recognition. Grasping things through symbols, establishing and maintaining practices, are things we do, are to be understood as activities, on Hegel's theory.

And so we have two related activities. There is a fundamental activity of Spirit, which it tries to grasp through the various levels of self-formulation. These mutually conditional activities are at first out of phase, but they are destined in the end to coincide perfectly. That is because it will become clear at the end that the end of the whole life-process was that Spirit come to understand itself, and at the same time the life-process itself will be entirely transparent as an embodiment of this purpose.

But this perfect coincidence comes only at the end. And it only comes through the overcoming of non-coincidence, where what the pattern of activity is differs from what this pattern says. And so the distinction between these two dimensions is essential for the Hegelian philosophy: we could call them the effective and the expressive. Each life-form in history is both the effective realization of a certain pattern, and at the same time the expression of the certain self-understanding of man and hence also of Spirit. The gap between those two is the historical contradiction which moves us on.

And so for Hegel, the principle of embodiment is central. What we focus on as the mental can only be understood in the first place as the inner reflection of an embodied life-process; and this inner reflection is itself mediated by our formulations in an expressive medium. So all spiritual life is embodied in the two dimensions just described: it is the life of a living being who thinks; and his thinking is essentially expression. This double shift from Cartesianism, from the psychology of immediate self-transparency to one of achieved interiority, of the negation of the negation, is obviously grounded on the qualitative understanding of action, and the central role it plays here. The mental life has a depth which defies all immediate self-transparency, just because it is not merely self-contained, but is the reflection of a larger life-process; while plumbing this depth is in turn seen as something we do, as the fruit of the activity of self-formulation.

Once again, we see that the Hegelian understanding of things involves our seeing activity as all-pervasive. But the activity concerned is as it is conceived on the qualitative view.

2

We can thus see that this offshoot of the qualitative view, which sees action as first unreflecting, and reflective understanding as an achievement, underpins what I call the principle of embodiment in Hegel's thought. But we saw above that for this conception reflective consciousness transforms action. And this aspect too is crucial to Hegel's theory.

His conception is of an activity which is at first uncertain or self-defeating because its purposes are barely understood. The search for recognition is, properly understood, a demand for reciprocal recognition, within the life of a community. This is what our activity is in fact groping towards, but at first we do not understand it in this way. In a still confused and inarticulated fashion, we identify the goal as attaining one-sided recognition for ourselves from others. It follows that our practice will be confused in its purpose and self-defeating. For the essential nature of the activity is not altered by our inadequate understanding of it; the true goal of the search for recognition remains community. Our inadequacy of understanding only means that our action itself is confused, and that means that its quality as directed activity is impaired.

We can see this kind of confusion, for instance, at the stage where we seek to answer our need for recognition through an institution like that of slavery. We are already involved here with what will turn out to be the only possible solution to this quest, viz., community; because even the institution of the master–slave relation will typically be defined and mediated by law, a law which binds all parties, and which implicitly recognizes them as subjects of right. Within this framework, the relations of domination, ownership of man by man, contradict the basic nature of law. If we think of our building and maintaining these institutions as an activity we are engaged in together, which is how Hegel sees it, then we can see that our activity itself is confused and self-contradictory. This is, indeed, why it will be self-defeating and why this institutional complex will eventually undermine and destroy itself.

A new form of society will then arise out of the ruins of this one. But the practices of this new society will only be higher than previous ones to the extent that we have learnt from the previous error, and now have a more satisfactory understanding of what we are engaged in. Indeed, it is only possible to accede eventually to a practice which has fully overcome confusion and is no longer self-defeating if we finally come to an understanding which is fully adequate.

But throughout this whole development we can see the close relation which exists between the level of our understanding and the quality of our practice. On this view, our action itself can be more or less firmly guided, more or less coherent and self-consistent. And its being one or the other is related to the level of our self-understanding.

We are reminded here of a common conception of the Romantics, well expressed in a story of Kleist, that fully coherent action must either be totally unreflecting or the fruit of full understanding. The birth of self-consciousness on this view disrupts our activity, and we can only compensate for this disruption by a self-awareness which is total. Hegel takes up this conception with an important difference. The crucial activity is that of Spirit, and it aims for self-recognition. As a consequence, there is no such thing as the perfection of totally unreflecting activity. The earliest phases of human life are even then phases of Spirit, and the contradiction is present between their unconsciousness and what they implicitly seek.

In sum, we can see that this ramification of the qualitative theory of action involves a basic reversal in the order of explanation from the philosophy that Cartesianism and empiricism bequeathed to us. It amounts to another one of those shifts in what is taken as primitive in explanation, similar and related to the one we mentioned at the outset.

There I pointed out that for the Cartesian-empiricist view, action was something to be further explained, compounded out of undifferentiated events and a certain kind of cause. The cause here was a desire, or intention, a "mental" event; and these mental occurrences are taken as primitives by this kind of theory, and part of the explanatory background of action.

But the qualitative view turns out to reverse this order. The "mental" is not a primitive datum, but is rather something achieved. Moreover, we explain its genesis from action, as the reflective understanding we eventually attain of what we are doing. So the status of primitive and derived in explanation is reversed. One theory explains action in terms of the supposedly more basic datum of the mental; the other accounts for the mental as a development out of our primitive capacity.

III

The qualitative view also brings about another reversal, this time in the theory of meaning, which it is worth examining for its own sake, as well as for its importance to Hegel.

I said above that for this view becoming aware of ourselves, coming to self-consciousness, is something we do. We come to be able to formulate properly what we are about. But this notion of formulation refers to that of an expressive medium.

One way to trace the connection is this: if we think of self-consciousness as the fruit of action, and we think of action as first of all unreflecting bodily practice, which only later comes to be self-understood; then the activity of formulating must conform to this model. That is, our formulating ourselves would be at first a relatively unreflective bodily practice, and would attain only later to the self-clarity required for full self-consciousness.

But this is just what we see in the new expressive theories of meaning which arose in the later eighteenth century, and which Hegel took over. First, the very notion of expression is that of self-revelation as a special kind of bodily practice. The Enlightenment theory of signs, born of the epistemological theories of the seventeenth century, made no fundamental distinction between expressive and any other form of self-revelation. You can see that I am afraid of a recession by the fact that

I am selling short; you can see that I am afraid of you by the expression on my face; you can see that it is going to rain because the barometer is falling. Each of these was seen as a "sign" which points beyond to something it designates or reveals. Enlightenment theorists marked distinctions between signs: some were by nature, some by convention. For Condillac, there were three kinds: accidental signs, natural signs, and signs by institution.

But the distinction they quite overlooked was the crucial one for an expressivist, that between "signs" which allow you to infer to their "designatum," like the barometer does to rain, and true signs which express something. When we make something plain in expression, we reveal it in public space in a way which has no parallel in cases of inference. The barometer "reveals" rain indirectly. This contrasts with our perceiving rain directly. But when I make plain my anger or my joy, in facial or verbal expression, there is no such contrast. This is not second best, the dropping of clues which enable you to infer. This is what manifesting anger or joy *is*. They are made evident not by or through the expression but in it.

The new theories of meaning, which start perhaps with Herder's critique of Condillac, involve a fundamental shift. They recognize the special nature of those human activities which reveal things in this special way. Let us call them expressive activities. These are bodily activities. They involve using signs, gestures, spoken or written words. And moreover, their first uses are relatively unreflecting. They aim to make plain in public space how we feel, how we stand with each other, or where things stand for us. It is a long slow process which makes us able to get things in clearer focus, describe them more exactly, and above all, become more knowledgeable about ourselves.

To do this requires that we develop finer and more discriminating media. We can speak of an embodiment which reveals in this expressive way as a "medium." Then the struggle for deeper and more accurate reflective self-understanding can be understood as the attempt to discover or coin more adequate media. Facial expressions do much to make us present to each other in our feelings and desires, but for self-understanding we need a refined and subtle vocabulary.

This amounts to another major reversal in theory. The Enlightenment account explained meaning in terms of the link of designation or "signifying" between word and object. This was a link set up in thought. In Locke's theory, it was even seen as a link set up through thought, since the word strictly speaking signified the idea of the object. Meaning is explained here by thought, which once again is seen in the role of explanatory primitive. In this conception, expression is just one case of the signifying relation, which is seen as constituted in thought.

But for the expressive theory, it is expression which is the primitive. Thought, that is, the clear, explicit kind of thought that we need to establish new coinages, new relations of "signifying," is itself explained from expression. Both ontogenetically and in the history of culture, our first expressions are in the public space, and are the vehicles of quite unreflective awareness. Later we both develop more refined media, in concepts and images, and become more and more capable of carrying out some part of our expressive activity monologically; that is, we become capable of formulating some things just for ourselves, and hence of thinking privately. We then develop the capacity to frame some things clearly to ourselves, and thus even to coin new expressions for our own use. But this capacity, which the Enlightenment theory takes as a primitive, is seen here as a late achievement, a change we ultimately come to be able to ring on our expressive capacity. This latter is what is now seen as basic in the order of explanation.

In our day, a similar radical reversal was carried out in the theory of meaning by Ludwig Wittgenstein, who took as his target the theory which emerges out of modern epistemological theory, to which he himself had partly subscribed earlier. What I have called the Herderian theory is very reminiscent therefore of Wittgenstein's.

But Hegel wrote in the wake of the earlier expressive revolution. And one can see its importance for his thought by the crucial place in it of what I have called the notion of medium. But the struggle to attain this is just the struggle to formulate it in an adequate medium.

Thus Hegel distinguishes art, religion and philosophy as media, in ascending order of adequacy. The perception of the absolute is embodied in the work of art, it is presented there (*dargestellt*). But this is in a form which is still relatively inarticulate and unreflecting. Religious doctrine and cult bring us closer to adequacy, but are still clouded by images and "representations" (*Vorstellungen*). The only fully adequate form is conceptual thought, which allows both transparency and full reflective awareness. But attaining our formulation in this medium is the result of a long struggle. It is an achievement; and one which builds on and requires the formulation in the other, less adequate media. Philosophy does not only build on its own past. For in earlier ages, the truth is more adequately presented in religion (e.g., the early ages of Christianity), or art-religion (at the height of the Greek polis). In coming to its adequate form, philosophy as it were catches up. True speculative philosophy has to say clearly what has been there already in the images of Christian theology.

Thus for Hegel too thought is the achievement whereby our expression is made more inward and clear. The attainment of self-understanding is the fruit of an activity which itself conforms to the basic model of action, that it is at first unreflecting bodily practice and only later attains self-clarity. This is the activity of expressing.

IV

I have been looking at how the qualitative theory of action and its ramification underlie Hegel's philosophy of mind, for which in the end everything is to be understood in terms of the all-pervasive activity of Spirit. I have been arguing that we can only understand the kind of activity involved here if we have in mind the qualitative view.

But there are also some important features of human historical action on Hegel's view which only make sense against this conception. I want to mention two here.

1

The first is this: all action is not in the last analysis of individuals; there are irreducibly collective actions. The causal view was inherently atomist. An action was such because it was caused by desire, intention some "mental" state. But these mental states could only be understood as states of individuals. The mental is what is "inner," which means within each one of us. And so action is ultimately individual. That is to say, collective actions ultimately amount to the convergent action of many individuals and nothing more. To say "the X church did so-and-so," or "the Y party did such-and-such" must amount to attributing converging action to clumps of individuals in each case. For what makes these events actions in each case is their having inner mental causes, and these have to occur or not occur discretely within individuals.

By contrast, the qualitative view does not tie action only to the individual agent. The nature of the agency comes clear to us only when we have a clear understanding of the nature of the action. This can be individual; but it can also be the action of a community, and in a fashion which is irreducible to individual action. It can even conceivably be the action of an agent who is not simply identical with human agency.

Hegel, of course, avails himself of both of these latter possibilities. In his conception of public life, as it exists in a properly established system of objective ethics (*Sittlichkeit*), the common practices or institutions which embody this life are seen as our doing. But they constitute an activity which is genuinely common to us; it is *ours* in a sense which cannot be analysed into a convergence of *mines*.

But for Hegel, there is a crucial level of activity which is not only more than individual, but even more than merely human. Some of what we do we can understand also and more deeply as the action of Spirit through us. In order to arrive at a proper understanding, we thus have to transcend our ordinary self-understanding; and to the extent that our common sense is atomist, we have to make two big transpositions: in the first, we come to see that some of our actions are those of communities; in the second, we see that some are the work of Spirit. It is in the *Phenomenology of Spirit* that we see these transitions being made. The first corresponds to the step from chapter V to chapter VI (here Hegel speaks of the community action by using the term "Spirit"). The second is made as we move through the discussion in the third part of chapter 6 into the chapter on Religion.

2

Following what I have said in earlier sections, human action is to be understood in two dimensions, the effective and the expressive. This latter dimension makes it even clearer how action is not necessarily that of the individual. An expression in public space may turn out to be the expression essentially of a common sentiment or purpose. That is, it may be essential to this sentiment or purpose that it be shared, and the expression may be the vehicle of this sharing.

These two features together – that action can be that of a community, and that it also exists in the expressive dimension – form the crucial background to Hegel's philosophy of society and history. The *Sittlichkeit* of a given society is not only to be seen as the action of a community, or of individuals only so far as they identify themselves as members of a community (an "I" that is "We," and a "We" that is "I");[7] it also embodies and gives expression to a certain understanding of the agent, his community, and their relation to the divine. It is the latter which gives us the key to the fate of the society. For it is here that the basic incoherence underlying social practice will appear as contradiction, as we saw with the case of the slave-owning society above. Hegel's notion of historical development can only be properly stated if we understand social institutions in this way, as trans-individual action which also has an expressive dimension. By contrast, the causal view and its accompanying atomist outlook induces us to explain institutions in purely instrumental terms. And in these terms, Hegel's theory becomes completely unformulable. We cannot even begin to state what it is all about.[8]

V

I have been arguing that we can understand Hegel against the background of a long-standing and very basic issue in modern philosophy about the nature of action. Hegel's philosophy of mind can be understood as firmly grounded on an option in favour of what I have been calling the qualitative view of action and against the causal view.

I have tried to follow the different ramifications of this qualitative view to show their importance to Hegel's thought. I looked first at the notion of agent's knowledge, and we saw that the system of philosophy itself can be seen as the integration of everything into a form of all-embracing agent's knowledge. I then followed another development of the qualitative view, which shows us action as primordially unreflecting bodily practice, which later can be transformed by the agent's achievement of reflective awareness. We saw that Hegel's conceptions of subjectivity and its development are rooted in this understanding. I then argued that the expressive revolution in the theory of meaning could be seen as offshoot of this same view of action; and that Hegel is clearly operating within the expressive conception. Finally we can see that his theory of history supposes not just the expressive dimension but also the idea of irreducibly common actions, which only the qualitative view can allow.

One part of my case is thus that Hegel's philosophy of mind can be illuminated by making this issue explicit in all its ramifications. This is just in the way that we make any philosophy clearer by spelling out more fully some of its deepest assumptions. The illumination will be the greater the more fundamental and pervasive the assumptions in question are from the theory under study. Now my claim is that for Hegel the qualitative theory of action is very basic and all-pervasive, and the above pages have attempted to show this. Perhaps out of deference for Hegel's shade I should not use the word "assumption," since for Hegel everything is ultimately demonstrated. But my claim stands that the thesis about action I have been describing here is quite central to his philosophy.

This is only one side of the gain that one can hope for in a study of this kind. The other, as I said at the outset, is that we should attain some greater understanding of the historical debate itself by situating Hegel in it. I think this is so as well, but I have not got space to argue it here.

What does emerge from the above is that Hegel is one of the important and seminal figures in the long and hard-fought emergence of a counter-theory to the long-dominant epistemologically based view which the seventeenth century bequeathed to us. This can help explain why he has been an influential figure in this whole counter-movement. But what remains to be understood is why he has also often been ignored or rejected by major figures who have shared somewhat the same notions of action, starting with Schopenhauer but by no means ending there.

Perhaps what separates Hegel most obviously and most profoundly from those today who take the same side on the issue about action is their profoundly different reading of the same genetic view. For Heidegger, for example, the notion that action is first of all unreflected practice seems to rule out altogether as chimerical the goal of a fully explicit and self-authenticating understanding of what we are about. Disclosure is invariably accompanied by hiddenness; the explicit depends on the horizon of the implicit. The difference here is fundamental, but I believe that it too can be illuminated if we relate to it radically different readings of the qualitative view of action, which both espoused in opposition to the epistemological rationalism of the seventeenth century.

NOTES

Reprinted by permission from Taylor, *Philosophical Papers*, vol. 1, *Human Agency and Language* (Cambridge: Cambridge University Press, 1985), 77–97.

1 D. Davidson, "Actions, Reasons and Causes," *Journal of Philosophy* 60, no. 23 (1973): 685–700; Ted Honderich, ed., "Freedom to Act," in *Essays on Freedom of Action* (London, 1973).

2 C. Taylor, "Action as Expression," in *Intention and Intentionality*, ed. C. Diamond and J. Teichman (London, 1979).

3 B. Williams, *Descartes* (London, 1978).

4 I have argued this further in C. Taylor, "The Validity of Transcendental Arguments," *Proceedings of the Aristotelian Society*, 1978–9, 151–65.

5 G.E.M. Anscombe, *Intention* (Oxford, 1957), pp. 13–15.
6 C. Taylor, *Hegel and Modern Society* (Cambridge, 1979), 18.
7 *Philosophy of Spirit*, 140.
8 I have developed this further in C. Taylor, "Hegel's 'Sittlichkeit' and the Crisis of Representative Institutions," in *Philosophy of History and Action*, ed. Yirmiahu Yoval (London, 1978).

8 Negativity: Charles Taylor, Hegel, and the Problem of Modern Freedom

KENNETH KIERANS

I will not attempt to sum up Taylor's account of Hegel, let alone offer an assessment of it. His contribution to our understanding of Hegel – and of the modern world – is too far-reaching, and we are all still trying to assimilate it.[1] What I will do, instead, is highlight some of the important issues and themes which Taylor's reading of Hegel has brought to our attention.

My focus will not be the same as Taylor's, but I hope to communicate some of the breadth and depth of his interpretation.

First of all, Hegel's work appeals to Taylor because it offers us a critique of modern freedom. Both Hegel and Taylor in the end affirm modern freedom. But they emphasize that it has a tendency to emptiness and negativity. As Taylor puts it, the problem is the modern focus on subjective freedom, which is difficult – in some ways impossible – to reconcile with the good of the community and with the higher calling of religion.

Second, Taylor is drawn to Hegel's philosophy because of its vision of the past, notably of ancient Greece, where in contrast to the narrow focus of modern subjective freedom a wider field of ethical life, of social and political experience, opens up. And beyond ethical life, ancient philosophy – Plato, Aristotle, and the Neoplatonists – sought a good that is the source of all things, an ultimate or unconditional good. Taylor's own reflections on history have much to do with this notion of a good, which points beyond life and the all-too-human demand to find satisfaction in it.

Third, Taylor thinks that we have much to learn from Hegel's concept of "spirit" in which modern and ancient standpoints are combined. In the various forms of spirit – subjective, objective or institutional, and the union of the two in art and religion – we find a profound synthesis of the human and the divine. Thus Hegel follows the ancients in tracing all things back to their divine origin, but he also affirms the subjective principle of the modern world in which everything that is other than the human is related back to it. Although Taylor differs from Hegel in significant respects, he too sees the unity of the human and the divine in Western history – a unity which preserves the difference, even to the point of enabling atheism.

Hegel's philosophy is similar to, but crucially different from, the circular monism of the Neoplatonists. The unity to which Hegel ascends from out of difference and multiplicity is not, as in Neoplatonism, the primal, undifferentiated unity of the beginning, but a unity which is higher, because in it all individuation and diversity persist. As Taylor explains it, the Hegelian system fuses the idea of the circular return with the idea of linear progress. The absolute is found not at the beginning but at the end of the developmental process, which has the form of an ascending plane or spiral.[2]

The notion of a spiral gives Hegel unshakable confidence in modern freedom. The same confidence can be found in Taylor, though it takes a very different form. Both see a movement from the division and conflict – the negativity – between subjectivity and objectivity to a unification of the two sides. But whereas Hegel everywhere sees an inevitable and desirable deepening of negativity, Taylor sees a need to contextualize and moderate it.

So Taylor can in no way be called a "Hegelian," but his emphasis on the movement from negativity to a moderate, affirmative, "situated" freedom reveals that he has much in common with Hegel. Furthermore, it exposes an issue of huge and ongoing significance for our understanding of the modern world – how the negativity of human freedom can be converted into an affirmative stance, and whether this conversion involves a temporal standpoint or an eternal one. Though Taylor by no means excludes the eternal, he thinks that affirmation can truly take place only in a temporal "horizon of the implicit," a linguistically and symbolically constituted social life.[3] I will argue that this is not so much a break with the Hegelian system as an adaptation and modification of it.

I

Hegel's critique of modern freedom, which Taylor follows closely, has to do with its powerful negativity. The immediate historical background to the rise of modern freedom and its negativity was the growing impatience of the medievals with the dualism between the sacred and the secular. Modernity grew out of that impatience: it is a radical revolt against medieval dualism, a sustained attempt to transpose the sacred onto the secular realm, and to resolve the conflict between them.[4] But modernity generates its own dualism, which appears in a host of ways, and most acutely in the unresolved tensions between the thinking ego and its object, morality and desire, the state and individual freedom. These tensions and oppositions are no doubt necessary to modern consciousness, but they also threaten to tear it apart.[5] How can they be overcome?

Kant and Fichte, inspired in part by Rousseau, thought that a new, radical idealism could bring about the great unification.[6] Fichte's version of this idealism is particularly important. At first a disciple of Kant, he transformed the master's system by eliminating the notion of an unknowable world of reality, the thing-in-itself. The result was a much more thoroughgoing conception of subjectivity. For Fichte, subjectivity ultimately is the basis of everything; he maintained that the objective world is posited, shaped, and formed by the "I think" and is thus not independent of it.

This ultimate, all-embracing subject can be known or felt – thanks to "intellectual intuition" – but it transcends the awareness of ordinary finite subjects.[7] Indeed, the infinite subjectivity that posits the world is what Fichte called God, and it played a greater and greater role in his system as his thought evolved. His system is not an atheistic one. But the explosive and revolutionary core of it is the notion of a moral subject that is unlimited in its activity, a subject that can surmount all barriers to its knowledge and will.

Fichte's great hope was that human beings – infinitely and boundlessly free in the world – would overcome the dualism of the Kantian moral subject. In the course of its development, the divided moral subject would be driven to an extreme where, in a triumphant act of self-assertion, it would absorb and overcome its opposition. That is how Fichte imagined the reconciliation of moral freedom with the world.

But Fichte was not really interested in reconciliation; he remained a Kantian in his insistence that the highest activity of the subject is the free will. The "I think" posits the world and is profoundly at one with it, but the positing takes place so that the subject may have barriers and obstacles to struggle against. That is, the moral subject is free only in struggling against a world of its own creation, and the struggle is endless. Any actual unity of the world and free will would bring the struggle between them to an end, and freedom would disappear. Thus a perfect unity of the world and human freedom can only ever be a goal; it is an ideal we should strive after and fight for, but it can never be realized.[8]

From Hegel's perspective, what Fichte was at least beginning to provide was a theoretical foundation for the unity of the world and human freedom.[9] Nature for him was not, as it was for Kant, a phenomenal object whose ultimate ontological foundation, the thing-in-itself, is unknowable; rather, nature is founded on a spiritual force which manifests itself in phenomena. The whole order of nature thus tends to realize spiritual goals, tends towards a form that is at one with subjective freedom. Nature both within and without unites with reason, moral freedom and our highest spiritual achievements.

But Fichte did not develop this idea far enough.[10] The world of nature is based on the spiritual force of the "I think," but is not the expression of its own underlying force; it is the object of human consciousness or human will. No doubt Fichte's God, his infinite subject, is distinct from finite human subjects who strive to unite themselves with it, but this infinite subject is concerned only with itself. It is essentially moral and regards the object only in relation to its own striving for perfection, its own freedom.

In point of form, Fichte's unity of subject and object is therefore an empty ideal, and it has enormous destructive potential.[11] But this destructiveness has implicit in it the demand for the nullification of the antithesis between idealism and empiricism. This is why some of the Romantics, who admired Fichte, sought to combine his position with Spinoza's. They hoped that such a combination would correct and overcome the emptiness of Fichte's idealism, while affirming its promise of freedom.[12] And surely they were right: the struggle to be free against all limits – natural and social – presupposes a recognition of these limits as one's own. Modern freedom is not just compatible with, but rooted in, the acceptance and affirmation of our limits.

The problem, as Taylor defines it, is to ground nature in a spiritual principle that is independent of human beings. If this could be done, and if this independent spiritual reality could act on its own to realize its unity with human freedom, then we would have a real unity of subject and object.[13] This unity would be liberating, but not in the sense that we could finally assert ourselves through some arbitrarily chosen goal. Rather, we would understand freedom as a response to – and acceptance of – a situation which is ours in virtue of our common condition or shared purpose.

Hegel famously turned to ancient Greece for help in envisaging such a unity of self and world, and insisted that the wisdom of the ancients is a necessary counterweight to the subjectivist tendencies of Fichte and other modern idealists. This is true not only from a philosophical, but also from a political and cultural point of view. In his commentary on the *Phenomenology of Spirit*, Taylor emphasizes the significance of Hegel's argument that pure individual freedom, particularly in the form of modern "morality," is not the ultimate form of self; that the true ethic is one lived in society, as in the ancient Greek city-state. The "spirit" of the ancient Greeks was not merely an ideal, or something demanded: it existed in their institutions, and was maintained by their allegiance. The basic lesson we must learn from the ancients is that the self lives within the spiritual reality of the city or state.[14]

In the end, however, Hegel found in ancient wisdom only the opposite of modern freedom: an independent substance into which the individual self disappears without a trace (or rather from which it must struggle to distinguish itself). What is needed, he thought, is a synthesis of ancient and modern standpoints. Taylor, for his part, is drawn to the notion of such a synthesis, though he also sees enormous, perhaps insuperable, obstacles to it.[15]

II

The Greek ethical world was one in which a substantial or infinite spirit appeared in social and political life. The freedom of the polis was not a subjective, finite, individualistic freedom, but the freedom of individuals who were devoted to the mutually supportive institutions of family and state. In such a world, individuals make their own what is already before them, i.e., an ethical life which is "given" but "which is at the same time the deed and work of the subject finding it."[16]

The religion which corresponded to this freedom and sustained it was to Hegel a "religion of art."[17] Confidence in the gods was at the same time human self-confidence, but a confidence which, though present in humans whose creativity perceived it, was divine (higher than the human). Here the world and human freedom, "substance" and "*actual* consciousness," were harmonized and reconciled.[18] And the harmony and reconciliation persisted so long as individuals were moved by the objective ends of the wider institutional order.

The harmony of Greek life was destroyed when subjective reflection asserted its independence: the sophists and Socrates began to question the validity of the objective order. For what justification can there be for confining the self to the appropriation of the already found? The spiritual bond between the ethical order and the individual self dissolved.

The resulting conflict prepared the ground for the rise of philosophy. Crucial was the rise of pagan thought from the finite to the infinite standpoint; it became, as Aristotle put it, "thought thinking itself," a thought at home with itself in everything. This claim to comprehensive truth is for Hegel an indispensable aspect of all genuine philosophy. Indeed, he says that "there is no higher idealism" than that of Aristotle, even among the moderns.[19]

Aristotle, building on Plato, disclosed an ideal, universal world at once human and divine on which the freedom of the polis was based. Hegel regarded the God of Plato and Aristotle as so lacking in "envy" as to reveal itself – or some of itself – to the human mind.[20] He believed that the Christian God could do much more. Taylor agrees, but (as we shall see) maintains that Hegel did not really understand the deep differences between the God of pagan philosophy and the Christian God of love.

After Aristotle, the problem was the relation of free individuals to the universal foundation of politics and religion.[21] The free individuals of Hellenistic-Roman culture, at first confident and worldly, increasingly descended into scepticism. The Stoic, for example, regarded himself as a free, self-made individual. In thought, they achieved freedom from the natural and human worlds, not by mastering them, however, but by turning away from them. Sceptical thought takes this free individuality a step further by negating the world altogether, even though from a practical point of view it acknowledged that we must all live in the world and deal with it.[22]

The free individuals of antiquity turned inward away from the world, abandoning it to the control of unreconstructed and increasingly irrational force. Confined to mere thought, the Stoic and Sceptic could not find happiness. They were superseded by a religious consciousness, which, though "unhappy," was able in the various forms of Neoplatonic philosophy to discover the absolute foundation of sensuous reality and individual freedom. This was a higher freedom than that known to either stoicism or scepticism. The Neoplatonists did not have to flee nature without and passions within, but could work through them both in an effort to reach a remote, unknowable God.[23]

In Neoplatonism, however, the movement to the absolute was from the side of the free individual, and not also from the absolute itself. The goal was to reach the intuition of an eternal universe, a unity before all division and difference. But the result, at least from the human side, was strictly negative: what was other than the principle was left unrelated to it, and to the free individual.[24]

Hegel says of Plotinus, for example, that, unlike Aristotle, he did not want to determine objects in their particularity, but rather to emphasize the universal in them as opposed to their fleeting, insubstantial existence. The essential point in Plotinus is this separation of the mind from externals, and the elevation of it to what is "good and true, to the absolute." This means that the highest activity of humans is the rational contemplation of the eternal, which is the source of our reason. In all of this, Hegel says, Plotinus thought that soul "brings itself nigh to the Deity," but this Deity "cannot be conceived as creative."[25] The descent of the individual mind to nature and to consciousness has the character of an "arbitrary" fall.[26] In short, humans lack definite connection with the divine.

Taylor says much the same thing about Plotinus, and he does so in order to highlight the modern dimension in Hegel's thought. Thus, while there are "affinities" between Hegel and Plotinus, "there is no exact parallel." In the philosophy of Plotinus, finite things arise from a descent or fall from the One. They "emanate" from the divine, but are not essential to it; they are absolutely dependent on the divine, but the divine is absolutely independent of them. For Hegel, by contrast, finite things and individual human beings play a necessary and essential role in the life of the divine: "finitude is a condition of the existence of infinite life." This, according to Taylor, is a "modern idea."[27] Hegel would only add, as Taylor would not, that it is also a thoroughly Christian idea.

With Neoplatonism, there was, from within the sphere of subjectivity, the promise of reconnection with objective reality. The inward world of Neoplatonic thought was wonderfully self-sufficient – rich and self-complete – but far from bridging the gap between inner and outer opened up by stoicism and scepticism, it deepened it and made it complete.[28] The truth is that Neoplatonism did not comprehend and embrace the world, but rather fled from it.

Relative to Neoplatonism, Taylor occupies a middle position: he wants to affirm a transcendent point of view, one which takes us beyond ordinary life and the demand for satisfaction in it, but he also wants to be able to stay with the world and ordinary life. The negativity of Neoplatonic thought points beyond the world, but also leaves the self attracted to it, and the result is uncertain: the free individual, infinitely turned in upon itself, no doubt needs connection with the finite world of nature and other human beings, but how from the Neoplatonic point of view can this be?

Hegel, so it seems, also had a middle position: on the one hand, he affirmed a transcendent, eternal divinity, and on the other hand, insisted that this divinity be totally immanent in the world. For otherwise we would be left with a worldless divinity – abstract, inaccessible even by thought – and a godless world, material and at some level accessible but meaningless. It is not at all clear how we can forge a synthesis of the two sides.

In speaking of the inward turn to pure thinking, a turn which the ancients experienced under the pressure of an increasingly oppressive external world, Hegel – coolly and objectively – notes that they were left with nothing but "a blank Destiny." And he strikes an existential note, one which has a contemporary ring: as the city fragments and succumbs to tyranny, atomistic individuals "become elemental beings raging madly against one another in a frenzy of destructive activity ... They exist, therefore, in a merely negative relationship, both to one another and to him who is their bond of connection or continuity." The desires and enjoyments of ruler and ruled alike become "monstrous excesses," and the individual consciousness "is *driven back into itself*."[29]

III

The free individual of antiquity had separated and distanced itself from the world: how was it to find or, better yet, create a world in which its freedom had reality? A new beginning was required in which the movement to the divine would be not only from the side of the free individual, but also from the divine itself.[30] The divine which is independent and prior to the world would have to enter into it, without however suffering loss of its divinity. It would have to act from its own side to save free individuals who are manifestly unable to save themselves. This divine movement would have to be accepted as fact, as an act of grace, but it would imply that "man is capable of the divine," which would in turn bring about a "revolution" in world history.[31]

The Christian religion satisfied the need for a reconciliation with the divine, for a new beginning. Neoplatonic philosophy led to "the One": the unknown God prior to the division of life and thought. With Christianity, God – a Trinitarian God – knows this division as his own. God the father, through the incarnation, death and resurrection of his son, reconciles the world with himself and draws free individuals from their division to a concrete freedom in him. There is a unity of "the divine and human nature," and the individual "is made worthy of attaining on his own account to this unity."[32]

This new beginning did not at first exist in a philosophical form. It took the form of faith, and only in that way could everyone come to know and will it. Individuals were purged of the finite, given limits through which the negativity of pagan freedom had found expression; they found in faith, in the revelation of absolute truth, a spiritual relation of God and humanity in which a concrete freedom became possible.[33]

A new philosophy emerged only after the Christian religion had inspired individuals to transform the human world and seek an institutional order which would unite nature and subjective freedom. This happened in the Protestant Reformation: the medieval church gave way to a religious community in which individuals regarded subjective freedom – conscience – as a necessary moment in the acceptance of religious authority. The concrete spirit of this religious belief led to equally concrete social and political changes: the medieval virtues of chastity, poverty and obedience were replaced by the modern ideals of family life, work and a free acceptance of political authority.[34]

The promise of modern philosophy was that it could do what ancient philosophy could not, i.e., affirm both divine and human freedom. At first, however, this synthesis of divine and human was only implicit: the history of modern philosophy is one in which the relation of human freedom and subjectivity to the God of faith and to the natural world was more and more systematically developed. Hegel saw this history as a gradual, step-by-step process in which subjective, one-sided forms of philosophy emerged, conflicted with faith, and then finally gave way to a perfected philosophical system – his own – which resolved the antithesis of reason and religious belief. In the same way, from within the political realm, subjective, one-sided forms of freedom emerged, conflicted with the state, and then finally gave way to a perfected, fully developed state – a post-revolutionary one – which had subjective freedom in it.[35]

For Hegel, it is not enough for moderns to have the divine substance as their foundation: their impulse is, with the divine substance in mind, to find themselves by going into the world, with which they are implicitly united. The ancient way to God takes us beyond the world, but if, as moderns think, nature is God's work, then humans need not lose contact with divine truth by turning to nature and busying themselves with it. God is present in the free worldly activity of human beings as well as in natural necessity and causality. Taylor, too, sees the importance to modernity of this notion of God's presence in the world, but denies that Hegel – or any other philosopher – has successfully reconciled natural necessity and causality with modern freedom.[36]

There are indeed problems in the relation of the modern self to what is other than and external to it, and Taylor may well be right to ascribe these problems to Hegel himself. Like the ancients, moderns no doubt have an intuition of unity prior to the division of the free subject from the world, but what they want and demand is knowledge that can comprehend that division. In seeking this knowledge, however, moderns discover that, however mightily they strive for unity, they cannot actually attain it: to the extent that they conceive of unity only through the human subject, the negativity of their experience is bound to conflict with – and fatally compromise – the intuition of its unity.

Still, like Hegel, Taylor thinks that modern history tends to overcome the division and conflict between the world and human subjectivity; the negativity brings to light an underlying spiritual unity to which we are called.[37] The movement is to a concrete unity of the free subject with the whole, in which the various forms of opposition between the ego and its object are overcome. This happens not only subjectively – i.e., emotionally and psychologically – but also objectively in the institutional order: individuals are subsumed in a self-governing community in which all – as free and equal – can affirm the community as their own good.[38]

Where does all this leave religion? Taylor agrees with Hegel that religion is central to our understanding of history and of ourselves. In religion, the subjective and the objective come together as one in a free, inward relation of human and divine. This ultimate unity of subjective and objective is a return of the divine to itself from out of division and conflict, suffering and evil. The divine acts from its own side to bring about this unification, though humans must also do their part. As Taylor understands it, again following Hegel very closely, everything in Christianity rests on the notions of the Incarnation and the Kingdom of God, which in the course of history inspire us to make our union with God real in various forms of human community.[39]

It would seem, then, that Taylor agrees with Hegel that the Christian religion is a religion of the "*reconciliation* of God and the world."[40]

He allows that Hegel re-interpreted "a surprising number of orthodox Christian beliefs in his system." But this is where Taylor draws a line: with regard to creation, revelation and salvation, "Hegel cannot accommodate the relations of God and man as they must be for Christian faith. He has no place for grace in the properly Christian sense." Indeed, for Taylor, Hegel's vision of reason triumphant, of our "identity with cosmic necessity," is incompatible with Christian faith. And so, a Hegelian philosopher really cannot "thank God," for what "he does is to contemplate his identity with cosmic spirit, which is something quite different."[41]

Certainly, Taylor sees in Hegel's account of Western politics and history as well as in his vision of Western philosophy a movement from unity to division and back to unity – in other words, a spiral. But he concludes that Hegel's attempt to demonstrate the rational necessity of this unifying movement is unconvincing. Hegel's central claim – on which his system depends – is that finite being is nothing outside of infinite being, i.e., God. This claim, however, cannot overcome the sceptical conviction that we are limited in what we can think by contingency and time. What Hegel gives us is not a compelling proof of his system, but merely "an incisive expression of his personal belief."[42]

Similarly, Taylor concedes that for Hegel the world is an emanation of spirit: the divine manifests itself in the work of human beings, and our freedom is therefore more than a subjective reaction to what is there in the world around us. But for Taylor, Hegel's notion that human freedom can be truly infinite when it affirms the world as the embodiment of the divine cannot prevent that notion of infinite freedom from fixating on the ego and falling back into the old antagonism between self and world. In fact, like many commentators, he thinks that Hegel's system, and the modern world on which it rests, gives rise to – even deepens – the dualism and feeling of estrangement they were supposed to overcome.[43]

Nevertheless, and despite the distance between them, Taylor is closer to Hegel than to the numerous post-Hegelian advocates of "absolute freedom," whether liberal, Marxist, or existentialist. Taylor's view is that Hegel brilliantly and decisively exposed the emptiness of the modern notion of a self-dependent freedom. The self which drives for freedom by setting aside all external obstacles and limits ultimately experiences a void in which there is no vocation or purpose, nothing inspiring or worth doing. Creative freedom, when centred in the individual, is too indefinite to ground human action or a way of life. Taylor embraces this Hegelian insight: only an established social order which gives us our goals can define the content of freedom and specify the purpose of creativity.[44]

So too with religion: Taylor's understanding – and acceptance – of atheism as an essential feature of modern spiritual life echoes Hegel's insistence that atheism, or the "feeling that 'God Himself is dead,'" is a "moment" in the rediscovery of the divine, i.e., the "highest totality." Crucial to the conversion from atheism to theism, in Hegel's account, is the "harsh consciousness of loss" which overwhelms unbelievers. Spiritual knowledge is not something simple and immediate, but a hard won victory over the "abyss of nothingness" both within and without.[45]

In an analogous way, Taylor traces the eighteenth-century transition from belief to unbelief, and then the jarring nineteenth-century journey from humanism to anti-humanism. With Nietzsche and his twentieth-century followers in view, Taylor says that anti-humanism is "a revolt from within unbelief" in which the primacy of "life" in atheistic humanism is rejected. Anti-humanism involves a meditation on "death," not just as the ultimate moment of loss, but as "an escape from the confines of life, to the paramount vantage point in which life shows its meaning."[46]

The connection between Nietzschean-style anti-humanism and religion – notably Christianity and Buddhism – is obvious: the notion that fundamental human problems cannot be solved within history brings us face-to-face with the boundaries of the human domain. For this reason, Taylor gives anti-humanism an important place in the contemporary theistic perspective. Like Hegel, Taylor acknowledges that the early moderns, in a remarkable burst of confidence, took themselves to be independent of the social order and its religious foundations. However, as a necessary counter-movement, he sees a dissolution of this modern confidence that we are independent of earlier forms. Moderns are both self-making and the product of a long history.[47]

From one perspective, Taylor and Hegel are poles apart: Hegel aims at the explicit clarity of conceptual necessity – the Idea – whereas Taylor accents the unreflective experience which precedes self-aware consciousness, and is (only partially) illumined by it.[48] From another perspective, however, they are really saying the same thing: human beings are spiritual creatures who cannot be satisfied with finite ends, and at the same time want more than the anarchism and scepticism of endless difference. Both Taylor and Hegel think it necessary to go beyond ever-receding limits to an experience and a knowledge of the historical process which makes an ordered freedom possible, a freedom which is at once finite and infinite, temporal and spiritual.[49]

The modern world is no doubt deeply conflicted and unstable: its humanistic confidence generates a scepticism which cannot reconcile the demands of sensual particularity with conceptual reason. In the ancient world, this kind of scepticism led to diverse forms of Neoplatonism – an upward or inward turn away from the corruption of temporal life to a rational world and a unity before all division. But pagan Neoplatonism posits an unmediated spiritual order, one which is absolutely separate and apart from us and what we love.[50] By contrast, and for all their differences, Taylor and Hegel bring to light a Christian spiritual order which removes that deep division of divine and human and establishes a new kind of desire and enjoyment, a modern secularity.

Hegel argues that the modern world is Christian in the sense that it conceives an objective order – natural and social – which humans can access only through their own freedom and creativity. The order is unavailable except through the medium of human consciousness and activity. The dangers of such a world are clear to both Hegel and Taylor: despair and rage in the face of the apparent impossibility of connecting with the objective order through our own free activity. Still, like Hegel, Taylor is hopeful that the modern standpoint can unite the intelligible world with the sensible, and with free individuals.[51]

Moderns, from at least the time of Rousseau, have felt the need to reflect on themselves, to grasp their own historical evolution from out of the ancient world. Hegel says that the reason in our history is evident in the conflict between substantial unity and subjective freedom, and in the unification of the two in modern political and religious life. Taylor does not deny that there is reason in history, but for him it is discernible only from our immediate social experience as interpreted by language and symbols. This is a more cautious and modest standpoint, to be sure, and yet Taylor does have a vision of history in which the world and the self come together as one. He does not contradict, but rather complements, Hegel: both offer us inspiring, affirmative visions of modern freedom and of the history which gave rise to it.

NOTES

1 There are several excellent commentaries on Taylor. Particularly helpful, in my view, is Brian J. Braman's *Meaning and Authenticity: Bernard Lonergan and Charles Taylor on the Drama of Authentic Human Existence* (Toronto: University of Toronto Press, 2008).

2 Charles Taylor, *Hegel and Modern Society* (Cambridge: Cambridge University Press, 1979), 8–11.
3 Ibid., 165.
4 G.W.F. Hegel, *Lectures on the History of Philosophy*, trans. E.S. Haldane and Frances H. Simon (New York: Humanities, 1968), 3:157–8.
5 In his account of "consciousness," Hegel criticizes Kant and Fichte for failing to reach a unified standpoint: see G.W.F. Hegel, *Philosophy of Mind*, trans. William Wallace (Oxford: Oxford University Press, 1971), s. 415, 155–6.
6 In what follows, I will draw on Taylor's account of Fichte. See Charles Taylor, *Hegel* (Cambridge: Cambridge University Press, 1975), 36–40.
7 On this point, see Emil Fackenheim, *The Religious Dimension in Hegel's Thought* (Bloomington: Indiana University Press, 1967), 15–16; and Fackenheim, *The God Within: Kant, Schelling and Historicity*, ed. John Burbidge (Toronto: University of Toronto Press, 1996), 76–7.
8 Taylor, *Hegel*, 188–92.
9 Hegel, *History of Philosophy*, 3:505–6.
10 Both Hegel and his erstwhile friend Schelling saw Fichte's idea of unity as valid but undeveloped and naive. For a superb account of Schelling's relation to Fichte, written in the nineteenth century from a Hegelian perspective, see John Watson, *Schelling's Transcendental Idealism: A Critical Exposition* (Chicago: S.C. Griggs, 1882), particularly chap. 4, 98–100 and chap. 8, sec. 1, 196–201.
11 See the remarkably vivid account of this destructive potential in Michael A. Gillespie, *Nihilism before Nietzsche* (Chicago: University of Chicago Press, 1995), chap. 3.
12 Taylor makes this point relative to Schelling in *Hegel*, 41–2.
13 Taylor's enthusiasm for this prospect shines through in his account of Romanticism. See Charles Taylor, *Sources of the Self: The Making of the Modern Identity* (Cambridge, MA: Harvard University Press, 1989), chap. 21.
14 Hence the transition in the *Phenomenology of Spirit* from *reason* (chap. 5) to *spirit* (chap. 6), which involves a leap from negativity to affirmation. See Taylor, *Hegel*, 16–170.
15 Taylor, *Hegel and Modern Society*, 111–18.
16 G.W.F. Hegel, *Phenomenology of Spirit*, trans. A.V. Miller (New York: Oxford University Press, 1977), 276.
17 Ibid., 425.
18 Ibid., 424.
19 Aristotle and Hegel cited in Alfredo Ferrain, "Hegel's Aristotle and Its Time," in *A Companion to Hegel*, ed. Stephen Houlgate and Michael Baur (Oxford: Blackwell Press, 2011), 445.

20 Very instructive on this point is Merold Westphal, *Transcendence and Self-Transcendence: On God and the Soul* (Bloomington: Indiana University Press, 2004), 82–3.
21 Hegel, *Lectures on the History of Philosophy*, 2:232–6.
22 Ibid., 328–33.
23 Ibid., 376–9.
24 For an exceptionally clear description of Neoplatonism and Hegel's relation to it, see James Doull, "Hegel's Phenomenology and Post-Modern Thought," in *Philosophy and Freedom: The Legacy of James Doull*, ed. David G. Peddle and Neil G. Robertson (Toronto: University of Toronto Press, 2003), 284–5.
25 Hegel, *History of Philosophy*, 2:407, 412, 415.
26 Ibid., 429.
27 Taylor, *Hegel and Modern Society*, 40.
28 Hegel does see an evolution within pagan Neoplatonism: Plotinus was superseded by the more "systematic" Proclus and his followers. Still, he says, the gap in Neoplatonism between the human and the divine, the world and the self, remained. See Hegel, *History of Philosophy*, 2:435.
29 Hegel, *Phenomenology*, 290–3.
30 Thus Fackenheim says that Hegel "affirms two Trinities: the pre-worldly trinitarian play eternally complete apart from the world, and the real trinitarian incursion into the world." See Fackenheim, *Religious Dimension*, 153. This is a vexed issue in Hegel scholarship. Taylor, for one, strongly denies that there is room for a pre-worldly trinity in Hegel's system; see Taylor, *Hegel*, 494, note.
31 Hegel, *History of Philosophy*, 3:4.
32 Ibid., 2–3.
33 Ibid., 23–5; G.W.F. Hegel, *The Philosophy of History*, trans. J. Sibree (New York: Dover Publications, 1956), 341–2.
34 Hegel, *History of Philosophy*, 3:146–55.
35 See, for example, Hegel's "Idea of a Concrete Universal Unity," and particularly his discussion of Montesquieu and Rousseau, in ibid., 3:397.
36 I refer to Taylor's comments on substance, causality, and freedom in Hegel, 286–96.
37 Taylor, *Hegel and Modern Society*, 160.
38 In Taylor's view, there is a deep connection between liberal "atomists" and communitarian "holists." See his "Cross-Purposes: The Liberal-Communitarian Debate," in *Philosophical Arguments*, chap. 10 (Cambridge, MA: Harvard University Press, 1995).
39 Hegel, 491–2.

40 G.W.F. Hegel, *Lectures on the Philosophy of Religion*, ed. Peter C. Hodgson and trans. R.F. Brown, P.C. Hodgson, and J.M. Stewart, vol. 3, *The Consummate Religion* (Berkeley: University of California Press, 1985), 65.
41 Hegel, 492–4.
42 *Hegel and Modern Society*, 67.
43 Ibid., 58.
44 Ibid., 157–9.
45 G.W.F. Hegel, *Faith and Knowledge*, trans. Walter Cerf and H.S. Harris (Albany: State University of New York Press, 1977), 190–1. In his mature phase, Hegel was for the same reason still convinced of the "consoling power" of Christianity. See G.W.F. Hegel, *Logic*, trans. William Wallace (Oxford: Oxford University Press, 1975), 210.
46 Charles Taylor, *A Secular Age* (Cambridge, MA: Belknap, 2007), 724–6.
47 So strongly does Taylor feel about this connection with history that, in his view, theories of modernity that reject the traditional forms on which they depend "richly deserve suppression." See *Sources of the Self*, 101.
48 See *Hegel in Modern Society*, 163–6, where Taylor explicitly identifies with the late Wittgenstein, Heidegger, and Merleau-Ponty, amongst others.
49 Ibid., 159–60.
50 Taylor, *Sources of the Self*, 275–6. For a similar, fuller treatment of Neoplatonism, see M.H. Abrams, *Natural Supernaturalism: Tradition and Revolution in Romantic Literature* (New York: W.W. Norton, 1971), chap. 3.
51 Taylor, *Sources of the Self*, 427–8.

PART TWO

Hegel in Canadian Politics

9 Early Canadian Political Culture: Hegelian Adaptations in John Watson

ELIZABETH TROTT

Introduction

Philosophy first arrived in Canada in the late 1600s in trunks full of books carried by Jesuit priests. For the next one hundred years philosophers in Quebec debated Descartes and Augustine and kept up to date on philosophical developments in Europe.[1]

When philosophy arrived in English Canada, well over one hundred years after its arrival in Quebec, adjustments to the philosophical traditions of the nineteenth century began.[2] Those adjustments produced articles and books written in Canada with patterns of problem-solving that reflected Kantian and Hegelian influences. *The Faces of Reason* documents those patterns and argues that they manifest innovative responses to standard philosophical questions about ethics, metaphysics, politics, religion, and nature – responses that can be understood as foundational to Canadian culture.[3]

Many of the early Canadian philosophers came from Glasgow and Edinburgh. James Beaven (1801–1875, arrived at University of Toronto 1843) and William Lyall (1811–1890, arrived at Knox College, Toronto 1848, left for Dalhousie University, Halifax 1850) did incorporate common sense traditions in their writings, but others did not. John Clark Murray (1836–1917, arrived at Queen's University, Kingston,1862, left for McGill University, Montreal 1872) and John Watson (1847–1939, arrived at Queen's University, 1872) used idealist theories to address philosophical questions in their new world.[4] Providing answers to the questions raised by cultural disparities in Canada was paramount.

Canada in the early nineteenth century was a country without any history of an evolving political order. There was a need to reconcile unities and pluralities, a need to develop political constructs that would incorporate dualities of individual and community, order and freedom, state and nation. There was a need to address the disparities of multiple cultures – disparities of religion, ethical customs and moralities, political orientations. In early Canada, individuals being able to set their own agendas often depended on coming to terms with cultural differences. Social order, over thousands of miles of sparsely populated land, would not result from imposing a political vision that was promoted by authorities from abroad. New ideas about social order needed to be developed using the logic of reason.

British political philosophy during the nineteenth century had not ignored Hegel.[5] Hegel had developed a logical method, one that could address goals of unity through synthesis, and enable change. His idealism could be modified to address multiple interpretations of experience, that is, an increasingly complex association of cultures. John Watson, teaching at Queen's University in 1872, needed to adapt British traditions to his new circumstances. Watson was known for his excellent contributions to Kantian scholarship.[6] In his political theory, *The State in Peace and War* (hereafter *SPW*), Watson appealed to and defended Hegel, but modified Hegel's methodology.[7] We turn, first, to the association between philosophy and culture; second, to an examination of the Hegelian model that is reflected, but not imitated, in Watson's writings; and third to Watson's adaptations of Hegelian theory.

Philosophy and Culture

In "Philosophy and Culture," Leslie Armour writes, "Culture is the meaning people put on their own behaviour and that of others. When the same behaviour is habitually given more than one meaning there are two or more sub-cultures involved. If the meanings thus separated form a whole way of life, there are two or more basic cultures involved."[8] For example, the arrival of the Queen in Quebec City will have different meanings for sovereigntists and separatists.

The philosopher enters the fray about multiple meanings associated with events in recognizing the need to coordinate multiple meanings. "Philosophy has always been an attempt to put together the elements of experience and conceptual arrangements so as to form a meaningful whole, or to show why such an enterprise must fail, and even, sometimes, to revel in its failure."[9] We can understand, from Armour's perspective, that unless a means is found to unify the disparate experiences that collectives of people associate with shared events, communication among them will be all but impossible. Armour argues that because philosophy is concerned with getting our experiences and social lives into some meaningful order, along with asserting some claims about what exists, and identifying what changes we have the power to make, culture is closely related to philosophy. It is "through a culture that one gets one's very notions of meaningful order."[10] The existence of different cultures means that our intuitions and beliefs about meaningful orders are not the same.[11] The recognition of reason, as a common tool of operation that facilitates arguments and defences, means that conflicts between meaningful orders can be discussed, and, it is hoped, resolved or reconciled.

Philosophical treatises can be thought of as records of reasoning about differences, that is, as records reflecting efforts to resolve conflicts between meaningful orders. And yet these records can be subject to interpretation and incorporated into different cultures, with very different meaningful orders being promoted as a result. For example, the analytic/continental divide produces very different readings of classic texts.[12] Plato has been regarded as both totalitarian and democrat;[13] Hegel has been read as authoritarian and liberating;[14] Marx has been referenced in remarkably different contexts by sociologists, economists, historians, political scientists, feminist writers, and critical culture theorists, as well as philosophers.[15]

If cultures are differentiated through multiple meanings being associated with the same event, then critical discussions of philosophers' works can be representative of different philosophical cultures. Hegel is the reference point for considering the philosophy of John Watson, thus one must first establish which set of meanings associated with Hegelian texts – which Hegelian culture – to adopt in connecting Watson to Hegel's writings.

Debate about Hegel's Philosophy

The proliferation of analyses of Hegel's writings is indicative of the range of Hegelian interpretive cultures. Thom Brooks, in *Hegel's Political Philosophy: A Systemic Reading of the Philosophy of Right*, identifies two main cultures associated with reading Hegel: the systemic reading of Hegel, and the non-systemic reading.[16] We shall address the difference in these two readings.[17]

The non-systemic reading assumes that particular topics, such as religion, politics, art, and history, that identify different Hegelian works, can be examined independently of their larger context, that is, their place within his whole body of writing.[18] The systemic reading understands Hegel's writings as a unified system, one that is constructed through a developing synthesis of universals and particulars throughout his writings. This systemic reading is the reading that will connect to Watson's philosophy.

The Systemic Reading of Hegel

Brooks identifies the systemic reading as one that recognizes Hegelian metaphysics and logic as necessary to understanding the *Philosophy of Right* (hereafter *PR*).[19] The non-systemic reading evades the methodological system, through which one can interpret Hegel's political philosophy. Brooks writes, "The debate between the non-metaphysical and the metaphysical approaches ... is not a question of whether or not metaphysics can be found, but how much there is to be found ... The non-metaphysical reading is, therefore, not a reading that denies *metaphysics*; but, rather, it is a reading that denies an explanatory role for Hegel's *system.*"[20]

Brooks defends the proposition that Hegel regarded the *PR* as part of his larger system, outlined in the *Encyclopaedia of Philosophical Sciences*. In his Preface to the *PR*, Hegel writes, "This compendium is an enlarged and especially a more systematic exposition of the same fundamental concepts which in relation to this part of philosophy are already contained in a book of mine designed previously for my lectures – *The Encyclopaedia of the Philosophical Sciences*" (Heidelberg, 1817).[21]

Brooks comments that a systemic reading has "fallen out of favour with contemporary philosophers."[22] This chapter will support the position that the systemic reading in particular helps reveal how Watson's metaphysical and political writings can be understood.

A very early account of Hegel's systemic philosophy can be found in *The Origin and Significance of Hegel's Logic*, by James B. Baillie – one of Hegel's early translators.[23] Hegel's thought, we learn, is an ongoing *synthesis* of the universal and the particular. Baillie considers Hegel's philosophy of logic to be a system for grasping reality. The system is developed dialectically over three stages in Hegel's writings. The *PR*, written towards the end of Hegel's body of works, demonstrates that the concept of self evolves through a rational progression of conceptual categories. Freedom is experienced when the self is realized through the highest order of conscious social experience – knowing oneself as a citizen within a state.

The first stage of Hegel's writings, 1797–1800, reveals his initial concerns with the role of ethics and religion in the life of the individual.[24] Gradually, Hegel confronts a contradiction: "The individual does and can exist in the world apart from the universal, and has a supreme value of his own; and yet, on the other hand, the life of the state seems to make real and concrete that of the individual."[25]

This recognition of contradiction as a hurdle to be overcome in understanding any phenomenon of experience will animate the rest of Hegel's writings. Hegel came to see "that the general opposition of individual and universal pervaded every sphere of knowledge and experience."[26] All concepts of reasoning require oppositional ones to make experience meaningful: the synthetic requires the analytic, negation requires affirmation. Contradictory concepts are necessary for understanding existence, and our experience of what exists is made intelligible through their dialectical frameworks. In resolving contradictions, one side of the dichotomy does not disappear; rather, a new conceptualization emerges that resolves the impasse. Hegel began to search for a universal concept from which all particulars could be differentiated. That concept was consciousness, revealed to us through our rational capacities.

The second stage, 1801–7, demonstrates the analysis of the rational concepts that enabled Hegel's recognition of our conscious awareness of contradictions.[27] This stage of his writings culminates in the publication of the *Phenomenology of Mind* in 1807 (hereafter *PHM*). Hegel shifts from the exploration of his two fundamental metaphysical concepts, Mind and Nature, to the procedure whereby those concepts can be discussed – the dialectic of reasoning. Mind and Nature are part of a system and are related, as both concepts are forms within the Absolute, or the totality of all reality. If we consider consciousness as the ground of all experience, then consciousness is always of a particularized being, and yet it can conceive of itself as the universal or home of all conceptions. Hegel writes, "Consciousness, however, *qua* essential reality is the whole of this process of passing out of itself *qua* simple category into individuality and the object, and of viewing this process in the object, cancelling it as distinct, appropriating it as its own, and declaring itself as this certainty of being all reality, of being both itself and its object."[28]

Hegel, in recognizing particularities as components of a system, also recognizes his progression of thinking to be a particular component in the holistic perspective he is working out. The concepts that structure a system can be analysed as the contents of that system. His earliest writings considered logic and metaphysics to be separate concerns.[29] In the second stage, he explains that logic is not only a subject matter of inquiry, logic is also the tool of analysis for itself, as a subject matter. To that extent, logic is both universal and particular. The emergence of logic, as definitive of all existence, begins to be most powerfully expressed towards the end of the *PHM*, in "Absolute Knowledge."[30]

The third stage, 1807–16, covers the years during which Hegel completed the *Science of Logic*, 1812–16 (hereafter *Logic*).[31] Reason is now both the tool of analysis and the object of study. But throughout the development of his system, that is, throughout the dialectical movement of logic towards the revelation of existential truth, Hegel continues to demonstrate the principles of logic as being essential to – the essence of – all other particular subjects. In the *Encyclopaedia of the Philosophical Sciences,* his writings once again address Logic, Nature, and Mind. A further transmutation of the metaphysical into the logical emerges as Hegel seeks the supreme reality, and the formal conditions of our awareness of this reality.

There is nothing beyond logic as the animating force of conscious experience. Logic *is* reality, hence Hegel's famous quote: *What is rational is actual and what is actual is rational.*[32] Even Absolute Spirit can be conceived only through the dialectic of universal and particular.

Throughout the third stage – his dialectical systemization – concepts originally thought of as universals (stage one) are reconceived as particulars, ones in partnership with their shared and unifying universal – logic or reasoning. If experience and change do not become meaningful through their relation to universals, or if things could not be grasped through concepts, no thinking would occur and nothing could be known to have happened.[33]

Hegel's development of ideas, first discussed in his early publications, and then again in the *PHM*, concluded in works about those same ideas: history (e.g., lectures on the philosophy of history, first delivered in 1822, then revised in 1830–1), nature, religion, and art. Included in this output was the *PR*, 1821.[34]

Hegel and the *Philosophy of Right*

In his Preface to the *PR*, Hegel writes,

> It will be obvious from the work itself that the whole, like the formation of its parts, rests on the logical spirit. It is also from this point of view above

> all that I should like my book to be taken and judged ... This book, then, containing as it does the science of the state, is to be nothing other than the endeavour to apprehend and portray the state as something inherently rational. As a work of philosophy, it must be poles apart from an attempt to construct a state as it ought to be. The instruction which it may contain cannot consist in teaching the state what it ought to be: it can only show how the state, the ethical universe, is to be understood.[35]

The *PR* is the exploration of dichotomies in our human experience (viz., the individual and the state, ethical life and law), ones that cannot be understood independently of the dialectical method as the unifying universal.[36]

The struggle of individuals to shape a concept of their individuality is the process whereby ethical life becomes known.[37] This evolution of moral awareness is not achieved by a community forcing external rules and restraining social actions on its members, nor is it achieved by developing an individual set of moral principles independently of the social world.[38] In the *PR*, the particularities of ethical life, and of civil society, are now presented as logically necessary components of the state. Yet their content is understood through grasping the concept of that of organic unity.[39] Hegel explores the idea of the organic in the *PHM*. His systematic approach to working with dualisms is evident when he writes, "Reason in observing organic nature only comes to see itself as universal life in general, it comes to see the development and realization of this life merely by way of systems distinguished quite generally, in the determination of which the essential reality lies not in the organic as such, but in the universal individual (the earth); and among these distinctions of earth (it comes to see that development and realization) in the form of sequences which the genus attempts to establish."[40]

In the *PHM*, Hegel associates the concept of organism with nature, and the particularities of nature that renew themselves. But he also means in his use of organic, organization. In the *PR*, an organic whole exemplifies the state.[41] "This organism is the development of the Idea to its differences and their objective actuality. Hence these different members are the various powers of the state with their functions and spheres of action, by means of which the universal continually engenders itself, and engenders itself in a necessary way because their specific character is fixed by the nature of the concept. Throughout this process the universal maintains its identity, since it is itself the presupposition of its own production. This organism is the constitution of the state."[42]

The concept of organism marks out the state as a particular developing agency, or organization, made determinate by the universal of reason (logic), which must animate the interaction of its particular components. This animation is explained through Hegel's concept of ethical life.

The Individual as Ethical Life, the State as Political Unity

Sittlichkeit, or ethicality, is Hegel's conception of "that form of the moral life which has embodied custom in the institutions and order of an organized state or commonwealth ... the visible and substantial realization of moral activity."[43]

Moral life and ethical life encompass the gradual realization by the individual that free will can be willed freely only where order can enable direction for action. Arbitrary acts, ones focused only on ourselves, will not, in and of themselves, qualify as being reflective of ethical life. When individuals recognize the importance of positive laws, through which maximum freedoms are made possible and can be exercised by everyone, they move from the particular to the universal in their understanding of social relations. In other words, they shift from moral to ethical life. The "most complete consideration of our freedom rests on a view of ourselves in a community with others."[44] The activity of rational minds, as they develop towards being functioning selves within society, determines the particularities of custom and ethical life in their historical context.[45] Each stage of a particular, moving through the dialectic of perpetual actualization, "must develop its content in the character which that content possesses."[46]

The *Sittlichkeit* (i.e., ethical life) referenced in the *PHM* is the *Sittlichkeit* referenced in the *PR*, but the latter (Hegel frequently refers to its consideration as philosophy of law) is now understood as a particular expression of the universal concept of a whole, or a state. Hegel writes, "Moreover, this form of universality – the Understanding, to which particularity has worked its way and developed itself, brings it about at the same time that particularity becomes individuality genuinely existent in its own eyes. And since it is from this particularity that the universal derives the content which fills it as well as its character as infinite self-determination, particularity itself is present in ethical life as infinitely independent free subjectivity."[47] He follows with "Since the state is mind objectified, it is only as one of its members that the individual himself has objectivity, genuine individuality, and an ethical life."[48]

Ethical life is a stage of particular content achieved by the rational grasp of the dialectic of self and other, such as of individual and community. Rationality is made concrete in the state.[49] The state is the concrete universal that grounds the individual in a social setting.

Systems of ethics (and religions) have character in relation to their historical conditions of the dialectic, through which they become actual and expressed. Hegel did not want one idea (either the state or the individual with his or her freedom to make ethical decisions) to be the overriding universal under which all other political concepts would be subsumed. The individual is not an extension or example of the universal, that is, a simple part of a larger whole. If there is any measure of a good state, it will be understood only through the stages of rational development that the state manifests. Rational development can mean the historical movement of the state towards the development of concepts that increase freedom: from families, to ownership of property, to political orders, such as democracy. Rational development can also mean the individual's living in his or her time, experiencing gradual recognition of increasing freedom. Allen Wood, in *Hegel's Ethical Thought,* explains: "The scaffolding of the *Philosophy of Right* is the developing image of the free will or self-knowing and self-concerned human agent, conceiving of itself successively, ever more concretely and adequately, first as a 'person' possessing abstract rights, then as a 'subject' with a moral vocation, then in the concrete spheres of ethical life as a family member, then a burgher, and finally as a citizen."[50]

Our free will seeks external expression through involvement with the world. This involvement develops through a refinement of abstract categories (such as "right") to their actualization in a world of particular determinations, whereby free choice makes sense and is more than arbitrary guessing.[51]

Hegelian logic gives us access to shared formulations of conflicts; we used the same dialectical categories of affirmation, and negation, and have the same capacities to recognize conflict. The role of reason, for those whose consciousness or cultural difference seems inconceivable to some selves and irreconcilable to some communities, is to find paths towards understanding each other, as having identities as reasoning selves, and thus, as having common human experiences.

In a developing country, such as early Canada, helping people realize their shared humanity meant that different meanings associated with shared events needed to be (through Hegelian systematic logic) eventually understood by everyone. Achieving shared understanding was not going to be easy. Reason had to do more than identify dichotomies and propose resolutions to conflicts between determinate particulars. Reason had to imagine possible interpretations of standard concepts, to examine them in detail, and to recognize individual determinations of meanings to be conveyed. John Watson's sensitivity to the task of teaching his students how to help others overcome oppositions finds an obvious source in his mentor, Edward Caird.

Watson's Mentor, Edward Caird (1835–1908)

Scottish Hegelian Edward Caird (1835–1908) followed the systematic interpretation of Hegel's writings. Oppositions could be overcome when one grasped that each was necessary for the meaningfulness of the other. Common conceptual structures could help us develop new ideas for understanding the world.

Yet the ongoing discoveries in science, during the post-Darwinian world, challenged previous systemic orders. When the concept of God served as the source of meaning and truth, science and religion could coexist as extensions of God, in that they could be thought of as being God's creations. During Caird's time, that overriding concept of God was coming under intense scrutiny. Increasingly, science and religion were carving out very distinct, possibly irreconcilable, conceptual worlds. Caird was worried that emerging knowledge claims were beginning to solidify the divide between science and religion.

Hegel's metaphysics sustained both religion and science as part of our experience. Both could be understood as particulars within the universal system of logic. Yet Caird did not see how situating concepts, such as religion and science, within a logical system would assuage the fear and anger of those who had not read Hegel. His Address to the Civic Society of Glasgow in 1897, *Individualism and Socialism* (promptly published by James Maclehose and Sons) maintained it was misleading to divide interpretations of conceptual paradigms, ones used in explaining existence, into sets of competing claims. A culture of power struggles, or warring economic ideologies, or contradictory schemata of conceptual orders left scholars who were thinking about practical social problems having to take sides. Doing so would only produce right/wrong, win/lose debates.[52] Caird's intent was to show that "the then current dichotomy of political and economic theorizing – the individual stands in some confrontational relation to the power of the state – was too simple to account for the multiple dimensions of human experience."[53]

Caird thought that supporting the perspectives of science, such as regarding persons as atoms in the universe, or as material packages with evolutionary tendencies, or as animal beings, struggling to survive in an arena of competing forces, was too simplistic. Portraying the current scientific theories as theories that have defeated previous ones would neglect the complexities of human endeavours. Abandoning one universal concept in favour of another could neglect important particulars associated with human life. "Everyone who has given himself to any kind of scientific investigation knows how difficult it is to grasp the full meaning of a body of facts, to see all of their aspects and to combine them in one view. Scientific men are constantly tempted to theorize on insufficient data, to make things simpler than they are."[54]

Caird thought there was great danger in letting the oppositions of individuals and classes, or individuals and society, "harden into dogmas that make it impossible for us to understand each other."[55] Adversarial modes of conceptualizing events and cultural differences were not going to be productive in creating new orders of meaning.

Hegel in Canada through John Watson (1847–1939)

John Watson (Edward Caird's protégé), Canada's first Gifford Lecturer, 1908, (the only other being Charles Taylor, 2008), arrived at Queen's University in Kingston, Ontario, in 1872. Watson commented on his new setting, "The university had taken seriously Aristotle's definition of a building, four walls and a roof."[56] He published eight books and more than two hundred articles in the major journals of his time. He participated in the much-publicized debate about the nature of God (the Absolute) held at the University of California at Berkeley during 1895/6.[57] He became a close friend and advisor to Queen's principal George Munro Grant. During Grant's reign (1877–1902), Queen's established the *Queen's Quarterly* and distance education courses, and it admitted women to classes. Historian Hilda Neatby cites Watson as being involved in, and vocally supportive of, every initiative Grant took towards making intellectual development possible for all Canadians.[58] Yet Watson's mission of teaching students, headed miles into the wilderness to educate multiple cultures gathered together in one small, cold, building, was a task of enormous complexity. Caird's concerns about oversimplification were in evidence everywhere.

In theory, Hegelian logic, as the systematic evolution of conscious experience, was adaptable when confronting the oppositions embedded in the developing colony of Canada. Hegelian categories such as nature, state, the individual, the community, religion, and ethical life, were applicable in Canada, but they were insufficient to deal with the multiple cultures of Canada. Individuals could be part of several (even warring) communities; they could lose family in one natural disaster; they could abandon cultural inheritances and expectations; they could find themselves isolated from patterns of moral development, trusting their animal support systems more than their human friends. Oppositional categories, such as French and English, immigrant and indigenous, scientific and religious, were insufficient to map out the ongoing conflicts to be overcome or synthesized.[59] This is not to say that those categories were abandoned; it is to say that their limitations were recognized by the early philosophers.

The Hegelian progression of dialectical reasoning, as the explanatory paradigm, would itself have to be reconsidered. But that reconsideration continued to sustain the perspective of idealist thought.

Watson's Metaphysics

Shortly after Caird published his Glasgow speech, Watson published *An Outline of Philosophy*, the first of his inquiries into metaphysics.[60] His political philosophy was formulated at the end of his writing career (similar to Hegel). We need to briefly consider Watson's idealism as it connects to the concept of the individual:

> What Speculative Idealism maintains is that, while the "world" is a "cosmos of experience" and therefore exists for each thinking subject only in experience, it is a "cosmos" just because the thinking subject is capable of grasping the permanent or essential nature of reality. There is no object apart from a subject, and yet it is only as the subject is capable of grasping the universal or necessary constitution of reality that there is for him "a world of things." This implies that, while in each subject there is a process of intelligent activity, through which alone his experience of a world of things originates, he yet is able to comprehend the true nature of the world because there is in him the principle which is involved in the actual nature of reality. The supposition that a world assumed to lie beyond intelligent experience is identical with what it is within intelligent experience is manifestly absurd, since it implies that the whole process in which the "cosmos of experience" is gradually formed through the exercise of intelligence is superfluous.[61]

In the above quote Watson shares with Hegel the idea of reality as a unified cosmos, one that unfolds as we struggle to understand experiences. Watson then situates the individual and her or his experience in relation to the experiences of, not just "the other" as opposition (I am this and not that), but in relation to multiple others, each different, and each with his or her own experience. Each difference of feeling, intuition, thought, and volition enables a particular individual to grasp his or her own individuality more fully with every encounter. "Assume, therefore, that I am absolutely limited to the consciousness of my own feelings and thoughts and volitions, and obviously I should be unaware that others have different feelings, thoughts, and volitions, and therefore unaware of my own peculiar individuality. The consciousness of self is therefore relative to the consciousness of other selves."[62]

The individual encounters multiple perspectives in his or her progress towards being a participant in any community or organization, but he or she never becomes anything other than an increasingly complex individual. (Hegel suggests, through a progression in understanding of a self through family, community, civil society, selves are conceptually transfigured into persons and citizens.)

Watson, while recognizing the process of reasoning and its capacity to differentiate particulars in increasingly detailed analyses, never loses sight of the individual and the perpetually changing communities of other selves. No single conceptual framework will enable me to know myself, nor will a single framework suffice as an explanation for all that exists. For example, should one try to offer a material explanation of all that is, that explanation will not account for self-consciousness.

Watson is not suggesting that the goal of rational thought and experience is to achieve a complete knowledge of the world. The cosmos of experience will always be that of a finite individual. One's finiteness is what one gradually comes to know as one differentiates oneself from others, and from the objects of experience in nature, and in social life. One can know that others are forming their own understandings of objects. Our understandings of the world, that each of us experiences, change as we revise previously held theories. In doing so we gain more knowledge. As one builds an understanding of a community of selves, one also recognizes that change happens. One *gradually* comes to know one's community as the source of oppositions in experience, and also as the source of solutions to those oppositions. Watson extends Hegel's dialectical system by emphasizing the need to incorporate multiple interpretations of events in each progression of understanding one's cosmos of experience. As Armour and Trott explain, "The relatively simple and undifferentiated structure of reality is capable of being represented by a comparatively large range of coherent structures. As it becomes more detailed, more clearly differentiated, more definitely structured, the truth about its earlier stages changes by becoming precise. For only those coherent systems which are capable of explaining its later states then have a claim to 'truth.'"[63]

Through the progression of understanding, from less specific to more specific particulars, we come to realize that being able to determine what is "real" may be a far more complex task than simply being able to identify oppositions. If identifying oppositions is all there is to conscious comprehension, there would be no real measure of having arrived at complete understanding or true knowledge. "Only a common capacity to reason about the differences between selves, and existences as parts of a common reality would unite people despite apparent insurmountable perceptions … Reason didn't just reveal opposition but enabled us to develop knowledge and new concepts in which oppositions could be accommodated."[64]

Watson's progression towards more comprehensive understanding is similar to Hegel's logical progression from abstract being to determinate particulars.[65] Hegel's inclusion of synthesis as a way to resolve oppositions (as if they could be resolved through recognition of a new concept) was for Watson too limiting.

Watson extends the role of reason, beyond the concepts of Hegel's logical system, to include our capacities to be curious, to wonder and speculate, to imagine, and to incorporate memory. Our curiosity about objects, and the attention we pay to them, indicates that we think all new phenomena studied will be intelligible. "Now interest, attention, belief in the intelligibility of the object, all involve the faculty of distinguishing one object from another by an apprehension of the properties of each."[66]

Including curiosity and imagination as essential to reasoning means we can do more than recognize oppositions; we can confront uncertainties and imagine several new contexts for their comprehension. We can include the generation of possibilities as activities of thought. Seeming impasses between customs and beliefs require that we reconceive the conflicts before we can try to resolve them. While some possibilities may become actual with every new problem solved, the process of possibilities becoming actual is endless. Every new interpretation of what is actual creates a new possibility for decision-making and change.

There is no absolute truth as an end goal; there are only endless, self-generated possibilities.

Much of Watson's recognition of the need to imagine possibilities as part of rational inquiry originated as he argued against the theory of evolution as a theory that would eventually explain the whole of the human condition. Watson agrees that the theory of evolution can be understood as a true theory, but he insists that it is one with limitations in its application. It can explain some aspects of our existence, but it can never account for attention, curiosity, speculation, and our use of higher knowledge to free ourselves from first impressions.[67]

Watson, Reason, and Ethics

Reason, as Watson understood it, was not just a tool for winning arguments; its primary function was to facilitate human curiosity by detecting differences, imagining multiple contexts for understanding differences, and then generating possible responses that could be grasped by other intelligent beings.

It would not be rational to develop different systems of understanding that were logically incoherent. For Watson, the principle of contradiction, which had animated much of neo-Hegelian thought, exists only when a concept is inadequate to serve as a determination of the whole. "Contradiction arises only when a limited way of determining Reality is taken as ultimate."[68] Contradiction signals that there may be more than one way of conceiving of an experience. Each way will contribute to our understanding of what exists. "To know ultimate reality, according to Watson, would be to have complete knowledge of all possible conceptions of experience and things."[69] This possibility of absolute knowledge remains as a possibility, for it contains no contradiction, but it is not locked down in some preconceived absolute. For Watson, "the rational order and the order of experience are not separable. An order must be an order of something. It must have a content."[70]

If there were contradictions between concepts of science and religion, then those concepts needed to be reconceived in new contexts. Possible interpretations needed to be furthered and explored. Watson did not believe that we were doomed to disagreement or, even worse, a state of incomprehension. Increasingly, a rich system of possible solutions would enable us to overcome the most obstinate disagreements. This capacity of reason, to reconceive of conflicts in different contexts, can be discerned in Watson's concerns about the quarrel between those who supported different ethical theories.

Watson's arguments against utilitarianism and extreme Kantianism, as discussed in the *SPW,* were based on his commitment to the individual and the community as necessary components of understanding, but ones that never would be subject to dialectical alterations in their essential nature. Utilitarianism would always neglect some contributing individual, and Kantian absolutism seemed unsuited to conceiving of reason as a tool for change, rather than as a tool for adjudicating right and wrong.[71]

When Watson writes, "The State cannot directly promote morality, because morality is a matter of will and motive, and though it can secure outward conformity to the law, it cannot penetrate to the inner self,"[72] he is aware that laws cannot make humans moral. In this respect he reflects Hegel.[73] Nor can laws, in virtue of their existence, guarantee that the individual will regard them as obligatory. Only if laws reflect the will of the community (by establishing conditions whereby the individual is able to be a person in his or her own right) will they contribute to individuals and communities accepting the state a moral agent. "Since man is ever striving after the highest moral good, or realization of his essential nature under special conditions, it is the object of the State to provide for the free development of the individuals under its superintendence."[74]

Watson did have high expectations of individuals, as being able to recognize that their very existence was contingent upon being in social conditions.

One the one hand, Watson tells us, "The personal, as distinguished from the common good, is not a legitimate end of action," and on the other hand, he writes, "The limits to public action are determined by reference to the common good, which cannot be secured by unlimited interference."[75] His position is that the law cannot be everywhere trying to impose and enforce moral rules. But acting as if one has free rein to do anything one wants, as an individual, will inevitably curtail and restrict one's survival in a community. In a country as vast and unpopulated as Canada was, developing ethical life or the custom of being self-disciplined, while recognizing that one's community was one's lifeline, required that the state reflect, not impose, ethical life. Watson's thoughts about ethical theory reveal his resistance to "moral law" solutions for every problem. He did not think there could be one moral theory such as Kant or Mill held. "Communities change as new knowledge develops and new ways of problem solving evolve. New rational orders will evolve through the interchange of ideas. The critical factor is to provide for such interchange in an atmosphere of freedom ... Balancing the rights of the individuals to seek new rational orders in conjunction with the community that supports his or her is the foundation of moral development."[76]

Watson and the Concept of State

Watson's concept of a state is better understood in terms of function, not logical ontology. At best Watson refers to the state as a "central regulative body ... Its function is to provide the external conditions of the free life, not to attempt the impossible feat of making its citizens religious or moral."[77] Political organization is not "absolutely supreme over other forms of organization ... it is the final means by which the other institutions are brought into harmony with one another."[78] This harmony best enables "the totality of citizens to realize all that is in them."[79] There could be no concept of the state that would be the universal that gave meaning to its particular components.

Watson knew that communities change as new ways of problem-solving emerge. Hegel had acknowledged that stages in history have their character, but he thought the prevalence of logical methods would direct change towards increasingly unified political orders. Watson thought no theory would ever provide solutions to every issue, because we cannot anticipate what conditions might exist from which new problems might emerge. New rational orders will evolve through the interchange of ideas. The critical thing is to provide for such interchange in an atmosphere of freedom. "The moral is not what is happening now because we could not have done anything else. The moral is that we must not expect to be able to solve all our social, political, and constitutional problems instantly because we may or may not have developed the regions of experience which would provide the basis for the discovery of the rational order which we require for a solution."[80]

For Watson, freedom and its increasing determinateness is achieved through the recognition that facing and coping with multiple oppositions can contribute to viewing one particular opposition from a different perspective. For example, if one could overcome one's resistance to a neighbour's religious views and recognize him as an individual with multiple characteristics, one might more readily invite him to share his knowledge of barn building. When one can overcome an opposition, a new determinate freedom is experienced. Each step towards freedom is also a step towards making individual decisions. Independent and willing collaborative decision-making is the beginning of the development of social customs, ones that require no enforcement by external law. The idea of an absolute good, or perfect end, or target for social justice and human fulfilment need not be invoked.[81]

Watson, the State, and Its Institutions

Watson distinguishes between government and the state in support of his imperative that neither the individual nor the state should take priority in understanding political order. The concept of the state denotes the exhibited stability, or "harmony," of multiple coordinated particulars, a hierarchy of institutions: family, trade, education, religions, and laws expressing the public perception of the general good.[82] Government is one of those particulars; it is not equivalent to the totality of all associations. Government may have to establish the means to coordinate conflicts between institutions, but that doesn't means it represents them or is in control of them. The freedom to seek new solutions to unforeseen problems, and to develop new orders, requires public spaces within which this freedom may be exercised. Thus Watson suggests that the individual "is not called upon to serve the State," as an unthinking duty-bound part of the state; he or she has only a duty to conform to the general will, or common good.[83] This suggests that all associations are self-determining, until they come into conflict. "The whole history of man is the process by which the discovery [of the general will] is made, and it may be assumed that while the process does not result in absolute comprehension, it is in a well-organized State at least in the line of development towards it."[84]

Throughout the *SPW*, Watson frequently rises to Hegel's defence when Hegel is under criticism from other philosophers Watson is discussing. Watson reminds us that Hegel presented the state as being singularly sustained by the will of the people, not through its use of force.

> It is strange that some who trace all our present evils back to Hegel do not see that one who held the inviolability of the State could not be at the same time an advocate of world-dominion, and that it is not possible that

> the exponent of the free will, which is also the moral will, should be the *fons et origo* of the immoral doctrine that the State has no limits but its own selfish interests.[85]
>
> The glorification of war as the nursery of manly virtues and the contempt for weak States which cannot defend themselves ... is a palpable distortion of the doctrine of Hegel, that the State rests upon Will, not upon Force.[86]

Watson's concerns are with the all-encompassing nature of Hegel's system. Watson described Hegel's state as "the custodian of the moral world," which seemed to allow little room for innovation or individual critique.[87] Hegel promotes common purpose as the phenomenon that shifts us from being merely together, like a herd, towards the next level of rational individuality.[88]

Watson is much less definitive about the process of change in the *SPW* being reflective of a dialectical system.[89] Change is propelled by free rational interaction among individuals and communities, institutions, artistic endeavours, and religious organizations. He qualifies his recognition of the need for institutional freedoms by adding, if the good of all is threatened by any one of these independent associations, the state must have ways to intervene. "Within their own sphere these associations will not be interfered with by an enlightened State, but, on the other hand, they cannot be allowed to threaten its own existence."[90] Conflicts between autonomous institutions, and between individuals and communities will be resolved by expanding possible conceptions of the conflict, not by rearticulating the oppositions through a new concept.

For example, if a school insists on a religious orientation, and yet is the only school for miles around, a non-religious student would have to be accepted on the ground that education is required for freedom of choice to be furthered. Religion, as a frame of reference for developing meanings, can be understood as a choice. Rather than considering belief in God as a mandatory truth, the belief in God can be understood as a choice. Reason must work to find *possible ways* that the proposition – beliefs can be chosen – can be made intelligible for believers. The belief in God is not wrong or contradictory when faced with those who don't believe in God, nor does it require being reconciled with some synthesis. Understanding what a belief is can create possible resolutions to conflict, while enabling a believer to keep his or her belief. Watson developed his theory of rational religion in his Gifford Lectures.[91]

Watson and Hegel on Property and the State

Watson insists that the state is required for freedom, in that it provides the arena for individual decision-making, and for individuating oneself from others.

A comparison of Hegel and Watson on property and the role it plays in their analyses of political orders and freedom will help to demonstrate additional differences between them.

Hegel observes, "When reflection is brought to bear on impulses, they are imagined, estimated, compared with one another,"[92] and the choice about content is the actualization of free will. Taking possession of something as property confirms this freedom to us. One's freedom is made actual in the world. When one negotiates with another, in agreement or disagreement, one engages in mutual recognition with another. This negotiation signals that both wills are now united. Hegel's concept of property is "*an illustration* primarily in order to advance an explanation of how the free will can begin to overcome arbitrariness,"[93] that is, how the will becomes actual in the social world. Hegel introduces property in his section on abstract right, as a way of making the universal right (to exist as a living being) particular. Initially, Hegel is not just talking about the things of life; owning property means possessing an understanding of oneself as a free person, and this understanding is made possible through education and social order.

The Hegelian system propels every individual towards becoming a determinate particular, within a universal concept: "society," or "family," or even as a "law-abiding citizen." These reconceptions of the self as a member of family or citizen can now be thought of as particulars within the universal concept, the state, or the embodiment of reason. An individual's existence becomes more actual (becomes the essence of being a free human being) as he or she reconceives of himself or herself as a participating member of the state. The first step to one's knowing freedom is to possess self-awareness as dialectically related to a community that recognizes each particular self within it.

Possessing a sense of oneself requires that others see one as an independent self; they do not possess each particular self. That recognition by others of being a self unto oneself enables individual selves to move towards understanding themselves as members of civil society. Hegel's discussion of property is now situated in the detailed particulars of an interactive objective world with families and laws.

Hegel will extend the idea of property to the "occupancy" (ownership) of things.[94]

Watson's view of property begins with the abstract idea of personality, or the individual. He writes that property "is essential to the free realisation of the higher life, being the external instrument for the realisation of that life."[95]

Watson favours neither the individual nor the community. There is no resolution (no synthesis) that subsumes every individual in a determinant particular called "family," "society," or "law-abiding citizen." The individual always remains a participant in the state but is not a determinate of, nor determined by, the state. The individual must be able to act, to have the means of self-determination, i.e., to have property, or freedom has no meaning at all. According to Watson, property is essential to understanding ourselves as free, and it incorporates the world of things and the means of life. "It may, however, be said generally that no arrangements which make it virtually impossible for a large section of the community to own property can be defended ... for without property, as Hegel says, a man cannot be a complete man. Hence the State has the right to interfere with anything that prevents a large number of people acquiring property."[96]

Without property we cannot participate in the community; we cannot be persons or even have the means to make free choices. But a way to balance competing interests must be established. An example of Watson's concern with seeking a balance between individual self-determination and the good of the people can be seen when we consider his views about land, as an example of property.

Watson defends the rights of states to exercise some control over land as property. Land is finite capital, that when possessed by one, is also denied to others. Watson supported capitalism as an expression of our competitive nature, but he also realized that land was a finite resource. "Land is unlike capital in this respect, that it cannot be possessed by one person without others being deprived of it, whereas capital benefits both its possessor and those who labour under its superintendence. The system of landed property which has led to a class of landless men requires some readjustment, and the State ought therefore to exercise some control over the rights of property in land."[97]

Hegel regards the concept of property as a way of understanding oneself as one moves through the dialectic of self and other. Regarding oneself as not being owned is a step towards realizing one can experience freedom as a member of a social world. Material property helps to actualize this freedom. Watson regards property as the means whereby we survive. Thinking about being owned is possible only if we can recognize the conditions of ownership. Realizing (making freedom actual) one's freedom must entail being able to recognize those conditions, not just by being able to eat, but being able to access education, and thereby gain an understanding of the principles of ownership.

Hegel, Watson, and Enlightenment

Both Hegel and Watson were disciples of Kant's celebration of enlightenment.[98] Hegel cites Kant in a footnote in the *PHM* and includes sections on enlightenment, superstition, and truth.[99] While any further discussion of Hegelian enlightenment lies beyond the scope of this chapter, Hegel's general view can be summarized as follows: Enlightenment is recognizing belief for what it is, explanation without knowledge. Enlightenment is being able to envision the unity of rational truth and to seek this unity.

Watson also appeals to enlightenment. His enlightened state knows when the interest of particulars (individuals, institutions) will thwart the general will or the common good. But paying attention to these conflicts between individual freedoms and the common good also requires the development of institutions, ones that can reflect a changing public understanding of enlightenment. The dialectic of individual and community, as abstract concepts, becomes actual when individuals participate in economic and political systems; yet persons must be able to continue to know themselves as individuals as well. Any progressions of understanding must take account of the multiple ways individuals create orders within society.

If Watson appeals to an indeterminate idea, such as goodwill or enlightenment, it is because he recognizes the dangers of absolutist theories. There is no political formula or logical methodology, that will explain and resolve all cases of conflict, because they may arise from multiple and disparate meanings associated with new events. When faced with perpetual unforeseen change, no political philosophy can lay out clear directives or provide formulaic principles of order. The need for legislation, and for agencies that can provide conflict resolution, will be publicly expressed, but only if individual freedoms and balanced understandings of the general good are also able to be expressed.

A fierce commitment to education is instrumental to Watson's whole way of thinking, one that resists hierarchical visionaries dictating what is in the interests of the people, but allows for a general will to be operative as a normative framework for sorting out multiple meanings, within cultural conflicts, in a multifaceted state. Education provides understandings that are multidimensional beyond individual interest, individual pleasures, and self-serving moralities. Enlightenment, revealed by an increasingly educated populace, can be realized as a conceptual universal that gives multiple orders of meaning, coherence. A target of peaceful coexistence will require patience while we learn about each other's differences, and also learn what accommodations must be made for that learning to take place.[100] Exposing people to each other's meanings and interpretations of events is a high-risk practice. Some cultures do not want to consider the possibility that different cultural meanings for the same event can be chosen. Yet without that choice, freedom has no meaning. Watson's emphasis on education reflected Hegel's observation that "education is the art of making men ethical."[101] The suggestion that education is an art, not a science, fit well with Watson's support of the imagination and the need for extended contexts of individual development. Art gives new ways of understanding familiar experiences to communities of individuals.

The more we know, the better able we are to imagine, propose, and create ways to help conflicting meanings become compatible. For Watson, political planning required a recognition that sustaining balance and creating harmony will always involve differences, not similarities.[102]

Watson's System

Does Watson have a system, a progression of concepts that culminate in experiential particularity and shared universal coherence? Does he regard consciousness, activated by experience and logic, as the ground of all meaning? Certainly he committed to consciousness as the ground of all claims about reality. Reason does follow patterns, and in Watson's earlier works (which display a pattern of progression similar to Hegel) dialectical reasoning gives credence to the evolution of thought in regards to concepts of God, science, truth and the material world. But Hegelian methodologies restricted the faculties of imagination, speculation, and critical reflection when responding to new problems. The concept of logic, as the definitive boundary of all universals, shut the door on radical innovation.

Watson's system, as we discover it in the *SPW*, is expressed at times with disregard for contradiction. Idealism, Watson writes, considers "the good of the individual is identical with the good of the community."[103] This sounds like a surrender of our individuality, but Watson means the exact opposite. The good of humanity, if enriched by educational enlightenment, is achieved through the slow and careful move towards balance and harmony in social orders, which allows for our ideal individuations to be pursued through both catastrophic and carefully planned changes. Watson supports a political order that will best enable persons to flourish as individuals. This process of individuating oneself from others will be limited by the cultures and customs of one's community. The meanings sustained will mark out the possible responses to events and problems by each social group, community, or political unit (e.g., city, province, nation state). A balanced state, focused on harmony among differences, will provide for locations, in which cultures/communities can (and may be required to) interact and participate in each other's cultural expressions. Doing so will encourage greater differentiations of meanings to be developed and experienced.[104] "A community that does not provide the means for a plurality of particular individuations does not give rise to individuals. If a community produces only conformities, there is little opportunity for development and growth. The intersections and interactions will be stilted by the community's limitations on actions, in mental, spiritual, and physical systems."[105]

Watson's statement against social contract theory clarifies his position.

> A social contract … makes society an arbitrary combination of individual wills. There is nothing to explain why individuals should enter into the contract … A larger amount of happiness doesn't explain why any man should be under obligation to assent … if he thinks he would attain more satisfaction by individual initiative … the theory can only explain the compulsion placed by society upon the individual by saying that the good of the greatest number is more important than the private interest of any individual. But this obviously identifies the State with the power of the majority to have its own conception of the good forcibly realized.[106]

Watson respects the Hegelian methodology of rational negotiations, but he resists the finality of any explanatory system. Only education, which is perpetually renewing itself, will further the evolution of political enlightenment.

The principle of universal consciousness and the logic of reality find powerful expression with Hegel; in the mind of John Watson, they are reliable starting points. The concept of reason, as existential consciousness, needs to be understood as having multiple capabilities that can work together simultaneously in experimental ways. Reason is a capacity for imagining and creating ways of preserving differences, and understood as such, is the metaphysical foundation of an enlightened state.[107]

Peace, order, and good government take on a new poignancy after a reading of John Watson.[108]

Conclusion

Multiple cultures existing in isolation from one another will never coalesce into a nation state. The possibility of reconceiving of oneself as a participant in a multicultural state, and of developing compromises required for cooperation are, for Watson, our best chances for peaceful individualization. Watson's support of imperialism is based on his perception that the empire offered security against the infusion of American culture, which Watson regards as much more uniform than his own.[109] The First World War confirmed for him the terrible dangers of invoking power over individuals, or declaring that, through efforts to snuff out cultural individuations, a single concept of the good will be administered.

The dialectic of individual and community, as abstract concepts, becomes actual when economic systems and laws enable persons to become citizens and to remain individuals. These concepts are, for Watson, progressions of understanding. But these progressions have to accommodate multiple orders in society. Government ensures that multiple individuations are possible. The Hegelian logical system manifests the human mind as a universal feature of existence. Watson agrees. But Watson knows that for there to be communication between disparate cultures, reason must be able to imagine and conceive of multiple orders of meanings beyond the orderly systems of Hegel. Reason is not a tool for winning arguments, but a tool for revealing possible solutions and multiple points of discussion. The Canadian nation state has to constantly readjust to make room for new visions and solutions to human conflicts.[110]

NOTES

I am very grateful for the thorough reading, critical commentary, and editing help from my former Ryerson graduate students Luke Bowman MA and David Collins MFA, MA; my former and current colleagues, James Cunningham, John Leslie, David Ciavatta, Boris Henniq; and my late mentor and friend, Leslie Armour. Thank you as well to Lucan Gregory PhD, LLB/BCL.

1 For a survey of early philosophers in French-speaking Canada, see Yvan Lamonde, *Historiographie de la philosophie au Québec* (Montreal: HMH, 1972); Lamonde, *Le philosophie et son enseignement au Québec, 1667–1920* (Montreal: Hurtubise HMH, 1980). See also Leslie Armour, Elizabeth Trott, "Faith and Reason: The Catholic Philosophers," *The Faces of Reason: an Essay on Philosophy and Culture in English Canada 1850–1950*, 478–506 (Waterloo, ON: Wilfrid Laurier University Press, 1981) (hereafter Armour and Trott, *FR*); Leslie Armour, "Culture, Communities, and the Basis of Diversity," *The Idea of Canada*, 77–91 (Ottawa: Steel Rail, 1981); A.B. McKillop, *A Disciplined Intelligence* (Montreal and Kingston: McGill-Queen's University Press, 1979); A.B. McKillop, *Contours of Canadian Thought* (Toronto: University of Toronto Press, 1987).

2 Armour and Trott, *FR*, is the first major research work on philosophy in English-speaking Canada. A thorough discussion of John Clark Murray can be found in chapter 5 (his political philosophy from 105–26). John Watson's work occupies chapters 7 and 8. Watson's political theory is discussed in chapter 7, 233–48, but it cannot be separated from his ethics and so the whole chapter requires the reader's attention. Watson and Murray have been the subjects of investigation in a compilation of articles published in J.D. Rabb, ed., *Religion and Science in Early Canada* (Kingston ON: Ronald P. Frye, 1988); and carried far afield to a conference in Russia sponsored by the University of Pennsylvania and Volgograd University, Russia, "Representations of Canada," Volgograd University, Centre for American Studies, 2002. The first volume of essays on Canada in an eight-volume series – Alexander I. Kubyshkin and Robert M. Timko, eds., *Representation of Canada: Cross-Cultural Reflections on Canadian Society* (Volgograd: Volgograd University Press, 2002) – includes one on John Clark Murray by Joan Whitman Hoff, "Reconciliations: Philosophy, Religion and Science in John Clark Murray's The Industrial Kingdom of God," 152–62; and highlighting Watson, a chapter by Robert M. Timko, "From Theology's Servant to Reason's Orphan: Philosophy in English Canada's Universities," 142–51. For further reference to Watson, see Elizabeth Trott, "Caird, Watson, and the Reconciliation of Opposites," in *Anglo-American Idealism, 1865–1927*, ed. W.J. Mander (London: Greenwood Press, 2000), 81–92.

3 See above note 1.

4 J.C. Murray (McGill University, 1872–1917) sought to reconcile the individual and the community, science and religion, the industrial property owner and the working man. John Watson (Queen's University, Kingston, 1872–1925), armed with glowing letters from Edward Caird, was no stranger to the dialectical strength of Hegelian theory. For Murray's social and economic views, see J.C. Murray, *The Industrial Kingdom of God* (Ottawa: University of Ottawa Press, 1982). This publication, with introductory notes by Leslie Armour and Elizabeth Trott, originated with a manuscript found in the McGill University Archives.

5 See William Sweet, ed., *The Social, Moral and Political Philosophy of the British Idealists* (Exeter, UK: Imprint Academic, 2009).

6 John Watson, *The Philosophy of Kant Explained* (Glasgow: J. Maclehose and Sons, 1908).

7 John Watson, *The State in Peace and War* (Glasgow: Maclehose & Sons, 1919), (hereafter Watson, *SPW*).

8 Leslie Armour, "Philosophy and Culture," in *Philosophy, Culture and Pluralism*, ed. William Sweet (Aylmer, QC: Éditions du Scribe, 2002), 179. This meaning of culture is also in Armour and Trott, *FR*, 4.

9 Armour, "Philosophy and Culture," 179. For example, those who promote Marxist analysis of politics or economics are intent on showing why freedom should not be a value of market-driven economies, and that capitalism stifles individual endeavours.

10 Amour alerts us to the following example: John Rawls's defence of liberalism arose within the post-McCarthy world of U.S. political muscle-flexing. "But no one can miss the association of John Rawls' political philosophy with American liberal culture." Ibid., 184.

11 Ibid., 188–200.

12 An explanation of the origins and implications of this divide can be found in Simon Critchley, *A Short Introduction to Continental Philosophy* (Oxford: Oxford University Press, 2008).

13 Karl Popper attacks Plato as totalitarian in *The Open Society and its Enemies*, vol. 1 (London: Routledge and Kegan Paul, 1945). Frank Cunningham cites Plato as the beginnings of democratic theory in *Democratic Theory and Socialism* (Cambridge: Cambridge University Press, 1987). The former was writing at the beginning of and throughout the Second World War in Europe; the latter was writing in the 1980s at the University of Toronto.

14 See Michael Hardimon, *Hegel's Social Philosophy* (Cambridge: Cambridge University Press, 1994).

15 Anyone who teaches in the social sciences and the humanities knows that Marx is included in the curriculum of courses in many different social science and arts course offerings.
16 Thom Brooks, *Hegel's Political Philosophy: A Systemic Reading of the Philosophy of Right* (Edinburgh: Edinburgh University Press, 2007).
17 Brooks is aware that simplification can distort. He includes, in his analysis, the possibility of a strong, and a weak systemic reading. Ibid., 27–8.
18 Brooks lists Michael Hardimon, Charles Taylor, and Peter Steinberger among those who support a non-systemic reading, and Stephen Houlgate, Michael Inwood, and Stanley Rosen among those who support a systemic reading. Ibid., 5–6.
19 T.M. Knox, trans., with notes, *Hegel's Philosophy of Right* (Oxford: Clarendon, 1962) (hereafter *Hegel's PR*).
20 Brooks, *Hegel's Political Philosophy*, 3.
21 Knox, *Hegel's PR*, 1.
22 Brooks, *Hegel's Political Philosophy*, 9–10.
23 J.B. Baillie, *The Origin and Significance of Hegel's Logic* (Bristol: Thoemmes Antiquarian Books, 1991), first printed 1901 (hereafter Baillie, *OSHL*).
24 Ibid., 21–56. For an extensive analysis of this period, see H.S. Harris, *Hegel's Development* (Oxford: Oxford University Press, 1972).
25 Baillie, *OSHL*, 15.
26 Ibid., 16.
27 Ibid., 57–98.
28 G.W.F. Hegel, *The Phenomenology of Mind*, trans. with introduction and notes by J.B. Baillie (London: George Allen and Unwin, 1966), 278–9 (hereafter *PHM*).
29 Baillie, *OSHL*, 30–4.
30 Ibid., 159–311.
31 G.W.F. Hegel, *Hegel's Science of Logic*, vols. 1 and 2, trans. W.H. Johnston and L.G. Struthers (London: George Allen and Unwin, 1966).
32 Knox, *Hegel's PR*, Preface, 10. Hegel is not saying that what exists is rational. By "actual," he means the synthesis of essence and existence. The actual is what we conceive the essence of a determinate particular to be.
33 Hegel, *PHM*; see esp. 804–8.
34 "This compendium is an enlarged and especially a more systematic exposition of the same fundamental concepts which in relation to this part of philosophy are already contained in a book of mine designed previously for my lectures – the *Encyclopaedia of Philosophical Sciences* (Heidelberg, 1817)." Knox, *Hegel's PR*, 1.
35 Ibid., 2, 11.

36 Knox writes, "[Hegel] takes for granted in the *Philosophy of Right*, the general conception of philosophy and the general mode of argument expounded in his *Encyclopaedia of the Philosophical Sciences*. The best introduction to the study of any part of his philosophy is probably the smaller *Logic*." Knox, *Hegel's PR*, "Translator's Foreword," vii.

37 The concepts of the individual, social order, and ethical consciousness that underlie the *PR* are introduced in *the PHM* in REASON, B. The Realization of Rational Self-Consciousness Through its Own Activity (374–89), and in SPIRIT BB "The Ethical World" (465–82) and "The Condition of Right or Legal Status" (500–6).

38 Brooks gives a clear explanation of the evolution of individual morality towards the ethical life. *Hegel's Political Philosophy*, 53–5.

39 Baillie describes the relation of the *Logic* to the *PHM*, 209–17: "Logic deals with the absolute truth of the highest mode of mind." Baillie, *OSHL*, 210. In the Introduction to the *PHM*, he writes, "The science of logic is straightway identical with metaphysic." 40. Mind does not have reason; it is reason. See Baillie's defence of the *PHM* as the origin of the *Logic*, *OSHL*, 206–16.

40 Hegel, *PHM*, 326, 327.

41 Knox, *Hegel's PR*, 174.

42 Ibid., 164.

43 Baillie, *OSHL*, 63n3.

44 Brooks, *Hegel's Political Philosophy*, 55.

45 Baillie, *OSHL*, 204, 205.

46 Hegel is not prescribing the components of a preconceived good state, one that is to be the measure of all states, future and past. His endeavour is not normative. States must be understood as portraying the customs and character of their time. "It is just as absurd to fancy that a philosophy can transcend its contemporary world as it is to fancy that an individual can over leap his age, jump over Rhodes. If his theory really goes beyond the world as it is and builds an ideal one as it ought to be, that world exists indeed, but only in his opinions, an unsubstantial element where anything you please may, in fancy, be built." Knox, *Hegel's PR*, 11.

47 Ibid., 126.

48 Ibid., 156.

49 Hegel explains this further in Knox, *Hegel's PR*, 156.

50 Allen W. Wood, *Hegel's Ethical Thought* (Cambridge: Cambridge University Press, 2009), 32. For a clear explanation of Hegel's theory of the self as it becomes a moral self, see David Ciavatta, *Spirit, the Family, and the Unconscious in Hegel's Philosophy* (Albany, NY: SUNY Press, 2009), 2–4 and 28–37.

51 Brooks explains Hegel's system further in *Hegel's Political Philosophy*, 41.
52 Community vs the individual, the individual v the power of the state, the environment of science vs. the social world of man, the progress of reason as a power struggle in nature vs reason as a God-given tool with defined goals – all of these dualisms fed into an atmosphere of fierce debate with few resolutions.
53 Trott, "Caird, Watson, and the Reconciliation of Opposites," 82.
54 Edward Caird, *Individualism and Socialism* (Glasgow: James Maclehose and Sons, 1897), 4.
55 Ibid., 6.
56 Armour and Trott, *FR*, 216.
57 The *New York Tribune* ("the debate of the century") and the *New York Times* ("the great debate") reported on a series of papers given at Berkeley (1895–6). Watson, a late invitee, Josiah Royce, Edward Mezes, Joseph Le Comte, George Holmes Howison, and Francis Ellingwood Abbot (not at the actual debates) defended their different interpretations of God and/or the Absolute. The major newspapers gave their lectures daily coverage. For further information, see John W. Buckham and George M. Stratton, *George Holmes Howison, Philosopher and Teacher* (Berkeley, CA: University of California Press, 1934), who report that, according to Howison, Watson's pluralistic views had won the day. A thorough analysis of the metaphysical issues can be found in Leslie Armour, "The Great Debate: Infinity and the Absolute, Individual and Community, Royce, Watson, Howison, & Abbot," *British Journal for the History of Philosophy* 13, no. 2 (2005): 325–48. Watson's views on God and the Absolute are most thoroughly spelled out in *Christianity and Idealism* (New York: Macmillan, 1896). The meetings of 1895/6 coincided with Watson's book being published. The subsequent publication of the American views came in 1897. Watson's contributions to the debate were based on his book, already in print, before the debate concluded. His original thoughts were not responses to the arguments of the others.
58 Hilda Neatby, *Queen's University*, vol. 1, *1841–1917* (Montreal and Kingston: McGill-Queen's University Press, 1978), 136–8, 163–4, 244.
59 The sorting out of priorities, between Cartesian theory and Thomism, was well under way by the time the English-Canadian philosophers had to confront the skirmishes between Catholics and Protestants. Watson, and before him Murray, realized that trying to establish arguments demonstrating the superiority of any one particular religious doctrine would only alienate various members of rural and urban communities.

At any point in time one might require help from a neighbour, regardless of his or her religious orientation. The philosophers had to develop a civilizing culture where cooperation in social development was recognized as a necessary, and therefore common, value.

60 John Watson, *An Outline of Philosophy*, 4th ed. (Glasgow: Maclehose & Sons, 1908).

61 Ibid., 439.

62 Ibid., 186.

63 Armour and Trott, *FR*, 289.

64 Elizabeth Trott, "Bradley and the Canadian Connection," *Philosophy after F.H. Bradley*, ed. James Bradley (Bristol: Thoemmes, 1996), 71, 72.

65 Watson's idealism would be directed towards accommodating religion and science, accommodating traditional religions, and ultimately inspiring his concept of a rational religion. See Armour and Trott, *FR*, 311–20.

66 Watson, *OP*, 135.

67 Watson spells out his concerns with evolution, as the only "scientific" theory available to explain human nature, in his discussions of Darwin, Paley, and Spencer. Ibid., 107–49.

68 Trott, "Bradley and the Canadian Connection," 65. This quote originates in Watson's lecture notes, 1904–1905, Queen's University Archives, John Watson, 1064 a, box 2.

69 Ibid., 66.

70 Amour and Trott, *FR*, 285.

71 Watson's arguments against Kantian moral theory can be found in *SPW*, 119–25. His attack on utilitarianism is in "Hedonism and Utilitarianism," *Journal of Speculative Philosophy* 10, no. 3 (1876): 271–90. See also Armour and Trott, *FR*, 250–66.

72 Watson, *SPW*, 215.

73 See above note 37.

74 Watson, *SPW*, 215.

75 Ibid.

76 Elizabeth Trott, "John Watson and the Foundation and Applications of Moral Theory," *The Moral, Social and Political Philosophy of the British Idealists*, ed. William Sweet (Exeter: Imprint Academic, 2009), 276.

77 Watson, *SPW*, 197.

78 Ibid., 203.

79 Ibid., 196.

80 Armour and Trott, *FR*, 235.

81 Leslie Armour discussed the role of the good in "Canadian Tradition and the Common Good," *Maritain Studies* 5 (April 1989): 23–40.

82 Watson, *SPW*, 208.
83 Ibid., 210.
84 Ibid.
85 Ibid., 168.
86 Ibid., 193. Watson has made this same point earlier: Hegel "just as decidedly declares that will, not force, is that which binds together the distinct elements" of the state. Watson, *SPW*, 167.
87 Ibid., 168.
88 Hegel, *PHM*, 418. Watson is concerned that Hegel allots to the state "an amount of power over the individual that would be intolerable to an Englishman or an American or a Canadian" (*SPW*, 207), but explains that Hegel is arguing that the trained official is better able to judge what is for the public good than the unenlightened citizen.
89 Watson appeals more to the dialectic of rational progression in his writings on nature (*OP*, 146–9).
90 Watson, *SPW*, 211.
91 Watson, *The Interpretation of Religious Experience: The Gifford Lectures 1910–12* (Glasgow: Maclehose, 1912), 2:125–8.
92 Knox, *Hegel's PR*, 29.
93 Brooks, *Hegel's Political Philosophy*, 35.
94 Knox, *Hegel's PR*, 40, 139–40.
95 Watson, *SPW*, 234–5.
96 Watson's concerns about the development of persons, included women. He cites the need for voting privileges, equality in opportunity, and the right to be educated, and defends his position by arguing they are necessary to the meaningfulness of rights to life and liberty. Watson notes the serious disadvantages children may have who come from "vicious parents." Their only hope for flourishing lies in education. Ibid., 233.
97 Ibid., 234–5.
98 Immanuel Kant, "*What Is Enlightenment?*," 1784.
99 Hegel, *PHM*, 561–98.
100 Watson's discussion can be found in *SPW*, 211–12.
101 Knox, *Hegel's PR*, 260.
102 Renaissance music was about balance and harmony. Today's music has extended those meanings and challenged every traditional demand. The world of music is not determined by rules, reflecting principles of order (such as right or wrong ways of composing), it has become more complex and hugely extended. Balance and harmony have acquired many new meanings in musical cultures.
103 Watson, *SPW*, 213.

104 In short, to survive in Canada at the turn of the twentieth century and any time before that as well, you needed all the help you could get. If you thought you had all the answers and the right method of problem solving and that your job was to go out and convince others of your wisdom, you were not going to make it down the first log road.

105 Trott, "John Watson," 271.

106 Watson, *SPW*, 194–5. Robert Sibley discusses Watson on the social contract, in *Northern Spirits* (Montreal and Kingston: McGill-Queen's University Press, 2009), 81–3; see also Robert Meynell, *Canadian Idealism and the Philosophy of Freedom* (Montreal and Kingston: McGill-Queen's University Press), 223–5.

107 Hilda Neatby writes of the hundreds of young men and women Watson sent out with a profound concern for truth and their responsibility "to make unselfish choices" (Neatby, *Queen's University*, 1:138). Queen's had long offered lectures to the public in Kingston, starting 1858. Watson was offering winter and summer lectures by 1885. By 1892 Queen's was offering extension courses to settlements in the NWT, and by 1894, as far west as Victoria (ibid., 228). Queen's students, once graduated, set out to serve in remote places and, since Watson's classes were a dominant force in the university, his ideas about community and service travelled with them. His students often served as both teacher and preacher, providing services in one desolate building that would house multiple religious cultures on Sunday, and then transform into the classroom for the children of those same families the next day (Trott, "Bradley and the Canadian Connection," 57–72). Watson's students also moved to Ottawa. The Ottawa connection came when in the late 1800s extension courses from Queen's were offered in Ottawa. With the first publication of the Queen's journal, *Queen's Quarterly*, in 1893 (to which Watson contributed regularly), his thoughts became accessible to hundreds more.

108 The Supreme Court of Canada's continued endorsement of the "living tree" metaphor for the Canadian Constitution arguably reflects Canadian enlightenment. It recognizes that the Constitution must be (judicially) interpreted in a flexible and organic fashion, so as to accommodate the multiple, evolving beliefs about justice that emerge from within Canada's ever-changing multicultural landscape. In *Canada (Attorney General) v Hislop*, [2007] 1 S.C.R. 429, 2007 SCC 10, the Court held:

> 94 The approach which our Court has adopted in respect of the crafting of constitutional remedies [page 468] also flows from its understanding of the process of constitutional interpretation, which the "living tree"

metaphor neatly describes. From the time Lord Sankey L.C. used these words to characterize the nature of the Canadian Constitution, courts have relied on this expression to emphasize the ability of the Constitution to develop with our country (*Edwards v. Attorney-General for Canada*, [1930] A.C. 124 (P.C.), at p. 136). This Court has often stated that the Canadian Constitution should not be viewed as a static document but as an instrument capable of adapting with the times by way of a process of evolutionary interpretation, within the natural limits of the text, which "accommodates and addresses the realities of modern life": *Reference re Same-Sex Marriage*, [2004] 3 S.C.R. 698, 2004 SCC 79, at para. 22; see also *Attorney General of Quebec v. Blaikie*, [1979] 2 S.C.R. 1016, at p. 1029; *Re Residential Tenancies Act, 1979*, [1981] 1 S.C.R. 714, at p. 723; *Law Society of Upper Canada v. Skapinker*, [1984] 1 S.C.R. 357, at p. 365; *Hunter v. Southam Inc.*, [1984] 2 S.C.R. 145, at p. 155.

95 It is true that the "living tree" doctrine is not wedded to a particular model of the judicial function. At times, its application may reflect the fact that, in a case, the Court is merely declaring the law of the country as it has stood and that a retroactive remedy is then generally appropriate. In other circumstances, its use recognizes that the law has changed, that the change must be acknowledged and that, from a given point in time, the new law or the new understanding of some legal principle will prevail.

The Supreme Court of Canada has chosen to remain engaged with helping to ensure the good of the Canadian people (including the good as constituted by the Canadian people). Might the idea of the Canadian Constitution as a living tree have been a characterization of enlightenment recognized over time through the spirit of John Watson? Perhaps. Yet its original conception came from Lord Sankey (1866–1948) in England, a British Labour Party supporter, lawyer, and Privy Council judge, in *Edwards*, the "Person's Case" (confirming the acceptance of women as persons, 18 October 1929). See Robert J. Sharpe and Patricia I. McMahon, *The Person's Case: The Origins and Legacy of the Fight for Legal Personhood* (Toronto: University of Toronto Press, 2008). Sankey, a graduate of Oxford, was no doubt familiar with the writings of T.H. Green (Oxford), himself a supporter of Labour, a colleague of Edward Caird, and follower of Hegelian rationalism. The writings of T.H. Green in the late nineteenth century were as dominant in the political philosophy world as those of John Rawls are today. It is inconceivable that anyone could be involved in political or legal theory at Oxford and not have encountered Green's publications. Sankey arrived at Oxford shortly after Green's death (1882). We do know that Watson studied with Caird, wrote with considerable respect about T.H. Green, and promoted the education of women. And we know his students travelled all over the country to help educate Canadians. Most philosophers are ahead of their time. Watson lived to see his visions begin to develop. To that extent Watson was profoundly in anticipation of Canada's future.

109 For Sibley's discussion of empire, which supports this claim, see *Northern Spirits*, 43–5. Meynell also confirms Watson's support for empire, in *Canadian Idealism and the Philosophy of Freedom*, 225. See above note 106.

110 It is reasonable to observe that the migration of Watson's students to the civil service in Ottawa, as well as to the isolated churches in the Prairies and the Maritimes was a big part of the development of Canadian customs (*Sitte*). Queen's University staffed the civil service, and almost every student from Queen's who headed to Ottawa soon after Confederation would have been at some point in Watson's classes. Queen's Humanities building is named after John Watson, though I doubt that many Queen's students, today, know who he was. Certainly change, as Watson anticipated, is part out our evolving society, but recognizing and evaluating change needs benchmarks.

10 Idealism and Empire: John Watson, Michael Ignatieff, and the Moral Warrant for "Liberal Imperialism"

ROBERT C. SIBLEY

Towards the end of the nineteenth-century, Prussian leader Otto von Bismarck remarked that the most important thing to know about the twentieth century was that Americans spoke English. His point was obvious: an alliance between the British Empire and the United States, the world's largest English-speaking polities, would create the most powerful political entity on the planet. Others made similar observations at the time – Rudyard Kipling, Winston Churchill, and Theodore Roosevelt, to mention a few.

Perhaps surprisingly, late nineteenth-century Canadians thought in these terms, too. Men such as George Monro Grant, George Robert Parkin, and, later, Stephen Leacock, Andrew Macphail, and James Cappon; they all spoke in one fashion or another of a grand alliance of the English-speaking people. For example, Parkin, the headmaster of Upper Canada College and an evangelist of empire, envisioned a new world order in which Britons (which, of course, included Canadians) and Americans worked together to become "the greatest secular instrument for good in the world."[1] At the time, the promotion of such a view of empire ensured that "the imperial idea became at once a popular enthusiasm and a reasoned political and ethical philosophy."[2]

The postcolonial era has largely discredited this notion of empire.[3] Even so, we should remember that these turn-of-the-twentieth-century Canadians had high hopes for Canada's future greatness, and their imperial dreams reflected the belief that Canada detached from the British Empire would become a "Little Canada," a political entity unable to satisfy the highest ideals and aspirations of its citizens. Only as an equal partner in the Empire, sharing in the benefits and responsibilities of imperial citizenship, would Canadians overcome their colonial mentality and achieve their potential greatness.[4] Leacock voiced this idealist view of empire on the eve of the 1907 Imperial Conference when he urged delegates to "find for us something other than mere colonial stagnation, something other than independence, nobler than annexation, greater in purpose than a Little Canada ... We must become something greater or something infinitely less."[5] For the imperialists like Leacock, the issue of Canada being part of an empire or succumbing to a lesser political destiny was "the greatest political question of the hour."[6]

The Canadian imperialists were sustained in their enthusiasm for empire by the then dominant philosophy of Idealism.[7] The philosopher most responsible for this was John Watson,[8] who taught at Queen's University for some fifty years and was a leading exponent of Idealism in the Anglo-Saxon world.[9] Watson's thought, as Brian McKillop observes, gave "the argument for an increased imperial connection much philosophical substance."[10]

Does a long-dead Idealist philosopher have anything to say to us when the geopolitical questions of the hour are Islamist terrorism and, as it sometimes seems, the breakdown of an international order amenable to the interests and inclinations of the liberal democratic West? Perhaps this: While the concept of empire was much maligned during the decades of decolonization in the mid-twentieth century, it has returned in the early twenty-first century as a subject of serious political discourse.[11] Whether regarded as an attempt to justify American global power or supported as a necessary response to terrorism and geopolitical disorder, while the old territorial-style "imperialism is over," a "new imperial form of sovereignty" is reshaping the geopolitical order, to borrow the phrases of Michael Hardt and Antonio Negri.[12] This "imperial turn"[13] is rather extraordinary, considering that the idea of empire was largely denounced in the postwar era as war-weakened European powers abandoned their colonial heritage. Yet, considering the ongoing "war on terror" in which the CIA projects American power with drone strikes on the Pakistani frontier or in the tribal areas of Yemen, or the way Western nations occasionally deploy battleships and warplanes to effect regime change in the Arab world under the guise of protecting civilians – the NATO intervention that helped bring down Muammar Gaddafi's dictatorship, for instance – it is hard to deny that the imperialist impulse, however euphemistically labelled, is enjoying something of a resurgence, and, perhaps, justifiably so. Indeed, several respectable intellectuals have promoted policies and practices that are de facto forms of imperialism as necessary and legitimate responses to world disorder.

Michael Ignatieff, the former leader of the Liberal Party of Canada, appeared very much like a nineteenth-century imperialist when he advocated the deployment of NATO jets as part of the United Nations mandate to protect Libyan civilians during the Arab Spring revolt against Muammar Gaddafi's dictatorship. Referring to his previous membership in an international commission that promoted the idea of "responsibility to protect," he said, "That is not a doctrine about armed military intervention and boots on the ground. That's a doctrine that says if Canada can stop a dictator massacring civilians, Canada should step up."[14] Similarly, Ignatieff sounded very much like those old-style imperialists who argued that empire could bring order out of disorder. "We need to be part of an international community action that isolates this regime, says Paul Martin to Gaddafi: 'Turn back before you precipitate civil war, understand that the international community will not tolerate this behaviour.'"[15] Ignatieff adopted a similar posture a decade earlier when he supported the United States' invasion of Iraq. "America's entire war on terror is an exercise in imperialism," he said, but then argued that imperialism undertaken for the right purpose cannot be wrong. "How can it be imperialist to help people throw off the shackles of tyranny? No one in his right mind can want liberty to fail."[16]

Ignatieff is not alone in arguing the necessity of liberal-style imperialism. Political economist Deepak Lal argues, "Empires have unfairly gotten a bad name,"[17] and he calls for the "beneficent exercise of power" to bring peace and order to the disordered regions of the world.[18] "There has never been a time in which the world seemed more in need of empire," says British theorist Robert Cooper. "The spread of democracy and of the liberal state has … become a foreign policy imperative" for the West.[19]

I shall expand on these arguments later, but the essential point to recognize is how closely contemporary euphemisms for imperialist practice – cooperative imperialism, defensive imperialism, and even liberal humanitarianism, for example – align with Watson's philosophic justification for empire, both in terms of description and prescription. That is to say, contemporary arguments for "liberal imperialism," "humanitarian intervention," and "responsibility to protect" strongly resemble Watson's Idealist hopes for the British Empire.

Watson's Moral Empire

Watson's most explicit linkage of imperialism and Idealism was made in the one book he devoted to political philosophy, *The State in Peace and War*, published in 1919. To understand his Idealist approach to imperialism, it is necessary to briefly consider his political philosophy as a whole as it pertains to his qualified endorsement of imperialism. For Watson, the essential task of politics is to reconcile the aspirations of the individual with the requirements of the larger community, of uniting public authority with individual freedom. He extended this notion to the international level, arguing that the British Empire was "the only thoroughly successful experiment in international government that the world has ever seen," in that it largely succeeded in "combining the freedom of the separate organs with the unity of the whole."[20]

For Watson, a legitimate state is not one that possesses absolute sovereignty or power over other institutions. Rather, the state is the net that holds all these entities together. And it holds them together not because of any intrinsic superiority, but because it is the most practical means by which these organizations can be harmonized so as not to interfere with one another and breed conflict. In other words, the state is not an arrangement for controlling individuals, nor does it have as its chief function that of keeping individuals from interfering with the "freedom" or rights of others. Rather, the state is the highest expression of human freedom as manifested through the objective institutions that make up the state – family, property, civil society, the courts, the government, and the constitution – and ideally it operates by the free assent of the individuals to those institutions. The Idealist state promotes individual autonomy while safeguarding the wish of individuals to belong to a community. Any state that fails to live up to this purpose loses legitimacy.[21]

Watson's theory of the state extends to the international arena in what might be called his theory of relative imperialism. Just as the state must not hamper the individuation of its citizens, so, too, must the imperial power make no attempt to eliminate cultural differences within or among states. Individual states are differentiations of the organic unity of humankind as a whole. The purpose of any system of states must be to enhance the independence and individuality of its members. The independence of each state is necessary for the good of humanity as a whole, since "each nation has its own special task, arising from differences in climate, economic, religious, artistic and scientific relations."[22]

In short, Watson's theory of relative imperialism asserts: Act imperially; think locally.

Watson believes that, regardless of its flaws and failings, the British Empire was a decent model for this reconciliation of the local and the imperial. While he supports the autonomy of nation states and cultures, he nevertheless argues for the legitimacy of imperialism on the grounds that a civilization with a more developed rational consciousness can exercise political authority over a less developed population – if that authority is wielded for the good of that state's citizens. On this basis, Watson judges the British Empire a "remarkable success" in that it was able to "combine the freedom of the separate organs with the unity of the whole."[23] Within the empire there existed the freedom for the self-development of each member state and, at the same time, a sense of belonging to a community of common sentiment and common ideals.

Watson's Idealism did not blind him to the abuses of imperialism. He was well aware that empires are often inaugurated in exploitation and violence, including the British Empire. "The first contact of the civilised trader with the savage races has often led to the most deplorable results; the natives have been robbed, corrupted by opium, murdered in cold blood and sold as slaves."[24] But following the imperatives of Hegelian synthesis and its notions of *Aufheben*, he also insisted that out of this conquest, and implicit in it, came the further development of freedom, and hence the development of a higher moral and social order. Bluntly stated, the development of consciousness has meant the use of violence, the conquest of some by other others, the forced submission of "savages" to a "superior force."[25]

No doubt, some will regard this as an illegitimate ends-justify-the-means warrant for imperialism. This would be to misread Watson's argument. Watson, like other Idealists of his time, was appalled at Britain's conduct in the Boer War. But even in denouncing the abuses of empire, he insisted, "there was a right kind of imperialism which entailed a responsible and sustained effort to prepare indigenous peoples for self-government."[26] Watson then is not promoting empire for the sake of conquest or material gain, although he does not deny that this is how many see it. Imperial rule is legitimate only if it is consciously directed towards preparing a subject people for the rational comprehension and practise of their inherent freedom. The imperial power must not expect or want to maintain permanent authority over its colonial subjects. If a civilized nation fails to live up to this principle, "its rule can only be regarded as an unjustifiable tyranny."[27] Or, as Watson put it in his penultimate statement on empire, "There is no justification for the rule of a foreign government which does not seek to promote civilisation, liberty and progress in the subject people, and does not take the necessary steps to fit them for self-government."[28]

Such a position clearly anticipates the arguments of contemporary liberal humanitarianism. Indeed, setting aside semantical differences, it is hard to see how Watson's prescription for moral imperialism differs from the arguments of those who insist Western powers intervene in failing states such as Bosnia, Liberia, East Timor, Sudan, Mozambique, the Congo, Afghanistan, Iraq or, more recently, Libya and Syria. Watson, however, is arguably more prudent than many humanitarian interventionists who seek to impose Western notions of liberal democracy on failing states. He qualifies his support for imperialism by arguing that even if one nation possesses all the highest qualities of civilization – "a preposterous supposition," as he says – it would still not have the right to impose its culture on other nations by unjustified force.[29] Thus, Watson is careful to impose moral boundaries on imperial rule:

> The rule of a foreign and subject people is a difficult and delicate task. The better elements in the older civilisation must be recognised and fostered. To destroy a people's faith in their traditional customs and laws can only lead to the overthrow of all moral rules and the introduction of moral anarchy. A whole foreign civilisation cannot be externally imposed upon a people. The foreign government must act so as to create a feeling of loyalty to itself in the minds of the subjects, while these must learn to look to it for security of person and property, for freedom of thought and speech, and for the defence of their special form of worship.[30]

Watson's Idealism thus promotes a positive notion of imperialism in which "empire" is less an economic and military enterprise and more an agent for furthering peoples' moral development.[31] Does such an Idealist conception of empire have any relevance in our postcolonial – and post-Idealist – era? His language of empire may not be that employed today, but his ideas are echoed by contemporary neo-imperialists who argue not only for the need to defend the values and traditions of Western liberal democracy, but also that the Western democracies have a responsibility to protect and a duty to defend human rights.

"Humanitarian Empire"

Such an argument is put forward by a variety of contemporary neo-imperialists. Deepak Lal, for example, argues that with large regions of the world in disorder, a return to empire offers the most practicable means for restoring order. For all their failings, "the major argument in favour of empires is that, through their *pax*, they provide the most basic of public goods – order – in an anarchical international society of states."[32] He also espouses a Watson-like notion of "relative imperialism," arguing that "the most urgent task in the new imperium is to bring the world of Islam into the modern world, without seeking to alter its soul."[33] While he is sceptical of Watsonian notions of "ethical imperialism," he nonetheless holds that through "the beneficent exercise of power" Western nations can see their democratic values emulated elsewhere in the world. Certainly, parts of the planet will continue to fear and loathe the West, but, as Lal observes, one of the essential tasks of imperial statesmanship is to prevent this inevitable and unavoidable hatred from creating global disorder. "Wishing the empire would just go away or could be managed by global love and compassion is to bury one's head in the sand and promote global disorder."[34]

Political theorist Robert Cooper likewise makes an act-imperially, think-locally argument for "defensive imperialism." The existence of what he calls pre-modern zones of chaos is too dangerous for established states to tolerate. Western countries might, under extreme circumstances, need to take charge of these countries and provide good government, administrative competence, and institutional order until the locals can do it themselves. Cooper describes this as the "imperialism of neighbours," a system in which "the strong protect the weak, in which the efficient and well-governed export stability and liberty." He admits that empire has often not operated this way, but it has generally been "better than the chaos and barbarism it replaced."[35]

Historian Robert Conquest shares Cooper's concerns about the increasingly fragmented and fractious post–Cold War world. He urges the establishment of an "association" of English-speaking nations and peoples, including the United States, Britain, Canada, India, Ireland, Australia, and New Zealand, as well as the peoples of the Caribbean and the Pacific Ocean. The "closer integration of the English-speaking countries can create a centre of power attractive to the other countries with a democratic tradition and form the basis for a yet broader political unity in the long run. And this in turn could eventually be the foundation for a full unity of the democratized world."[36] In an argument that closely resembles the arguments of Canada's nineteenth-century imperialists in favour of Canada being part of a "Greater Britain," Conquest points out that countries such as Canada, Australia, and now Britain lack the power to act autonomously with any but local effect. Yet their interests, like those of the United States, are deeply involved in the world scene, and in acting together they can influence events and effect geopolitical changes far beyond their own areas, changes that would help the whole world community. Arguably, Canada's military presence in Afghanistan and its contribution to NATO's activities in Libya reflected this imperial outreach.

Conquest even suggests that Canada's membership in such an association would mitigate separatist aspirations in Quebec, as well as offset secessionist inclinations in Western Canada: "On an Association basis, the former trend might be muted and the latter largely satisfied." And if Quebec ever did secede, English-speaking Canadians would have even more reason to look positively on such an association.[37]

While these various neo-imperialist ideas might lack the theoretical substance of Watson's Idealist philosophy, they nonetheless echo his moral imperative that an empire must exist for a good beyond its own self-interest. Interestingly, this is Ignatieff's argument, too. Ignatieff might eschew the idea of an English-speaking association – or Anglosphere, as it has been called – but he nonetheless favours a closer alliance within the West as a response to Islamist terrorism and other forms of disorder. "In the old imperialism, the empire had a single capital ... In the new humanitarian empire, power is exercised as a condominium, with Washington in the lead, and London, Paris, Berlin and Tokyo following reluctantly behind."[38] Ignatieff may be critical of Western involvement in less developed, non-liberal regions of the world, but his prescription for those regions is, as David Long argues, "a more systematic and substantial embrace of empire."[39]

This ascription to imperialism highlights the quandary facing the liberal mind in an illiberal world. Ignatieff is perhaps the present-day "imperialist" who most closely resembles Watson, both in terms of substance and form. In the same way that Watson regarded membership in the British Empire as a vehicle for moral development and, thus, an escape from a "Little Canada" mindset, Ignatieff criticizes Canadians who indulge in the "naïve narcissism"[40] of believing that Canada can immunize itself against Islamist terrorism and other forms of disorder.[41] The failure of so many states in the post–Cold War era has reached such proportions that it has created "an ongoing crisis of order in a globalised world."[42] The only coherent response to this disorder, Ignatieff says, is the application of imperial power to help these states get back on their feet. And since power ultimately requires military capacity, the United States is the singular power in the world for any nation-restoring enterprise and, thus, must accept the burdens of empire. But Canada must carry its share of the imperial burden, too. Canadians cannot claim to believe in multilateralism and international institutions as the way to maintain order in the world if they are not prepared to defend those beliefs and those institutions, by force if necessary.[43]

Ignatieff sounds distinctly Watsonian (and Hegelian) in arguing that the key to order and good governance, as well as the protection of human rights, is stable institutions. And institutional order, domestic or international, ultimately depends, like it or not, on the threat of coercive force by governments acting to represent and maintain the integrity of the state. Soft-power appeals to tolerance and diversity, or notions that Canada can influence the world as a "model citizen,"[44] are dangerously insufficient when faced with opponents who do not subscribe to such values and, indeed, reject the principles and assumptions underlying those values. As Ignatieff states,

> If chaos rather than tyranny is the chief cause of human rights abuse, then activists will have to rethink their traditional suspicion of the state and of the exercise of sovereignty ... As long as populations are menaced by banditry, civil war, guerrilla campaigns, and counter-insurgency by beleaguered governments, they cannot be secure. In such conditions, international human rights and humanitarian organizations can do no more than bind up the wounded and protect the most vulnerable. These Hobbesian situations teach the message of the Leviathan itself: that consolidated state power is the very condition for any regime of rights whatever. In this sense, state sovereignty, instead of being the enemy of human rights, has to be seen as their basic precondition.[45]

In other words, when order is threatened by disorder, when dissent descends into civil war, there is "a case for temporary imperial rule, to provide the force and will necessary to bring order out of chaos."[46] In this fashion, Ignatieff reveals "the imperial character of humanitarian intervention."[47]

Ignatieff also clearly resembles Watson in asserting a moral dimension to contemporary liberal imperialism. Just as Watson argued that imperialism could be justified so long as its intention is not to rule others for self-serving purposes, so, too, does Ignatieff maintain that the exercise of imperial power is not discreditable, "provided that empire does more than reproduce itself, provided that it does eventuate in self-rule for nations and peoples."[48] Ignatieff understands that the primary purpose of contemporary imperialism is to bring order to the "barbarian zones" because it is only out of order that human rights, the rule law, and other institutions of democracy emerge. "Armed intervention can only be justified in two instances: First, when human rights abuses rise to the level of a systematic attempt to expel or exterminate large numbers of people who have no means of defending themselves; second, when these abuses threaten the peace and security of neighboring states."[49] Such a sentiment is little different in substance from Watson's claim that the British Empire's "special mission" was to bring order and civility to the "savages."

Recall, too, another of Watson's claims about moral imperialism: "The only justification for the rule of a superior over an inferior people is that the former should regard as its special task the elevation of the latter to its own level."[50] This is not substantially any different from Ignatieff's promotion of nation-building "as an exercise in solidarity between rich and poor, the possessors and the dispossessed."[51] Ignatieff may deploy politically correct language, couching his neo-imperialism with phrases like "humanitarian intervention" and "responsibility to protect," but his arguments are much the same as Watson's: "Bringing order is the paradigmatic imperial task, but it is essential, both for reasons of economy and for reasons of principle, to do so without denying local people their rights to some degree of self-determination."[52] In this regard, it is not out of line to see Ignatieff's "empire lite" as a contemporary version of Watson's relative imperialism.

Admittedly, given the historical abuses of imperial power, the rejection of colonialism after the Second World War, and the post-war ascendancy of notions of national self-determination, words like *empire* and *imperialism* still possess near-demonic connotations for many. That history, no doubt, goes a long way to explaining why the neo-imperialists prefer kinder and gentler phraseology. Be that as it may, as sociologist Lewis Feuer points out, there is also no denying that in many cases Western imperialists brought improvements in social, economic, and political conditions to those they ruled – everything from better education and health to an end to slavery and tribal warfare.[53] Such claims can be – and often were – self-serving, a way to hide "imperialist" exploitation behind a mask of self-righteous morality. It is also highly questionable whether the ostensible promotion or protection of a peoples' well-being by some imperial power supersedes the right to self-determination. It can – and should – be asked whether notions of nation-building or spreading democracy warrant the imposition of imperial power.

The only intelligible answer to such questions is, I suggest, that it depends on the situation. As Hegel might observe, there can be no genuine freedom when you are starving or dying of AIDs, or your community is under attack from its neighbours. Nor does a minority's abstract "right" to self-determination do a lot of good when it is too weak to defend against the concrete actions of a hostile regime. Imperial power – call it humanitarian intervention, if it makes you feel better about yourself – might well be necessary to enforce those rights and guarantee those freedoms. Of course, there are some who seem to think that asserting abstract ideals constitutes the existential achievement of those ideals. But it is utterly naive, and dangerous, to think such principles can be actualized in any substantive fashion without the active institutional presence of a strong, stable, and when necessary, aggressive political order at hand.

In this regard, it is time to consider a more balanced view of empire. Feuer, for example, distinguishes between regressive and progressive imperialism.[54] The former, he argues, is devoted to pillaging colonies, while the latter seeks, at least to some extent, to improve social and economic conditions. Feuer offers Mongolian, Spanish, and Soviet imperialism as examples of regressive imperialism. The Alexandrian, Roman, French, Dutch, and British Empires were more progressive forms of imperialism in that, for all their errors and arrogance, their rule was generally beneficial in the long run. Bad as it could be, imperialism in modern times also brought improvements in social conditions and economic wealth to many regions of Asia and Africa. As well, Britain's outlawing of slavery throughout the empire largely put an end to the slave trade, except in the Arab world.[55] Thus, Feuer concludes, "Imperialism brought with it a tremendous rise in the populations of Africa and Asia. From West Africa to Java it put an end to the tribal wars that, periodically decimating populations, made genocide a recurring phenomenon. The death toll of epidemics was reduced by health measures. Although most of the colonial areas remained backward in technology, and prefeudal, feudal or absolutist in their social systems, they received at the hands of the imperialist power a set of medical and political services that were the high achievements of the Western capitalist nations."[56]

Feuer's argument on behalf of imperialism would likely receive Watson's endorsement, and maybe even a nod from Ignatieff and others. Former British prime minister Tony Blair has also said something similar in speeches and articles that resurrect, unconsciously or otherwise, the ideals of nineteenth-century imperialism. Speaking to the British Labour party in the fall of 2001, Blair defended Britain's participation in the fight against Islamist terrorism in distinctly Idealist terms: "The starving, the wretched, the dispossessed, the ignorant, those living in want and squalor from the deserts of North Africa to the slums of Gaza to the mountain ranges of Afghanistan: they too are our cause."[57] Elsewhere, Blair advocated "progressive pre-emption" in an era where "globalization begets interdependence. Interdependence begets the necessity of a common value system to make it work."[58]

Ignatieff says much the same thing when he argues, "Nation-building is the kind of imperialism you get in a human rights era."[59] Thus, if Ignatieff, Lal, Cooper, Conquest, and Blair, among others[60] are right to claim ours is a new age of imperialism – *relative imperialism* is as good a term as any – then Watson's moral prescription for empire offers guidance even in our post-Idealist age. His Idealist conception of empire – the imperial power must act in such a way as to preserve diverse cultures and encourage responsible government – certainly fulfils the requirements of liberal humanitarian interventionists, as well as that of multiculturalists who require the recognition and preservation of diverse cultures. Nor does Watson's idea of empire preclude the desires of liberals to spread the benefits of democracy. Indeed, as far as Ignatieff is concerned, "imperialism has become the precondition for democracy."[61] Equally important, though, Watson is realistic in recognizing the legitimacy of defensive imperialism. All of which leads to the conclusion that this nineteenth-century Idealist philosopher has much to say to Canadians regarding their future in the new imperial order taking shape in the twenty-first century.

NOTES

1 Carl Berger, *The Sense of Power: Studies in the Ideas of Canadian Imperialism 1867–1914* (Toronto: University of Toronto Press, 1970), 217.

2 Donald Creighton, *Canada's First Century* (Toronto: St Martin's, 1970), 91–2.

3 Not everyone accepts this view, though. Lord Max Beloff has argued that on the whole the British Empire had been a force for good in the

world. "There's no question in my mind that Britain, through its colonial administration, brought quite a lot of benefit to people around the world. There is little doubt that the positive outweighed the negative." Quoted in "Three Cheers for the Empire," *Ottawa Citizen*, 29 June 1997.

4 Berger, *Sense of Power*, 120. He writes, "All the imperialists identified imperialism with an extension of Canadian freedom and her rise to nationhood."

5 Stephen Leacock, "Greater Canada: An Appeal," *University Magazine* 6, no. 1 (April 1907): 132–41.

6 George Robert Parkin, "Imperial Federation," *University Magazine* 1, no. 1 (April 1902): 193.

7 A.B. McKillop, *A Disciplined Intelligence: Critical Inquiry and Canadian Thought in the Victorian Era* (Montreal and Kingston: McGill-Queen's University Press, 1979), 195–6. See also Terry Cook, "George R. Parkin and the Concept of Britannic Idealism," *Journal of Canadian Studies* 10, no. 3 (1975): 15–31; Robert J.D. Page, "Canada and the Imperial Idea in the Boer War Years," *Journal of Canadian Studies* 5, no. 1 (1970): 33–49; D.L. Cole, "Canada's 'Nationalistic' Imperialists," *Journal of Canadian Studies* 5, no. 3 (1970): 44–9; Allan Smith, "Conservatism, Nationalism and Imperialism: The Thought of George Monro Grant," *Canadian Literature* 83 (Winter 1979): 90–116.

8 A.B. McKillop, "The Idealist Legacy," in *Contours of Canadian Thought* (Toronto: University of Toronto Press, 1987), 96–110.

9 John Irving, "Philosophical Literature to 1910," in *Literary History of Canada*, ed. Carl F. Klinck, vol. 1, *Canadian Literature in English* (Toronto: University of Toronto Press, 1976), 454. Irving writes, "One of the great teachers of philosophy in Canada during the last hundred years, Watson was the first philosopher in this country to achieve an international reputation through his writings. British and American historians of philosophy always list him as one of the leading representatives of the Idealistic movement in the Anglo-Saxon world."

10 McKillop, *Disciplined Intelligence*, 196.

11 A few examples should suffice to make the point. Niall Ferguson, *Colossus: The Price of America's Empire* (New York: Penguin, 2004); Andrew J. Bacevich, *The Imperial Tense: Prospects and Problems of American Empire* (Chicago: Ivan R. Dee, 2003); Max Boot, "The Case for American Empire," *Weekly Standard*, 15 October 2001; and Boot, *Savage Wars of Peace: Small Wars and the Rise of American Power* (New York: Basic Books, 2002); Sebastian Mallaby, "The Reluctant Imperialist: Terrorism, Failed States, and the Case for an American Empire," *Foreign Affairs* 81, no. 2 (March–April 2002): 2–7;

Ramesh Ponnuru, "The Empire of Freedom," *National Review*, 24 March 2003. Even before the 11 September 2001 attacks there was some discussion of neo-imperialism. See Thomas E. Ricks, "Empire or Not? A Quiet Debate of U.S. Role," *Washington Post*, 21 August 2001; Ernest W. Lefever, *America's Imperial Burden: Is the Past Prologue?* (Boulder, CO: Westview, 1999); and David Rieff, "A New Age of Liberal Imperialism?," *World Policy Journal* 14, no. 2 (Summer 1999): 1–10.

12 Michael Hardt and Antonio Negri, *Empire* (New Haven, CT: Harvard University Press, 2001), xiii–xiv.

13 Michael Cox, "Empire, imperialism and the Bush doctrine," *Review of International Studies* 30 (2004): 589.

14 Steven Chase and Jane Taber, "Canada Won't Put Boots on the Ground in Libya, Harper Says," globeandmail.com, 31 March 2011, http://www.theglobeandmail.com/news/politics/ottawa-notebook/canada-wont-put-boots-on-the-ground-in-libya-harper-says/article1965371/.

15 Stephanie Levitz, "Send in the Troops: UN Must Intervene in Libya, Says Ex-PM Paul Martin," Canadian Press, 23 February 2011, http://www.ipolitics.ca/2011/02/23/united-nations-must-intervene-in-libya-says-paul-martin/.

16 Michael Ignatieff, "Nation-Building Lite," *New York Times Magazine*, 28 July 2002, http://www.nytimes.com/2002/07/28/magazine/nation-building-lite.html.

17 Deepak Lal, *In Defense of Empires* (Washington, DC: AEI, 2004), 37.

18 Ibid., 2.

19 Robert Cooper, *The Breaking of Nations: Order and Chaos in the Twenty-First Century* (Toronto: McClelland and Stewart, 2005), 176–7.

20 John Watson, *The State in Peace and War* (Glasgow: J. Maclehose Sons, 1919), 271–4.

21 Ibid., 200–3, 208, 224.

22 Ibid., 214.

23 Ibid., 272–3.

24 Ibid., 271.

25 Ibid., 228.

26 Ibid., 274. On this point it is worth quoting an 1881 letter to British Prime Minister William Gladstone from King Bell and King Acqua in West Africa: "We want to be under Her Majesty's control. We want our country to be governed by the British Government. We are tired of governing this country ourselves, every dispute leads to war, and often to great loss of lives, so we think it is the best thing to give up the country to you British men who no doubt will bring peace, civilization, and Christianity in the country … We

are quite willing to abolish all our heathen customs." Kings Bell and Acqua to William Gladstone, 6 November 1881, Foreign Office 403/18, Public Record Office, Kew, in M.W. Doyle, *Empires* (Ithaca: Cornell University Press, 1986), 162. Some, no doubt, will dismiss the letter as born of ignorance of imperialism; the kings did not know their own best interests. Such a response is condescending because it assumes "savages" know less about their real needs than the anti-imperialist liberal who has the natives' best interests at heart when insisting on their right to self-determination.

27 Watson, *State in Peace and War*, 274.

28 Ibid., 274–5.

29 Ibid., 181.

30 Ibid., 275.

31 Robert Meynell, in his critique of *Northern Spirits*, seems to agree with my remarks about Watson's insistence that the national sovereignty of the empire's members must be respected for imperial rule to have legitimacy. See Meynell, *Canadian Idealism* (Montreal and Kingston: McGill-Queen's University Press, 2011), 224. Indeed, I explicitly quote Watson on this point: "A whole foreign civilisation cannot be externally imposed upon a people" (*The State in Peace and War*, 275). So I am puzzled at Meynell's assertion that I promote the surrender of Canada's sovereignty to an American empire. Meynell seems to assume describing Watson's positive view of imperialism is a de facto assertion on my part that Watson would endorse "American expansionism" and, by implication at least, an endorsement of American empire to which, he assumes, I subscribe. Meynell goes on to argue that Watson would see "American imperialism" as having failed to protect diverse political cultures because, unlike the British political tradition, it gives the individual precedence over the community. Watson was certainly critical of the social contract theories present in the American political tradition, but as his close ties with American Idealists suggest, he was also aware of a more communitarian strain in American society. Nevertheless, Meynell asserts without theoretical evidence that Watson would have regarded contemporary American-style liberalism as "a threat to freedom." I doubt that, particularly in the wake of the Second World War, the fall of the Soviet Union, and the willingness of the United States to expend blood and treasure in fighting fundamentalist Islam. To say this is not to deny the failings of American foreign policy in the post–Cold War world, or, indeed, to defend every American military action in the post-9/11 world. But to see American political traditions as a "threat to freedom" is more an indulgence in ideological posturing than rigorous political theory. To borrow from Barry Cooper's review of *Canadian*

Idealism, Meynell is misreading the text. See Cooper, "An Invented Tradition," *Review of Politics* 74, no. 3 (June 2012): 335–8.

32 Lal, *In Defense of Empires*, 2.

33 Ibid., 27, 37.

34 Ibid., 26–7.

35 Robert Cooper, "The New Liberal Imperialism," *Guardian*, 7 April 2002, http://www.guardian.co.uk/world/2002/apr/07/1.

36 Robert Conquest, *Reflections on a Ravaged Century* (New York: W.W. Norton, 2001), 281.

37 Ibid., 276–8.

38 Michael Ignatieff, *Empire Lite: Nation-Building in Bosnia, Kosovo and Afghanistan* (Toronto: Penguin, 2003), 209.

39 David Long, "Liberalism, Imperialism, and Empire," *Studies in Political Economy* 79 (Autumn 2006): 204.

40 Michael Ignatieff, "Canada in the Age of Terror: Multilateralism Meets a Moment of Truth," *Policy Options* 24, no. 2 (February 2003): 14.

41 Ibid., 14–15.

42 Ignatieff, *Empire Lite*, 124.

43 Ignatieff, "Canada in the Age of Terror," 14–18.

44 Derek Burney, the former Canadian ambassador to the United States, makes a similar point in challenging the soft-power attitudes of Jennifer Welsh's 2004 book, *At Home in the World: Canada's Global Vision for the 21st Century*. Where Welsh argues that Canada can be an example to the world by promoting multilateralism, human rights, pluralism, and basic decency, Burney regards such thinking as dangerously naïve, the kind of thinking that makes Canada increasingly irrelevant on the international stage. He argues that a foreign policy based on "values" and "model citizenship" will relegate Canada "more permanently to the periphery as a dilettante, not to be taken seriously." Quoted in "Still Waiting," *Ottawa Citizen*, 28 March 2005.

45 Michael Ignatieff, "Intervention and State Failure," *Dissent* (Winter 2002): 114–23.

46 Ignatieff, *Empire Lite*, 125.

47 Long, "Liberalism, Imperialism, and Empire," 209.

48 Ibid., 23.

49 Michael Ignatieff, *Virtual War: Kosovo and Beyond* (New York: Picador, 2000), 76. It is worth noting that Ignatieff's writings on the Balkan crisis in the 1990s, including *Virtual War* and *Empire Lite*, were instrumental in the adoption of the ideas of "humanitarian intervention" and "responsibility to protect."

50 Watson, *State in Peace and War*, 274.
51 Ignatieff, *Empire Lite*, 25.
52 Ibid., 21–2.
53 Lewis Feuer, *Imperialism and the Anti-Imperialist Mind* (Buffalo, NY: Prometheus Books), 1986, esp. chapters 2, 4, and 5. In fact, Feuer observes that "the abrogation of imperialism brought a resurgence of tribal massacres in independent African states," 166. Feuer notes, for example, the massacres in 1962 and the 1970s when Tutsi and Hutu tribesmen began killing each other by the thousands in Rwanda and Burundi.
54 Ibid., 1, 20. Feuer defends his ideas about empire by arguing that "anti-imperialist literature has perhaps beclouded the great fact that the world's advances have been associated with the eras of progressive imperialism … A progressive imperialism is one in which energies are liberated for the advancement of civilization and creative activity … A rising, progressive people will be a correspondingly commercial, scientific, and imperialist people; such imperialism is not atavistic but creative. Decay comes when those energies have become effete."
55 Ibid., 104. Feuer writes, "Between the years 1860 to 1876 at least four hundred thousand natives, it has been estimated, were enslaved for use in the Middle East and North Africa," 104. He also notes that thousands of African boys were castrated by Arab slave traders, and questions why "the writings of Arab and black ideologists alike evince no trace of an Arab-Muslim guilt" comparable to the guilt Westerners are supposed to feel about their imperial past. He goes on to observe, borrowing an argument from Bernard Lewis, that somehow the idea of the "white man's burden" has transmuted into a burden not of power but of guilt that was enthusiastically taken up by leftist intellectuals after the First World War.
56 Ibid., 105.
57 Quoted by Robert Cooper, "The Next Empire," *Prospect*, 20 October 2001, http://www.prospectmagazine.co.uk/features/thenextempire.
58 Tony Blair, "Our Values Are Our Guide," *Globe and Mail*, 27 May 2006. Cited in Long, "Liberalism, Imperialism, and Empire," 212.
59 Ignatieff, *Empire Lite*, 106.
60 Pascal Bruckner, *The Tears of the White Man* (New York: Free Press), 1986.
61 Ignatieff, *Empire Lite*, 24.

11 Beyond "Hegel's Time": Made in the USA, Not Available in Canada[1]

DAVID MACGREGOR

> To speak of "Hegel's time" is to utter a riddle. For it was Hegel's fortune to live in two widely different times. The Bastille was stormed when he was nineteen; and all his early work was done under the shadow of the Revolution, and of Napoleon. His two great books, the *Phenomenology of Spirit* and the *Science of Logic*, belong properly to the Napoleonic age – though the last of the three volumes of the *Science of Logic* appeared only after Waterloo. So with the advantage of hindsight, we can fairly say that "Hegel's time" was that of the French Emperor who was only one year older than he ... In that first time, however, when he did his most important work, Hegel remained almost invisible ... It was after Napoleon was dead and buried on St Helena that Hegel became almost as visible and as predominant in his own sphere as the Emperor had been in the political world before 1815 ... Hegel at Berlin, the dominant figure in what was then, without dispute, the intellectual capital of the world, was still ... "in hiding." Behind the façade of the great philosophy professor, soon to be Rector Magnificus of the University for his appointed term, there was still the committed believer in a Napoleonic "new order."
>
> H.S. Harris, Preface to *Hegel in His Time*

I

The title of this chapter refers in part to a former market condition, rendered extinct by globalization and free trade, when industry-poor Canadians looked with envy across the border to the gargantuan manufacturing output of the United States. But the title also suggests that Hegel's philosophy may have more relevance for America than for Canada – the under-populated (former) British colonial outpost.

The reason for this is closely bound up with a little-noted relationship between Hegel and the German-American political economist Friedrich List.[2] Hegel may have had a decisive impact on List's approach to political economy. List's writings contributed to what Henry Clay called "the American system" – a revolutionary mode of thought and social organization that "would constitute the rallying point of human freedom against all the despotism of the Old World."[3] Though I do not have sufficient space here for a detailed argument, I speculate that the democratic ideal informing Hegel's philosophy flowed from the momentous Revolution of 1776. Thus, the riddle of "Hegel's time" mentioned by Harris goes beyond the philosopher's attitude towards Napoleon and the French Revolution.

I explore three aspects Hegel's relationship with Friedrich List (belief in democracy, opposition to empire, and critique of British political economy) that are also central elements of the American Revolution. By reading Hegel in light of this connection, I hope to demonstrate Hegel's lifelong interest in the American upheaval of 1776. Unlike with the French Revolution, however, my contention meets a necessary paradox. There are countless instances where Hegel deals concretely with momentous events in France, but he admits few lines to the New World insurgency. The argument here must go beyond "Hegel's time" as warranted by his writings, for there are few surviving transparent indications that the philosopher even heard the famous "shot that rang 'round the world."[4]

Before considering Hegel's relationship with List, the next two sections of this chapter provide the political context that may have encouraged Hegel's silence on the American Revolution.

II

Harris's monumental biography of Hegel includes only three references to the American Revolution, compared to almost two dozen for the French Revolution.[5] Most Hegel commentary is similarly preoccupied by the impact of the French Revolution on his philosophy while the American Revolution goes missing. Why is this so? First there is Hegel's silence on the issue. Yet taciturnity itself might have provoked some investigative curiosity. How did Hegel miss the significance of what Doull calls "the first post-national state, the first state based not on national particularity but on rational principles"?[6] As Wood relates,[7] for most of the last century historians misinterpreted the founding of the United States. A "progressive" generation of historians who dominated until the close of the Second World War perceived the American Revolution as conflict between agrarian populists and an aristocratic or business minority.[8] In the 1950s and 1960s "consensus" historians blasted apart the progressive analysis. They argued that hardly any change took place in the American revolutionary period that had not already occurred during the colonial era. Given these prevailing standpoints – both of which downplayed radical democratic turbulence in the New World – the absence of the Revolution from Hegel's writings did not ignite scholarly inquiry. As far as I know, my own effort to assay Thomas Paine's influence on Hegel's thought stands mostly alone.[9]

Recent interpretations of the American Revolution stress its absolute break from the British Empire and the terrible price paid by the United States in blood and social division. The revolutionary impulse accelerated as Americans erected powerful republican institutions bearing little resemblance to what Edgar Allan Poe later called "the heraldic display in monarchial countries."[10] This revised view of the American Revolution also throws into prominence Alexander Hamilton's radical republican vision of "government-sponsored national economic development,"[11] which Clay later named "the American System." Because of Canada's centrality within the New World movement, an assessment of Hegel's relationship with the American Revolution must also consider this enigmatic outpost of empire.

The British nearly swapped Canada for the sugar-rich French island of Guadeloupe in 1763,[12] but the American Revolution breathed new life into the frigid northern colony. Canada could serve as a counterrevolutionary fortress against the raw energy of liberty rising from a fledgling American republic. George Washington recognized that an independent Canada would forever pose a British threat against the United States,[13] and William Blake pointed ominously to "A Serpent in Canada."[14] For some, Canada provided a fancy picture window decorated by the British to entice errant Americans to drift upwards and huddle under the English Crown.

Reckoning Hegel's thought from the perspective of New World rebellion may yield important benefits. "Dangerous experiments in France," Hegel averred, "turn[ed] out to the ruin of their authors or at least produce[d] a very ambiguous result."[15] Unlike the French upheaval of 1789, the American Revolution did not consume the founders, and the republic's accomplishments, while incomplete, were not ambiguous. "By the early years of the nineteenth century the Revolution created a society fundamentally different from the colonial society of the eighteenth century. It was in fact a new society unlike any that had ever existed anywhere in the world."[16] No one knew better than the Americans themselves the momentous quality of the Revolution.[17] The audacious American experiment may carry special meaning in a twenty-first-century universe where many of our capitalist institutions have been characterized as unaccountable oligarchies beyond the rein of state power. What lessons can be learned from Hegel – the philosopher of revolution – regarding momentous times "when the Princes fade from earth, scarce seen by souls of men"?[18]

III

The fantastic effort of the infant democratic republic to relinquish a debased dichotomy of nobles and commoners, lords and serfs echoed throughout Europe, impinging decisively on Hegel and his circle. Thus, Harold Jantz contributes a remarkable account of the impact of the American Revolution on the early life and work of Hegel's mentor and friend, Goethe. Already in Germany circa 1776, Jantz writes, "Groups of young people were fond of creating imaginary republics on the American model."[19] As documented by Harris,[20] the American Revolution powerfully affected both Schiller and Goethe, and it is difficult to believe that Hegel did not share his older friends' enthusiasm for the Revolution. Goethe remained a staunch advocate of America throughout his long life (he died a year after Hegel), protected perhaps by his venerable literary prestige but also by the fact that he put pro-American utterances mostly in the mouths of his characters rather than articulating them himself.[21]

Blake's expectation that the British lion would shrink from the shores of America was sorely disappointed. Another civil war – the war with Canada – erupted in 1812 that nearly permitted the English to snuff out American liberty. The charged atmosphere of the times may explain Hegel's decades-long reluctance explicitly to address the American Revolution and its relationship to empire. Indeed, Hegel would not have been alone in his "silent advocacy"[22] of earth-shaking events in the United States. Heinrich Heine, who attended Hegel's lectures and abandoned Germany for the freer atmosphere of France after the 1830 July Revolution, provides a pertinent example of this peculiar code of omerta. The German poet shelved a manuscript version of an 1832 essay that "inveighs against attempts by ... [the] *Gazette de France* to turn the French against ... American ideas of liberty." S.S. Prawer notes that "as for genuine democracy, [Heine] proclaims the USA and the short-lived French Republic as the only realizations of that idea in the whole of human history. No wonder that Heine never thought it safe to publish these thoughts either in Louis Philippe's France, or in the Germany of his day!"[23] Among other German expatriate figures of the period, Friedrich List – perhaps like his older colleague Hegel, as we shall see – presciently feared a third American civil war, and Karl Marx played the fraught role of an interested observer surveying from afar bloody Union victories at Antietam and Gettysburg.

IV

In his classic 1941 study, *From Hegel to Nietzsche*, Karl Löwith presents a discussion of Hegel and Friedrich List, based on a 1904 book by J. Plenge. Plenge offered perhaps the earliest comparison of List and Hegel available in the literature.[24] However, Plenge (and Löwith) seem unaware that Hegel and List, as will be discussed below, worked together on constitutional reform in Württemberg, or that they shared a circle of friends, including Germany's most eminent publisher, J.F. von Cotta. Moreover, Löwith and Plenge ignore important similarities between Hegel and List that contrast sharply with the outlook of Karl Marx. According to Plenge (quoted by Löwith), an "epochal boundary" divides Hegel from List and Marx. After Hegel, the nineteenth century is characterized by force generated through "science as a method ... Material ... as energy! Friedrich List and Karl Marx both put their faith in force. This is the world of the real nineteenth century of which Hegel had no idea, although it was coming into being under his very eyes."[25] Transfixed by the French Revolution, writes Löwith, "Hegel intentionally overlooked the possibilities arising from it, even though in his own period it was obvious that the Age of Revolutions was just beginning." Hegel's system ends with "radical hostility between warring nation states ... and a Protestantism split up into sects, itself still an irreconcilable opponent of Catholicism."[26] The flaw in Hegel's remarkable "achievement in the study of history ... was only corrected ... by F. List and Marx," both of whom understood the new world of "technical and socioeconomic advances." Plenge (as quoted by Löwith) writes,

> Without overmuch concern for Hegel, List viewed the nation state as the vehicle of history and provided it with the economic weapons with which

> to secure its equal rights with other nations, upon which the world system was to grow. Marx, the spiritual heir of Hegel, like List, considered economics and science to be the real job and basis for existence of mankind; just for this reason he saw them as the seedbed of class conflict and of class wars, which he considered would have to be undergone until the final world system of work was achieved. We take them both only as examples of the way the facts of the age shoved Hegel's system aside, showing more simple ways for thought.[27]

Now an influential thinker for twenty-first-century economists critical of neoliberalism,[28] List began to study economics after 1815 in order to comprehend unfortunate economic circumstances then prevailing in the German states. Napoleonic Wars had devastated Germany, and cheap British goods flooded the impoverished country. Each German state posted severe tariffs and customs duties against the others, but most gave English wares easy entry. Alexander Hamilton's 1791 *Report on Manufactures* provided central themes that inspired List and allowed him to comprehend an emerging capitalist world of technology and science, and its relationship to the state.[29] Although I cannot develop the argument here, it is likely that Hamilton's report also influenced Hegel when he began his own study of political economy about twenty years before List. Further, I conjecture (following Friedrich Lenz, the biographer of List[30]) that Hegel's thought may have played a central role in List's seminal approach to political economy.

Born in 1789 at Reutlingen in Württemberg, about forty kilometres distant from Hegel's 1770 birthplace of Stuttgart, List held a post and attended lectures at Tübingen University. (Hegel graduated from the seminary attached to Tübingen two decades earlier). At Tübingen, List enjoyed close friendship with Johannes Schlayer, later to become secretary to the minister of education and religious affairs, Karl August Wangenheim, formerly registrar at Tübingen University. List and Schlayer shared lodgings in Stuttgart when Wangenheim and the minister of the interior, Karl Freiherr von Kerner, set out to reform Württemberg, in face of powerful opposition. Wangenheim appointed the brilliant and promising List as member of the Court of Audit in 1816. One of List's duties was to investigate why 700 citizens of Württemberg suddenly opted to leave Germany for the United States. He concluded that civic corruption, arbitrary officials, and brutal treatment by feudal lords precipitated the mass exodus.[31]

King Frederick offered Württemberg a new constitutional charter in 1815, but the giant 6′ 11″ monarch could not sway the Estates, including wealthy aristocratic families and corrupt officials. They insisted on keeping the old constitution and their enshrined privileges. In the resulting stalemate, the Estates drew up a contract based on the former constitution. Frederick died shortly afterwards, to be succeeded by his son William, who proclaimed freedom of the press and inaugurated the previously mentioned "reform ministry" of Wangenheim and Kerner.[32] Harris writes that Hegel was sympathetic to earlier democratic reforms in Germany. He had close friends in the group around Georg Forster, admirer of Tom Paine, acquaintance of Benjamin Franklin, and a major figure in the Jacobin Club that in 1793 founded the Mainz Republic, Germany's first republican state.[33] Hegel published in *Heidelbergische Jahrbücher* a detailed 1817 article, the "Proceedings of the Estates Council in Württemberg," in response to the Estates' proposals.

Meanwhile, Friedrich List started the *Württembergisches Archiv* "to bring to the attention of the public the urgent need to reform the administration."[34] Hegel, then teaching at Heidelberg University, agreed when List encouraged him to republish the Württemberg essay as a popular stand-alone *Archiv* pamphlet.[35] List published three tracts concerning the constitutional debate, all written after Hegel's original intervention.[36]

Critics have accused Hegel, with no discernible proof, of publishing his Württemberg essay in order to win Baron Wangenheim's approval and thereby secure chancellorship of Tübingen University and a seat in the Diet.[37] Somehow this story seems mixed up with the actual experience of Friedrich List, who obtained in 1818, through Wangenheim's patronage, a controversial post as professor in the new Department of Public Administration at Tübingen University. The fresh academic unit originated from a memorandum List prepared for Wangenheim, reflecting his own desire to create a professionalized body of civil servants inoculated against petty corruption and abuse. Significantly, a primary focus of Hegel's *Philosophy of Right* is the role of competent public servants in the rational state.[38] In an appendix to his 1818 introductory lectures in public administration, List includes a discussion of corporations that might almost have been lifted from the pages of the *Philosophy of Right* – except that List's remarks appeared before the 1821 publication of Hegel's book.[39] In fact, List's biographer Friedrich Lenz points out that List learned from Hegel the role of corporations in political life.[40] List offered, "Up to the present the slight attention paid to the nature of corporations or guild-organizations has been a great gap in political theory, for through them alone can true freedom and order be preserved. A great indivisible state without any organization is a French chimera, either an aberration of liberty or an attempt to introduce an Eastern despotism according to the proverb 'Divide et impera.'"[41]

Hegel allegedly earned favourable treatment from Wangenheim, because his essay "takes the side of the king and favours him while the estates are scathingly censured."[42] However, this makes little sense, given the experience of Hegel's younger colleague. List received his position at Tübingen after publishing critical essays on the constitution that declared against the king's influence in the proceedings and soundly rejected the reactionary standpoint of the Württemberg estates. While Hegel's essay warmly acknowledges King William's progressive role in opening constitutional debate, List and Hegel took very close positions regarding key issues at Württemberg.

List's three pamphlets applied ideas of democratic representation and constitutional government to the kingdom of Württemberg.[43] He argued for municipal autonomy and democratic practices and opposed traditional rights held by the Estates. List contended that corporations intermediate between the individual and the state were required to protect individual rights and ease participation of citizens in higher levels of government. On the same lines, Hegel severely impugned the draft constitution submitted by the Württemberg Estates that would preserve traditional corporate rights. "They acted," wrote Hegel, "like a merchant who proposed to ply his trade just the same on a ship, in which his capital was sunk, even though it had gone to the bottom, and to expect others to advance the same credit to him on the strength of it as before."[44] In his third essay, List detailed an overall agenda for German unity that included "freedom of the press, freedom of speech, freedom to engage in any trade or profession and freedom to emigrate and travel abroad": "He wanted to see the very loose federation of 1815 replaced by a constitution that would give much greater powers to the central government. He proposed the establishment of a national parliament, a national army, and a federal court of appeal. There should be federal institutions to foster the arts, science, and education. Germans should be allowed to move freely from one state to another. And a German customs union should be established."[45]

Hegel did not mention German unity in his Württemberg essay, but List's proposals echo concerns Hegel would subsequently expand upon in the *Philosophy of Right*. I hypothesize that List may have been aware of Hegel's unpublished essay, written two decades before, on the

German constitution. Hegel wrote, "The state requires a universal centre, a monarch, and Estates, wherein the various powers, foreign affairs, the armed forces, finances relevant thereto, &c., would be united, a centre which would not merely direct but would have in addition the power necessary for asserting itself and its decrees, and for keeping the individual parts dependent on itself."[46]

Democracy was hardly a novel idea introduced in recent times.[47] Representative government, noted Hegel, was a German invention that appeared in urban communities during the feudal period, but suffered erosion due to absolutist monarchies installed by foreign occupiers. As we shall see, Hegel felt that the American Revolution had revived these central principles. "Most of the European states were founded by Germanic peoples, and out of the spirit of these peoples their constitution has been developed. Amongst the Germanic peoples every free man's arm was counted and his will had its share in the nation's deeds. Princes were chosen by the people and so were war and peace and all acts of the whole. Anyone who wished participated in council; anyone who did not so wish forebore of his own will and he relied on a similarity of interest with the others."[48]

At Tübingen, List attracted attention from spies and informers who complained to the royal court about his lectures. After King William abruptly terminated Wangenheim's reform ministry, List resigned from his teaching post in 1818. He continued with some friends to push for political change in a new journal, *Der Volksfreund aus Schwaben,* which lasted until 1822. The young activist started a weekly trade journal that reached across Germany[49] and won a seat in the new Württemberg Chamber of Estates. In the Preface to his *National System of Political Economy,* List describes the hopeful atmosphere current in Germany.

> In 1819 all Germany teemed with schemes and projects for new political institutions. Rulers and subjects, nobles and plebeians, officers of State and men of learning, were all occupied with them. Germany was like an estate which had been ravaged by war, whose former owners on resuming possession of it are about to arrange it afresh. Some wanted to restore everything exactly as it had been, down to every petty detail; others to have everything on a new plan and with entirely modern implements; while some, who paid regard both to common sense and to experience, desired to follow a middle course, which might accommodate the claims of the past with the necessities of the present. Everywhere were contradiction and conflict of opinion, everywhere leagues and associations for the

> promotion of patriotic objects. The constitution of the Diet itself was new, framed in a hurry, and regarded by the most enlightened and thoughtful diplomatists as merely an embryo from which a more perfect state of things might be hoped for in the future.[50]

German experiments in democracy collapsed after Prince Metternich proclaimed the 1819 Karlsbad decrees, outlawing free speech and republicanism in most of the German states. List and the other originators of the *Der Volksfreund* would eventually serve time in jail. It is instructive for our purposes that List went to prison for essentially putting forward a program of democratic reform resembling proposals he and Hegel had earlier mooted for Württemberg.

List joined the Württemberg assembly in October 1820, and submitted a petition that reflected the desires of his constituents. Württemberg officials banned the leaflet, dumped List from the Chamber of Estates, and charged the neophyte politician "with insulting the king, slandering judges and civil servants, and breaking the press law."[51] List abandoned Stuttgart upon receiving a ten-month jail sentence that shocked public opinion in Germany. Sought by police in France and Switzerland for two years, List decided to throw his fate upon a possible pardon from the king. Instead of a pardon, he was condemned to a jail cell in the fortress of Hohenasperg. Halfway through his sentence, List accepted exile to the United States. He and his family quit Germany in early 1825.

Hegel may have had some connection with List's journey to the United States. While in France, List became friends with American War of Independence hero, General Lafayette, who invited List in 1824 to join him on a trip to the United States. The financially destitute List had to decline. Hegel's friend, the French philosopher Victor Cousin, provided List with a letter of recommendation to ease his entry into the United States. Cousin dedicated his 1826 translation of Plato's *Gorgias* to Hegel in recognition of the latter's persuading Prussian authorities to release him from jail in Berlin two years earlier.[52] Was the French philosopher's letter of introduction connected to Cousin's rescue by Hegel from internment in Germany?

V

Hegel's writings seem at first glance barely to note the American experience and the bitter break with England. By contrast, Friedrich List became a U.S. citizen, a well-known economist, and diplomat trumpeting the American system of political economy.[53] List achieved international fame and notoriety before his untimely death in 1846. Metternich in the mid-1830s labelled him "one of the most active, crafty and influential German revolutionaries."[54] List successfully promoted Germany's first railway[55] and inspired the Zollverein customs agreement that eventually ended internal tariffs dividing the German states, paving the way for a united Germany.[56] "As a foreign observer remarked, the Germans were prisoners who could only hold intercourse with one another through iron bars."[57] Germans helped imprison themselves while England, said List (who alludes to the interesting geopolitical function of Canada),

> held the keys of every sea, and placed a sentry over every nation: over the Germans, Heligoland; over the French, Guernsey and Jersey; over the inhabitants of North America, Nova Scotia and the Bermudas; over Central America, the island of Jamaica; over all countries bordering on the Mediterranean, Gibraltar, Malta, and the Ionian Islands. She possesses every important strategical position on both the routes to India with the exception of the Isthmus of Suez, which she is striving to acquire; she dominates the Mediterranean by means of Gibraltar, the Red Sea by Aden, and the Persian Gulf by Bushire and Karrack. She needs only the further acquisition of the Dardanelles, the Sound and the Isthmuses of Suez and Panama, in order to open and close at her pleasure every sea and every maritime highway. Her navy alone surpasses the combined maritime forces of all other countries, if not in number of vessels, at any rate in fighting strength.[58]

The economic and constitutional reforms urged by List for Germany (and that achieved reality under Bismarck) followed the U.S. model and reflected "American freedom, " achieved constitutionally "through a distinction of federal and state institutions which within their respective powers ... secure individuals in their liberty and draw them into a common will." As with Revolutionary America, Germany in the late nineteenth century thus developed "a unified will forged in opposition to British dominion."[59]

Perhaps we can consider List, who escaped the Old World, as a public voice for those like Hegel who remained shackled in Germany? Prince Metternich and his allies dominated the Continent under British tutelage until the revolutions of 1848 when the Austrian chancellor fled to England. Albion's influence did not rely on Metternich alone. "The King of England [remains] an estate of the German Empire," lamented Hegel in his unpublished essay "The German Constitution" (written between 1797 and 1802). Under the 1648 Peace of Westphalia, England (among other Great Powers) occupied Germany through the royal house of Hanover and regularly exerted "legal interference in German internal affairs."[60] Hegel neglected to mention in his essay that conscripts from the German state of Hesse, some of them direct subjects of King George III, made up a quarter of British troops in the American Revolutionary War.[61]

Hegel had to be extremely careful in his writings (even those that did not go to print), given what he called "the truth that lies in power."[62] According to German law, states were treated "in the legal form of private property" belonging to the prevailing royal house. A few ill-chosen words about royalty might place the offender in prison or worse. King Frederick of Württemberg, which embraced Swabia, Hegel's birthplace, was son-in-law of George III and brother-in-law of the English Prince Regent, later George IV. It is worth mentioning in this regard that Heinrich Heine "matriculated at the University of Göttingen, whose rector (as Heine pointed out with glee) doubled as King of England."[63]

Hegel resided amidst an English system badly shaken by continued success of the American Revolution. In terms of ideological threat to the British, the compromised and defeated French Revolution could never hold a candle to the wild revolutionary lover, red Orc.[64] Hegel was not deported to the United States as was List; nor did he embrace the cold rule of Britannia. His philosophy, I speculate below, may form a powerful rebuke to English oligarchical thought and rule. "Nowhere more than in England," Hegel observed, "is the prejudice so fixed and so naïve that if birth and wealth give a man office they also give him brains."[65]

VI

Returning to Germany in 1841, List found himself opposed by a group including the young Karl Marx for editorial leadership of the newly relaunched Cologne newspaper, the *Reinische Zeitung*. "Free trade was considerably more popular to ... [Cologne's] business men than were the protectionist ideas that List espoused and that his protégé ... wanted to make the center of editorial policy."[66] A neophyte in economics,[67] Marx had List's candidate for editor removed in January 1842, and replaced by someone closer to his liking. A few months later, Marx took over the editorial office of a newspaper fast becoming one of the most controversial in Europe.[68]

This was no flash-in-the-pan dispute between bourgeois liberals, as Marx's biographers Nicholaievsky and Maenchen-Helfen suggest.[69] The English saw List, the pre-eminent German political economist, as a mortal enemy. London's potentates despised him as an influential supporter of the American challenge to English hegemony. List pulled no punches regarding empire. "English national economy," he wrote in 1827, "has for its object to manufacture for the whole world, to monopolize all manufacturing power, even at the expense of the lives of the citizens, to keep the world and especially her colonies in a state of infancy and vassalage by political management as well as by the superiority of her capital, her skill, and her navy."[70] Canada – or British North America – was a key victim of English economic practices, as detailed by List. London allowed hardly any manufacturing in its North American colony while encouraging primary industries such as fur and lumber that would supply British industry. Like other British colonies, Canada could not export material that might compete with English exports, and protective tariffs were frowned upon.[71]

Marx's intellectual partner Friedrich Engels, in 1845 campaigned in Germany against List's theories about tariff protection and industrial development, and Marx wrote a screed against List in 1845, complete with the usual unfounded charges of plagiarism.[72] A few years later Engels joined the Manchester branch of his father's textile firm that relied on tariff-free slave cotton from the American South. It is often noted that Engels's generous financial support for Marx's work was funded by profits extracted from the blood and sweat of exploited proletarians. Less often mentioned is that Engels's earnings, and those of other British textile manufacturers, relied heavily upon, and may have exacerbated the split between the slave South and the industrial North of the United States.[73]

For List, the massive influence of the British (or cosmopolitan) school of political economy, with its enthusiastic supporters among key opinion-makers – including radicals like Marx and Engels – in Germany and elsewhere on the Continent stemmed from deliberate English policy. Employing tariffs and other policy instruments recommended by the American system, both the United States and Germany would surpass British industrial production by the end of the nineteenth century. In a memorable passage, List summarizes the ideological barriers employed by the English to slow American and German industrial development.

> All the scientifically educated Government employés, all the newspaper editors, all the writers on political economy, had been trained up in the cosmopolitical school, and regarded every kind of protective duty as a theoretical abomination. They were aided by the interests of England, and by those of the dealers in English goods in the ports and commercial cities of Germany. It is notorious what a powerful means of controlling public opinion abroad is possessed by the English Ministry in their "secret service money"; and they are not accustomed to be niggardly where it can be useful to their commercial interests. An innumerable army of correspondents and leader-writers, from Hamburg and Bremen, from Leipzig and Frankfort, appeared in the field to condemn the unreasonable desires of the German manufacturers for a uniform protective duty, and to abuse their adviser in harsh and scornful terms; such as, that he was ignorant of the first principles of political economy as held by the most scientific authorities, or else had not brains enough to comprehend them. The work of these advocates of the interests of England was rendered all the easier by the fact that the popular theory and the opinions of German learned men were on their side.[74]

In view of List's critical stance towards the English system and its supporters, he maintained a buoyant outlook. He personally approached Metternich twice in the early 1840s, believing the chancellor was open to persuasion on the subject of industrial policy and a customs union. "But if List thought he was now in Metternich's good books he was mistaken. Metternich still regarded List – as he had regarded him in 1834" – as a dangerous revolutionary.[75] List visited London in a hopeless 1846 effort to recruit prominent free-traders Cobden, Bright, and MacGregor to the cause of industrial development. Despondent, broke, and fearing assassination, List evidently shot himself in the head while staying alone in Tyrol, where he had hoped "a warmer climate would restore him to health."[76] List's death came almost exactly fifteen years after that of Hegel.

VII

In "Hegel's America," George Armstrong Kelly cautions against a reading of the Berlin philosopher that frames the American Revolution as "a likely candidate to overcome history's previous forms." Hegel's "brief, rather perfunctory" 1830 remarks in his lectures on the philosophy of history about America as "land of the future," says Kelly, merely concern "the United States [as a] rather inchoate part of what Hegel calls the 'Germanic world.' [America] reveals a tantalizing incompleteness, not a higher consciousness of its own making." The destiny of the New World experiment "cannot be of profound interest," submits Kelly, primarily because "it lies in a future that no historical research can penetrate ... and it presents no features that would appear to illuminate the philosophy of history."[77]

I have conjectured, on the contrary, that there are reasons to suspect that Hegel may have held an emancipatory vision of America (and an extremely critical view of the British system) resembling that of Friedrich List. Karl Löwith observes that Hegel's writings contain "scattered references to America, ever since the beginning of the [nineteenth] century, thought of as the future land of freedom [which] admit the possibility that the world spirit might emigrate from Europe."[78] In this concluding section, I speculate that Hegel's philosophy drew substantially from the American experiment.

Under a pseudonym, Hegel translated and published in 1798 a revolutionary pamphlet written five years earlier by Swiss author J.J. Cart, just before he fled to the United States. Cart celebrated victory by the people of the Swiss Canton of the Pays de Vaud over the abusive Berne nobility. The success of the revolt in Switzerland mirrored events in the New World. "The American Revolution," writes Harris, "was in Hegel's view another example of the Nemesis that looms over all political authorities who are deaf to the voice of 'justice.'" However, Hegel objected to J.J. Cart's naive acceptance of myths surrounding the British system, including its liberal constitution. The British pay high taxes, conceded Cart, "and yet there is no people ... in Europe which enjoys greater prosperity or so much individual and national respect. Because the Englishman is free, because he enjoys the rights inherent in freedom, in a word, because he taxes himself."[79] Hegel's frosty assessment of English constitutional monarchy ought to be quoted in full:

> The author has not lived to see how gravely in these latest years the security of property has been compromised in many respects and the rights of domestic property restricted by the power conceded to the receivers of higher taxes, how personal freedom has been limited by suspension of the constitution on one hand [the allusion is doubtless to the suspension of the

> right of habeas corpus in 1794] and civil rights limited by positive law on the other; – how strikingly clear it has become that a minister can scorn public opinion if he has a parliamentary majority at his command ... that the nation is so inadequately represented that it cannot make its voice effective in Parliament, and its security depends more upon fear of its unconstitutional might, upon the prudence of the minister, or upon discretion of the House of Lords ... Through this insight and on account of these facts even the respect toward the English nation itself of many of its strongest admirers, has fallen ...
>
> The tax, which the English Parliament imposed on tea imported into America, was very small; but the feeling of the Americans, that along with the quite insignificant sum which the tax would cost them, their most important right would be lost to them, made the American Revolution.[80]

The anti-oligarchical theme sounded by Hegel infused his (and List's) contribution to the Württemberg constitutional debate almost twenty years later, as we have seen. However, Hegel's 1831 article on the English Reform Bill provides perhaps the most spectacular example of bitter antagonism to the British system. I surmise that Hegel's withering analysis of English aristocratic hegemony – delivered in the last few months of his life – perhaps should be understood in light of the revolutionary New World alternative. The Berlin philosopher's article offended the Prussian monarch and received finishing touches from state censors.[81] Electoral reform in Britain offered nothing like the achievement of the American Revolution, but it did promise to widen political representation and minutely restrict the power of wealth and nobility. In his introductory remarks on Hegel's article, Pelczynski acknowledges Hegel's expert acquaintance with "English conditions" gained through "assiduous reading of current English newspaper articles and parliamentary reports." But Pelczynski is agonized by the results. "What mars the work is its strongly anti-English flavor and a tone of patronizing superiority ... His particular scapegoat seems to have been oddly enough, the nationalism of the English."[82] Pelczynski continues, "The extremely critical tone of The English Reform Bill lends plausibility to the hypothesis that one of the objects of the article was to counteract a current wave of Anglomania in Prussia, but even so the work remains something of an enigma."[83]

To be sure, Hegel never mentions the American Revolution while writing about the depravity of British electoral practices, but the U.S.

republican experiment was likely always in his mind. "The reason why England is so remarkably behind the other civilized states of Europe in institutions derived from true rights is simply that there the governing power lies in the hands of those possessed of so many privileges which contradict a rational constitutional law and true legislation."[84] Hegel notes the incredible political power of the East India Company – the company's tax on tea precipitated the famous events in Boston Harbour mentioned by the young Hegel in his essay on J.J. Cart – and the common practice of buying seats in the House of Commons. "It has been calculated that the majority of the House is controlled by 150 persons of eminence." The supposed superior character of English democracy stood as a hollow sham. "It would be difficult to discover a comparable symptom of political corruption in any other people."[85]

Hegel often reflected on blind British patriotism in his lectures. Accordingly in his *Lectures on the Philosophy of World History,* Hegel observes, "If he is asked, any Englishman will say of himself and his fellow citizens that it is they who rule the East Indies and the oceans of the world, who dominate world trade, who have a parliament, and trial by jury, etc. It is deeds such as these which give the nation its sense of identity."[86]

Similarly, List noted the jingoism of the English hidden beneath a thin cosmopolitan veneer. For ideologists of empire, all nation-building was bad except the English variety. Thus, Adam Smith and his followers developed a lexicon of cosmopolitanism that obscured the extremely protectionist character of industry in England.[87]

In a reference to John Locke's philosophy, which is "still for the most part, the philosophy of the English and the French, and likewise in a certain sense of the Germans," Hegel anticipates Friedrich List's critique English political economy: "To the English, Philosophy has ever signified the deduction of experience from observations; this has in a one-sided way been applied to physical and economic subjects. General principles of political economy such as free-trade in the present day, and all matters which rest on thinking experience, the knowledge of whatever reveals itself in this sphere as necessary and useful, signifies philosophy to the English."[88]

List grew convinced that the ruling British school of political economy, headed by Adam Smith, David Ricardo, and J.B. Say – and at the time immensely popular in Germany – paid no attention, in fact, to political economy.[89] British economists concentrated on economic relationships among individuals and groups, setting these in the context of a utopian world economy that existed nowhere while mostly ignoring economic relationships integral to nation states and the relations between them – the exact content of political economy, as List understood it. In his 1841 *National System of Political Economy*, List would write, "How pitiable and unpractical seems that theory of political economy which would have us refer the material welfare of nations solely to the production of individuals, wholly losing sight of the fact that the producing power of all individuals is to a great extent determined by the social and political circumstances of the nation."[90]

Here we find another key similarity between List and Hegel. The latter built his philosophy around a contrast between reason and the understanding. Reason encompasses broad relationships between the individual, civil society, and the state, but the understanding (which Hegel identified with the English school of Adam Smith) flounders in a sea of half-digested facts and vulgar opinion: "Political economy ... [shows] how thought extracts from the endless multitude of details with which it is initially confronted the simple principles of the thing ..., the understanding which works within it and controls it ... To recognize, in the sphere of needs, this manifestation ... of rationality which is present in the thing ... and active within it has, on the one hand, a conciliatory effect; but conversely, this is also the field in which the understanding, with its subjective ends and moral opinions, gives vent to its discontent and moral irritation."[91]

Both Hegel and List shared a deep antipathy to English governance, unlike Marx, who spent most of his life in London, thoroughly captivated by British thinkers like Adam Smith, David Ricardo, and David Urquhart.[92] If Marx projected capital as the dominant power in England, thereby obscuring the fundamental difference between democratic America and aristocratic Europe, Hegel offered a strikingly different assessment. "The nobility," he suggested, forms "the very heart and vital principle of the constitution and condition of Great Britain."[93] In the *Philosophy of Right*, the Roman Empire stands as Hegel's coded term for the British Empire, as I argued in *Hegel, Marx and the English State*.[94] Both List[95] and Hegel believed that a world united under English rule would be a disaster – one nearly accomplished in their own era. List's and Hegel's conception of an autonomous nation state is totally lost in Marx's vision of a cosmopolitan world united by capitalism and free trade – influenced as the latter was by the British trinity of Smith, Say, and Ricardo.

Lenz suggests that "Marx's thought remains at the level of social critique, while List vividly understands the reality of state organization [*staatliche Gestaltung*]." Accordingly, "List – beyond Marx – already outlines the imperialistic market expansion central to the worldview of a few imperial powers and draws from that conclusions which post-Marxist critiques of modern imperialism will only later answer to." Lenz refers to List's prediction that "after the US, Great Britain with its dominions and colonies will endure as the second 'giant power.' In his knowledge of the historical forces of this expansion – how they have formed over centuries in the battles of the Venetians, the Hanseatic League, the Spanish etc. – List, as proven by his 'natural' and his 'national system,' is in no way lagging behind the Marxist critique. He surmounts it through his insight into the national forces which flow through and shape the social world."[96]

Hegel, as I argue in *Hegel, Marx and the English State*, assembled the first modern theory of imperialism in the *Philosophy of Right* – one that, I conjecture, likely influenced List's writings.[97] List's socio-economic account of the formation and dissolution of nations and empires in the 1841 *National System of Political Economy* – in which the American system ultimately challenges the British Empire for world supremacy – perhaps offers an elaboration of the following passage in the *Philosophy of Right*:

> Since states function as particular entities in their mutual relations, the broadest view of these relations will encompass the ceaseless turmoil not just of external contingency, but also of passions, interests, ends, talents and virtues, violence ..., wrongdoing, and vices in their inner particularity. In this turmoil, the ethical world itself – the independence of the state – is exposed to contingency. The principles of the *spirits of nations* ... are in general of a limited nature because of that particularity in which they have their objective actuality and self-consciousness as *existent* individuals, and their deeds and destinies in their mutual relations are the manifest ... dialectic of the finitude of these spirits. It is through this dialectic that the *universal* spirit, the *spirit of the world*, produces itself in its freedom from all limits, and it is this spirit which exercises its right – which is the highest right of all – over finite spirits in *world history* as the *world's court of judgement*.[98]

There is no space here to present my speculative argument in full, but Hegel's account of U.S. social conditions in his famous passage on America as the land of the future includes many parallels with List's

1827 *Outlines of American Political Economy*. A significant example of this commonality may involve List's polemic against the writings of Thomas Cooper, a prominent pro-slavery economist and enemy of the American system. In 1827, Cooper advocated succession of the Southern states from the United States, originating the ideological movement that culminated thirty-four years later in the American Civil War.[99] List pointed out that the agricultural regime in the South made America dependent on the goodwill or enmity of the British, who provided the primary market for American cotton. Meanwhile, cheap English imports repeatedly devastated manufacturing in the North. Aware of the danger of succession outlined earlier by Cooper, List called for harmony in America between agriculture, manufacturing, and commerce promoted by "judicious laws, fortresses for securing our productive powers (as we erect them for securing our territory) against foreign aggressions, foreign events, foreign laws and regulations."[100] Equally, Hegel averred that America's federal make-up encouraged division among the states and rendered the United States extremely vulnerable to imperialist penetration. "This was already obvious in the last war with England. The Americans could not conquer Canada and the English were able to bombard Washington simply because the strained relations between the provinces prevented them from mounting a vigorous campaign."[101]

List predicted that U.S. policies promoting harmony between agriculture, manufacturing, and commerce would heal the divide between North and South and eventually eliminate slavery. "In time, I hope the slaves of this country will be made of iron and brass, and set in motion by stone coal instead of whips."[102] Arguably in the same vein as List, Hegel wrote in 1830 that America's "world-historical importance" perhaps might be revealed "in the ages which lie ahead ... in a conflict between North and South ... It is up to America to abandon the ground [the struggle between master and slave] on which world history has hitherto been enacted."[103]

Hegel rejected the negative perspective on the state originated by Hobbes and Locke, and their followers. Adherents of this English viewpoint mocked the American revolutionary conception of government as the means to bring about human fulfilment.

> To imagine that freedom is such that the individual subject, in its coexistence with other subjects, must limit its freedom in such a way that this collective restriction, the mutual constraint of all, leaves everyone a

> limited area in which to act as he pleases, is to interpret freedom in purely negative terms; on the contrary, justice, ethical life, and the state, and these alone, are the positive realisation and satisfaction of freedom. The random inclinations of individuals are not the same thing as freedom. That kind of freedom on which restrictions are imposed is mere arbitrariness, which exists solely in relation to particular needs.[104]

For Hegel, "the real state is animated by [the national spirit] in all its particular transactions, wars, institutions, etc."[105] The spiritual content of the state ("life, liberty, and the pursuit of happiness" as the founders of the American revolutionary state themselves wrote in the Declaration of Independence[106]) "is the sacred bond which links men and spirits together. It remains one and the same life, one great object, one great end, and one great content, on which all private happiness and all private volition depend."[107]

Hegel's philosophy has for too long been considered mostly in light of the (failed) French Revolution. We need to see Hegel from the viewpoint of vast changes set in motion by the American Revolution. The ramifications of this perspective will be felt, I would speculate, not only in further studies of Hegel's political writings but in all facets of his thought. Even though the names of American revolutionaries hardly appear in his surviving work, Hegel, no less than his younger friend Friedrich List, was aware of "the souls of warlike men, who rise in silent night / Washington, Franklin, Paine & Warren, Gates, Hancock & Green."[108] Harris informs us that Hegel once considered drafting revolutionary pamphlets along the lines of J.J. Cart's tract on the revolutionary upheaval in the Vaud.[109] In a sense, we already have these radical pamphlets informed by the great figures and events of the American Revolution, though they are in the form of the *Phenomenology of Spirit, Philosophy of Right*, the *Science of Logic*, and other works of Hegel's maturity.

NOTES

1 This chapter is dedicated to H.S. Harris's groundbreaking work, "The Social Ideal of Hegel's Economic Theory," in *Selected Essays on G.W.F. Hegel*, ed. Lawrence S. Stepelevich (New Jersey: Humanities, 1993), from which the epigraph is drawn (187). Harris's work on the political context of Hegel's thought is a key inspiration of this chapter.

2 Writes Gunther Chaloupek, "It is hardly ever mentioned that it was List who encouraged Hegel to relaunch his essay [on the constitution of Wurttemberg] which first appeared in the *Heidelberger Jahrbucher* as a separate publication." "Friedrich List on Local Autonomy in His Contributions to the Debate about the Constitution of Württemberg in 1816/17," in *Two Centuries of Local Autonomy*, ed. Jurgen Georg Backhaus (New York: Springer, 2012), 8. Chaloupek cites Friedrich Lenz, *Friedrich List: Der Mann und das Werk* (Munich: Verlag Von R. Oldenbourg, 1936).

3 Robert V. Remini, *Henry Clay: Statesman for the Union* (New York: W.W. Norton, 1991), 174.

4 Ralph Waldo Emerson, "Emerson's Concord Hymn," National Park Service, http://www.nps.gov/mima/historyculture/index.htm.

5 H.S. Harris, *Hegel's Development: Towards the Sunlight, 1770–1801* (Oxford: Clarendon, 1972), 535, 544.

6 James Doull, "The Philosophical Basis of Constitutional Discussion in Canada," *Animus* 2 (1997), http://www2.swgc.mun.ca/Animus/Articles/Volume%202/doull1.pdf.

Peddle and Robertson suggest that Hegel did not deal with the United States, because for him "North America could only be 'the land of the future.'" David G. Peddle and Neil G. Robertson, eds., *Philosophy and Freedom: The Legacy of James Doull* (Toronto: University of Toronto Press, 2003), xxii. The notion that the United States held considerable promise for future development was widespread in Germany, as elsewhere in Hegel's time. It was certainly Goethe's opinion, for example, but this did not prevent the great German poet from saying a great deal about America (see below).

7 Gordon Wood, *The Idea of America: Reflections on the Birth of the United States* (New York: Penguin Group, 2011).

8 Progressives suggested that radical elements pushed America toward revolution but then lost control to conservative aristocratic and business interests. From this viewpoint, gradual change following the Revolution favoured the agrarian majority and eventually turned America into a land of "the common man."

9 See David MacGregor, *Hegel and Marx after the Fall of Communism*, 2nd ed. (Cardiff: University of Wales Press, 2014), 63–88. The perspective of consensus historians is taken for granted in my discussion of Paine and Hegel in this book. Interestingly, Doull quotes Paine on the English constitutional monarchy in order to illustrate Hegel's views on the excesses of privilege and tradition. James Doull, "Hegel and Contemporary Liberalism, Anarchism and Socialism: A Defense of the Rechtphilosophie

against Marx and His Contemporary Followers," in *The Legacy of Hegel*, ed. J.J. O'Malley, K.W. Agozin, H.P. Kainz, and L.C. Rice (The Hague: Martinus Nijhoff, 1973), 240.

10 "The Revolution not only radically changed the personal and social relationships of people, including the position of women, but also destroyed aristocracy as it had been understood in the Western world for at least two millennia." Gordon Wood, *The Radicalism of the American Revolution* (New York: A.A. Knopf, 1992), 6.

11 See, for example, Michael Lind, *Land of Promise: An Economic History of the United States* (New York: HarperCollins Books, 2012), 47.

12 Ron Chernow, *Alexander Hamilton* (New York: Penguin Books, 2004), 7.

13 Ron Chernow, *Washington: A Life* (New York: Penguin Books, 2010), 184, 715.

14 William Blake, "America: A Prophesy," in *The Complete Poetry and Prose of William Blake*, ed. David Erdman, 2nd ed. (Berkeley: University of California Press, 2008), 52.

15 G.W.F. Hegel, "The German Constitution," in *Hegel's Political Writings*, trans. T.M. Knox, intro. by Z.A. Pelczynski (Oxford: Oxford University Press, 1964), 207.

16 Gordon Wood, *The Radicalism of the American Revolution* (New York: Knopf Doubleday Publishing Group, 1992), 6.

17 They were, observes Doull, "from the first conscious that they attempted something new, and of consequence for the human race: there began with their independence a *'novus ordo saeclorum.'*" "Philosophical Basis of Constitutional Discussion," 142.

18 Blake, "America," 59.

19 Harold Jantz, "America and the Younger Goethe," *MLN* 97, no. 3 German issue (April 1982): 530.

20 On the close relationship between Hegel, Schiller, and Goethe, see H.S. Harris, *Hegel's Development: Night Thoughts (1801–1806)* (Oxford: Oxford University Press, 1983), xxiv.

21 "There was a … [pro-American] vein in Goethe, if we may take the sentiments he ascribes to Wilhelm Meister as his own … [He] too, saw a vision of America as a land better off than old Europe, only to conclude that such ideas were a dream, and that the world of the here-and-now was the best to be hoped for – *Hier oder nirgends ist Amerika*. Goethe's other famous lines on America – *Amerika, du hast es besser Als unser Continent, das Alte* – were not written until his extreme old age, in 1827." R.R. Palmer, *The Age of the Democratic Revolution: A Political History of Europe and America, 1760–1800. The Challenge* (Princeton, NJ: Princeton University Press, 1959), 257.

22 I owe this phrase to an anonymous reviewer for University of Toronto Press.
23 S.S. Prawer, *Frankenstein's Island: England and the English in the Writings of Heinrich Heine* (Cambridge: Cambridge University Press, 1986), 153.
24 Arno Mong Daastol offers a brief, valuable comparison of the two in his PhD thesis, "Friedrich List's Heart, Wit and Will: Mental Capital as the Productive Force of Progress" (University of Erfurt, 2011), http://www.academia.edu/8405129/Friedrich_List_s_Heart_Wit_and_Will_Mental_Capital_as_the_Productive_Force_of_Progress, 294–300.
25 Karl Löwith, *Hegel to Nietzsche: The Revolution in Nineteenth-Century Thought*, trans. David E. Green (Garden City, NY: Anchor Books, 1967), 132–3. See also Roman Szporluk, *Communism and Nationalism: Karl Marx and Friedrich List* (New York: Oxford University Press, 1988), 11.
26 Ibid., 134.
27 Ibid.
28 See, for example, Ha-Joon Chang, *Bad Samaritans* (London: Bloomsbury, 2009).
29 Keith Tribe, "Friedrich List and the Critique of 'Cosmopolitical Economy,'" *Manchester School* 56, no. 1 (March 1988): 26.
30 Lenz, *Friedrich List*, 20–1.
31 W.O. Henderson, *Friedrich List: Economist and Visionary 1789–1846* (London: Frank Cass, 1983), 20.
32 Ibid., 15–16.
33 Harris, *Hegel's Development*, 432. Forster died in Paris in 1794 at the age of forty; at that time, Paine was also in Paris – occupying a prison cell and awaiting the guillotine. Hegel annotated Forster's work on the French Revolution in 1793 while working as a tutor in Berne. Forster violently opposed Edmund Burke's interpretation of the French events. Domenico Losurdo, *Hegel and the Freedom of Moderns*, trans. Marella and Jon Morris (Durham, NC: Duke University Press, 2004), 303.
34 Henderson, *Friedrich List*, 16.
35 Chaloupek, "Friedrich List on Local Autonomy," 3–4.
36 Lenz, *Friedrich List*, 31.
37 Z.A. Pelczynski, "Part I: An Introductory Essay," in *Hegel's Political Writings*, 19. See also Brady Bowman and Allen Speight, "Introduction," *Georg Wilhelm Friedrich Hegel: Heidelberg Writings*, trans. and ed. Brady Bowman and Allen Speight (Cambridge: Cambridge University Press, 2009), xx.
38 David MacGregor, *The Communist Ideal in Hegel and Marx* (Toronto: University of Toronto Press, 1984).

39 Hegel began his lectures in Heidelberg on the *Philosophy of Right* in 1817, and List likely was aware of those lectures.
40 Lenz, *Friedrich List*, 23.
41 Margaret Esther Hirst, *Life of Friedrich List and Selections from His Writings* (New York: Charles Scribner's Sons, 1909), 9.
42 Pelczynski, "Part I," 19.
43 Chaloupek, "Friedrich List on Local Autonomy," 3–4.
44 Hegel, *Political Writings*, 281.
45 Henderson, *Friedrich List*, 17.
46 Hegel, *Political Writings*, 150.
47 Ibid., 206.
48 Ibid., 202.
49 Henderson, *Friedrich List*, 32.
50 Friedrich List, "Some Extracts from the Author's Preface to the First Edition," in *The National System of Political Economy*, trans. Sampson S. Lloyd (London: Longmans, Green, 1916), xl.
51 Henderson, *Friedrich List*, 54.
52 MacGregor, *Hegel and Marx after the Fall of Communism*, 102.
53 Parts of this chapter are drawn from the "Afterword," ibid.
54 Henderson, *Friedrich List*, 73.
55 Ibid., 78.
56 See Szporluk, *Communism and Nationalism*, 105–6.
57 Hirst, *Life of Friedrich List*, 12. As List recounts, tariff barriers between German states began to disintegrate with reforms in Prussia in 1818, and in Wurttemberg, Bavaria, and other states after 1820. List, *National System of Political Economy*, 109–10.
58 Ibid., 60.
59 Peddle and Robertson, *James Doull's Recent Political Thought*, 485, 487.
60 G.W.F. Hegel, *Political Writings*, ed. L. Dickey and H.B. Nisbet (Cambridge: Cambridge University Press, 1999), 198.
61 Also omitted in Hegel's essay was the French/German Deux Ponts (Zweibrucken) Regiment, "that fought on the American side with such distinction, on through the final encounters that led to the surrender of Cornwallis at Yorktown." Harold Jantz, "America and the Younger Goethe," 515.
62 Hegel, *Political Writings*, 199.
63 Prawer, *Frankenstein's Island*, 4.
64 Orc appears in Blake's "America" (51) as the passionate lover of revolution who wrests the American colonies from Albion's angel.
65 Hegel, *Political Writings*, 311.

66 Jonathan Sperber, *Karl Marx: A Nineteenth-Century Life* (London: Liveright Publishing, 2013), 82.

67 At the time of his initial conflict with List, Marx had no knowledge of economics. According to Engels, he did not begin investigations into this science until 1843. Friedrich Engels, "Preface," *Capital* (New York City: International Publishers, 1967), 2:89.

68 Following complaints in early January 1843 by the Russian czar to Prussia's ambassador to St Petersburg, the king of Prussia ordered closure of the Rheinische Zeitung. Francis Wheen, *Karl Marx: A Life* (New York City: W.W. Norton, 2001), 48; Boris Nicholaievsky and Otto Maenchen-Helfen, *Karl Marx: Man and Fighter* (London: Penguin, 1976), 59–65.

69 Nicholaievky and Maenchen-Helfen, *Karl Marx*, 53.

70 Hirst, *Life of Friedrich List*, 167–8.

71 Ha-Joon Chang, *Kicking Away the Ladder* (London: Anthem, 2002), 52–3.

72 Draft of an article on Friedrich List's *Das Nationale System der Politischen Oekonomie*, in *Karl Marx Frederick Engels Collected Works*, vol. 4, *Marx and Engels 1844–45* (London: Lawrence and Wishart, 1975), 265. Later a confirmed enemy of List, the young Friedrich Engels vacillated on List's economic prescriptions for Germany. See Franz Mehring, *Karl Marx: The Story of His Life* (Ann Arbor: University of Michigan Press, 1962), 106, 130.

73 Lind, *Land of Progress*, 60. "North and South," writes Doull, "diverged further from each other with a rapid growth of manufacturing in the one, while the other drew its wealth in great part from the export of cotton grown by slave labour … The North required tariffs for the protection of its industries; tariffs against British goods threatened the export market for Southern cotton." Doull, *Philosophical Basis of Constitutional Discussion in Canada*, 416.

74 Friedrich List, "Some Extracts from the Author's Preface to the First Edition," in *National System of Political Economy*, lxi.

75 Henderson, *Friedrich List*, 108.

76 Ibid., 88.

77 George Armstrong Kelly, "Hegel's America," *Philosophy and Public Affairs* 2, no. 11 (Autumn 1972): 6. Despite these negative opening remarks, Kelly later offers that Hegel's political philosophy includes much that is relevant to modern America.

78 Löwith, *From Hegel to Nietzsche*, 42.

79 Harris, *Hagel's Development*, 423–4.

80 Ibid., 424.

81 For my account of Hegel's commentary on the English Reform Bill, see *Hegel, Marx and the English State* (Boulder, CO: Westview, 1992).

82 Pelczynski, Introduction to Hegel, *Political Writings*, 23.
83 Ibid., 24.
84 Ibid., 300.
85 Hegel, *Political Writings*, ed. Dickey and Nisbet, 236.
86 G.W.F. Hegel, *Lectures on the Philosophy of World History*, trans. H.B. Nisbet (New York: Cambridge University Press, 1975), 103.
87 See Erik Reinert and Arno M. Daastøl, "The Other Canon: The History of Renaissance Economics," in *Globalization, Economic Development and Inequality*, ed. Erik Reinert (Cheltenham, UK: Edward Elgar, 2004), 39.
88 G.W.F. Hegel, *Lectures on the History of Philosophy* (London: Routledge and Kegan Paul, 1968), 3:298, 313.
89 List, *National System of Political Economy*, vol. 2, *The Theory*, 6–7.
90 List, *National System of Political Economy*, vol. 1, *The History*, 100.
91 G.W.F. Hegel, *The Philosophy of Right*, ed. Allan Wood (Cambridge: Cambridge University Press, 1991), 226.
92 Engels, *Anti-Dühring: Herr Eugen Dührings Umwälzung der Wissenschaft* (Peking: Foreign Language, 1976), condemned List's critique of key figures within British political economy, including Smith and Ricardo.
93 Ibid., 295.
94 MacGregor, *Hegel, Marx and the English State*, 32.
95 Szporluk, *Communism and Nationalism*, 119.
96 Lenz, *Friedrich List*, 287. Translation by Marlo Alexandra Burks, PhD candidate in German Literature, Culture and Theory, University of Toronto.
97 MacGregor, *Hegel, Marx and the English State*, 1–2. I do not mention List's concept of imperialism in this book.
98 Hegel, *Philosophy of Right*, para. 340, 371.
99 Dumas Malone, *The Public Life of Thomas Cooper* (New Haven, CT: Yale University Press, 1926), 309–10.
100 Hirst, *Life of Friedrich List*, 240.
101 Hegel, *Lectures on the Philosophy of World History*, 169.
102 Hirst, *Life of Friedrich List*, 207.
103 Hegel, *Lectures on the Philosophy of World History*, 172–3. "America" at various points in Hegel's reflections on the New World in the philosophy of world history sometimes refers to both South America and North America (including the United States and Canada) and sometimes only to the United States. Hegel may have cultivated a deliberate ambiguity in this passage. The notion of a war between "North [America] and South America" – one possible interpretation of this passage – hardly makes any sense in this context. However, starting with the 1820 dispute

over admission of Missouri (a slave state) into the Union, "the strained relations between the American provinces" contained the germ that would later erupt into civil war between North and South.

104 Hegel, *Lectures on the Philosophy of World History*, 94.

105 Ibid., 97.

106 See Danielle Allen, *Our Declaration: A Reading of the Declaration of Independence in Defense of Equality* (New York: Liveright Publishing, 2014), 153.

107 Hegel, *Lectures on the Philosophy of World History*, 97.

108 Blake, "America," 52.

109 Harris, *Hegel's Development: Towards the Sunlight*, 418.

12 Freedom and the Tradition: George Grant, James Doull, and the Character of Modernity

NEIL G. ROBERTSON

With the publication in 1965 of *Lament for a Nation* George Grant initiated a national debate about the nature, indeed the very reality, of Canada. Grant's own standpoint was captured succinctly in the subtitle to that book: "The Defeat of Canadian Nationalism." While it was the defeat of Diefenbaker's government in 1963 that clarified for Grant the desire of Canadians to give up their independence from the United States, the causes that he pointed to lay deeper than any particular political event. For Grant, the sources of Canada's demise lay in the forces at work in modernity and its expression in technology: the noble folly of Canadian nationalism lay in its belief that a more stable, conservative society could exist on the borders of the United States, the nation that more than any other embodied this technological modernity.

In April 1965, George Grant's friend and former colleague James Doull wrote to him about the newly published work: "Your book is as exasperating as it is brilliant. The worst is that you, incapable as any could be of inaction and mere lament, encourage Canadians to give up the battle before it has been fought."[1] Three years later Doull wrote again to Grant, now expressing how some of their difference over Canada had affected their friendship: "Sometimes I have spoken or written harshly about your attachment to Upper Canadian conservatism, not evidently without giving offence I had not intended. What moved my comments was that you know young Canadians, can speak to them as no other: that this being so, you did not speak a little more hopefully to them – did not prepare them to resist a little more strongly absorption into the American Empire. For my part, I can only act as though resistance makes some sense."[2] Doull would go on to refer to Grant's *Lament for a Nation* at a number of points in his own continuing reflections on

Canada. For example, in 1983, in an article published in a Festschrift for Grant, Doull again suggests that Grant is mistaken in his lament and by contrast argues for the possibility of a distinctive and independent Canada; even in the 1990s, after Grant's death, Doull is moved to distinguish his position from Grant's and suggest the insufficiency of Grant's account of Canada.[3]

This disagreement about the fate of Canada points to and opens up a set of deeper disagreements between Doull and Grant: the nature of the state, the essence of technology, the character of modernity, and the relation of God to history. If one wanted to sum up these disagreements in a phrase, it was a disagreement about the truth of the Hegelian philosophy. However, Grant and Doull did not always have this disagreement. Though Doull and Grant's friendship predates Doull's own immersion in the Hegelian philosophy, according to Grant, it was he who introduced Grant to Hegel, with such success that Grant was able to say concerning his first book, *Philosophy in the Mass Age* (1959),

> At the theoretical level, I considered Hegel the greatest of all philosophers. He had partaken of all that was true and beautiful and good in the Greek world and was able to synthesize it with Christianity and with the freedom of the enlightenment and modern science. It cannot be insisted too often how hard it is for anyone who believes the western Christian doctrine of providence to avoid reaching the conclusion that Hegel has understood the implications of that doctrine better than any other thinker. I therefore attempted to write down in non-professional language the substance of the vision that the age of reason was beginning to dawn and first in North America.[4]

However, by the time *Lament for a Nation* came to be written, Grant had broken his attachment to Hegel, and indeed came in that work to define his own position in opposition to that of Hegel.[5] Grant's Hegelian-based hopes for the dawning of a new age in North America had turned to lamentation for the death of an independent Canada. Doull never shared Grant's rejection of Hegel nor his turn to resignation at the fate of a vanishing Canada.

In this chapter, I want to leave to one side the question of whether Grant's Hegel was the same as Doull's Hegel (and if they differ, which is a truer reflection of the historical Hegel), and I also wish to leave aside the exact extent of Grant's "Hegelianism" during the 1950s.[6] That is, while there is clearly a biographical context for a consideration of what distinguishes Grant's from Doull's position, it is to the substance of the thought of these two Canadian thinkers that I wish to turn, for it is here we can enter into a debate of a more universal concern. It can appear that Grant's passing Hegelianism is indeed only of biographical concern; and yet, that he came to his later position through a rejection of Hegel is not without consequences for the shape and scope of that position: Grant came to see as an implication of his mature position, the need to turn from the whole Western Christian standpoint, which he saw expounded most fully in the thought of Hegel.[7] However, rather than turn directly to Doull's and Grant's differing assessments of the Hegelian philosophy, a more approachable way into the substance of their disagreement might be to return to the question of Canada. For what distinguished Grant's position from Doull's was not simply a factual question – was Canada over or not? – but a substantive question: what is Canada? For both Doull and Grant (and this is a testimony to the depth and thoroughness of both thinkers) their whole philosophical reflections were drawn into this question.

Grant and Doull on Canada

In *Lament for a Nation,* Grant argues that "to be a Canadian was to build, along with the French, a more ordered and stable society than the liberal experiment in the United States."[8] Canada was, for Grant, an inherently conservative society, and one built upon a rejection of the United States and its directly humanistic individualism. Through Canada's relation to Britain and France, a connection was maintained with a culture that preceded what Grant called "the age of progress." For Grant, this meant that English and French Canada sought to keep open through their institutions – above all their institutions of higher learning, but also their political forms, their sense of what the economy was for, and the place of religion in society – a connection to the premodern cultures of Jerusalem and Athens that saw human life in terms of purpose and goodness and not simply humanly enacted values and the individualistic pursuit of them.[9] For Grant, a relation to the Good, a sense of one's creatureliness and fellow-creatureliness, belonged to this older European tradition with which Canada sought to keep in contact.

The decision to build a nation more stable and less given to the illusions of modernity than was the case in the United States was a noble one, but, according to Grant, one born for failure. The British connection (and in Quebec's case, the French connection) was vital not because of its specific ethnic characteristic but because it was the only living connection Canadians had collectively and institutionally with this older European conception of society. Thus for Grant, the failing of this connection, the decision of Liberal politicians to weaken rather than strengthen it, was equivalent to the end of Canada. Grant combines here a sense of *fate* – that Canada could not hope in the face of the dynamism and sheer massiveness of American modernity to be able to sustain this connection – with a sense of *betrayal*, that specific politicians and specific social groups acted, even underhandedly and manipulatively, to break this British connection.[10] For Grant these two moments of fate and betrayal came together in the defeat of John Diefenbaker in 1963: the slick and ambitious in Canada's metropolitan centres turned against this apotheosis of pure loyalty, used his personal follies and weaknesses to ridicule his great and specifically Canadian virtue of loyalty – the attachment to the given, to one's own. When Canadians turned their backs on their own, their loyalty to the connection with an older European sense of stability, they gave up, except in name, all that distinguished them from the United States.[11]

For Grant the failure of Canada cannot be seen as merely the failure of a small cultural experiment: rather, that failure is emblematic of the truth of modernity, the very vanishing of older, more sustaining forms: "The impossibility of conservatism in our age is the impossibility of Canada. As Canadians we attempted a ridiculous task in trying to build a conservative nation in the age of progress, on a continent we share with the most dynamic nation on earth."[12] And so Grant tells us, "The confused strivings of politicians, businessmen and civil servants cannot alone account for Canada's collapse. This stems from the very character of the modern era."[13] The unravelling of Canada was the unravelling of the contradiction of conservatism in the modern age: Canada sought in its institutions both to retain a relation to the traditions of Jerusalem and Athens and, at the same time, to release and support its citizens in the pursuit of a modern dynamic society. The modern technological state in which, according to Grant, "no appeal to human good, now or in the future, must be allowed to limit [individuals'] freedom to make the world as they choose"[14] was clearly incompatible with the desire of Canada's founders to "build a society in which the right of the common good restrains the freedom of the individual."[15] Canada was caught between attachment to older forms through the British and French traditions received from Europe, and participation in modernity in terms not only of the overwhelming presence of the United States, but also of the inherent corruption of the British and French traditions insofar as they were already modern. In contrast to Doull, what Grant denied was that tradition and modernity, community and technology, could actually be united. The impossibility of this meant that, in Grant's eyes, Canada was a contradiction waiting to unravel; the defeat of Diefenbaker was merely the manifestation of this having, in fact, occurred.

According to Doull, however, Canada is not established in its difference from the United States by an attachment to a conservative tradition. Doull does not deny that such a conservatism and attachment have been part of Canada's history and were vital to Canadian founders, both English and French: however, he argues that such a difference is passive and indefinite, making Canada's independence rest upon the external and – as it turned out – unstable realities of the British Empire and the Tridentine Catholic Church. Indeed, according to Doull, Grant may be right to lament, but his lamentation is not properly of Canada but of a specific British connection to Canada that Grant by education and family tradition saw as equivalent to Canada itself: "Professor Grant calls his lament 'the failure of a nation.' There is much confusion in his use of the word 'nation.' What has failed in his account is British America. The failure Professor Grant speaks of is of the effort to establish British culture directly in Canada from above through higher education and the arts. It would be better described as the failure of colonialism."[16]

Doull agrees with Grant that the quiet revolutions of both Quebec and English Canada in the period after the Second World War destroyed the older forms of Canadian self-definition, but he thought this a positive development and not to be equated with absorption into American culture. For Doull, the death of loyalist Canadian culture is not to be equated with the death of Canada itself. He sees it, rather, as a moment necessary for any possibility of real self-definition and independence on the part of Canadians. In his reaction to Grant's lament, Doull was by no means blind to the possibility that Canada could exchange colonialism to the United States for that to Britain, but he saw it as being in no way a necessity. This judgment was the source of Doull's opposition to Grant's stance: he saw Grant's fatalism as contributing to, rather than resisting, any tendency to absorption into American culture.

Doull argues that Canada's independence from the United States rests not upon certain qualitative measures (such as "traditional" versus "technological"), but upon a substantial difference. Doull wants to press more firmly Grant's own point that Canada is distinguished from the United States in its history and its institutions by arguing that, if this difference is real, it cannot be a simply passively received difference, a difference resting on a colonial attachment to Europe. Rather, the demand is that Canadians appropriate these institutional and cultural forms as their own. Indeed Doull would contend that from the beginning, even in their colonialism, Canadians transformed what they received. As Doull once put it, "The mere continuance of the old and customary has no power to educate, but can only impart an external order to the savagery of the natural will."[17] Thus for Doull, the demand for Canada is that it come to define itself, not principally through either Europe or the United States (though these are undoubtedly elements of Canada's self-definition), but through itself, and so bring these elements, and others, into a concrete relation. That is, Doull's contention is that Canada is substantial or real in its history and institutions and so is capable of relating and integrating seemingly opposed qualitative distinctions. On Doull's account, then, Canada is not – or at least need not be – a confusion or mixture of technology and tradition, but rather a certain form of the unity of the two.

It was a contention throughout Doull's intellectual career, resting – as we shall see – upon his larger Hegelian standpoint, that Canada should not be consigned, as Grant claimed, to a fatal dissolution. What especially distinguishes Doull's political thought in the last decade and a half of his life (coincidentally, approximately from the death of Grant) is a clarification of his grounds for upholding his confidence in Canada as a sovereign state. Central to this clarification was a re-evaluation of the United States.

For a long time Doull shared Grant's view that the United States was a technological empire. In the 1960s, 1970s, and much of the 1980s, Doull saw in the United States a technological naturalism liberated from the rationality and constraint of its older Enlightenment constitution: "In place of the older order, one had come to assume in the later nineteenth century a naturalism and against it an abstract moralistic idealism. Marx and the socialists would draw these elements into one view: the free natural individuality they proposed combined these elements. Such in general is the technological culture of the present time. In the United States, where it occurs in its purest and simplest form, it is commonly assumed that technology and a free naturalistic individuality can sustain each other."[18]

Certainly the New Deal and the emergence of the welfare-consumer state in America led Doull, as well as Grant, to see in the United States the most complete embodiment of technology. So long as Doull held to this view, his account of Canada as at least implicitly beyond the opposition of technology and tradition was hard to justify: why should Canada escape the corruption and revolution besetting the rest of the Western world? Grant's assessment that what remained of Canada's sense of its difference from the United States rested on a residual traditionalism that was at least as plausible.

By the late 1980s, however, Doull broke with this account of the United States, and in doing so, reconfigured his account of Canada and of the possibilities of the contemporary period. In a lecture Doull gave in 1992, he contrasted this new account to Grant's position in *Lament for a Nation*:

> Some years ago George Grant in a well-known book lamented the demise of Canada; a Canadian nation, betrayed by politicians, had fallen prey to the great technological empire to the south. But in truth neither was Canada a nation nor … is the United States rightly defined as a centre of "global technology." What then were we to lament? George Grant grew up in the ruins of Victorian culture in Ontario and Heidegger was for him a principal interpreter of the culture which took its place. *Amicus Plato, sed magis amica veritas*. The effect on Canadians of this twofold relation to the Old World has been to make possible the question, what are we as a North American people, whose freedom and its political articulation has a different basis than for Europeans?[19]

Doull's reconsideration of the United States and regrounding of his hopes for Canada lay in his recognition of what he came to call "North American freedom."[20] This freedom belongs to and defines the character of the "post-national," federal states of North America. It is necessary to the understanding of Doull's fully developed account of Canada and its contrast to Grant's to see more clearly his conception of North American freedom. Doull's claim is that North American freedom can be put on the side of neither technology nor of tradition. Rather it encompasses and integrates both sides: in North American freedom, Jerusalem and Athens come together with modernity. However, before we can make sense of Doull's account of North American freedom it is necessary that we explore in more detail the character of technology and its relation to modernity. As is clear already, for Grant, technology is at the very centre of the modern, and it is technology that renders conservatism (and, in turn, Canada) impossible. If Doull's account of

Canada and of North American freedom is to have any plausibility, it must confront Grant's analysis of technology and modernity.

Technology and Modernity

While it is possible to contrast Grant's and Doull's considerations of Canada in terms of lamentation and hope respectively, it is important to see that their differences are more deeply rooted than the emotional or subjective and that their disagreement is of wider than simply biographical interest. Nor is it sufficient to say that Doull's response is that of a naive liberalism or modernity, or Grant's of a narrow traditionalism. It cannot be said that Doull does not recognize the "technological" and its power to annihilate an apprehension of those sources upheld in the traditions of Jerusalem and Athens. Nor can it be said that Grant does not see the powerful appeal, and, indeed, claims to justice and legitimacy of the technological. Rather, the contrast between Doull and Grant is in a different assessment of the character and origins of "technology" and its relation to modernity.

According to both Grant and Doull, the fundamental question of the contemporary is posed by the presence of technology. And according to both thinkers, technology is not to be understood simply as the devices before us, nor as the science that gave rise to those devices, nor even as the various developments in moral, political, and religious thought that made possible the coming to be of those sciences. Deeper than these levels is the characterization of technology as a mode of being, what Heidegger characterizes as an ontology. Doull and Grant agree that the standpoint of technology involves a break with the European tradition of contemplation and a rise to the eternal. For both, technology is the assertion of a radical, "this-worldly" mastering of nature and humanity that is essentially atheistic and destructive of the givenness of all traditional forms.

What principally distinguishes Doull's accounts from Grant's here is that Grant takes technology so understood as a complete or comprehensive ontology, while Doull, though acknowledging the profound contemporary experience of technology as ontological, would question this status. That is, Doull fully accepts that the contemporary era encounters technology as the underlying standpoint that shapes all encounters with the world, that is, as an ontology. However, Doull also asserts that a deeper and historically informed analysis reveals this ontological experience to be, in fact, historically constructed or mediated. What we contemporaries experience as an all-pervasive immediate ontology, is, in truth, a mediated relation. In short, Doull does not so much reject Grant's account of technology and its fundamental role in shaping the contemporary, as he does seek to place it in a larger context that frees our understanding of the contemporary from the apparent fatality of technology that Grant perceives. In Grant's view, Doull's claims fail adequately to grasp the inner nature of technology, and assert an Hegelian standpoint that makes the impossible claim to mediate technological ontology and the ontology of ancient and Christian accounts. To assess the relative merits of Grant and Doull's claims, it is necessary to consider in more detail their respective enucleations of technology.

The experience of the society he lived in as "technological" was fundamental to Grant's thinking throughout his life. The titles of a number of his writings bear simple testimony to this fact. For the purposes of this brief exploration of Grant's account of technology it is useful to divide the development of his thinking, after his break with Hegel in the early 1960s, into two stages. The first stage comprises most of the 1960s when his thinking about technology was principally guided by Jacques Ellul and Leo Strauss. The second stage began in the late 1960s with his encounter with the writings of Nietzsche and Heidegger. It should be said that underlying these developments there was a common structure to his thinking about technology, and one that relates him to a set of contemporary thinkers. Like Heidegger, Nietzsche, and Strauss, but also like figures such as Karl Löwith, Etienne Gilson, and Alasdair MacIntyre, Grant argues that technological modernity is nihilistic, and that this nihilism reveals a suppressed, forgotten, or overlooked principle that we can now recover through a return to an older tradition or standpoint refused by modernity, but nonetheless presupposed by it. For Heidegger or Nietzsche, this return was to the pre-Socratics: for Löwith, it was to the Stoics; for Strauss, to Plato; and for Gilson and MacIntyre, to Aquinas. In Grant's case the return is to a Christian Platonism, especially as expounded in the writings of Simone Weil. This basic structure – the nihilism of technology and the corresponding return to a hidden Christian-Platonic standpoint – remains constant in Grant, once he broke with the thought of Hegel. What develops in his thinking is a deepening of the two sides: a deepening that involves a growing clarity about the irreconcilability of technology with Christian-Platonism.

Grant began his account of this division through the work of Ellul and Strauss. What they taught Grant was to see the contemporary world, especially North America, as fundamentally given over to a civilizational order incompatible with ancient or Christian accounts of virtue or piety. Grant had learned from Strauss that, built into all forms of modernity is a certain dynamic leading to the "universal and homogeneous state." Grant agreed with Strauss that the universal and homogeneous state that both liberalism and Marxism pursued would result, not in a liberated humanity released from all former limits and structures of oppression, but in a total tyranny inherently obstructive of all forms of higher life – religion, philosophy, and so on. Grant, however, disagreed with Strauss's assertion that the most completely modern forms were to be found in the second and third waves – those he associated with communism and national socialism respectively. Strauss made fundamental the level of the political order and the ideology underlying that order. At that level Grant agreed that communism and national socialism represented more "advanced" forms of modernity. But for Grant (and here he drew on Ellul), the actual dynamic of modernity, what underlay and informed its civilizational hold upon the world, was not at the level of political thought so much as at the level of "technology." For Grant, the best way to characterize the contemporary was, in Ellul's phrase, as a "technological society." The principle articulated in this society is "the conquest of human and non-human nature."[21]

When the dynamic of modernity is understood in terms of the conquest of human and non-human nature, the analysis of the contemporary world is importantly reconfigured. According to Strauss, but also according to Marxist analysis, communist regimes informed by the more developed thinking of figures from Rousseau to Marx are more modern than a regime such as the United States, informed by the earlier thought of Hobbes and Locke that emphasized natural rights. However, in pointing to the deeper role of technology, Grant suggests that in fact American liberalism is the more modern form – not because it is a more advanced form politically, but because it is less developed and more pragmatic at the level of political thought, and is thus, ironically, more permissive of the unconstrained unfolding of technological dynamism: "Liberalism is, then, the faith that can understand progress as an extension into the unlimited possibility of the future. It does this much better than Marxism, which still blocks progress by its old-fashioned ideas of the perfectibility of man."[22] In liberalism the dynamic modern account of man's essence as freedom is allowed untrammelled development.[23]

The implication of Grant's analysis of the role of technology as the dynamo of modernity is the recognition of the United States as the centre of modernity. This is obviously going to be a vital point when we turn to Grant's account of the impossibility of Canada. But here what is worth noting is that Grant sees that the United States is inherently imperialistic precisely because of its technological character. American imperialism, however, while sharing many similarities with traditional European imperialism, is distinctive in its fundamentally technological character. American imperialism is not primarily realized through conquest and colonial expansion, as were the older European empires; rather it is accomplished by the willing or coerced accession of other peoples and civilizations to the expansion of technological civilization. For Grant, in the 1960s, the clearest expression of American technological imperialism was the Vietnam War. As Grant put it, there the Americans were willing to commit genocide rather than allow the Vietnamese to stand apart from the American liberal technological empire.

What the reading of Nietzsche and Heidegger brought to Grant was not so much a revision of his earlier conception of technology, as a deepening of that conception. One way to refer to the account Grant held of technology while he was writing *Lament for a Nation* was that it was fundamentally a "civilizational" account. Technology was, centrally, a certain civilizational form given over to the mastery of human and non-human nature. Following *Lament*, Grant's reading of Nietzsche and Heidegger allowed him to see the ground of this civilization as "ontological." What makes technology so enveloping and fateful is that it enfolds the very fundamental ways of our thinking and being:

> To put the matter crudely; when we represent technology to ourselves through its common sense we think of ourselves as picking and choosing in a supermarket, rather than within the analogy of a package deal. We have bought a package deal of far more fundamental novelness than simply a set of instruments under our control. It is a destiny which enfolds us in its own conceptions of instrumentality, neutrality and purposiveness. It is in this sense that it has been truthfully said: technology is the ontology of the age. Western peoples (and perhaps soon all peoples) take themselves as subjects confronting otherness as objects – objects lying as raw material at the disposal of knowing and making subjects. Unless we comprehend the package deal we obscure from ourselves the central difficulty in our present destiny: we apprehend our destiny by forms of thought which are themselves the very core of the destiny.[24]

How this ontology of technology came to be is a real question for Grant. Precisely because it is nihilistic and historically specific, technology cannot be seen as belonging simply to the nature of things: but neither can it, as ontological, be attributed to a self-conscious human agency. The ontology of technology arises specifically out of the historical development of the West, but not as willed or consciously constructed. In this sense the origins of technology are inherently obscure. Certainly modernity is, for Grant, through and through technological. But the roots of technology lie deeper than modernity, which Grant argues (with Heidegger) presupposes technological ontology rather than initiates it. Grant points to these deeper roots in a late essay:

> I do not mean by "technology" the sum of all modern techniques, but that unique co-penetration of knowing and making, of the arts and sciences which originated in Western Europe and has now become worldwide. Behind such descriptions lies the fact that "technology" is an affirmation concerning what is; it remains unfathomed, but is very closely interwoven with that primal affirmation made by medieval Westerners as they accepted their Christianity in a new set of apperceptions. That affirmation had something to do with a new content given by Western people to the activity of "willing." "Technology" is the closest, yet inadequate word for what that new affirmation has become as it is now worked out in us and around us.[25]

What Grant chiefly learned from reading Nietzsche was that the heart of technological ontology was what Nietzsche characterized as the will-to-power: a will to mastery, a will to more free and creative willing in which all otherness or givenness is reduced to being but a moment of the will. As the above quotation suggests, Grant saw the roots of this pure willing in the Western Augustinian turn to the will. It is in reaction to this development of the Western tradition that Grant turns to a Christian Platonism more consonant – in his eyes – with the Eastern development of Christianity.[26] What this non-Western tradition preserved was a sense of the Good or God as participatively, but not wilfully, present in the world. God and the order of creation, especially the order of justice, were present in the very being of the world, not through a self-active will – whether divine or human. All of this is clearly related to Grant's break with the Hegelian account of history as God's activity.

The centrality of the will in the West, Grant suggests, is ultimately generative of the standpoint of technology, of an ontology of the will to power that necessarily, as Grant puts it, "has meant for all of us a very dimming of our ability to think justice lucidly."[27] What Nietzsche clarified, above all, for Grant was that the ontology of technology was inherently incompatible with the ancient accounts of justice and the Good: "Nietzsche's writings may be singled out as a Rubicon, because more than a hundred years ago he laid down with incomparable lucidity that which is now publicly open: what is given about the whole in technological science cannot be thought together with what is given us concerning justice and truth, reverence and beauty, from our tradition."[28] In the older account, there is an order "we do not measure and define, but by which we are measured and defined."[29] The standpoint of technology necessarily must elide this order: the very possibility of a self-active will requires a break from the given order. The very being of technology, of modernity, of a self-contained secularity can only be ontologically established by a negating or occluding of the order of what is. For Grant the very nihilism that is manifested in pure technological willing brings to light the negativity present in the very being of technology.

A crucial implication of the ontological character of technology is that it cannot be itself mastered or taken in hand or subordinated to higher human ends. All such efforts to get control of technology are themselves technological, not only in the obvious sense that one cannot master mastery, but in the more deep-seated sense that, for the contemporary person, the viable forms of moral and political thought that are supposed to give direction and purpose to technology are themselves implicated in technological modernity: "The result of this is that when we are deliberating in any practical situation our judgement acts rather like a mirror, which throws back the very metaphysics of the technology which we are supposed to be deliberating about in detail."[30] For Grant, the only possibility for getting "beyond" technology is, on the one hand, through the recollection of a pre-technological ethic evoked by those remnants of pre-modernity still present (this is Grant's conservatism) and, on the other hand, through the radicalizing of technological civilization to the point of its collapse from its own inner nihilism (here appears Grant's radicalism). What is crucial in this prognosis is that Grant's account of technology allows no mediation between technology and a humanly liveable order. As ontological, technology is corruptive of all efforts to humanize it by relating it to human ends. Technology must rather be allowed to fulfil its self-dissolution, purging the Western tradition of all voluntarism and opening us to a participatory and receptive relation to the divine.

For James Doull, Grant is right in characterizing technology as ontological – but only in a relative and conditional sense. Doull argues that technology in the ontological sense is not to be seen as modern or pre-modern in its origins – though he would certainly concede technology is not possible without the whole development of modernity. Rather, Doull argues that "technology" in the sense Grant intends is a nineteenth- and twentieth-century phenomenon. According to Doull, technology arises out of the corruption and later collapse of the nineteenth-century nation state. He argues that technology is in fact one aspect of a two-sided corruption of the nation state: the other side Doull speaks of as nationalism, existentialism, or fascism. Doull contends that technology is in truth an element of the nation state, but an element that takes itself to be self-complete and immediately actual. The other element, the existentialist or nationalist, suffers the same immediacy. In the nineteenth century, these two elements had their radical and revolutionary theorists, the most developed of whom were Marx, on the one side, and Nietzsche, on the other. Doull suggests the twentieth-century is where these elements take on a life of their own as the European nation state is destroyed in the trenches of the First World War. The history of twentieth-century Europe is a gradual development from the two elements assuming themselves to be self-constituted wholes in the forms of communism and fascism to the dissolution of this assumption to the point of the present European Union in which the two sides remain as irresolvable but restrained aspects of European life.[31]

What is crucial to grasp in Doull's analysis of technology is that he places technology in a wider context in which it can be seen not as the whole reality but as one element of a more comprehensive dialectic. There is alongside technology (to which it is necessarily related) the existential or nationalist aspect and which, for lack of a better term, I will call the "communitarian" aspect. The communitarian side of the contemporary, like the technological, takes on a variety of forms. Some of the anti-technological positions are religious and traditionalist, others more radical and revolutionary. However, according to Doull, they share a common logical and structural character informed through the relation to technology: to preserve a realm of being from the technological reduction, there is the need to uncover a principle whose being is beyond the technological. From Doull's perspective, then, Grant himself takes up just such an anti-technological account and so occupies a one-sided aspect of the contemporary. Grant thus dogmatically asserts the radical difference of technology from the standpoint that would recognize the Good and order of justice that informs the world. Now Doull would allow that this is a true perception, so long as one leaves undisturbed the immediate distinction of the forms in which the contemporary experiences itself. But it is Doull's argument that this assumption is misplaced. These forms that take themselves to be directly what they claim to be – and this is what it is to speak of them as ontological – are in fact dialectically related to one another and in three senses.

First, according to Doull, the two sides of the contemporary are in truth historically derived forms arising from the nation state where, so long as the nation state had life, they could be related and connected to one another. This took especially the form of the relation between civil society and the state, where universality and particularity were able to be concretely related and united. In the dissolved state of the twentieth century there tends to be either the collapse of the state into civil society in communism, socialism, or liberalism, and later in a global economy, or the separation of the two in nationalism, fascism, or Nazism and later in communitarianism. As Doull states,

> In their time the thought of Marx and Nietzsche was not of general interest. Both perceived the national political community in a partial and unbalanced way through one of its elements. With the decline of the national state their thought came into its own, since the decline is nothing else than that elements contained before in the whole came to have rather a life of their own. The assumption on which the independence and completion of the national state rested was that life and nature were capable of containing technology – that the concreteness of the Christian principle existed naturally in the state. The history of these communities has been rather the disintegration of these elements.[32]

Doull maintains that what each side of the contemporary takes as immediate, the free individuals of the technological society or the rooted individuals of the particular community, are, in truth, historical results that do not know themselves as such. Indeed, according to Doull, not only are the two sides results of the whole development of the nation state, but also the very immediacy that hides this history is itself a historical result. In his view, it belongs to the inadequately self-conscious character of the nineteenth-century nation state that it should so readily collapse at the point that it is fully developed into opposed forms.

There is a second sense in which there is an undisclosed dialectic at work in the relation of technology to community. Doull's claim is not only that the two sides share a common origin, but that, even in their claim to be self-grounded, they are in fact defined negatively through one another. The technological defines its activity relative to an anti-technological standpoint that resists the freedom of technological universality by holding, for "superstitious" reasons, to a particularity that can only be understood as oppressive and limiting. Equally the communitarian standpoint is drawn to a principle that is defined precisely in its being beyond the technological – whether this be Heideggerian Being, Straussian nature, or Gilsonian God. Further, the immediacy of the one side is precisely necessary to the self-grounding of the other side. Now in each case, the immediacy of the opposed standpoint turns out to be false: a false particularity or a false universality. For the technological will, the attachment to the particular is simply a negation of the universal and the attachment to what is in truth nothing. For the communitarian, the attachment to technology is a nihilism premised on negating rootedness and so is, in truth, the attachment to nothing. So long as these forms – the technological and the communitarian – stay in their distinction from one another, they can at best be alternately balanced, but not in truth related or reconciled. Doull argues that this describes the contemporary state of the European Union.[33]

This leads to the third form of dialectic that Doull points to: precisely because of the two earlier forms of dialectic, there is both the possibility and need to move beyond the contemporary opposition of the sides of technology and community, to an actual relating and uniting of the two sides. Not technology simply, but the relation of technology to community through the institutional order of the state, Doull took to be the question before the contemporary era: "The practical interest of the present age is transparently that science and technology be brought under universal will, and that individuals have their particular freedom explicitly and primarily therein – not through the blind conflict of aggressive wills."[34] By contrast with Grant, Doull contends that technology can and must be subordinated to human ends. He states,

> In antiquity Prometheus could be subdued and taught to live under the power of Zeus. But now he has captured the citadel of Zeus and founded technology on the sovereign right of the individual. The principle of the modern age is the unity of theoretical and practical. A more dangerous principle there could not be. But Hegel would, as before, see no other

> course than to awaken in men a clearer knowledge of this principle. Danger he would see to lie exactly in a seeming modesty which left open to human passions and false certainties to seduce reason and science from their natural end of serving humanity.[35]

For Doull, the course of the twentieth century in Europe, from the rise of fascism and communism where community and technology took themselves to be complete wholes and accrued to themselves the whole power of the state, through to the unstable relation of global technology and community in the European Union, there has been a coming to clarity that the truth that both sides of the contemporary are in themselves nothing. This result is already known, in Doull's eyes, in postmodernity, where the instability of both universal and particular is known in an all-dissolving scepticism. Doull sees postmodernity as the philosophy proper to the European Union. Thus, the nothingness that each side of the contemporary took to be the truth of the other side is found to be its own truth. But this is to suggest a purely negative result.

For Doull, this negative postmodern result is one aspect of the contemporary, that it comes to nothing in its effort to establish itself in itself. But equally for Doull, the contemporary is the fullness of the whole historical development. What Doull takes to be at work in the period between the Hegelian nation state and a return to the fullness of the historical development is not simply revolt, corruption, and denial. That is to say, the return to the lost content of the European nation state is not simply a return. The old nation states are, in Doull's eyes, gone for good. What the collapse of the older European order has accomplished is the liberation from received forms that can readily lose their actuality as forms of spirit. The contemporary has been, according to Doull, a painful education beyond the immediacies that the old Europeans fell prey to. Doull suggests, especially in his last political writings, that it belongs to North America, and its more directly universal and self-conscious forms of polity, to realize the returned dialectic that knows technology and community as aspects of one totality in a freer and more complete form than even the nation states that Hegel had before him.

But from Grant's perspective, Doull's claim can appear contradictory. On the one hand, Doull claims that the state – that is, the Hegelian concept of the state – can comprehend the difference between technology and community, and yet the historical realization of this in the nineteenth-century nation state was in fact unable to hold together these "elements" and suffered disintegration. Grant's argument is that, given the actually experienced division of technology and community, it is more compelling to see in technology a principle destructive of community, virtue, religion and life, than to suppose there can be a uniting of technology and community, freedom and virtue, secularity and religion. Doull insists that this sense of division is in fact the true experience of contemporary Europe and sees in Heidegger, especially, the most powerful and profound articulation of this experience. But what undergirds Doull's whole account are two claims: (1) that even in the division of technology and community the Idea of the State is still effective (this is what allows Doull to articulate a three-fold dialectic even in the very opposition of technology and community in contemporary life), and (2) that the nineteenth-century European state was only an immediate instantiation of the Idea, and its more universal and adequate realization is in the New World and especially the federations of North America.[36]

For Doull, North American states are to be differentiated from the European nation states because the North American states are founded explicitly on rational principles and have not been subject to a radical division between the Enlightenment principles of universal freedom and equality and attachment to a particular culture and language. As a result, whereas the European nation states suffered in the Second World War the virtual destruction of independent sovereignty and required a European Union to secure political life in the global technological economy, the states of North America are in principle beyond the nation state and not subject to its history. The United States is, for Doull, in his later political thought, the most well-developed example of North American freedom, a freedom that retains the concreteness that Hegel saw to belong to the nineteenth-century nation state, now realized in a more adequately universal and self-conscious form. This freedom can hold together as one reality what contemporary Europe assumes only in a divided form: technology and tradition, the particularity of community and the universality of rights and liberties. It belongs to these North American states that they are federations, capable of uniting and drawing into a common life a multicultural, multi-ethnic populace and yet able to retain local distinctions – and, in the case of Canada, even national differences.

It is this North American freedom that Doull suggests Grant does not sufficiently recognize. From Doull's perspective, Grant is still thinking in a European context when he puts on one side the "nation" of

British North America and on the other side the technological "empire" of the United States. Put in these terms, Doull would certainly allow that Grant's analysis is correct. Canada has experienced the dissolution of British North America and, equally, of French Catholic Quebec. But Doull's argument is that these terms are insufficient to the reality of Canada as a form of North American freedom. To get hold of Doull's argument, it is not enough to say that North American states, in contrast to the European nation states, escaped the direct destruction of institutions and culture wrought by the world wars – this is largely true of Great Britain also, especially if one finds, as Doull does, the imperial expansion of nineteenth-century Europe to be a corruption and not an essential aspect of those states. But Britain, as much as the other nations of the European Union, has found itself incapable of holding together technology and tradition. What is distinctive about North American forms is that they are post-nation states and, as such, are not technological empires that dissolve and destroy particularity and tradition. Rather, the federal structure of these states, their capacity to promote and uphold local differences, which are not at the same time simply frozen into external givenness of pure custom, points to a concreteness, a holding together of technology and community, that is beyond and yet comprehensive of the dividedness that contemporary Europe experiences.

This distinctive character of North American freedom is crucial to understand Doull's critique of Grant's account of Canada. Grant sees Canada's distinctiveness to lie in its determination to conserve the presence of English and French culture in Canada and so to have access to a tradition of contemplation, virtue, and political stability. The role of Canada is to act as a means to defend the institutions and ways of being that sustain these cultures. These cultures are received by Canadians as received forms they are to participate in, and, as Grant understands the heart of these cultures to be a participation in the Good, there is a coherence to this receptive or passive attitude. But Doull disagrees with Grant, not only on the content of these cultures, but also on the Canadian relation to them. Doull outlines a history of Canada whose purpose is to question the claim that English and French Canadian cultures were ever simply participatory and conservative. Rather Doull wants to argue that from its beginning Canadians appropriated and transformed their received cultural forms in the new context of North America.[37]

What Doull's account means for Canada is that its technological and traditional sides need not be seen as ultimately opposed. Canada, and

North American federations generally, are capable of containing and mediating technology together with a preservation of a specific sovereignty. This active uniting of past and present, universal and particular, is, according to Doull, the very character of North American freedom: the actuality of the state as explicated in the Hegelian philosophy. For Doull, at the heart of Grant's account of Canada is a colonial passivity where tradition can be preserved only when not actively appropriated through a self-determining freedom. This contrast takes us to the theological-philosophical heart of the debate: the truth of the Hegelian philosophy, the claim that in the modern state – which for both Doull and Grant, from their opposed perspectives, is most fully realized in the North American state – there is a uniting of God and history, of human self-activity and the eternal, of freedom and the traditions of Jerusalem and Athens.

Doull and Grant on God and History

Grant tells us that the context of his lament for the demise of Canadian nationhood rested in an understanding of history fundamentally opposed to the liberal conception of history as the development of freedom and equality. By the time he wrote *Lament for a Nation*, Grant had broken with the doctrine of progress in which he had been raised and to which in his first book, *Philosophy in the Mass Age*, he subscribed, in what he believed was the form articulated by Hegel. In the concluding chapter of *Lament for a Nation*, Grant turned explicitly against what he found most disturbing in the Hegelian doctrine of progress, namely the claim that "Die Weltgeschichte ist das Weltgericht." Here Grant argued that "the doctrines of progress and providence have been brought together."[38] Historical development was both towards higher forms of human life and at the same time made God's will scrutable as accomplished through these higher forms. This doctrine of progress was connected to Grant's account of Canada because he saw in its hold upon Canadians a source of their blindness to what was being lost in the passing away of what was specifically Canadian through ever greater integration with the United States and its dynamic modernity. In this doctrine, Canadians could see this integration not as loss, but rather as part of the beneficent, liberating movement of history, a stage in the fuller realization of freedom. In portraying the future as a necessarily higher stage than the past, the doctrine of progress, in Grant's eyes, reconfigures evil, loss, destruction, and the whole suffering of historical life as good, as redeemed through its role in the higher achievement of future development:

> But if history is the final court of appeal, force is the final argument. Is it possible to look at history and deny that within its dimension force is the supreme ruler? To take a progressive view of providence is to come close to worshiping force. Does this not make us cavalier about evil? The screams of the tortured child can be justified by the achievements of history. How pleasant for the achievers, but how meaningless for the child. As a believer, I must then reject these Western interpretations of providence. Belief is blasphemy if it rests on any easy identification of necessity and good.[39]

Grant saw in the doctrine of progress, and most fully in the Hegelian expression of it, a confusion between what he referred to as the order of necessity and the order of the Good. Grant argued that Plato, and the ancients generally, preserved a distinction between the eternal or the Good and necessity, a realm of becoming that participates in the eternal, but remains as other to it. It was only by so distinguishing the historical and the eternal that the distinction of good and evil could be retained. Grant found the same distinction in Christianity that he found in Platonism in the notion that, for Christianity, God's will, Providence, is not scrutable, and so we are called to look not to human history but to Christ, and most fully, to his crucifixion, for our theology. Using Luther's terms, Grant distinguished a theology of glory – above all embodied in the doctrine of progress – from a theology of the cross. In the one, Grant saw a triumphalism where human will or subjectivity was seen as an agent of divine activity in the world; in the other, he saw a deep humiliation of Christ not asserting his will, but rather giving it away both to his Father and, in forgiveness and love, to those who had persecuted him. For Grant, Christ's greatness lay in his giving his will away to the eternal order and, even in the face of extreme affliction, in the very abandonment of God, not conforming to the wilfulness of the realm of necessity and historical life.

Grant saw in the Hegelian uniting of progress and providence a radical reduction of all otherness to human historical life, ultimately to human subjectivity and will. Grant saw otherness – both the otherness of God and of other beings – as preservable only in the recognition of an order of the good, an order of justice, that precedes human willing and activity. Grant here saw two levels of recognition: (1) a Platonic recognition that affirmed justice as the love of the beautiful in otherness and so the limitation of one's will through virtue made possible by the illumination of one's intelligence by the Good, and (2) the still more radical Christian form of love of otherness in the giving away of one's self for the sake of otherness in the face of radical affliction or the experience of the absence of the Good. In spite of these distinctions between what Grant took to be the Platonic and Christian accounts of the Good, what they together affirmed was a relation of the human to the Good as receptive or participatory and not as generative or determining. For Grant, religion, art, and philosophy are all forms of participation and so, in a broader sense, they are all religious. There is certainly a human activity in each, but only as responsive to and within a "gift" from the eternal source. It is only this standpoint of receptivity or openness, as Strauss and a number of other contemporary thinkers also suggest, that makes possible an apprehension of the eternal as eternal and not simply as a moment of human self-activity.

Doull argues on the basis of Hegel's philosophy of religion that Grant's account of the separation of God and history, or necessity, is neither true nor Christian. On Hegel's account it belongs to the full philosophical articulation of the Christian *Vorstellung* that the human relation to God is mediated by the activity of the thinking subject and by the development of history. The contemplation of God, from an initial withdrawal from the world in early Christianity, is inwardly transformed so as to bring forth a recognition of the Logos present in human activity, both in its contemplative and practical dimensions. History is not conceived then as a merely external necessity or Fate but as the activity of an infinite actuality, a necessity that has as its telos the Good conceived as self-conscious freedom, what Hegel calls Spirit. It belongs to the Hegelian philosophy to know that the Trinitarian God revealed in Christianity is at the same time the ground of historical, worldly existence. Doull makes this point relative to the Hegelian position: "The movement of this thought, as in the Vorstellung, is to a relation of equal 'persons' within which are contained all subjective and objective concepts. On this foundation rests a *Sittlichkeit* in which 'life' or the immediate existence of spirit, and its relation of individuals in their particularity, are comprehended in a self-governing community wherein the unity of freedom and nature in family, society and state is equally the unfolding of an objective end, and, from the side of individuals, the realizing of that end is their concrete good."[40]

It is the state, and above all the modern state, that is, according to both Doull and Hegel, the focus of God's relation to historical life and is, as such, the precise object of world history in general and so also the substance of Hegel's theodicy.[41] Doull wrote to Grant in 1956, "Hegel is able to say with perfect accuracy that the state is the *civitas dei* on earth; for what was for Augustine, as far as practice goes, a regulative idea, is in the state, so far as true to its idea, the practical good."[42] Doull at the conclusion of his final writing, some forty-five years later, expands on the point that the Augustinian *civitas dei*, which relates, as Doull puts it, "the absolute creative God of Judaism and the subjective freedom mediated by the Greek world," is made historically actual in the state:

> Christian history mediates between Augustine's *civitas dei* – as possessing the absolute truth in separation – and historical existence. There takes shape a world more and more conformed in its institutions, and in the spirit moving in them, to the unchanging belief of all peoples. And philosophy, in responding to the reason of the world that has broken from the *Vorstellung*, gives to its religious content the form of thought. At first in this work one drew on the ancient philosophy. Then, finding that this could not contain the concreteness of the *Vorstellung*, the need of which the structure of medieval institutions made felt, a new philosophy emerged founded on the religious belief itself and able to relate that belief to a secularity apparently radically opposed to it. And from that modern world in turn has emerged a more deeply Christianized secularity and a new philosophy.[43]

Doull argues that the historical reality of the *civitatis dei*, the state in its full and ideal development, comprehends modern freedom so that this freedom is not corrupting of pre-modern virtue and piety, but is rather the fulfilling of the promise of the ancient world: "In Plato's polities the ruling power was freed from the special interests of classes. The difficulty then occurred how the ruling part could be in the state. How this uncorrupted independence of the ruler could move effectively the classes to the realization of the good is shown in Hegel's concept of the state."[44]

But this is just what George Grant denies. Fundamental to Grant's denial of the Hegelian account of history is his claim that modernity is fundamentally corruptive of virtue and the human participation in Justice, and thus, rather than fulfilling the Platonic philosophy, is its ruination. For Grant, the synthesis of ancient and modern, of Christian and secular, that Hegel took himself to have effected is seen to be impossible. The ancient account that preserves the distinction between the necessary and the Good cannot, with integrity, be united with an account that dissolves this distinction. In the doctrine of progress and its turn to human historical activity, Grant sees not a realization of the divine, but rather an obscuring of the divine and of genuine otherness – their reduction to moments of the will. For Grant, otherness is preserved as otherness by being seen as grounded in the Good as its source and so as having a being apart from human willing. The destruction of otherness, however much it belongs to the order of necessity to bring this about, is therefore secured as irreducibly evil. In the doctrine of progress both the realm of natural and human otherness and divine otherness or the order of the Good, are drawn into human will and subjectivity and so obscured. From this perspective, Hegel's understanding of history must be seen, if not in intention, at least in result, to involve the dissolution not only of religion, but of every relation, philosophic, artistic, civic, or moral, of the human to an order transcending and defining the human. Grant sees built into the modern conception of the state, not, as Doull and Hegel would have it, a fulfilling of the ancient forms, but their dissolution.

We seem to have arrived at an impasse, or at least at the limits of this chapter. The judgment of the validity of Grant's or of Doull's account would seem to rest on an ability to determine rightly the relation of God to historical life. Indeed, its full exploration would require as a beginning an inquiry into the Hegelian system as a whole as (both Doull and Grant agree) the most comprehensive consideration of this question in the Western tradition. But then, there is the need of a further reflection on whether the history of the West since Hegel has been disclosive of the underlying falsity or truth of this account.[45] Are we then left with our various intuitions, experiences, and inclinations about these issues?

Throughout his career Doull could defend his claims by referring to the Hegelian system, and he could explicate with a depth of knowledge that astonished Grant the history of philosophy and of the West more generally and so display the historical reality of the Hegelian system and the inadequacy of accounts of that history that assumed one or another of the aspects of the contemporary standpoint. He could also point to the experience of the contemporary that seemed to undermine the Hegelian position as in fact confirming it. For while each side of the contemporary divide between technology and community recognized the divide, they could explain it only one-sidedly, and in turn could not explain the ground of their own position or its relation to the whole history it nonetheless presupposed. But of course the claim to be able to rise to a standpoint beyond the opposition of technology and community and that can be "objective" and mediate in thought their division is precisely what Grant denies.[46] In the last decade and a half of his life Doull argued that the Idea of the state is not only available to a philosophical comprehension of the divisions of contemporary European culture, but is in fact actual and effective in the societies of the New World, especially in the United States and (somewhat more obscurely) in Canada. During Grant's life, Doull and Grant tended to agree that the United States was a technological empire as much given over to one-sided contemporary corruption and revolution as Europe in the disintegration of the nation state. In the period after Grant's death, however, Doull began to see in the United States an actual integration of technology and community.[47] From this standpoint, Doull could not only point above contemporary life to the Idea as comprehensive of what was experienced dividedly, but argue that this division was being actually and effectively overcome not in Europe, but in the New World.

Equally, for Grant, there is a connection between the truth of Hegel's philosophy and the possibility of Canada in the modern age. His turn away from Hegel in the early 1960s gave birth to a deepening insight into the fragility, indeed the impossibility, of Canada – or perhaps it was a deepening sense of the impossibility of Canada in the context of North America that gave him insight into the problematic character of the Hegelian philosophy.[48] The point that for Grant fused these two insights was the question of modernity. Grant "came to the conclusion that Hegel was not correct in his claim to have taken the truth of antique thought and synthesized it with the modern to produce a higher (and perhaps highest) truth."[49] For Grant, Jerusalem and Athens, Christ and Socrates, while they could be brought together in some manner, could not, without corruption and distortion, come together in and with modernity. Grant's turning away from the claim in Hegel that the modern and ancient are not, in the end, opposed, but united and completed in one another, belonged with his turning from hope to lamentation about the fate of Canada. Grant saw the coming to Canada of technological modernism as one with the occluding of the light cast by the contemplation of Athens and the piety of Jerusalem. For Grant, as much as for Doull, the possibility of Canada and the reality of the Hegelian philosophy were interconnected.[50]

We have, then, a more direct, if also limited, route by which to consider the debate between Doull and Grant, and this is to return to the question of Canada. For Doull, the actuality of Spirit is present not only to the Hegelian philosopher, but, precisely if it is Spirit, is also present – no doubt incompletely and inarticulately – in the institutions and social life of Canadians and North Americans generally. For Doull, it belongs to the confusion of post-Hegelian culture that we tend to see this reality one-sidedly: we see Canada either as liberal and progressive or equally as conservative and traditional. Canada is portrayed as a nation built either on universal rights or on specific communities. Grant, by contrast, opposes these two sides. On this ground, Canada as traditional cannot be united with Canada as liberal and progressive. But Doull suggests that, while Canadians tend to take up one side in opposition to the other, the country from its beginning could not be simply one side or the other. An implication of this more self-active account of Canadian history sketched by Doull is the claim that Canada's history cannot be understood as the histories of two distinct "nations" – British and French – that out of a shared determination to avoid assimilation into the United States have formed a marriage of convenience. As Doull puts this, "Were the history of the 'two nations' such as nationalists recount, they would already have separated painlessly enough, seeing mutual benefit and little loss in their separation."[51] Doull's criticism of Grant is that he in fact leaves Canada as just such a compact, without real unity.[52] However, Grant argues that what unites Canadians, whether French or English, is an attachment to the universality of the pre-modern tradition that is instantiated in differing forms in Quebec and in English Canada – a shared standpoint deeper than the differences of culture and equally opposed to American modernity. Doull in one sense does not disagree with this, but says that if it is this universal culture that is the truth of Canada, then the national forms become secondary, and this is what the history of Canada has been. As Doull puts it, "There is not only a separate history of Quebec and another of a British 'nation'; there is also a common Canadian history more basic than either of these abstractions."[53] It is this common history that Canadians have made to which Doull wishes to turn our attention, and which, for him, points to a reality that escapes Grant's account.

The very confusion and indecision of Canadians suggests this larger reality. Canadians can neither agree to separate along linguistic lines and dissolve what appears a marriage of convenience, nor accept the Constitution as settled and separatism put to rest by the patriation of the Constitution and the Charter of Rights. In this incapacity of Canada to settle into one or other side of our current self-understandings, Doull suggests there is present a deeper substantiality than is anywhere given expression: the truth of Canada is both universal rights and specific community. Canadians would not feel caught in indecision, Doull argues, unless they knew implicitly that the truth is on both sides: we belong to received traditions, which we also transcend in a comprehensive universality. The same ambiguity can be seen, according to Doull, in Canada's vexed relation to the United States.[54] Canada seems through the Free Trade Agreement to give itself over wholly to American technological consumerism and "globalization," and yet in this Canada seems to experience at the same time its difference from the United States in social programs, in the relation of provinces and regions to one another, and in foreign policy. For Grant, such experiences of substantiality and independence can be understood as only the last glowing embers of an extinguished fire. What is the truth here?

For both Doull and Grant, contemporary Canadians live in ambiguous times: we are either a state unable to articulate the sovereignty we in fact possesses (Doull) or we are people without sovereignty and independence and yet still think ourselves a state (Grant). For both there is a problem of articulation or recognition. For both what is required for an articulation adequate to our situation is not only a recollection of the whole history of Canada, nor only an understanding of its constitutional order, but also a reflection on the character of the contemporary as a whole – on the nature of technology and its relation to the sovereignty of political institutions in this era. This last reflection, in turn, requires a consideration of how higher ends and human freedom and self-activity relate: how God can be present or absent in historical life. It is a testimony to the depth of both thinkers that they are opposed to one another consistently and at the same points. To put the matter in its simplest form, Grant argues that there is a fundamental divide at each level, whereas Doull acknowledges this division at every point but argues that it is overcome. Beyond the division between the British/French connection and American technology, Doull argues for the possibility of a sovereign, post-national Canada. Beyond the division between community and technology, between tradition and modernity, Doull argues for the possibility of a sovereignty in the state capable of uniting these aspects. Beyond the division between God and human historical life, Doull argues for the possibility of their effective and scrutable unity. Grant denies such possibilities on the basis of both an experience of their total division and a philosophical analysis that argues for the irreconcilability of these divisions. Doull, in his turn, allows that short of the absolute standpoint of the Hegelian philosophy, there can be no known overcoming of these opposed aspects. It is not the purpose of this chapter to ultimately decide between Doull's and Grant's accounts – but, rather, to suggest that in the relation of their thought is experienced the most fundamental questions for contemporary reflection: in their difference the reader can experience in contrasting ways the deep presence and absence of Jerusalem and Athens in our contemporary living.

NOTES

This chapter owes a great deal to the collaborative work I have done with David Peddle, and in particular to our paper "Lamentation and Speculation: George Grant, James Doull and the Possibility of Canada," *Animus* 7 (2002): 94–123.

1 James Doull to George Grant, 26 April 1965 deposited in Library and Archives Canada, Collected Works of George Grant project [textual record] (2015-00341-X) (hereafter cited as LAC).
2 James Doull to George Grant, 11 October 1968, LAC.
3 James Doull, "Naturalistic Individualism: Quebec Independence and an Independent Canada," in *Modernity and Responsibility: Essays for George Grant*, ed. Eugene Coombs (Toronto: University of Toronto Press, 1983), 29; Doull in *Philosophy and Freedom: The Legacy of James Doull*, ed. David G. Peddle and Neil G. Robertson (Toronto: University of Toronto Press, 2003), 375 and 395–6.
4 George Grant, *Philosophy in the Mass Age* (1959; repr., Toronto: University of Toronto Press, 1966), vii (hereafter cited as *PMA*).
5 George Grant, *Lament for a Nation* (1965; repr., Toronto: University of Toronto Press, 1978), 89 (hereafter cited as *LN*).
6 There is good reason to think two things: (1) Grant never fully internalized the Hegelian position in the way Doull did, and (2) Doull thought Grant had an inadequate understanding of Hegel. See Grant, "Comments on Hegel," in *Collected Works of George Grant*, ed. Arthur Davis, vol. 2, *1951–1959* (Toronto: University of Toronto Press, 2002), 521–6; Grant to Sheila Grant, August 1957, in *George Grant: Selected Letters*, ed. William Christian (Toronto: University of Toronto Press, 1996), 194–5; Larry Schmidt, ed., *George Grant in Process* (Toronto: University of Toronto Press, 1978), 64; Doull to George Grant, 26 April 1965, unpublished, LAC.

7 Grant, *PMA*, vii; *LN*, 89. For a helpful consideration of the sense in which Grant remained influenced by Hegel, even in his very repudiation of him, consider Robert Sibley's argument in chapter 13 of this volume. Also valuable is Barry Cooper's account of Grant in chapter 15. Doull would clearly reject the account of Hegel provided by Kojève that Cooper finds most compelling and that he argues is also the one that Grant upholds, though Grant is careful to distinguish Kojève from Hegel. As Jim Vernon points out in chapter 6, even while ultimately critical of his account, Grant shares with Fackenheim the desire to discover a "middle position" between and yet also comprehensive of both left and right approaches to Hegel.

8 Grant, *LN*, 4.

9 The expression "Jerusalem and Athens" has great resonance for Grant, who takes it up from various sources, but especially as it was developed by Leo Strauss as connoting a basic dividedness in the roots of the Western tradition. Leo Strauss, "Jerusalem and Athens," in *Jewish Philosophy and the Crisis of Modernity*, 377–405 (Albany: SUNY, 1997). However, Simone Weil points for Grant to a need and possibility of seeing these roots as belonging together. Consider Grant's important essay "Faith and the Multiversity" in *Technology and Justice*, 35–77 (Toronto: House of Anansi, 1986), especially "Appendix," 71–7. For Doull's very different way of thinking of the relation of "Jerusalem" to "Athens," consider "The Christian Origins of Contemporary Institutions," *Dionysius* 6 (1982): 111–65.

10 Grant made himself clear in his 1970 foreword to a reissuing of *Lament for a Nation*, that he was not attached to the British connection (a) ethnically, for he saw such unthinking attachment as part of the demise of that connection, or (b) without ambiguity, especially given what he perceived as the British abasement before the United States in the twentieth century. As Grant states, "I emphasise this failure in irony because many simple people (particularly journalists and professors) took it to be a lament for the passing of a British dream of Canada. It was rather a lament for the romanticism of the original dream." Grant, *LN*, xi.

11 "The argument that Canada, a local culture, must disappear can, therefore, be stated in three steps. First, men everywhere move ineluctably toward membership in the universal and homogeneous state. Second, Canadians live next to a society that is the heart of modernity. Third, nearly all Canadians think that modernity is good, so nothing essential distinguishes Canadians from Americans. When they oblate themselves before 'the American way of life,' they offer themselves on the altar of the reigning western goddess." Ibid., 54.

12 Ibid., 68.
13 Ibid., 69.
14 Ibid., 70.
15 Ibid., 87.
16 Notes to a lecture on *Lament for a Nation*, unpublished, Doull Archive, 3.
17 James Doull, "Naturalistic Individualism: Quebec Independence and an Independent Canada," in Coombs, *Modernity and Responsibility*, 44.
18 Ibid., 39.
19 James Doull, "Heidegger and the State," in Peddle and Robertson, *Philosophy and Freedom*, 357–77.
20 See Graeme Nicholson's illuminating consideration of Doull's account of North American freedom in his chapter in this volume.
21 Grant, *LN*, 70.
22 Ibid., 71.
23 Ibid., 71.
24 George Grant, *Technology and Justice* (Toronto: House of Anansi, 1986), 32.
25 William Christian and Sheila Grant, eds., *The George Grant Reader* (Toronto: University of Toronto Press, 1998), 435–6.
26 On Grant's relation to Eastern Christianity, especially through the work of Phillip Sherard, see Harris Athanasiadis, *George Grant and the Theology of the Cross* (Toronto: University of Toronto Press, 2001), 134–7 and 168–71.
27 Christian and Grant, *George Grant Reader*, 437.
28 George Grant, *English Speaking Justice* (Toronto: House of Anansi, 1985), 77.
29 David Cayley, *George Grant in Conversation* (Toronto: House of Anansi, 1995), 82.
30 Grant, *Technology and Justice*, 33.
31 See Doull in *Philosophy and Freedom*, 360–70 and 399–402.
32 James Doull, "Augustinian Trinitarianism and Existential Theology," *Dionysius* 3 (1979): 121.
33 Doull, *Philosophy and Freedom*, 399–402.
34 James Doull, "Hegel and Contemporary Liberalism, Anarchism, Socialism: A Defense of the *Rechtsphlosophie* against Marx and His Contemporary Followers," in J.J. O'Malley, K.W. Algozin, H.P. Kainz, and L.C. Rice, *The Legacy of Hegel* (The Hague: Nijhoff, 1973), 229.
35 Doull, *Philosophy and Freedom*, 341.
36 For Doull on Latin America, see Doull, *Philosophy and Freedom*, 406–7.
37 Doull's history of Canada is found in *Philosophy and Freedom*, 434–59. For a fuller discussion of Doull's history of Canada in contrast to Grant's, see David Peddle and Neil Robertson, "Lamentation and Speculation: George Grant, James Doull and the Possibility of Canada," *Animus* 7 (2002): 16–19.

In this volume, Barry Cooper suggests that Doull's account falls within the terms of the "Laurentian" account in which he also places George Grant and Charles Taylor. It can at least be asked whether this is entirely sustainable in that Doull continually argues for the need for Canadians to acquire an independence from colonial postures, whether towards Britain or the United States.

38 Grant, *LN*, 99. That Doull disagreed with Grant's portrayal of Hegel's argument is an understatement. In a letter he wrote to Grant, "When Hegel writes that 'die Weltgeschichte is das Weltgericht' he means nothing remotely resembling the sense his words have in your quotation of them. It would be easy to find statements in Aquinas and Hooker equivalent to Hegel's. You and Strauss in turning from Hegel show yourselves still liberals at heart. America is omnipotent, you think, because its virtues of direct concerns for individuals are also for you the highest virtues. Whatever one may think about this, classical conservatism was on the other side." Doull to Grant, 26 April 1965, LAC. Doull considered the thought of Leo Strauss on a number of occasions, but see especially "Hegel's Critique of Hellenic Virtue," *Dionysius* 9 (1985): 3–17.

39 Grant, *LN*, 100.

40 Doull, *Philosophy and Freedom*, 288.

41 Hegel, trans. Leo Rauch, *Introduction to the Philosophy of History* (Indianapolis: Hackett Publishing, 1988), 18 and 42.

42 Doull to George Grant, December 1956 (unpublished).

43 Doull, *Philosophy and Freedom*, 298–9.

44 Doull, "Hegel's Critique of Hellenic Virtue," 14. For Doull's summary of Hegel's concept of the state, see ibid., 14–15. Also useful are the discussions of the *civitas dei* at the end of both "Christian Origins," 162–5, and "Christian Origins of Contemporary Institutions Part 2," *Dionysius* 8 (1984): 53–103, 100–3. In an unpublished lecture, "The Augustinian *Civitas Dei*," Doull made clear that he does not equate the *civitas dei* with modern historical life and sees the confusion between the two as a problem in contemporary thought and culture that tends to see "the *civitas dei* as historical and not as overcoming history." He argues against such a conflation of the *civitas dei* and *civitas terrena*: "In the light of Augustinian theology and the course of Christian history one would say of this conflation of the two cities that it draws the *civitas dei* into the realm of finite interests and that its history must be the process in which the assumption that finite interests are primary is destroyed." Unpublished, undated manuscript, Doull Archive, 6.

45 See the Doull-Fackenheim debate and Ken Kieran's commentary on this debate in *Philosophy and Freedom*, 330–53, as a beginning to this reflection.

46 Indeed, from Grant's position, Doull is not beyond the division, but has rather sided with modernity. This is clear from Grant's comments about Hegel in the new introduction to *PMA*, viii.
47 Doull did not see the United States as the most perfect form of this integration, but nevertheless saw the integrity there achieved as real and as capable of further development. See Doull, "The Philosophical Basis of the Constitutional Discussion in Canada," in *Philosophy and Freedom*, 393–465.
48 In his new preface to *Philosophy in the Mass Age*, Grant wrote, "To state quickly why one has changed one's mind is always difficult. Experience and reflection are too intricately bound for any ease of intellectual relation." *PMA*, x–xi.
49 Ibid., viii.
50 But, it should be said, not united: neither thinker would confuse the limited question of Canada's reality with the absolute question of the relation of God to the world.
51 Doull, *Philosophy and Freedom*, 396.
52 Ibid., 395–8.
53 Ibid., 398.
54 Ibid., 455–6.

13 Grant, Hegel, and the "Impossibility of Canada"

ROBERT C. SIBLEY

The publication of George Grant's *Lament for a Nation* in 1965, it is said, sparked an intense period of nationalism in Canada.[1] Yet Grant consistently denied having nationalistic motives for the book. Indeed, he explicitly refers in *Lament* to "the impossibility of Canada."[2] Moreover, he is straightforward about why Canada has come to an "end": the principles or ideas upon which the country was founded have given way to those of the American republic. These "American" principles promote social and political arrangements that make particular cultures and nations like Canada redundant. Since Canadians on the whole believe the principles of modernity are right and proper, they have little reason to maintain an independent political existence. Hence, Grant concludes that Canada is impossible as a sovereign nation state because of the "character of the modern age."[3]

How can the "disappearance" of Canada be attributed to "the character of the modern age"? The question brings forward the central concern of this chapter – how Grant's linkage of modernity and Canada's political fate is bound up with his philosophic relationship to Hegel. The German philosopher's influence on Grant is well known. So, too, is Grant's "turn" from Hegel. However, insufficient consideration has been given to the connection between Grant's Hegelianism, both in its initial appeal and its later repudiation, and Grant's claim about the impossibility of Canada. I argue that Grant's "lament" is bound up with his interpretation of and response to the thinker he once described as the greatest philosopher.[4]

In the 1959 edition of *Philosophy in the Mass Age*, Grant praised Hegel as the one philosopher who had been able to synthesize classical reason, Christian theology, and modern freedom. Hegel, he said, reconciled the concept of moderns as autonomous, history-making beings with the pre-modern account of humans as dwelling under the dispensation of an eternal, divinely given natural law. This positive appraisal of Hegel did not last long. Grant eventually recognized that it was impossible to bring together classical natural law and its imperatives with the modern ontological notion of time as the history created by humans free to make of themselves what they will. Grant's "turn" from Hegel and liberal progressivism has been called his "era of retractions,"[5] that period when, under the influence of such thinkers as Leo Strauss, Jacques Ellul, Friedrich Nietzsche, Martin Heidegger, and Simone Weil, Grant reconsidered his attachments to the modern project. Seven years after *Philosophy in the Mass Age*, Grant had undergone an intellectual conversion: "I came to the conclusion that Hegel was not correct in his claim to have taken the truth of antique thought and synthesised it with the modern to produce a higher (and perhaps highest) truth; that on many of the most important political matters Plato's teaching is truer than Hegel's. Particularly, I have come to the conclusion that Plato's account of what constitutes human excellence and the possibility of its realisation in the world is more valid than that of Hegel."[6]

However, despite Grant's disavowal, Hegel continued to have an abiding influence on his thought, providing a theoretical perspective that enabled him to account for the character of the modern world. Grant implied as much in his 1966 repudiation of Hegel, when he said it is difficult for anyone who ascribes to "the Western Christian doctrine of providence to avoid reaching the conclusion that Hegel has understood the implications of that doctrine better than any other thinker."[7]

To the degree this comment demonstrates that Grant continued to regard Hegelian philosophy as the fullest expression of modernity, his subsequent thought constitutes an ongoing reappraisal of Hegel in light of what he saw as the failings of the modern project, especially as it was manifested in North American society. Even in rejecting Hegel, then, Grant could not excise the German's influence in any absolute sense, because he retained throughout his work the "truth" of the Hegelian account of modernity.[8] Grant's "turn" from Hegel should therefore be interpreted not so much as a rejection of Hegel but as a shift in consciousness on Grant's part akin to the psychology reflected in Hegel's concept of *Aufheben*: that is, a conversion of consciousness that incorporates and sublates a previous mode of consciousness.

Such a claim naturally raises questions about the accuracy of Grant's interpretation of Hegel. These questions, however, are beyond the purview of this inquiry. This chapter is an exercise of intellectual history rather than philosophic analysis or exegesis of Hegelian thought. I am concerned with what Grant's appropriation of Hegel meant for Grant, not whether his understanding of Hegel is a particularly valid or a "correct" reading of the German thinker's work. Nor am I offering my own interpretation of Hegel.

It is necessary to make this latter point because Robert Meynell makes much of my ostensible "misinterpretations" of Hegel in his 2011 study, arguing that I cast Hegel as a social contractarian.[9] I can only respond by noting that I state explicitly in several places in *Northern Spirits* that I am not offering any specific interpretation of Hegel, least of all suggesting that he is a social contract theorist. Rather I emphasize how I am drawing solely on Hegel's general concept of reconciliation, because doing so "lets me side-step planting a flag in any particular Hegelian camp." As I say, "whether Hegel is interpreted as a revolutionary, a reactionary, a free-market liberal, a communitarian, a conservative or a Christian metaphysician, there is little dispute that he ultimately sought the 'reconciliation' of the various diremptions in human life, social, political, and spiritual. Because the term reconciliation is so inclusive, as it were, I am lifted above the ideological fray to gain a broader overview of Hegel's thought."[10]

Elsewhere, too, I observe that "Hegel goes beyond Hobbes's contractarian solution" and, in reference to Hegel's *Philosophy of Right*, note that "Hegel clearly says the state cannot be based on a social contract." Indeed, I conclude by highlighting Hegel's criticism of social contract theory: "Hegel's point seems to be that the contractarian model confuses the distinctions between state and civil society by taking an instrumental view of the state and its institutions. Such a position treats the ties of citizenship and sovereignty as relations of interest and, thereby, undermines that which gives civil association its ethical weight – the overarching authority of political order."[11] Perhaps, though, my most explicit refutation of the Hegel-as-contractarian critique is this: "In the Hegelian state, both self-consciousnesses's mutually acknowledge their interrelationship by recognising themselves as members of a political community. It is this shift to intersubjectivity that allows Hegel to avoid charges of excessive unity because he replaces modern atomism with intersubjective relatedness ... Hegel's community is the idea of individuals as self-conscious beings who fulfil themselves and find their freedom in their participation in a community."[12]

That said, I also point out that while Hegel would certainly agree with the communitarian argument about the importance of membership in families, society, and the state, and how that membership cannot be reduced to the mere satisfaction of individual needs and desires, he would, I suggest, disagree with the communitarians. What Hegel values in these relationships, whether as a family member or a citizen, is how they enhance an individual's freedom (in the fullest and most positive sense of that word).[13] This is not to assert, as Meynell claims, that I give moral freedom priority over community – "community membership is not optional for Hegel, but it is for Sibley"[14] is how he puts it – but rather to recognize that ethical life is bound up with the individual's moral freedom. For Hegel, the relationship of the individual and the community is a mutually sustaining one in that each provides purpose and meaning – and, hence, reconciliation – to the other.

In this regard, it is puzzling to be charged with casting Hegel as a social contractarian, and, given all this, it is perhaps not too strong to suggest Meynell deliberately misinterprets my "reading" of Hegel, the result of which is to misrepresent my argument as a whole.[15] Meynell does not distinguish between my "reading" of Hegel's concept of reconciliation and how Hegel's thought manifests itself in those thinkers with whom I am concerned. In this regard, then, the question to be asked is not regarding the validity of Grant's appropriation of Hegel, but rather what was it about Hegel's thought that Grant could not abide, even though he recognized it provided the most comprehensive account of the modern condition? Responding to this question penetrates to the heart of Grant's judgment about the impossibility of Canada.

Before I approach this question, though, it is worthwhile to provide some context to Grant's Hegelianism through a brief comparison of Canadian and American appropriations of Hegelian thought, a comparison that underscores Grant's claim regarding the Canadian surrender to American principles.

Hegel in Canada

Even a brief survey of the literature shows a long-standing interest in Canada in Hegel.[16] Hegelian philosophy was introduced into Canada through Scottish immigrants who imbibed the thought of the Scottish Enlightenment.[17] In the century after 1850, "the mainstream of philosophy in English-speaking Canada was more often than not Hegelian."[18] According to scholars, certain Hegelian principles have sunk deep roots in Canadian political culture because of this country's political and geographical circumstances. As Leslie Armour and Elizabeth Trott observe, "We needed ideas that were capable of spanning spaces and which could link sub-cultures which, because of their distribution, tended to grow in significantly different ways."[19] With a population divided by language, religion, and culture, a vast territory that needed to be held together, and that territory's historical domination by other powers, the attractiveness of a philosophy that sought to reconcile such diversity was valuable in helping to comprehend the Canadian experience. Hegel appeared to provide a theoretical framework that allowed cultures to maintain and develop their distinctive features, even while uniting them in a single political order.

Grant's initial employment of Hegelian thought reflects this attitude. Given Grant's concern with Canada maintaining its independence on a continent dominated by the United States, what perhaps most appealed to him about Hegel was the philosopher's understanding of how pluralistic societies can use legal and political systems and institutions to mitigate those forces that threaten to tear society apart. In the *Philosophy of Right*, for example, Hegel argues that modern societies are to be understood by reference to the fundamental concepts that guide them, and that the modern state seeks to enable citizens to assert those rights and freedoms that reflect the truest purposes of human life while, at the same time, reconciling them to a common good.[20] Grant asserts this sentiment in *Lament* when he says, "A society only articulates itself as a nation through some common intention among its people."[21] Canada existed as a nation state so long as its citizens held intentionally to the essential idea on which it was founded: "an inchoate desire to build, in these cold and forbidding regions, a society with a greater sense of order and restraint than freedom-loving republicanism would allow."[22] In other words, Grant's concern was not simply whether Canada was "over or not," as Neil Robertson puts it in chapter 12 of this collection, but rather that Canada continued to exist as a nation state in a way distinctively and substantively different from the United States.

Grant's initial appropriation of Hegel stands in sharp contrast to that of American thinkers, who tend to link Hegelian concepts to variations on manifest destiny. For example, Francis Fukuyama drew on Hegel's notion of historical progress to conclude that with the collapse of communism, humankind had come to the end of its ideological evolution. The kind of liberal democracy practised in the United States was the final form of human government, the best way to organize human affairs, and was destined to transform the globe into a homogeneous likeness of itself.[23]

This triumphalist appropriation of Hegel also appears in the nineteenth-century St Louis school, whose members introduced the German philosopher to the United States. One of the founding members, Denton J. Snider, argued that the United States embodied the most recent form of World Spirit: "The odyssey of the Hegelian World Spirit is clear – the United States has already arrived on the scene, bearing in its political structure the principle destined to become the *Begriff* of all future political reality."[24] Others saw in Hegel's philosophy the means of fostering national unity. Josiah Royce recast Hegel's principle of reconciliation to replace the Hegelian Absolute with a community united by a common understanding of and feelings towards the world. That is to say, Royce sought to apply Hegelian concepts – the identity of identity and non-identity, for instance – to differences among people in such a way that these differences collapsed into a new identity, a new loyalty that transcended difference.[25]

Grant eventually saw this triumphalist appropriation of Hegel as the one that has the most meaning for the modern world, at least in the sense that the technological society of North America was the most complete embodiment of Hegel's thought. But what was it about the Hegelian project that Grant could not accept?

The Problem of History: Necessity contra the Good

Grant's confrontation with Hegel begins in *Philosophy of the Mass Age* when he asserts the problematical nature of the concept of history. History, he says, presents difficulties for anyone attempting to make moral judgments about the right or wrong of any action.[26] With this claim Grant makes history a central concern of his thought. He seeks to show how history displaced the ancient understanding of nature as the overarching concept by which people comprehend themselves and the world. History, according to Grant, is not one idea among others that shapes the modern world, but rather the core theoretical concept by which moderns understand themselves and their purposes. Historicism, in essence, posits the claim that humanity's knowledge and experience of the world is to be understood only in and through historical movement.

Grant contrasts historicist consciousness with ancient consciousness.[27] The former regards the world as an unending flow of unique and irreversible events that have to be dominated and controlled through creative will. The latter considers time "as the moving image of an unmoving eternity and in which the passing events of life only have meaning as they lead men to the unchanging reality of God."[28] Ancient consciousness, in short, provided a doctrine of natural law by which people sought perfectibility in the union of temporal and divine reason.

Grant, of course, stands against historicism. He cannot agree that humans are ultimately knowable as a historical beings, and much of his philosophic effort was devoted to countering this notion. In particular, his attempt to understand the significance of historicism reflects his confrontation with Hegel, who, for Grant, was the great exemplar of historicist thinking. What turned Grant from his initial acceptance of Hegel's notion of historical development was his recognition that it carried too much of the positivist idea of progress as the ultimate aim of humanity and, worse, made it possible to justify even horrific events as serving some purposive good. Such a claim ignores the idea of human existence having a given highest purpose or good that transcends time or history and by which people are judged as moral beings. According to Grant, Hegel's conflation of historical necessity and transcendent good ultimately meant that history is the judgment of those possessed with the power to impose their will. For Grant, though, to make history "the final court of appeal" for determining the meaning and purpose of human life is tantamount to "worshipping force."[29]

Grant's rejection of historicism is stated most clearly in the final chapter of *Lament for a Nation*: "I must dissociate myself from a common philosophic assumption. I do not identify necessity and goodness. This identification is widely assumed during an age of progress. Those who worship 'evolution' or 'history' consider that what must come in the future will be 'higher,' 'more developed,' 'better,' 'freer' than what has been in the past … They identify necessity and good within the rubric of providence. From the assumption that God's purposes are unfolded in historical events, one may be led to view history as an ever-fuller manifestation of good."[30]

Against this historicist perspective, Grant sets Plato and classical philosophy. The ancients distinguished between eternity, or the Good, and Necessity, the realm of becoming that remains distinct from the Good even while participating in it. For Grant, it is only by maintaining this distinction between Necessity and the Good, between Time and Eternity, that can we retain the distinction between good and evil. Grant, however, sees in Hegelian thought the collapse of this distinction.

By identifying progress and providence, the realm of becoming and the realm of eternal being, Hegel reduces all that is "Other" to human subjectivity – that is, to historical development – and human willpower. The otherness of God that allows humans to maintain a concept of goodness separate from and not subject to their history-making is lost.

Adopting Martin Luther's terms, Grant describes Hegelian philosophy and its doctrine of progress as a theology of glory that exalts human will and makes the realm of necessity or history, and not the Good or eternity (or nature), the arena for redemption. A theology of glory regards historical events as manifestations of divine will, setting up the claim that such events are unique and irreversible because their meaning is derived from God's will. This claim, in turn, tends to exalt human will and, in the absence of a belief in divine order, implies that action must be future-directed because humans have their fulfilment not in the present but in the future.[31] For Grant, though, as he writes in "Faith and the Multiversity," this was the fundamental "mistake" of Western Christianity: it "simplified divine love by identifying it too closely with immanent power in the world."[32] That is to say, Christianity in the West became triumphalist because the historicist consciousness within which it came to function denied the infinite distance between necessity and the good.

In Grant's view, this conflation of necessity and the good received its fullest expression in Hegel and his notion of world history as the unfolding of Reason: "*Die Weltgeschichte ist das Weltgericht*," or "World History is the world's judgement."[33] Such a notion is anathema to Grant: "Hegel makes God's providence scrutable, and that is a teaching that offended me then and now at the deepest level."[34] In identifying progress and providence, Hegel effectively calls evil good and good evil in the sense that he casts the future as necessarily better than the past, thus justifying suffering as necessary for the sake of historical progress.

Grant thought this reliance on historical activity obscured the good and any genuine Otherness – including the "Other" that was Canada. Indeed, Grant connects the conflation of progress and providence to his assertion regarding the "impossibility" of Canada by arguing that nowhere has Hegel's doctrine of progress manifested itself more vigorously than in North America.

The "Fate" of North America

According to Grant, North American mass society epitomizes modernity's history-making consciousness. It incarnates more than any other society the values and principles of the age of progress, including an unquestioned subscription to mass production and its techniques, standardized consumption and education, wholesale entertainment, and almost wholesale medicine.

Grant identifies two basic characteristics of mass society. First, a scientific-technological epistemology and the attempt to apply that theory of knowledge to the domination of nature, including human nature; second, the use by an economic and political elite of various institutions and structures to extend this control such that even the elite is subjected to technology's dominion. Under the sway of modern epistemology, even reason comes to be an instrument to satisfy subjective purposes. The innate capacity of humans to reason becomes part of the apparatus for enclosing them in an ever-tightening circle.[35]

Nowhere, Grant argues, does this technological encirclement reveal itself more completely than in the United States, making it the centre of the modern project. According to Grant, this makes the United States inherently imperialistic because it is technological in the deepest ontological sense. This imperialist intention does not necessarily express itself through colonies and territorial conquest; rather, it manifests itself through the imperatives of a technological society that gives priority to market forces, techniques of efficiency, and mass culture.

How did Grant see this "American" technological imperialism reflected in the "necessity" of Canada's disappearance, and how is that disappearance related to his confrontation with Hegel? Responding to this question entails returning to *Lament for a Nation*. On the surface, *Lament* is the tale of how John Diefenbaker's Progressive Conservative government came under attack from Canada's political, corporate, and bureaucratic elite. It is a story of how a national debate about stationing American nuclear warheads on Canadian soil turned into a conspiracy by Canada's liberal establishment and business elite to defeat Diefenbaker in the 1963 election. Grant had little admiration for Diefenbaker – before the defence crisis he "saw nothing in his [Diefenbaker's] favour," as he said in a 1965 CBC interview[36] – but he regarded his electoral defeat as concrete evidence of the "impossibility" of Canada and, by extension, "the fate of any particularity in the technological age."[37]

Furthermore, Grant saw in Diefenbaker a form of conservatism akin to his own. This conservatism should not be misconstrued; Grant was not hostile to change or opposed to technology.[38] Rather, Grant's conservatism required maintaining connections to the older institutional orders and social traditions of Britain and, for Quebeckers, to France.

So long as those connections and the traditions embedded in them held sway in Canadian society, particularly among the dominant elite, then Canada was possible. The fall of Diefenbaker's government revealed how tenuous these ties had become among the elite, especially in English-speaking Canada. They welcomed the influence of the United States as it expanded continent-wide and globally through the growth of corporate capitalism. Because expansion brought wealth, it was in the interests of Canada's ruling classes to attach themselves to the forces of continentalism, which, as one scholar observes, is a catch phrase that in the Canadian context "signifies the loss of identity, sovereignty and distinctness."[39] Or, as Grant puts it, "The impossibility of conservatism in our era is the impossibility of Canada. As Canadians we attempted a ridiculous task in trying to build a conservative nation in the age of progress."[40]

It is easy to understand why for the sake of money Canada's corporatists were so willing to forgo the country's independence. As Grant sardonically states, "No small country can depend for its existence on the loyalty of its capitalists."[41] But even the federal public service "did not have the stuff of loyalty" and, as a result, became the instrument of a policy that left Canada a satellite of the United States. To be sure, Grant knows that no modern state can function without the civil service having considerable authority. Especially in "uncertain nations" such as Canada, "the civil service is perhaps the essential instrument by which nationhood is preserved." Nevertheless, Grant still asks why Canada's senior federal bureaucrats were so amenable to becoming "more and more representative of a western empire rather than civil servants of a particular nation-state?"[42]

Grant may fault the elite for its betrayals, but he also recognizes that the deeper sources of Canada's disappearance are rooted in the modern ontology. "The confused strivings of politicians, businessmen and civil servants cannot alone account for Canada's collapse. This stems from the very character of the modern era." Even if the bureaucrats, politicians, and businessmen had been more loyal, they could not withstand the imperatives of the modern project. A conservative Canada is impossible because "the aspirations of progress have made Canada redundant."[43] Conservatism must give way to the imperatives of technology.

Grant sees that the essence of contemporary liberalism is the identification of freedom and technology. Secularized humans believe their freedom requires control of the world, and this is to be accomplished through technology. But it is this unthinking ascription to the technological imperative that fated Canada to disappear. When Grant declares "the impossibility of Canada," he means that the nation abandoned its former intention to preserve itself as conceptually different from the United States. Canada ceased to be a sovereign nation, not because its formal political existence had come to an end, but because the "ideas" that provided its reasons for a distinct existence were no longer seen to be worth preserving in any substantive way. With no common intention beyond the liberal-progressivist promise of freedom and material acquisition, Canadians gave themselves over to the technological ethos exemplified in the American technological empire. The result was a "country" that, as Donald Creighton put it, had become merely "a good place to live."[44] Grant made much the same argument in later years about free trade between Canada and the United States. This, too, was another move towards Canada's economic and political integration into the United States. Such an integrative process was the fate of any particularity in the age of technology when economic efficiency holds sway, and there was little to stop it.[45]

Grant's understanding of Canada's fate is captured in the phrase "the universal and homogeneous state"[46] that he appropriated from Alexandre Kojève, the French Hegel exegete. Kojève interpreted Hegel's philosophy to be a philosophy of Time as History, and, with this interpretation, originated the now famous end-of-history thesis, according to which the end of history is consistent with the universal and homogeneous state. Kojève's interpretation of Hegel is, of course, much questioned, particularly in regard to the notion of "the universal and homogeneous state," and in that regard bears some consideration, given its influence on Grant.

Hegel regarded history as a long, drawn-out effort by human consciousness to understand itself and its relation to the world. There may have been some original unity in this consciousness at some early point in history, but by force of circumstance consciousness became divided. The history of thought reflects humanity's attempt to overcome these diremptions. Hegel postulated the idea of reconciling these divisions into a new unity of consciousness. Hegel cast this possibility as the attainment of "absolute spirit" and the moral unification of humanity as a whole, and regarded such an achievement, if it came to pass, as effecting the "end of history." Kojève took over this concept of the historical development of consciousness and the possibility of its ultimate reunification. But he mixed it with Marxist materialism and Heideggerian notions of radical temporality and effectively inverted

Hegel by making the transformation of human consciousness as strictly a worldly process of development. That is to say, Kojève offered a version of Hegelian thought in which the historical disunity of human consciousness is overcome at the "end of history" in the establishment of a universal and homogeneous state that provides mutual reconciliation, recognition, and affirmation, physical and psychological, to humanity as a whole. Where Hegelian idealism restored the unity of human consciousness in the spiritual totality of the Absolute, Kojève cut out the transcendent aspect of Hegel's reconciliation and makes the possibility of human unity and reconciliation a strictly humanistic and secular matter, realizable through materialist productivity and the satisfaction of human desire. In short, Kojève cuts Hegel's God out of history and makes humans the new gods. Where Hegel regards the end of history as humanity's reunification with some Absolute consciousness, Kojève sees the end of history as the end of humanity's attachment to the illusion of an eternal transcendent realm.[47]

Clearly, Kojève's Hegel is not Hegel's Hegel, at least not in any traditional by-the-book interpretation of Hegel. But to say Kojève's interpretation of Hegel is wrong is to fail to recognize that what a thinker meant is not necessarily what he comes to mean. In Grant's case it is the meaning of Kojève's Hegel that he adopts as his own. And it is through his particular appropriation of Kojève's Hegel that Grant sees the "impossibility" of Canada. The universal and homogeneous state, if realized, requires an end to the idea of Canada as a sovereign nation state on the top half of the North American continent. Grant's "conservative" Canada disappears with the fulfilment of Kojève's Hegelian project.

Conclusion: Tyranny, Philosophy, and the "End" of Canada

Grant was persuaded to this view of the universal and homogeneous state, in part at least, by his understanding of the debate between Leo Strauss and Kojève. A detailed consideration of this debate is beyond the scope of this chapter – Neil Robertson and Barry Cooper address the topic much more fully in this volume – so I shall restrict myself to noting Grant's general acceptance of Strauss's judgment that the universal and homogeneous state would be a tyranny and not, as Kojève contended, the culmination of humankind's historical struggle for recognition.[48] As Grant put it, "If the best social order is the universal and homogeneous state, then the disappearance of Canada can be understood as a step towards that order. If the universal and homogeneous state would be a tyranny, then the disappearance of even this indigenous culture can be seen as the removal of a minor barrier on the road to that tyranny."[49]

Beyond the social dimension, though, Grant also sees the establishment of the universal and homogeneous state in theological terms, recognizing that it necessitated the de-divinization of the "Other" that is God. As Kojève argued, the universal and homogeneous state could be achieved only by secularizing Christian theism in favour of an anthropomorphic historicism in which Christian eschatological hopes for the perfection of humanity in a transcendent realm are recast as a goal to be realized in the here-and-now of this world. But this can be attempted, Grant argues, only if philosophy takes its ground not from "an ahistorical eternal order," which is to say, from the Good, but from an eternity that is "the totality of all historical epochs."[50]

For Grant, though, an avowed Christian Platonist attached to the notion of a Good beyond Necessity, such a goal is not one for which humans are best fitted. The universal and homogeneous state, far from being the best social order, would, if actualized, result in a tyrannical order harmful to humankind, as conceived by classical philosophy. Hence, Grant follows Strauss's judgment on Kojève: "Modern philosophy, which has substituted freedom for virtue, has as its chief ideal ... a social order which is destructive of humanity."[51] Moreover, the universal and homogeneous state also means the end of philosophy, or, what is the same thing, the end of human excellence, since it is no longer acceptable to think that only a few are fitted for asking the most serious questions (never mind that there are no serious questions about human purposes to be asked at the end of history). For Kojève-Hegel, human satisfaction is grounded in historical recognition, or freedom and equality; for Grant-Strauss, human satisfaction is rooted in thought, in the contemplation of what is unchanging: "Philosophy is the excellence of the soul. There cannot be philosophy unless there is an eternal and unchangeable order."[52] The coming-to-be of the technological order means the end of philosophy, because the lowering of horizons that brings about the universal and homogeneous state requires the denial of substantive distinctions among people, cultures, and even nations. The universal and homogeneous state, the end point of the Hegelian project, means the end of the "distinct" political order that was Canada. Or, to put it differently, modern philosophy makes Canada impossible.

In conclusion, I have tried to show that for Grant the character of modernity means the end of a sovereign and independent Canada. And that this removal of what makes Canada "Other" to the United States is but one example of the erasure of alternatives that results from the fulfilment of Hegelian philosophy. This is not anti-Americanism on Grant's part: he simply recognizes that because of certain geopolitical and economic realities, Americanization is the way modernization is unfolding. Americans were the first members of the planet to be fully modernized. Canadians came second.

By Grant's argument, then, we now dwell in a post-Canadian world. While we might retain the formal trappings of nationhood – a flag, a border, Parliament, Canada Day, etc. – little of significant "national" substance or sovereignty remains.[53] Nor can there be any serious prospect of recovering a substantively distinct Canada. As Grant learned from Nietzsche, all horizons are "man-made perspectives by which the charismatic impose their will to power," expressions of "the values which our tortured instincts will to create."[54] Our historicist consciousness tells us that nationalism is a fiction. So how can we sustain any authentic patriotism when we are self-consciously aware that our nation is an invention that exists at the sufferance (or indifference) of the modern project as embodied in the United States?

Hegel's thought thus enabled Grant to comprehend what the modern project ultimately means. But this means he could not have rejected Hegel, even if he so desired, because his own thinking constitutes a response to Hegel. Grant's analysis of technology, his judgments on liberalism as a theology of glory, his lament for Canada, all reflect variations on an ongoing confrontation with Hegel. As one critic puts it, Hegel is "the true voice of all that Grant opposes."[55] In this regard, Grant's reputation as a "father of Canadian nationalism" needs to be re-evaluated. This reconsideration should be accompanied by a rejection of the notion that Grant's lament for the nation once known as Canada was little more than an indulgence in "longing for the past," an "Anglo-Saxon lament" or nostalgia for some pre-war myth of Canada's Britishness.[56] Certainly, Grant knew his thought was informed by his "being part of a class which is disappearing."[57] But he also insisted that only "simple people" would settle for interpreting *Lament* as mere nostalgia for "the passing of the British dream of Canada."[58]

If Grant's views on the relationship between philosophy and the political reality of Canada can be parsed to a single statement, it is this: if modernity constitutes the end of philosophy in favour of technology, then Canada was fated to disappear. This might seem an outlandish notion, but this is what Grant's diagnosis of modernity implies. If Hegel is right, if necessity and goodness are identical, and the tyranny of the universal and homogeneous state is the political result of that identification, then Grant is correct to pronounce Canada's impossibility.

NOTES

1 See, for example, Mel Hurtig, "One Last Chance: The Legacy of Lament for a Nation," in *By Loving Our Own: George Grant and the Legacy of Lament for a Nation* (Ottawa: Carleton University Press, 1989), 44. Clifford Orwin refers to Grant as "a father of Canadian nationalism." See "Review of Grant's English-Speaking Justice," *University of Toronto Law Journal* 30 (1980): 106.

2 George Grant, *Lament for a Nation: The Defeat of Canadian Nationalism* (Ottawa: Carleton Library Series, 1989), 68. Even in later years, while acknowledging the "traces of care" shown by Pierre Trudeau's nationalist policies, Grant maintained that "below the surface the movement towards integration continues." See Grant, "Introduction," in *Lament for a Nation,* viii–ix. As late as 1985, Grant insisted he had not been trying to promote the nationalist cause in *Lament*: "Because people quite rightly want finite hopes, people have read a little book I wrote wrongly. I was talking about the end of Canadian nationalism. I was saying that this is over and people read it as if I was making an appeal for Canadian nationalism. I think that is just nonsense. I think they just read it wrongly." Quoted by Larry Schmidt, "An Interview with George Grant," *Grail* 1, no. 1 (March 1985): 36. Cited in William Christian, "George Grant's Lament," *Queen's Quarterly* 100, no. 1 (Spring 1993): 211.

3 Grant, *Lament*, 53.

4 Grant, *Philosophy in the Mass Age*, ed. William Christian (1959; repr., Toronto: University of Toronto Press, 1995), 120.

5 Frank Flinn, "Bibliographical Introduction," in *George Grant in Process*, ed. Larry Schmitt (Toronto: House of Anansi, 1978), 197.

6 Grant, *Philosophy in the Mass Age*, 121–2.

7 Ibid., 120.

8 Grant, *Technology and Empire* (Toronto: House of Anansi, 1969), 104.

9 Robert Meynell, *Canadian Idealism and the Philosophy of Freedom* (Montreal and Kingston: McGill-Queen's University Press, 2011), 217–23. Elizabeth Trott, in her contribution in this volume, examines the differences in my and Meynell's views of "Hegel in Canada."

10 Robert C. Sibley, *Northern Spirits: John Watson, George Grant and Charles Taylor – Appropriations of Hegelian Political Thought* (Montreal and Kingston:

McGill-Queen's University Press, 2008), 10–11, 15–16. I must thank Sacha Ghanderharian, a graduate student in one of my seminars, for drawing my attention to the interpretive differences between myself and Meynell.

11 Ibid., 28–30.

12 Ibid., 44, 51.

13 Ibid., 53.

14 Meynell, *Canadian Idealism*, 220. In this volume, Trott appears to accept Meynell's view as her own – "Sibley misreads Hegel's position on the concept of freedom" – but she makes no reference to the actual argument in my book, which, as I have demonstrated here, refutes her view.

15 Barry Cooper highlights Meynell's "misreadings" in a review of *Canadian Idealism*, "Invented Tradition," *Review of Politics* 74, no. 3 (June 2012): 535–8. As he puts it, "With respect to those who understood Canadian intellectual history and the political division between the United States and Canada on rather different grounds, Meynell again indulged a regrettable tendency to pronounce ex-cathedra judgments on their arguments. Such individuals made 'major missteps' or 'common errors' and 'erroneous interpretations'; but he did not supply detailed analysis and refutation of, for example, Janet Ajzenstat and Peter Smith, J.G.A. Pocock, or Bernard Bailyn." More particularly, Meynell discovered similar "misreadings of Grant's intellectual development" on the part of "just about anyone who has written on Grant, and George Grant himself." In effect, Meynell claimed "to have understood Grant better than Grant understood himself. He did so, moreover, without the bother of showing that he understood Grant on Grant's own terms." I would suggest something similar applies to Meynell's understanding of *Northern Spirits*.

16 David MacGregor has written that proportionately, "Canada may produce more original work on Hegel than any other nation." See "Canada's Hegel," *Literary Review of Canada*, February 1994, 18–29.

17 Leslie Armour and Elizabeth Trott, *The Faces of Reason: An Essay on Philosophy and Culture in English-Canada 1850–1950* (Waterloo, ON: Wilfrid Laurier University Press, 1981), 1–32.

18 Leslie Armour, *The Idea of Canada and the Crisis of Community* (Ottawa: Steel Rail Publishing, 1981), 79.

19 Armour and Trott, *Faces of Reason*, 19.

20 Hegel, *Philosophy of Right*, trans. T.M. Knox (Oxford: Clarendon, 1952), 160–1.

21 Grant, *Lament*, 68. I have argued elsewhere that Grant may have absorbed Hegelian principles even before he read Hegel, through the

influence of his grandfather, George Monro Grant, who, as head of Queen's University in the later decades of the nineteenth century, was a friend of the Idealist philosopher and Hegel scholar John Watson, who taught at Queen's for several decades. See Sibley, *Northern Spirits*, 121–3.

22 Ibid., 70.

23 Francis Fukuyama, *The End of History and the Last Man* (New York: Free Press, 1992).

24 Quoted by James A. Good, "A 'World Historical Idea': The St Louis Hegelians and the Civil War," *Journal of American Studies* 34, no. 3 (December 2000): 450.

25 Josiah Royce, *The Philosophy of Loyalty* (New York: Macmillan, 1908).

26 Grant, *Philosophy in the Mass Age*, 3.

27 On this topic, I have greatly benefited from Harris Athanasiadis's study, *George Grant and the Theology of the Cross: The Christian Foundation of His Thought* (Toronto: University of Toronto Press, 2001), 112–15.

28 Grant, *Philosophy in the Mass Age*, 19.

29 Grant, *Lament*, 89.

30 Ibid., 88–9.

31 Athanasiadis, *George Grant and the Theology of the Cross*, 207–8.

32 George Grant, *Technology and Justice* (Toronto: House of Anansi, 1986), 76.

33 Grant, *Lament*, 89.

34 Quoted by Schmidt, *George Grant in Process*, 64.

35 Grant, *Philosophy in the Mass Age*, 4–8.

36 Cited by Christian, "George Grant's Lament," 205, 207–8.

37 Grant, "Introduction," *Lament*, ix.

38 As Grant writes in *Lament*, 94, "Those who criticize our age must at the same time contemplate pain, infant mortality, crop failures in isolated areas, and the sixteen-hour day."

39 Yusuf Umar, "George Grant's Political Philosophy," in *George Grant and the Future of Canada*, ed. Yusuf Umar (Calgary: University of Calgary Press, 1992), 14–15.

40 Grant, *Lament*, 68.

41 Ibid., 69.

42 Ibid., 18, 51–2.

43 Ibid., 53.

44 Creighton's scathing statement deserves being quoted in full: "Well, it's still a good place to live, but that's all Canada is now – just a good place to live." Quoted by Charles Taylor, *Radical Tories* (Toronto: House of Anansi, 1982), 23. In short, Canada is a comfort zone for lifestyle consumers.

45 Grant, "Lament for a Nation Revisited: An Interview with George Grant," by Monica Hall, *International Insights: A Dalhousie Journal on International Affairs* 4, no. 1 (1988): 7. Tim Thomas, "George Grant, the Free Trade Agreement and Contemporary Quebec," *Journal of Canadian Studies* 27, no. 4 (Winter 1992–3): 180–96. On this point, it is worth nothing Elizabeth Trott's argument in her contribution to this volume in which, echoing Meynell's critique, she suggests that my exploration in *Northern Spirits* of Hegelian thought and my analysis of Canada's "present cultural state" amounts to my "promoting ... assimilation policies" that would provide "more freedom for each of us were we to join the United States." This is a puzzling assertion for any reputable scholar to make. Such a claim, echoing Meynell's, implies that analysing Grant's views on the "impossibility of Canada" and describing Watson's positive views on empire (see chapter 10) amount to the promotion of Canada's political assimilation into the United States.

To be sure, I acknowledge the "uncertainty" of Canada's political future, but I also clearly state in both the beginning and in the conclusion to *Northern Spirits* that my task was to seek a deeper philosophic comprehension of Canada's political culture, not entertain finite hopes about its political future. See *Northern Spirits*, 6–7, 298–9. For Meynell and Trott to conflate theoretical analysis and prescription is to abandon political theory in favour of ideology.

46 Grant, *Lament*, 53. This is Grant's first use of Kojève's phrase in *Lament* and it is worth quoting him on what he takes it to mean: "The universal and homogeneous state is the pinnacle of political striving. 'Universal' implies a world-wide state, which would eliminate the curse of war among nations; 'homogeneous' means that all men would be equal, and war among classes would be eliminated."

47 On this distinction between Hegel's actual thinking and Kojève's recasting of that thought, I recommend H.S. Harris, "The End of History in Hegel," in *Hegel Myths and Legends*, ed. Jon Stewart (Evanston, IL: Northwestern University Press, 1996), 228.

48 Grant's exposition of and commentary on the Strauss-Kojève debate is contained in his 1963 essay, "Tyranny and Wisdom." See Grant, *Technology and Empire*, 81–109. The debate was raised in Strauss's *On Tyranny: An Interpretation of Xenophon* (Chicago: University of Chicago Press, 2000), in which Strauss argues that Xenophon, in his dialogue *Hiero*, showed a better understanding of the relationship between politics and philosophy than modern thinkers. The book contains Kojève's response to Strauss and a rejoinder from Strauss to Kojève. In essence, Strauss claims the

philosopher can possess a knowledge that transcends particular historical circumstances. Kojève contends that philosophical knowledge and, hence, political order are dependent on and determined by the historical process, the end of which brings the universal and homogeneous states into being as the best and last political order. Grant accepts Strauss's refutation of Kojève's argument: The actualization of the universal and homogeneous state would be a tyranny and not the culmination of the historical struggle for recognition. In this regard, it is understandable why Grant describes the Strauss-Kojève debate as "the most important controversy in contemporary political philosophy." Grant, *Technology and Empire*, 81.

49 Grant, *Lament*, 44.

50 Grant, *Technology and Empire*, 88–90.

51 Ibid., 92–3.

52 Ibid., 98.

53 Hans Hauge, "George Grant's Critique of Modernity: Canadian Refractions of Continental Ideas," *Canadian Issues* 12 (1990): 109–3.

54 Grant, *Time as History* (1969; repr. Toronto: University of Toronto Press, 1995), 40.

55 Zdravko Planinc, "Paradox and Polyphony in Grant's Critique of Modernity," in Umar, *George Grant and the Future of Canada*, 31.

56 Arthur Kroker, *Technology and the Canadian Mind* (Montreal: New World Perspectives, 1984), 25, 50–1; R.K. Crook, "Modernization and Nostalgia: A Note on the Sociology of Pessimism," *Queen's Quarterly* 73 (1966): 269–84; Robert Blumstock, "Anglo-Saxon Lament," *Canadian Journal of Sociology and Anthropology* 3 (1966): 98–105; Abraham Rotstein, "Running from Paradise," *Canadian Forum*, May 1969, 26; Dennis Duffy, "The Ancestral Journeys: Travels with George Grant," *Journal of Canadian Studies* 22, no. 3 (Autumn 1987), 90–103.

57 Grant, "Conversation," *George Grant in Process*, 63.

58 Grant, *Lament*, xi.

14 Hegel and Canada's Constitution

GRAEME NICHOLSON

A lifetime spent in the study of Greek epic, tragedy, politics, and philosophy gave to James Doull a perspective on Hegel that differentiated him from much of the Hegelianism of the twentieth century. It counterbalanced our tendency to situate Hegel mainly in reference to modern philosophy – in politics, as replying to Hobbes and Rousseau; in metaphysics, as replying to Hume and Kant. My intent here will be to show some Hegelian themes that are at work in a number of Doull's articles, and to point to the Hellenic grounding for them. Many of them appeared in the online journal *Animus*, some in the classics journal *Dionysius*, offering interpretations of ancient poetry and philosophy. Some of these studies were clearly Hegelian, some less so; the most important of them are included in the volume *Philosophy and Freedom*.[1] In addition, all through the 1980s and 1990s he devoted a number of articles to questions of the Canadian Constitution, culminating in "The Philosophical Basis of Constitutional Discussion in Canada"[2] – which, along with accompanying commentaries in *PF*,[3] will be my main source here. Not every classicist and not every Hegelian has worked with such intensity on the country's law and constitution; it is, I believe, family tradition that we have to thank for this – Professor Doull's father had been chief justice of the Nova Scotia Supreme Court.

In my opening section, I shall pay attention to the appropriation of Hellas by both Hegel and Doull. This will lead me, in the second section, to propose an interpretation in English of Hegel's famous doctrine of *Sittlichkeit*: I shall call it "civilization." Third, I hope to show that this Hegelian structure can be found realized in the Canadian Constitution, and in some recent expressions of our Supreme Court that bear on our constitution. I shall conclude with some observations on nation and

Volk, even though it is well known that they are not central to Hegelian political philosophy.

Hellas and Hegel

The Greek beginning of philosophy remained permanently significant for both Hegel and Doull, and through Doull we understand that the studies of antiquity that fill the pages of Hegel's lectures and his *Phenomenology* were anything but a decorative adjunct: "The ground was prepared for that philosophy by the political freedom of the polis – not an abstract subjective freedom, but an ethical freedom in which individuals knew themselves free in realizing the concrete objective ends of family and state."[4]

For Doull and Hegel, the Greek achievement is everlasting, even though qualified by a limitation. In Greek religion, the spiritual is for the first time decisively elevated above the natural, expressed in the central story of the victory of the gods over the titans, Prometheus and the rest, natural beings banished to the edge of the earth,[5] and obliged to serve the gods. The Olympian gods are pure spirit, and the worship of them in the festivals is cheerful and free;[6] the beauty of the gods is the idealization of human beauty. But these gods, while spiritual, are finite, and Greek life, accordingly, is "not yet the subjectivity that is inwardly universal."[7] "The Greeks are not free in the sense that we are free, i.e., in their self-consciousness; they let themselves be determined from without," i.e., by oracles and the like.[8] As Doull too says, later in the essay we quoted,[9] "The ancient philosophy ... did not have in it the free rational individual or person." But the main point is that without this first, immediate, beautiful freedom, there would never have been a free humanity!

The theme of freedom is undeniably central to Hegel's whole project, and the Greeks are for him an emblem of one central element in freedom, one that, in his view, tended to be lost in modern accounts – for instance, in Kant and Fichte – in which the factor of subjectivity predominated. Hegel treated this modern one-sidedness in the *Phenomenology of Spirit*, in the sections devoted to "Reason," and to "Spirit," especially "Reason as lawgiver" in the former section, and "Morality" in the latter. Moreover, in the *Philosophy of Right* (*PR*),[10] the entire "Second Part: Morality" was devoted to these modern subjectivist views. Both books in their later course accomplish a fusion of the Greek-objective and the modern-subjective elements of freedom.

All Hegel interpreters acknowledge this fused or "concrete" sense of freedom. There are recent challenges[11] to the mainstream liberal reading of Hegel – the Hegelian Middle, so-called; but I do not think that that argument affects the concrete composition of freedom itself. It does not move Hegel from his mediating position between Kant, Fichte, etc., on one side, and Greek antiquity, on the other side.

When we turn to the Hegelian constitutional discussion, we find the framework for it mainly in the introductory paragraphs on the state,[12] and the remarks on sovereignty.[13] They are both comprehended under the heading of Will, for the sovereign state determines what is to be done. The Introduction to *PR*[14] offered a lengthy phenomenology of the Will, starting from the assumptions common to Kant and Fichte, that Will is a function of the single subjective Ego. But the argument of the whole book, culminating in the account of the state, is that there is a collective Will, in the sovereign state, and that cannot be grasped without reference to the beautiful freedom expressed in ancient Greek art and thought.

The *Philosophy of Right* criticizes the modern doctrine of the social contract, a contract that, according to Hobbes, brings into being the sovereign, who is provided with so much greater power than anyone else that all are kept in awe of his fearsome power. Paragraph 258 repudiates any effort to derive the state from "contingencies such as distress, need for protection, force, riches, etc.,"[15] a derivation that would make it depend on "the interest of individuals as such," implying that their "membership of the state is something optional."[16] All this he ties to the very idea of a "contract" (*Vertrag*),[17] which has been falsely applied to the case of the state. Though it is Rousseau he quotes, his critique certainly encompasses Hobbes as well.

Hegel says in these pages that the social contract doctrine exhibits only an alleged or reputed rationality (*das vermeinte Vernünftige*).[18] The contract-philosophy aims to answer the question, What is the reason for the state? Is it not for securing the safety, welfare, and property of the individuals it embraces? Hegel is aware that many individuals would think in such a fashion, i.e., that this would express the appearance (*Erscheinung*) of the state to an individual located in it with some point of view. But the developing *Philosophy of Right* wants to offer a concept that is not dependent in that way upon some "point of view": it wants to be *Wissenschaft*.

We have to understand that the state – that structure of Reason and Will – is in fact one mode of Spirit, which comprehends Reason and

Will, one embodiment of that particular modality of Spirit that Hegel calls *Sittlichkeit* (usually but not helpfully translated "ethical life"), along with the family and civil society. Hegel is well known for having differentiated the state clearly from civil society (economic relationships and the institutions that regulate them), a separation that had not been achieved by any of his predecessors. But he was also the first to conceptualize *Sittlichkeit* as distinct from morality (*Moralität*), the former fusing the subjective domain of freedom and right with the objective domain that Greek life had exemplified so well. If Duty was understood in *Moralität*[19] as pure and formal in the Kantian way, Hegel's family, civic life, and the state, on the other hand, offer us a multitude of varying specific duties, rooted partly in custom, partly in legislation, differentiated by person, profession, and role.[20] Our theme now is not any one of these three main existing institutions but rather the idea, the principle, by which they operate, *Sittlichkeit* itself. The key point is that these many duties, practices, customs, and rules are not merely what ought to be – they are real and effective all the time. A *Sitte* (as perfectly expressed in the Greek *ēthos*, and perfectly exemplified by the figure of Antigone) is "the familiar ordinance and the custom which is observed ... its truth is its effective validity, open and apparent";[21] therefore it is a law that has existence and is not only something commanded. Precisely this feature means that *Sittlichkeit* is the very Idea of the Right that is guiding Hegel, the concept of right together with the actualization of the concept.[22] Given the concrete or fused character of Hegel's freedom and Right, we recognize that such a law has two sides:[23] it is alive in the consciousness of the individual,[24] yet it is also objective, a reality surrounding the individual, expecting him or her to participate.[25] The central issue that now confronts Hegel as over against a moralist such as Kant is why these *Sitten* should prevail with an obligatory character. Where Kant's free subject had been expected to appraise every empirical command and custom reflectively, bringing it under the categorical imperative of reason, Hegel argues that *Sittlichkeit* fulfils the rational idea of the Right more completely than morality. The fact that state authority is not grounded in a social contract is one expression of this point.

The state with its legislature and executive certainly embodies a *will* – i.e., such-and-such is to be *done*. But this is not the will of a singular person; it is collective. Hegel identifies it as the will of the objective mind, or the universal will. It expresses itself in laws and regulations that have the authority of reason behind them. This includes the constitution. Hegel uses a number of phrases to express what is special about the state: it is rational in itself, *an und für sich*;[26] it expresses the very idea of reason, *das an sich in seinem Begriffe Vernünftige*;[27] it is the unmoved end in itself, *unbewegter Selbstzweck*.[28] Negatively, it is clear that Hegel is denying that the state can be justified or derived from some other aim or purpose. It is not that it lacks an aim or purpose; rather the aim has to be intrinsic to it.

The way to understand this is to think not only of the state as an institution but also all the laws and policies that it promulgates. Laws themselves are judged, in the first instance, according to previous laws. And just as distinct laws are judged according to other laws, so the institution as a whole, the state itself, finds its rationale through the laws that it authorizes. There is a circular structure: the laws have their legitimacy by virtue of the state that has decreed them, but in the other direction, the state finds its own rationale in the laws that it has decreed. It is not justified through the preferences of contracting individuals. Hegel himself poses the Hobbesian question of the origin of the state,[29] but he says, "If we look for grounding for the authority of an actually existing state, this can only be derived from the laws themselves that are valid within that state."[30] Those who legislate do so according to an existing code of law that is operative on any occasion of legislation. Here we discover another sense of the term *universal*: state and law embody reason universally, because reason is already operative in the deliberation that brings forth constitutions and laws. The law is universal in that all occasions of making law and applying law are guided in advance by a law that is always already in effect. That is characteristic of reason, and it marks this reason off from the calculating rationality of contracting agents.

As a next step in interpretation I should like to propose a concept to capture what is particularly salient for the discussion. No English expression will capture every nuance of Hegel's idea, but one application of it can guide our discussion further: *Sittlichkeit* means "civilization."

Civilization

This concept (Hegel would have called it an Idea) is familiar from the study of the remotest past and anthropology, where we represent the transition of humanity from an uncivilized state to civilization, comprehending here the regularization of marriage and kinship practices, the emergence of agriculture, the development of language, and some form of writing. Historically, civilization in this sense is the bedrock on the basis of which later forms of polity and government would arise. But we also use the term in another sense, plural and comparative, when we identify distinct civilizations, e.g., in East and West. Here we do not merely intend that there is some kind of kinship structure and some form of agriculture, etc., but we recognize that distinct customs and rules (e.g., for kinship) prevail within one civilization and other ones elsewhere. Indeed these are not ultimately distinct concepts; in fact, civilization is both prehistoric and historic, both pre-political and political; the civilization that is the condition for polity and government to emerge continues to mark society after the polity has emerged. A common aspect of civilization in all its senses is that this is at once a descriptive and a normative concept. Not only do we describe the structure of a given civilization according to certain features; we also recognize an obligation upon human beings to be civilized. This is the case with the anthropological concept and with the plural differentiated concept.[31] The dual character of it – both descriptive and normative – replicates the feature we saw in Hegel's Idea. There is an objective order, definite customs and rules that surround every individual subject; equally, that person's consciousness recognizes these customs as binding.[32] Such is the civilized person. So I shall use this term instead of Hegel's German word *Sittlichkeit* in the rest of my exposition, looking for something that can serve as justification for laws and constitutions.

I think that Hegel's treatment of the modern state is applicable to Canada – indeed, Doull has made the case that it provides the best optic for understanding Canada. That is owing above all to the correlation Hegel has formulated between civil society and the state, assigning supremacy to the latter within the general structure of civilization. This supremacy is not realized everywhere, and in particular not in the United States through a good portion of its history. Doull's outline in "The Philosophical Basis of Constitutional Discussion in Canada" is guided by a lengthy historical comparison between Canada and the American federation, a comparison guided by two different correlations. On the one hand, there is the Hegelian correlation of state and civil society, which is fundamental for characterizing both countries and clarifying their difference. On the other hand, there is also the correlation between central governments and the governments of the provinces or states. It is crucial to understand this second correlation as one within the state, for in federal unions sovereignty is divided, some aspects assigned to the centre, others to the provinces or states. Divided sovereignty, the essence of federalism, is not a feature of Hegel's theory in *PR* (even though Germany was to become a federal state when it was created, and is today a remarkably successful federation). Where Hegelian thought can guide us is in grasping how the oscillations of power throughout the life of a federation are shaped through the interactions of state and civil society, differently realized in the United States and Canada.

Doull treats the U.S. Constitution in a lengthy, interesting historical narrative[33] that begins from the adoption of the Constitution in 1787 and its interpretation by such founders as Hamilton, Jefferson, and Madison: "The American federation is a relation of sovereign States to a sovereign Union, but that as ordinarily viewed from the standpoint of free individuals."[34] The subsequent history concerns the different weightings, over time, of the different elements in this structure. The test of the power of the union over the states came eventually in the Civil War. But with the supremacy of the union established at that time, there came a period of reform with the progressives in combat against the barons of the Gilded Age – "the rapid growth of an industrial society tended to make obsolete the concept of the independent individual as the bearer of American freedom"[35] – this is the matrix of pragmatist philosophy, according to Doull.[36] Then the limits of this culture appeared in the Depression, that required a new initiative of the state on behalf of society. To skip to the end of the story, Doull sees the modern neoliberal attack on state power – deregulation, for instance – as once again exposing the need in the United States for a state structure to define the common good. Writing in 1997, he appeared to believe that this need would be met, with a new swing in favour of state activity; reading the article today, one is far from reassured that the United States will develop in the direction Doull was hoping. The story as a whole is that the United States, beginning from a supposed primacy of society over state, is led by its detailed experiences to come to understand that the state "might emerge more clearly as the basis and support of the society of free individuals."[37] Doull's history of the United States is illuminated by many discerning comments on the philosophers who belonged to the history, especially Rawls and Rorty.

That treatment of the United States was undertaken to highlight a different development in the course of Canada's history. "There is not the aversion of Americans to the state when it is felt to impinge on individual freedom."[38] Thus from its foundation the state in Canada was not subordinated to the varying interests of society. Likewise, in the foundation of modern Canada in 1867 the central government was intended to have clear supremacy over the provinces – at least, in the opinion of the first prime minister, John A. Macdonald.[39] This, however, coexisted with the duality of French and English cultures, languages, and religions, with the historic weight of this difference evident in Quebec. As Doull reads the whole course of the history, Canada's development has been from a preponderantly centralized state authority to a more balanced federation where provincial sovereignty will receive its due[40] – in a sense, therefore, in the opposite direction from developments in the United States.[41] With this account of history we need to take note of the urgency of the occasion of Doull's article, seeking to provide a "philosophical basis for discussion of the constitution." It was prompted by central events of the 1980s and 1990s: the proclamation of the Constitution Act of 1982, with its Charter of Rights and Freedoms; Quebec's refusal to sign this constitution; the history of the Meech Lake Accord from 1987 to 1990; its final rejection by a combination of authorities in Canada; the 1995 Sovereignty Referendum in Quebec, which lost only by a tiny margin. The torrents of constitutional discussions during the 1980s and 1990s would have benefited, Doull believed, from closer attention to history and philosophy. Doull comes at the end of his essay to the question of Quebec's right of secession. He does not acknowledge such a right, and our interest now is to understand his treatment of the historical and philosophical principles, and then to see how they are deployed on the question of Quebec's rights. Understanding of principles is inherently worthwhile, even apart from the secession question.

Throughout the article, there are many occasions on which Doull leads the reader back behind sovereignty and divided sovereignty, back behind the correlation of state and society, to something lying at their basis – a deep stratum of civilization, corresponding to the Hegelian Idea of *Sittlichkeit*. In the old union of Canada West and East, there was a common political experience that led to the proposals for Confederation – we had "a common political formation in which we passed from colonial dependence to complete independence."[42] But this applies not merely to committees of legislators: on the land, in the towns, there was a "common Canadian spirit."[43] It was the "basis of a unified Canadian sovereignty."[44] It is true that there were "two cultures,"[45] but both were "based on a common European culture."[46] How did the Canada of today come into existence? "To know how the common polity of these peoples which now exists, if imperfectly, came to be, one must attend not only to the events of their common and special histories but to the spirit moving in them."[47] Throughout this account, Doull uses the term *Western freedom* to characterize this common spirit, or civilization. "One reads with admiration of the heroic characters who made New France – Champlain, Frontenac, and many another."[48] It is the given basis of the country, *Sittlichkeit* or civilization, that stands in the way of a unilateral declaration of independence – Doull argues that Canada could not accept such a venture.[49]

Canada's Constitution

Our concern up to here has been to work towards a philosophical understanding of civilization. As for the practical consequences to be drawn from the idea, we may be best advised to turn our attention away from philosophy as such to law. We shall turn to a statement of the Supreme Court of Canada (which was issued very shortly after Doull's article was published) in which the question of the secession of Quebec was examined according to Canada's constitutional law. The result, in my view, will show still that there is a Hegelian idea of civilization operative in our Constitution.

Our focus is now on the "Supreme Court Reference re Secession of Quebec" of 1998. Subsequent to the events of the 1980s and 1990s that I mentioned above, the Government of Canada, in 1996, referred three questions to the Supreme Court, which I may paraphrase:

1. Does the Constitution of Canada permit Quebec's government to effect the secession of Quebec from Canada unilaterally?
2. Does international law bestow such a right upon Quebec?
3. If domestic law conflicted with international law over this question, which would take precedence?[50]

It is in accord with Hegel's idea of Right and *Sittlichkeit* that our inquiry should turn first, not to the opinions of one person or group, but to the actually existing law, in this case, the constitutional law. It is also in accord with Hegel's philosophy that it is the mandate of an existing court to declare what the law is. And the court that issued this statement knew its terrain and did not stray into those issues that politicians had to decide. It was not considering whether secession would be wise or beneficial, nor by what methods it could be achieved, but only how such methods would be appraised according to the law.

First, the judgment showed that the three questions were within the jurisdiction of the court and were of a nature to receive a judicial answer.[51] Then it outlined the history of Canada before and after Confederation, highlighting the extensive consultations that led up to 1867 and the legal continuity of the confederation since then.[52] This narrative portion allowed the court to introduce a number of principles that it found working in the history, that also came to characterize the Constitution itself as the outcome of this history. They are part of the "unwritten constitution"[53] and constitute a condition for its "legitimacy," which is something more than legality.[54] The principles "dictate major elements of the architecture of the Constitution itself and are as such its lifeblood."[55] "The principles assist in the interpretation of the text and the delineation of spheres of jurisdiction."[56] We shall proceed next to examine the four principles, but it is worth noting at the start that the court was not appealing to some authority of the "founders" or "framers," their original intention, as is common in constitutional debates in the United States. As we shall see, these are impersonal norms, emergent from a history, not authored by any "founder," norms that underlay not only the legislatures that existed before and after Confederation, but also the civil society before and after Confederation – in short, as I shall try to demonstrate, norms of civilization or *Sittlichkeit* that have been at work, and are at work, not only in legal interpretation but also in concrete political life. The court's text makes it clear that the four principles are interwoven: no one of them can be invoked in isolation.

Federalism. Perhaps the most evident feature of Canada's Constitution, it has been adopted not for its own sake, or for efficiency in delivering government services, but as "a political and legal response to underlying social and political realities … it recognizes the diversity of component parts of Confederation."[57] Most notable is Quebec, whose "social and demographic reality … was one of the essential reasons for establishing a federal structure,"[58] but regional cultural diversity was and is true of the Maritime provinces too, i.e., their civilization.

Democracy. Our democracy is not merely a technique of management; democracy embodies "respect for the inherent dignity of the human person, commitment to social justice and equality, accommodation of a wide variety of beliefs, respect for cultural and group identity,"[59] i.e., elements of our wide Western civilization. It is this principle, undoubtedly fundamental to Canada and all its parts, that is taken by sovereigntists to justify a right to secession. They interpret it to mean self-determination of a people, recognizing the people's right to chart their future inside or outside any alliance or federation. In particular, the court has been asked for its ruling on Quebec's right to a unilateral secession, i.e., not dependent on the consent of other members of the federation. The answer of the court consists mainly in showing that democracy is not a separate principle in Canada, but rests in the context of the other three principles under discussion. "Quebec could not, despite a clear referendum result, purport to invoke a right of self-determination to dictate the terms of a proposed secession to the other parties to the federation. The democratic vote, by however strong a majority, would have no legal effect on its own and could not push aside the principles of federalism and the rule of law, the rights of individuals and minorities, or the operation of democracy in the other provinces or in Canada as a whole."[60] Nevertheless, the democratic principle in Quebec also cuts in another direction, too, as we shall see after we review the other principles.

The Rule of Law. This expresses a deep-seated moral principle that citizens have the right to be free from arbitrary actions of governments. And this is also a reason why the question of secession must meet tests imposed by the Constitution: its partisans cannot simply set the Constitution aside.

Protection of Minorities. A principle connected to the rule of law is the limitation of the power of majorities to impose their will on those whose position in the jurisdiction is weaker. Canada has not always acted so, but its history expresses an aspiration to that ideal.

Now we must turn to the positive force of the democratic principle, when it is not violating federalism, rule of law, and minority protection: if there were a referendum on a clear question with a clear majority, there would be a reciprocal obligation on the other members of the federation to enter into negotiations towards the secession of Quebec.[61] Such an expression of the democratic will of the Quebec people would confer legitimacy on the efforts of the Government of Quebec to initiate the negotiations. The court issued no directives concerning such negotiations – that would be a political process, not a judicial one, and it would remain to the politicians to declare what would count as a clear question and a clear majority. Thus, to conclude, the court did not declare secession unlawful – there is a possible constitutional path that the government of Quebec could pursue towards secession.

The court also answered the second question, whether international law would sanction the unilateral secession of Quebec from Canada. It found reasons for answering in the negative.[62] While this reasoning is important, it does not bear directly on our present theme, the *sittlich* foundations of Canada's own constitution. The argument does, however, turn upon *Sittlichkeit*, civilization. In fact, this is the principal norm that regulates international relations, supplemented by treaties. The court's opinion is that the self-determination of the people of Quebec has been achieved within the Canadian framework. They are not a colonial or oppressed people whose self-determination would require rupture from the Canadian federation, so Quebec could expect a frosty reception in the international arena in the event of a unilateral secession. We may note that international law constitutes the climax of Hegel's treatment of the state. He does not foresee, in Kantian style, a world government or league of nations. But while he is a realist, he is not a bloodthirsty one, for he recognizes that international relations are appropriately governed by a *Sittlichkeit* of their own.[63]

I may conclude my remarks on the Supreme Court Reference by observing that, since it found no conflict between domestic and international law on the issue at hand, it did not need to make a reply to Question 3.

Volk and Nation

A few years after this declaration of the Supreme Court, the Parliament of Canada passed a resolution recognizing that the people of Quebec constituted a nation. A resolution of that sort is not a constitutional initiative, and the term *nation* is not in the terminology of the Constitution. But since the resolution is part of the parliamentary record, we may well ask about it as a political question, though keeping one eye on the Constitution.

What does the resolution mean for Quebec? Among other things, it means that the long struggle of the Quebec people to survive, to maintain their language, culture, and identity, is now recognized as being in the interest of the country as a whole, that it has served Canada and its federation. Thereby the legislature of Canada has repudiated a view that is at times heard among some sectors of the anglophone population, that Quebeckers (or French Canadians) are just one of the ethnic groups in Canada, another linguistic minority who need to assimilate like the others. The legislature of Canada has thereby endorsed the measures that have seemed necessary in Quebec – through their government – to secure the primacy of the French language in Quebec, to prevent the assimilation of the people to a North American average culture, and to bring the immigrant families and children into the francophone sphere. A political question that still divides the Quebec people, however, is whether this national project can be achieved within the frame of Canada's Constitution. According to the understanding I have of Hegel's philosophy, he would give that an affirmative answer: the members of the nation will find their freedom through law and constitution. It does not seem, however, that there is anything in his philosophy that would convert a sovereigntist.

We ask further what that parliamentary resolution means for the anglophone majority outside Quebec. It is noteworthy that it did not awaken much resistance in Canada, by contrast with the stormy controversy that surrounded the Meech Lake Accord with its proposed constitutional recognition of Quebec as a distinct society. Does that prove that it is a harmless, empty gesture? I think not. Perhaps the actual effect of the resolution is to indicate that Canada, as such, is not a nation. Canadians now seem to be less ready to apply this term to their country than they were in decades past, in part because of recognizing that the country is a broad federation containing a Quebec nation and a number of Aboriginal groups known as the First Nations. It seems now that there are three possible responses to this situation that are implicitly at work in public opinion.

(1) There is the possibility that "English Canada" would be constituted as a nation, standing beside a Quebec nation, both contained in Canada. This is the deux nations concept that was current some decades ago, informing the policy of the Progressive Conservative Party at the time, and as the name suggests it expressed a vision of many Conservative Quebec federalists. It may be, too, that this solution is nearest to a Hegelian preference. At a deep level, there is a common civilization expressing itself both in Quebec and in the English-speaking part of Canada, what Doull has called "Western freedom." Such a grounding could sustain the doctrine of a Canadian nation expressing itself in two languages, but it could sustain as well a deux nations solution, recognizing that, just as in French Canada, there is an anglophone nation, constituted not only by language but by historical memories, religion, fraternal organizations, intertwined family histories, and countless other communal bonds.

It is true that Hegel was not pre-eminently a philosopher of the Nation (or *Volk*). It does not play a role in the constitution of the Right. Yet it appears all over the text of *PR* as a factual, empirical circumstance that he no more puts in doubt than he does town-and-country, East-and-West, man-and-woman, and many other constants of the world he knew. Thus his thought could recognize two nations within the one state.

(2) There is also the possibility that "English Canada" would be constituted as a nation, standing over against a separate, independent Quebec nation. In the event of Quebec secession, this nation would be properly called "Canada," but a national definition of "English Canada" now would be an anticipatory move, preparing for a future separate life. This nation would have the same conditions of memory, family, and fraternity that we mentioned above, but on this conception such a nation would continue its life after the political rupture than gave Quebec its sovereignty.

There are many currents in the Canadian scene that seem to assume such an identity.[64]

(3) But it may also be possible for the federation to continue, with a Quebec nation sharing in the Constitution along with a post-national, multicultural entity living on without a strong identity, "the English-speaking part of Canada" that is not a nation. Is this in fact possible? A people who were not a nation? Could there be one large part of a federated state with a population lacking national identity? The identity of such a people would be "unencumbered" by nationality. Such a form of freedom could also be sketched, and has been sketched, in other terms: the world after the nation state; a world come of age; a disenchanted world; a post-national world.

I believe that such a development would be difficult and paradoxical for a Hegelian to entertain. The "concrete" freedom that is at the foundation of his philosophy fuses a subjective, Kantian freedom together with the objective domain of custom and rule to constitute *Sittlichkeit*. It might seem that there would be nothing in a post-national community to attach the people to the state, no memories, no history, no heroes, no patriotic societies, no fraternal institutions. Thus their freedom would not be concrete in Hegel's sense. Hegel might see such a people as encountering the laws of the state purely as rational Duty, lacking all affective, emotional promptings – a bare, grey world of Fichtean rationalists.

I think, however, that despite Hegelian objections, we could imagine a Canada containing a Quebec nation and a post-national

English-speaking community, sharing in a common constitution out of different motives. Instead of expressing a "concrete" freedom, as Hegel did, that was made possible through law and the state, our sketch is expressing an "existential" freedom. Such a "freedom without identity" could well serve to introduce us to a stratum of civilization lying deeper than nationality.

NOTES

1 David Peddle and Neil Robertson, eds., *Philosophy and Freedom: The Legacy of James Doull* (Toronto: University of Toronto Press, 2003), (hereafter cited as *PF*).
2 James Doull, "The Philosophical Basis of Constitutional Discussion in Canada," *Animus* 2 (1997): 393–465; *PF*, 393–465.
3 Henry Roper, "James Doull's Political Thought," in *PF*, 466–75; David Peddle and Neil Robertson, "North American Freedom: James Doull's Recent Political Thought," in *PF*, 476–504.
4 James Doull, "Hegel's Phenomenology and Post-modern Thought," in *PF*, 284.
5 G.W.F. Hegel, *Lectures on the Philosophy of Religion: One-Volume Edition: The Lectures of 1827*, ed. Peter Hodgson (Berkeley: University of California Press, 1988), 333–4 (hereafter *LPR*). A similar story is told in Hegel's lectures on the *Philosophy of History*, *Aesthetics*, and the *History of Philosophy*.
6 Ibid., 352.
7 Ibid., 355.
8 Ibid., 356.
9 *PF*, 286.
10 G.W.F. Hegel, *Grundlinien der Philosophie des Rechts* [1821], ed. J. Hoffmeister (Hamburg: Philosophische Bibliothek, 1955) (hereafter *PR*). I shall be quoting the old, classical translation by T.M. Knox (London: Oxford, 1952), but page references are to the German edition of 1955.
11 Renato Cristi, *Hegel on Freedom and Authority* (Cardiff: University of Wales Press, 2005).
12 *PR*, paras 257–60.
13 Ibid., paras 278–9.
14 Ibid., paras 4–31.
15 *PR*, 210.
16 Ibid., 208.

17 Ibid., 209.
18 Ibid., 210.
19 *PR*, para. 133.
20 Ibid., para. 151.
21 G.W.F. Hegel, *Phenomenologie des Geistes*, ed. J. Hoffmeister (Hamburg: Philosophische Bibliothek, 1952), 319.
22 *PR*, paras 1, 142.
23 Ibid., para. 143.
24 Ibid.
25 Ibid., para. 144.
26 Ibid., para. 208.
27 Ibid., para. 210.
28 Ibid., para. 208.
29 Ibid., para. 209.
30 "In Rücksicht auf die Autorität eines wirklichen Staates, insofern sie sich auf Gründe einlässt, sind diese aus den Formen des in ihm gültigen Rechts genommen." Ibid.
31 All the anthropological works of Claude Lévi-Strauss afford a detailed grasp of this Idea, though he does not generally use the term *civilization.*
32 In my book *Justifying Our Existence: An Essay in Applied Phenomenology* (Toronto: University of Toronto Press, 2009), chap. 6, I tried to show how nations, states, and specific laws could find justification through the factor of civilization.
33 *PF*, 407–34.
34 Ibid., 409.
35 Ibid., 419.
36 Ibid., 420.
37 Ibid., 432.
38 Ibid., 405.
39 Ibid., 440, 443.
40 Ibid., 441, 443.
41 Ibid., 443.
42 Ibid., 393.
43 Ibid., 394.
44 Ibid.
45 Ibid., 458.
46 Ibid., 456.
47 Ibid., 436–7.
48 Ibid., 437.
49 Ibid., 456–62.

50 Reference re Secession of Quebec [1998] 2 SCR 217.
51 Ibid., paras 1–31.
52 Ibid., paras 32–48.
53 Ibid., para. 32.
54 Ibid., para. 33.
55 Ibid., para. 51.
56 Ibid., para. 52.
57 Ibid., paras 57, 58.
58 Ibid., para. 59.
59 Ibid., para. 64.
60 Ibid., para. 2.
61 Ibid., paras 85–95.
62 Ibid., paras 109–46.
63 Hegel, *PR*, para. 339.
64 This seems to be the thesis of Ian Angus's *Identity and Justice* (Toronto: University of Toronto Press, 2008), implicitly anticipating secession.

15 Hegel's Laurentian Fragments

BARRY COOPER

Introduction

An unexpected discovery by twentieth-century Canadian intellectual historians was the presence of Hegel in the early spiritual life of the country, sometimes mediated by Victorian English thinkers such as Bernard Bosanquet or L.T. Hobhouse, sometimes presented directly in classrooms by Canadian professors.[1] Summarizing this discovery at the beginning of *Northern Spirits*, Robert C. Sibley remarked that although Hegel had little to say about Canada, Canadian scholars from the nineteenth century to the present have found in Hegel's thought a secure source on the basis of which they could understand their own country and its place in what Hegel called "world history."[2] More specifically, Sibley, along with the thinkers included in his subtitle, particularly George Grant and Charles Taylor, along with several contributors to this volume, apparently thought Hegel could provide a way of understanding the major divisions, contradictions, fault lines, or tensions in Canadian politics.

As Sibley summarized the argument, Hegel "offered theoretical tools for working out how different groups might be united politically regardless of their seemingly irresolvable differences."[3] The question of "seemingly irresolvable differences" is said to have been a perennial problem in Canada's political life. Posing the question in terms of Hegel's influence on political thought about Canada narrows the topic to a manageable size.[4] In this chapter the focus is on Sibley's two twentieth-century "northern spirits," Grant and Taylor, whom I shall refer to collectively as the Canadian political Hegelians.

Among the seemingly irresolvable differences of interest to these two Canadian political Hegelians are the linguistic and to a degree cultural and religious divisions of the inhabitants of the St Lawrence Valley or what I have called Laurentian Canada;[5] the ambivalence of Canadian liberals and the anxieties of Canadian conservatives on the losing side of the rebellion of the Thirteen Colonies; the conflicts in the interests of the Maritime colonies (and later the Maritime provinces) with Laurentian Canada; following Confederation the conflict in the interests of the old Canadian colonies with the western and the northern territories; and the distinctive attitudes of Canadians in different parts of the country towards the United States.

For these Canadian political Hegelians, however, these were only *seeming* differences, and as all Hegelians know well, seeming differences exist only as constituent elements of an *Aufhebung*, which in this context we may translate as a reconciliation that elevates and synthesizes the previously existing differences into a common national purpose for British North America and later for the Dominion of Canada. We may allow as that they could be reconciled, but were they? To this commonsensical question Grant and Taylor give rather different answers.[6]

A second preliminary observation: central to the argument that Hegel was a source of clarity about Canada's purpose and about the meaning of Canadian political life is the account of the state that Hegel developed in what he called his textbook, *The Philosophy of Right*. There he argued that philosophy of right was first of all a part of philosophy, which in turn was "the apprehension of the present and actual, not the construction of a beyond, supposed to exist, God knows where, or rather that exists and we can perfectly well say where, namely in the error of a one-sided empty ratiocination."[7] Because, moreover, "what is rational is actual and what is actual is rational," a book on the science of the state has as its subject matter the conceptualization of "the state as something rational in itself. As a work of philosophy it must be a long way from any attempt to construct the state as it ought to be."[8]

Hegel's admonition against constructing an imaginary state as it ought to be, according to the one-sided empty ratiocination emerging from the dreams of subjectivity, is of great significance and poignancy for the Canadian political Hegelians, particularly when they are compelled to confront the actuality or reality indicated by so many books reflecting the aforementioned political divisions and conflicts and bearing titles such as *Divided Loyalties* or, indeed, *Lament for a Nation*.[9] Moreover, when one considers that the locus from which these Canadian political Hegelians have spun their arguments is Laurentian Canada, Canadians whose formation has been untroubled by the anxieties and prejudices of that part of the country (including the present author) have good reason to suspect the rationality and thus the actuality of their accounts. That is, the limitations of the accounts of the Canadian political Hegelians come into view when they are subjected to historical and theoretical analysis.

The foregoing language is, broadly speaking, Hegelian, but not unconnected to classical common sense. Any number of commentators have remarked that Hegel's language is often a problem for common sense. Here we would observe only that a common sense understanding of the political realities indicated by the titles of the books by Black or Grant (or many others) must be the starting point for any detailed analysis, whether Hegelian or not. Let us begin with Grant.

The Universal and Homogeneous State

By his own account, *Philosophy in the Mass Age* (1959) was his most "Hegelian" book.[10] Under the influence of Jacques Ellul and Leo Strauss, Grant changed his mind about what he called the validity of Hegel's account of human excellence as compared to that of Plato.[11] Grant alluded to Strauss on several occasions but cited him infrequently and wrote but one sustained analysis of his work, a 1963 essay, "Tyranny and Wisdom." It discussed Strauss's interpretation of a dialogue by Xenophon and responded to a review of Strauss by Alexandre Kojève.[12] Of the conflicting and contested versions that fill academic libraries on both sides of the Atlantic, the interpretation of Hegel that Grant found persuasive (as does the present author) was provided by Kojève. Accordingly, by rejecting Hegel in favour of Plato, Grant was rejecting Kojève's Hegel. We begin a second sailing (*Phaedo*, 99d) therefore, with a brief account of Kojève's Hegel. For reasons of space we will not discuss Kojève's or Hegel's metaphysics or philosophy of history but, as did Grant, consider only the result, which Kojève called the universal and homogeneous state, or UHS as it is often abbreviated.[13] We are concerned first of all, therefore, with the insights Kojève's argument affords our understanding of Canada, rather than our understanding of Hegel. As Taylor said in the opening sentence of his chapter in this volume, Hegel's philosophy of mind, but not just his philosophy of mind, "can be reconstructed from many perspectives," and "some are more illuminating that others."

Kojève accepted and indeed was committed to the view that Hegel's was the final philosophical teaching and that Hegel's intention, that philosophy "give up its name love of knowledge and become actual knowledge" or wisdom, had been fulfilled.[14] The scandalous implications of such an interpretation have inspired respectable academic Hegelians to distinguish Kojève from Hegel, to praise Kojève as a fine but eccentric mind, and one who got his Hegel all wrong.[15] That Hegel's claim regarding "actual knowledge" was an outrage to philosophy as love of knowledge is clear enough when read in the context of Plato's *Phaedrus*, 279d, because the implication was that Hegel had become divine. Naturally enough such a claim has also outraged the conventional understanding of Hegel as a great German philosopher. But that, of course, was just what Kojève disputed. One political philosopher who accepted the philosophical implications of Kojève's interpretation of Hegel as well as its philosophical implications was Eric Voegelin.[16]

In consequence, the System of Science must be singular, which is to say that Hegel, Kojève, and anyone else who is willing and competent could understand it. One might expect Hegel to understand it better than anyone else, but if the System embodied Wisdom, it must be the same for everyone who knew how to read it, especially as the author already indicated that the share of the "particular individual" was small so that he should receive no special recognition for the patient labours of the Concept.[17] According to Kojève, Hegel was not being modest but merely honest in acknowledging his own place as "a blind link on the chain of absolute necessity by which the world builds itself up."[18] Priority being given to the System as creator, so to speak, of Hegelianism, it is quite possible that Kojève understood it better than Hegel. All one needs to do is show where Hegel was unfaithful to the System, which is precisely what Kojève claimed to have done.[19]

The political consequence, Kojève explained in the *Introduction à la Lecture de Hegel*, was

> that history was over ... At first I thought quite simply that Hegel miscalculated by a hundred and fifty years. The end of history had come not with Napoleon but with Stalin, and it was I who was charged with saying so, with the difference that I did not have the chance of seeing Stalin pass beneath my window on a horse ... Later, with the war, I understood. No, Hegel was not wrong; he truly gave the date of the end of history as 1806. Afterwards, what has happened? Nothing at all but the *realignment*

of provinces. The Chinese Revolution is just the introduction of the Code Napoléon into China.[20]

Pro forma one must insist that this extraordinary claim was not a joke. There are several fascinating "theoretical" consequences that flow from the notion of the end of history,[21] but our focus is on the practical and institutional outcome, the UHS. According to Kojève it was a "total" and "definitive" reality. It united the whole of humanity that counted historically and repressed all specific differences of class, family, and religion: "Wars and revolutions are henceforth impossible."[22] Accordingly, the painful labours of humanity, the historical role of Hegel's Slave, have succeeded in imposing human will on the givenness of nature; and the bloody fights of humanity, the historical role of Hegel's Master, have come to a final end. As a result, Kojève said, "The man participating in this State understands himself and is understood completely; he lives in accord with himself. Thus he is completely satisfied (*befriedigt*) and he is so by *the mutual recognition of all*. The Napoleonic Empire did not just proclaim the ideals of liberty, equality, and fraternity, it actualized them once and for all."[23]

Several implications followed. First of all, as Kojève's friend Eric Weil observed, "The end of history is the end of our unhappiness, of that unhappiness for which we are not responsible but that overtakes and crushes us."[24] The Machiavellian hope for an end to nature's caprice (see *Prince*, chap. 25) has been replaced with an active desire to overcome all otherness by technological activity, a central concern to Grant. Technology has thus become the foundation for the final "politics of recognition," a major concern of Taylor. Indeed, according to Kojève, the free recognition of each by all is possible only in the UHS, which in turn is sustained by the technological mastery of nature, including "human nature." It turns out, however, that such promised recognition was not the everyday experience of ordinary citizens. Unlike Marx, Hegel did not dream of a universal and homogeneous *society*, nor did he expect the state to wither away. "Only the Leader of the universal and homogeneous State (Napoleon) is *really* 'satisfied' (recognized by all in his reality and his personal value) ... But all the citizens are fully 'satisfied' because *each* can *become* this Leader whose personal ('particular') action is at the same time the action of all." Because heredity, an "'inhuman,' 'natural,' 'pagan,' element" has been abolished as a relevant political factor,

each can actualize his [or her] Desire for recognition: on condition of accepting the risk of death (element of Mastery) that implies competition

> (= political Struggle; this risk guarantees the "seriousness" of the candidates) within the State, and on condition also of having previously taken part in the constructive activity of the Society, in the collective Labor that maintains the State in its reality (element of Servitude, of Service, that guarantees the "competence" of the candidates). The "satisfaction" of the citizen is thus a result of the synthesis, in himself, of the Master-warrior and the Slave-labourer. In addition, what is new in this State is that *all* are (on occasion) *warriors* (conscription) and *all* also take part in social labour. As for the Wise Man (Hegel), he is content to *understand*: [first] the State and its Leader, [second] the Warrior-and Labourer-Citizen, and lastly himself.[25]

This outline of the UHS, the final regime, Kojève argued, has increasingly been actualized since Hegel's day. This interpretation is plausible even in Canada, where federally, provincially, and municipally the executive (the elected council and the higher civil service) are by and large composed of serious, that is, competitively successful, individuals who are (at least in theory) competent administrators. Lower members of the bureaucracy are state functionaries employed in the dispassionate and technical application and enforcement of rules rather than in the making of them. Assemblies represent the welfare of citizens, authorize the collection of taxes, and are responsible for debating, refining, and articulating public opinion and the supervision of the police. All these textbook commonplaces conform to Hegel's commonsensical teaching in the *Philosophy of Right* so that "the Hegelian theory of the State is correct because it correctly analyzes the actual State of his era and of ours."[26] Kojève's understanding of Hegelian political science thus can provide the standard by which to judge the adequacy of the arguments of the Canadian political Hegelians: like every modern state, Canada is a "province" of the UHS.

But what does this "provincial" status mean? Obviously, the actual Canadian (or any other) modern state is not the nineteenth-century national monarchy familiar to Hegel, which simply means that the gestalt of the *Geist* had changed shape.[27] Thus, it remains generally true in modern states: (1) that citizens attain their legal majority between the ages of sixteen and twenty-one; (2) that children who are legal adults no longer live under the authority of the paterfamilias so that love alone, not law, holds the family together; (3) that social, economic, and political advancement is not legally impeded by "natural" factors such as ethnicity, religion, and gender; (4) that will and competence are the main factors governing one's advancement; and (5) that all these attributes of the UHS are dispassionately enforced by competent and serious bureaucratic human-rights commissions, entitlement-administrators, equal-opportunity enforcers, and so on. In sum, no modern political party or leaders could hope for office if they denied the slogans of the French Revolution, and no one can successfully oppose the notion that all citizens must be recognized as legally equal or that all people are properly speaking sisters and brothers.[28]

Two additional comments (*Zusätze*) in conclusion: First, Hegel's political science as interpreted by Kojève is the most resolutely modern and comprehensive account of the present or actual world known to me. To be modern is to adopt a specific self-understanding or self-interpretation: one sees oneself as autonomous, independent of natural or given constraints, independent of God, and therefore free to create personal and social meaning. The absence of natural constraints even for post-historical humans is not, however, absolute. Humans are not angels; they still have bodies. But for modern self-consciousness, one's body, one's gender, for example, does not constrain the meaning of one's sexuality: gay, straight, or kinky, the options of an androgynous and unformed polymorphous or transgendered existence may be everywhere displayed in public. To despise homosexuality as an unnatural vice is now merely a subjective prejudice unworthy of our permissive modern times. In some provinces of the UHS, articulating such prejudices is illegal. Of course, one can hold such views, just as one can postulate divine restraints, but they are not modern views or postulates and so are not publicly acceptable in modern provinces of the UHS. Likewise, the natural consequences of gender differences have effectively been circumvented by the widespread use of the technologies of contraception and abortion and by the legal and social legitimacy of divorce or of serial monogamy unhallowed by marriage. And finally, what could be more commonplace than to observe that all this has been described and justified in terms of freedom and the recognition of, and the gay pride in, who we are? Why else would one leave the closet, take the pill, or submit to surgical therapy?

A second comment: The essential element of all provinces in the UHS may be summarized as follows: it is a regime where natural or quasi-natural factors, that is, inherited status, religious belief, cultural tradition, gender, ethnicity, etc., play no role in the conduct of public affairs. In principle it is a homogeneous social order where recognition is accorded the free, historical, and entirely mortal individual who anticipates no "afterlife." The widespread acceptance of these attributes makes Canada a modern state. These observations obviously must apply to the province of the province of the UHS, namely Quebec. As a consequence there is something highly "inauthentic" regarding claims to the contrary. This has been true since Lord Durham's day and is discussed further below.[29]

Strauss's Objections

Of the many implications of Kojève's interpretation of Hegel that Grant rejected, his atheism and thus his rejection of the sacramental dimension to marriage or the sanctity of unborn humans are the most obvious. In this sense, Grant "rejected" Hegel-Kojève's account of modernity and *ex hypothesi* of this chapter, Grant's rejection led him astray in his understanding of the Kojèvian actuality and rationality of Canada. His rejection, in short, provoked his lament for a nation. In addition, however, there are the mostly commonsensical objections made by Strauss to Kojève's and to Hegel's understanding of what politics is like in the UHS, namely competition for the Napoleonic role of Leader among the serious and competent candidates for office. In this respect, Grant was more ambivalent.

"Syntheses effect miracles," Strauss observed, and Kojève's or Hegel's synthesis of classical and biblical morality produced "an amazingly lax morality out of two moralities both of which made very strict demands on self-restraint." Biblical and classical moralities do not, or rather did not, encourage us to oust perfectly capable persons solely for our own self-promotion or to extend political rule over as many persons as possible so as to gain extensive and potentially universal recognition. Strauss detected an element of bad faith in Kojève's synthetic morality because he "encourages others by his speech to a course of action to which he would never stoop in deed." He did so, moreover, by suppressing "his better knowledge" and, by way of Hobbes and Machiavelli, argued "from the untrue assumption that man as man is thinkable as a being that lacks awareness of sacred restraints or as a being that is guided by nothing but a desire for recognition."[30] Strauss's first commonsensical objection, very simply, was that Kojève's (or Hegel's) anthropology was inadequate – or as Grant said, invalid.

Strauss explicitly indicated there was no need to discuss the Kojèvian-Hegelian "sketch of the history of the Western world," because it amounted to a *petitio principii* that presupposed "the truth of the thesis which it is meant to prove."[31] Moreover, when one looks at the result, namely the UHS, Strauss argued that "men will have very good reasons for being dissatisfied," first because only the Leader is truly free and so truly satisfied by universal recognition, which on Hegelian grounds means that the UHS is no more than another Oriental Despotism.[32] Worse, citizens of the UHS are syntheses of warriors, or Masters, and labourers, or Slaves; but there are no wars to fight and no genuine transformative labours to perform: "There is nothing more to *do*."[33] According to Kojève, fighting and labouring elevated human beings above the brutes; according to Strauss, an end to fighting and labouring necessarily destroys the humanity of this being or, *at best*, ushers in the era of Nietzsche's "last man," a point that was made at great length by Fukuyama.[34] In other words, if the UHS is what humanity has spent history striving to attain, when it has been achieved it amounts to a destruction of humanity and a return "to the prehuman beginnings of History," which seems a colossal waste of time.[35] No wonder there was a resurgence of boredom (*Langweile*) from which humans have sought post-historical diversions, which amount to yet another act of bad faith.

Strauss added that there is no reason for despair to long as there are real men, *andres*, or "hombres" as he sometimes said, "who will revolt against a State which is destructive of humanity or in which there is no possibility of noble action and great deeds."[36] Even if it amounts only to a "nihilistic revolution" of the sort portrayed by Anthony Burgess in his post-historical novel, *A Clockwork Orange*, such violence still amounts to the assertion of one's humanity.[37] For Kojève, however, there was still the possibility of competition for the top job by serious and competent aspirants.[38] But they will always be a few, and for Strauss this was "a hideous prospect: a State in which the last refuge of man's humanity is political assassination in the particularly sordid form of the palace revolution?"[39] These commonsensical objections of Strauss are sufficient for our purposes.[40] Political assassination and palace coups are only for the most serious aspirants to the position of Leader and need take place only under conditions where violence and bloodshed are required. For other provinces of the UHS that are softer, "political assassination" can be undertaken by newspaper columnists and on radio talk shows; palace coups can be arranged by rigging celebratory political conventions and even elections. These alternatives may not be "hideous" as Strauss said, but they are hardly noble or edifying either.

Grant's View of the UHS

Grant accepted Strauss's criticism of Kojève, but his emphases were different. The title of his 1969 book, *Technology and Empire*, indicated his chief concerns: the Machiavellian basis or foundation of the UHS, namely technology, had as its chief consequence the hegemony of an administrative empire that Grant identified chiefly with the United States. As with the more extensive work of Charles Taylor, there are major insights and criticisms of the modern, liberal, technological, secular politics that owe little to Hegel or a fortiori to a Kojèvian version of Hegel.[41] In this chapter, however, I would like to indicate the inchoate presence of Hegel and Kojève in Grant's view of Canada, the *locus classicus* being the aforementioned *Lament for a Nation*.[42]

During the 1960s, Dennis Lee, a friend of Grant and a poet, reported that, because of the American war in Vietnam, his muse departed and he was silenced for four years.[43] Then, after reading one of Grant's essays, he grasped what it was to be a Canadian. He was still a colonial, he said, but he could speak. The source of what Hegel would call the particularity from which Lee found again his (perhaps subaltern) poetic voice was his ability to identify with the conservative losers of the American Revolution, the Loyalists. This experience, and the myth that expressed it, was what made Canadians different from the triumphant liberal winners. Lee found it intensely meaningful, especially as a way "to criticize our new masters," the Americans. Lee, no doubt, spoke for many who read *Lament for a Nation* as a criticism of the "masters." And Grant was enough of a Hegelian to know that criticism of masters can come only from slaves. As with the Loyalists' criticism of the Patriots, the servility that comes from the immediacy of defeat was transfigured into moral superiority.

There is always something faintly comical about moral superiority, and Loyalist moralism is no exception. To begin with, there is compelling evidence that by and large the Loyalists were as much modern liberals as the Patriots.[44] Second, if the "gorgon's face" of liberalism and behind it the UHS appeared most vividly in the Unites States and the Americans' conduct of foreign affairs in Vietnam, then the Americans were suffering even more than Canadians. This meant, as Clifford Orwin remarked in a review of one of Grant's later books, that although Grant may be "the father of Canadian nationalism," it is also true, by Grant's logic, that "the gravest crisis Canadians face is not one that they face as Canadians."[45] If the advent of the UHS constitutes the advent of an endless crisis, then all North Americans are facing it together.[46] On the other hand, an inability to stomach war at all would be expected from the last men.

Lament for a Nation was not Grant's first reflection on what it was like to be a part of an empire. Shortly after the war he argued that the British Empire and Commonwealth were the "chief hope for survival" of "Western Christian civilization."[47] Granted, he made these remarks prior to encountering Kojève, but they surely embody "the error of a one-sided empty ratiocination," even taking into account the immediate postwar context. *Lament for a Nation* expressed fewer illusions, but it remains a peculiar document not so much because of a crude anti-Americanism that inspired "Canadian nationalists" to which Orwin referred (and of which Lee was an example), but because of a blindness to the "gorgon's face" that this same so-called nationalism presented to non-Laurentian Canada.

The collapse of John Diefenbaker's government and its electoral defeat at the hands of Lester Pearson and the Liberal Party of Canada in 1962–3 was for Grant a signal event that showed Canada had no future independent of the United States.[48] Diefenbaker was initially characterized as a "small-town Protestant politician" and later as a courageous lawyer whose rhetoric did not translate well on television. Grant indicated that Diefenbaker was excluded from a central place in the party by "the old Conservative elite" who "ensured the control of the party remained in Toronto." It was also true that the Liberals "did not pay sufficient attention to the farmers or the outlying regions. Such regions existed for them as colonies of Montreal and Toronto."[49] Grant was silent as to the adequacy of the Liberals' perception and said nothing about how those who, like Diefenbaker, lived in the "colonies" and might have experienced matters. That is, Grant seemed oblivious to the fact that, for most Westerners, the chief importance of the Chief was that he was "one of us."[50] In Hegelian language the particularity of Diefenbaker as a Westerner was paramount. This meant that, so far as his Western supporters were concerned, the East, the "old Conservative elite" presented the face of "Canadian" homogeneity, if not universality. Grant was certainly aware that the old Conservative elite embodied the interests of Laurentian Canada, which were not those of the West. The spiritual significance of that conflict, however, seemed to have eluded him.

For Grant, what was of greatest significance was that "Ontario was determined it would be integrated into the Great Lakes region" and that loyalty to Britain "still survived in the less-modern parts of Canada," which was one way of referring to the West.[51] In fact, however, the "Great Lakes region" did not seem particularly significant to Diefenbaker's constituents. Even stranger was Grant's assertion that prairie farmers found any sustenance whatsoever in their loyalty to Britain by way of Canadian trade patterns. "The British connection," Grant claimed, "has been a source of Canadian nationalism. The east-west pull of trade – from the prairies, down the Great Lakes and the St Lawrence, to Western Europe – provided a counter-thrust to the pull of continentalism." Moreover, Macdonald's National Policy was invoked as a model of nationalist integration.[52]

It is no more than a cliché to say that the slightest acquaintance with Western Canadian political and economic history and Western self-understanding, from the free-trade movement at Red River in the 1840s to the free-trade movement of the 1980s, ought to be sufficient to disabuse anyone of the support that Westerners have given to "national" economic policies or "national" energy programs. Indeed, the agitation for free trade with the United States has been precisely the site of resistance to the colonization from Montreal and Toronto. Diefenbaker knew this. His National Development Policy, his "vision of the North" or advocacy of "roads to resources" were slogans that had at their core the meaning that technology could be used to decentralize power and wealth from Laurentian Canada.

Grant's interpretation ignored the common experience of Diefenbaker's strongest supporters and substituted another: Diefenbaker's understanding of Canada was in two respects defective and unrealistic.[53] First he did not understand that "if Canada was to survive, the cornerstone of its existence was the Great Lakes region," and second, the "keystone of the Canadian nation is the French fact."[54] He went on to explain that Diefenbaker's "prairie populism" meant he was unable to understand French Canada, just as his being a "prairie lawyer" meant he could not grasp the "economic implications of Canadian nationalism."

This interpretation was not self-evident. Alvin Hamilton, Diefenbaker's highly popular minister of agriculture, and Gordon Churchill, from Winnipeg, had formulated a successful electoral strategy that achieved victory without leaving hostages to fortune in Quebec. The subsequent political history of Canada has not refuted or even seriously challenged their wisdom.[55] So far as the Great Lakes region is concerned, its spiritual significance has surely been overrated. It is far from being the *fons et origo* of a single Canadian national myth expressing the meaning of what it is to be "Canadian." This is why Diefenbaker was entirely correct to ignore Professor Donald G. Creighton, whom Grant identified as the man who "had defined the conservative view of Canada to a whole generation."[56] Creighton's conservatism was expressed perfectly in the title to his first and frankest book, *The Commercial Empire of the St Lawrence* (1937). It would be more accurate to say that Diefenbaker was less a populist ignoramus than a commonsensical Westerner who was perfectly well aware what the commercial empire of Laurentian Canada had done for – or rather to – Saskatchewan.

One additional remark may clarify the limits to Grant's understanding of the gestalt of the Canadian *Geist*. The first is that he seemed genuinely to be of the opinion that the Ottawa civil service could serve as an agent of national preservation. Diefenbaker's failure to win the respect of unelected Ottawa was "a disaster," because "no modern state can be run without great authority in the hands of its non-elected officials. In such an uncertain nation as Canada, the civil service is perhaps the essential instrument by which nationhood is preserved."[57] Later in the book, Grant discussed the possibility of a "Gaullist" response to *le défi américain*. "The only possible basis for a Gaullist elite," he said, "would have been the senior civil servants working closely with politicians who knew what they were doing."[58] Considering the importance of French Canada in Grant's vision, it is surely odd to have to point out that Canada is a federal state and that, for whatever reasons, some Canadians look more to their provincial governments than to the mandarins of Ottawa to preserve what is important to them.

In other words, Grant's vision of Canada, his sustaining myth of "Canadian" nationalism was the parochial Loyalist myth of Laurentian Canada imaginatively expanded by the Ottawa mandarins from sea to sea, the same myth that Denis Lee appropriated to recover his poetic voice, which was a particular voice of his place, southern Ontario. This was made as plain as could be when Lee recommended Margaret Atwood's book *Survival* as a splendid account of the major themes of Canadian literature. In fact, of course, it is a splendid expression of the experience of southern Ontario. If such a vision ever approximated the actuality of Canada, it lapsed long before the Confederation of British North America. From the beginning, ambitious men in Laurentian Canada had designs on the Maritimes and the Northwest. Perhaps the tradition of Maritime Loyalism, particularly the experience of being pensioners and placemen, abetted their submission to the Canadians at Confederation.[59] Lacking such experience may explain why the strongest supporters of Diefenbaker were able to resist the power of Laurentian Canada with greater success.

Lament for a Nation exalted Canada over the United States by claiming that Canada was somehow pre-modern and that the most pre-modern part of Canada was in the West, which showed great allegiance to Britain. But neither Canada nor Western Canada is now or ever was in the past pre-modern. Grant was right to argue that Canada and the United States both depended on the historically most advanced technologies of the day to sustain their respective provinces in the UHS, but what does this mean? Even if we accept that the "colonies" west of Ontario rejoiced in their subordination to Laurentian Canada, which the history of the region in fact contradicts, their subordinate place in the nation has been secured precisely by the hardware technologies such as the railway and administrative technologies such as the National Policy, the Canadian Wheat Board, and the National Energy Program.

On the other hand, if the commonsensical regional conflicts in interest and contrasting political myths of Laurentian and Western Canada (to say nothing of the contrasts and conflicts with Maritime Canada and Newfoundland) are simply understood as constituting different sub-provinces of the UHS, the possibility of "conquest" by the West of Laurentian Canada remains as much a possibility as the colonization of the West by the Laurentians. What such a conquest would entail is precisely a reversal of the use of the Canadian state by Laurentian Canada to promote its own particularity, whether in the form of direct political control or by means of such notorious myths as that the "French fact" actually matters in the West. In this context the "unhyphenated Canadianism" of John Diefenbaker entailed a reversal of the domination of the Laurentian sub-province and would entail a serious and significant reduction of the importance of those "senior civil servants" whom Grant, in accord with Hegel's and Kojève's political teaching, apparently admired.

Finally, it may be true that the Canadian province of the UHS, whether divided into sub-provinces or not, is incapable of fulfilling the deepest desires of human beings. But what political order is? And no one, certainly not George Grant, would dream of actually aiming at a pre-modern world where various attributes of Kojève's understanding of nature such as ethnicity or gender were politically important. If there is a genuine relief for human longing, it will come only through an *Aufhebung* of politics; but that was already what Socrates taught, to say nothing of Jesus.

Charles Taylor and Canadian Federalism

In contrast to Grant, Charles Taylor is an internationally acclaimed political philosopher in the conventional sense that he is a professor of philosophy who has more or less coherently articulated his views on political things. In *Philosophical Arguments*, for example, Taylor indicated that three "basic themes" had been "worrying" and "bothering" him, the third of which was concerned with "the political culture of modernity," particularly the way that moderns "have come to imagine society," which conventionally is indicated by terms such as nationalism, liberalism, and modernity. He was, however, quick to dismiss the "fashionable notion" of the end of history: it looks good on "a superficial level," but on "a deeper level … it's dead wrong."[60] Not for Taylor does modernity debouch in the UHS, nor does he anticipate or desire that Quebec would someday be a full-fledged province of the UHS rather than a sub-province and part of Canada. One reason for his position, apart from his interpretation of Hegel, may be connected to Taylor's self-identification as a Quebecker and as a Canadian, which identification carries with it a commitment to particularity and heterogeneity. That self-identification can also be interpreted in light of Kojève's understanding.

In his McDonald Lecture delivered at the University of Alberta, in Edmonton, in March 1991, Taylor raised two questions: (1) why should Canada exist? and (2) why should Quebec be part of Canada? In the beginning, Taylor said, Canadians existed because they were distinct.[61] They were *British* North Americans and the triumphant revolutionaries were not. As the British connection faded, new attributes arose to distinguish Canadians from their southern neighbours. These were initially identified by Taylor as a commitment to "peace, order and good government" and to "collectivist" provisioning. The first, which was in origin a Victorian legal formula, has come to symbolize Canadian self-understanding as a cooperative and peaceful society, unlike what Canadians think of as a violent, litigious, and conflict-ridden American society. The collectivist aspect of Canada is contrasted with American individualism and initiative. Both attributes, as noted above, are often coloured with the unedifying tones of moral superiority.

Unity, Taylor said, follows from distinction. Accordingly, "we need to hang together in order to maintain this alternative political culture as a viable option in North America." In this way, the collective provisioning finds logical expression in a third attribute, "a solidarity of mutual help between regions" institutionalized as regional equalization policies and fiscal transfers from productive tax-paying individuals, provinces, and regions to unproductive ones.[62] More important than who benefits whom, as Taylor candidly admits, these policies have not worked. In the east, they have not improved economic standards of living; in the west, interests have been ignored. Taylor equates the two: "In one version, the implicit contract, which is seen as unfulfilled, calls for redistribution to poorer regions. In the other version, it calls for a redress of power and influence in favour of the regions with less demographic and economic clout. In one case, the implicit promise is of equalized incomes; in the other it points to more equalized power between regional societies."[63]

Taylor then considered the second question: "Why Quebec?" In some respects Quebec shared an allegiance to the attributes enumerated to describe Canada's distinctiveness. In addition, of course, language and culture set Quebec apart not only from the United States, but from Canada. When one poses the question "What is a country for,?" in the context of Quebec, one finds a clear and distinct answer: "To defend and promote the nation," where the latter term has come to mean, more or less, *la nation canadienne-française* in Quebec. The only thing to debate is whether the state doing the provisioning is Canada or Quebec.

In practice, said Taylor, the question of purpose meant "some kind of dualism" with two equally important parts: (1) the French language must be equal to English, and (2) there must be autonomy of some kind for the Quebec nation so that it might act as a body politic. In fact, of course, French is not as useful and practical as English is in North America, so that giving French equal status with English by statutory enactment "seemed like indefensible favouritism." So too did any proposal to give constitutional force and effect to the demand for autonomy or "special status," even though the social distinctiveness of Quebec is self-evident. Taylor called the refusal by Canada to grant constitutional distinctiveness to Quebec a "rather abstract judicial issue" concerned with "the relative constitutional status of provinces."

According to Taylor, the real difficulty lay elsewhere, in "a new conflict of purposes." Canada and Quebec answered the question "What is a country for?" in different ways. "More grievously," he said, special status for the Government of Quebec entailed "a collective goal. The aim is to ensure the flourishing and survival of a *community*," and this purpose is in conflict with the doctrine of individual rights that, he said, serves as the basis of the Charter and of Charter provisions in favour of non-discrimination. Consequently, "the *Charter* and the promotion of the nation, as understood in their respective constituencies, are on a collision course." There are some well-known collective *rights* protected in the Charter, but they are unlike the collective *purpose* of the French-speaking community, inasmuch as the latter aims to ensure the existence of another French-speaking generation, not guaranteeing the rights of existing French-speaking individuals to accept, for example, their traffic tickets only when written in French.

Taylor did not make the implications explicit, so far as I am aware, so I will do it for him. The Charter by his reading seems to be more than "a common reference point of identity" for Canada. It also provides an answer to the question "What is the country for?" and whatever answer is given to this question, it will be different from ensuring the survival and flourishing of *la nation canadienne-française*. Hence the aforementioned "conflict of purposes." Leaving aside the question of whether a country can have two purposes, it seems clear enough that there will be a conflict of some kind between Quebec and Canada. What gives the current conflict its seriousness, according to Taylor, is that for the first time independence is not just an abstract possibility or a threat. "It is," he said, "really thinkable," in the sense that the admittedly steep economic costs could be afforded and that the political costs are considered to be non-existent.[64]

On the other hand, "the emotional drive behind independence," he said, "lies not in questions of interest, of the costs and benefits of federalism or of fear of political retaliation." Rather it is "much more a failure of *recognition*," which we know from Kojève is a very modern difficulty. Accordingly, the famous problem of "Canadian dualism," which nowadays is not acknowledged beyond the borders of Quebec as much more than a cynical and self-serving slogan, "was the only form in which Confederation could be ultimately acceptable to French Canadians in a way which could engage their hearts and respect their dignity." What is involved, therefore, is a matter of pride, not interest. "The root cause of our impending fracture," Taylor said, "can be put in one word: recognition."[65] The conflict of purposes, it seems, can be resolved only if Canada recognizes that the purpose of the country includes the flourishing and survival of *la nation canadienne-française* in Quebec. To which most Canadians would reply: *Pourquoi pas*?

Unfortunately, such a sensible reply will not do. As Taylor observed, "Those who are frustrated in their desire for recognition understandably do not want to present their case in those terms." This "self-occlusion of the politics of recognition," he said, "plays a very negative role. It makes it all the harder to bring things to a resolution."[66] There is an obvious sense in which this is so. The Meech Lake Accord, for example, would have given constitutional force and effect to the social distinctiveness of Quebec by endowing the government of that province with the responsibility under the terms of s. (2)(2), "to preserve and promote the distinct identity of Quebec referred to in paragraph (1)(b)" of the Accord, which read: "The recognition that Quebec constitutes within Canada a distinct society." On the one hand, these provisions were said to be "just symbolic" but also a minimally acceptable position to Quebec. What could this mean? Taylor understated the problem when he observed, "Anyone who can use the expression '*just* symbolic' has missed something essential about the nature of modern society."[67] If the Meech Lake Accord, for example, were "just symbolic," in the sense of being trivial, why was it even an issue – for either side?

The Hegelian answer seems to be that no one *can* admit the search for recognition before it is granted. Meech Lake, therefore, looked like another *beau risque* and might have actually become one, at least from the Quebec point of view, had it been accepted by Canada. Quebec then would have accepted the Constitution, as modified by the amendments contained in the accord, *"dans l'honneur et l'enthousiasme,"* a phrase apparently coined by Lucien Bouchard but uttered by his then good friend, the prime minister, Brian Mulroney. But Meech Lake was rejected; and the rejection was seen in Quebec as an insult to their pride, their honour, a "refusal of recognition," and so on.

On the other hand Canadians were surprised that Quebeckers saw only a point of honour. So let us then consider Taylor's version of this central Hegelian question of recognition more closely. "Mutual recognition between groups," Taylor wrote, "has come to be a crucial issue in modern politics because of the very nature of modern society." So far as the intellectual sources of this issue are concerned, "Hegel comes to mind right off, with his famous dialectic of the master and the slave."[68] Central to the self-understanding of modern society (and here he followed Kojève) is the formal requirement that it comprises equal and autonomous citizens. "If one is unequal, or is dependent on another, then one's own voice does not count, or is weighed at a discount, in the decisions of this sovereign entity."[69] If the actual divergence of equality and autonomy from this standard grows too great, then the self-understanding of society itself will be questioned, and that is a recipe for strife.

As we have seen, regarding the contours of the UHS, the demand for equality is easier to meet if the "province" or "sub-province" is also homogeneous. Pluralist societies generally deal with this problem by means of anti-discrimination laws, which have as their formal objective the treatment of citizens as equals. Citizen equality turns out not to be enough for some superior people, since their superiority seems unacknowledged. According to Taylor, we may be recognized as citizens and taxpayers "and yet still be unrecognized in our identity. In other words, what is important to us in defining who we are may be quite unacknowledged, may even be condemned in the public life of our society, even though all our citizen rights are firmly guaranteed."[70] This is true enough, but there is an objection – to my mind a fatal one – that must be raised here.

One can be recognized, Taylor stated, only in terms of "what defines us as human agents."[71] And Kojève and Hegel argued that what we are is both given and the result of our action. By this argument, all that is not the result of what we have become cannot be recognized as having any relationship to human agency. In Kojèvian-Hegelian language, it is part of our natural "given-being," *Sein*. In other words, if it is part of our natural or sexual or ethnic being, it is not a consequence of our agency, of our acts or deeds. In Kojève's account, all these terms have a precise meaning, so that precisely what is *not* recognized in an individual is her race, her family, her gender, her nation, her community.

If we now apply this insight more directly to modern and contemporary pluralist society such as is found in North America, recognition on ethnic or gender or even class grounds, it seems to me, can be only implicit or informal. One may, therefore, agree that "most people need a secure cultural context to give meaning to their lives" without concluding that there must be public or political recognition of a culture. The Northwest Territories at the present time, for example, has an Aboriginal majority of citizens much as Quebec has a French-speaking majority. But like Quebec it is a territorial polity run along recognizably liberal democratic and constitutional lines. Similarly Nunavut is a territory within which an Inuit majority controls a modern liberal democratic government. It will not be an Inuit ethnic or cultural polity.[72] Or, put another way, if some or most people have a need for a secure cultural context to give meaning to their lives and more important, if they cannot get that security without public assistance, does this characteristic not immediately make them unequal, because they are dependent upon public authorities, as compared to those who do not need such assistance? And worse, does it not also mean that this dependence can never be admitted, for no one can at the same time demand recognition and ask for protection by another in order to receive it?

It seems to me, therefore, that the politics of collective or community recognition, insofar as it involves cultural or linguistic particularity, is inauthentic and simply not serious. Consider the following: First, Taylor is surely correct to say that a "judgment about identity is a judgment about me in particular, or about some particular person or group," and that "the question about identity is a modern one." Second, the demand for recognition, particularly by cultural groups, "is given urgency by the supposed links between recognition and identity, where this latter term designates something like a person's understanding of who they are, of their fundamental defining characteristics as a human being." Third, this urgent and modern and particularist demand can fail so that a refusal or a "mis-recognition" can "mirror back to them [who demand recognition] a confining or demeaning or contemptible picture of themselves. Non-recognition or mis-recognition can inflict harm, can be a form of oppression, imprisoning someone in a false, distorted, and reduced mode of being."[73]

There is no question that "mis-recognition" or even contempt *can* be hurtful, but it is also true that for others mis-recognition may be understood simply as the stupidity or barbarism of others. Notwithstanding the fact that there may be "reduced modes of being," are there no barbarians? Have the stupid or the malicious vanished from the face of the earth? Taylor provides an example that puts the politics of recognition in a proper perspective. Quebec nationalists, he said, care "passionately how their society is seen abroad, and particularly in the United States. This is why a Mordecai Richler who presents an unflattering portrait of our language legislation in the *New Yorker* is seen as a mortal enemy of Quebec."[74] But Richler was not really a *mortal* enemy, no more than Jacques Parizeau or Lucien Bouchard or Pauline Marois were traitors to Canada. On the contrary, intensifying the misunderstandings has not meant either sobriety and measured words or seriousness either. As Taylor has said, there are nationalist intellectuals in Quebec who are proud of knowing nothing of the cultural life of Vancouver but are quite up to date on what is happening in Prague or Rio. And for their part, many Canadians are growing indifferent towards the whole Quebec question ("why don't they make up their mind?"), as if Quebec had a single mind collectively dispersed. Others found the spectacle provided by the October 1995 referendum mildly droll: the solemn moralizing stiffness of Bouchard contrasted nicely with the Oxbridge Edwardianisms of Parizeau. By Jove! For the same reason, the more recent student protests against raising the lowest university tuition in the country and the *Chartre des valeurs québécoise*, which was proposed in response to the problem of "reasonable accommodation" proposed by the commission directed by Gerard Bouchard and Charles Taylor, were widely seen outside Quebec as silly.

The first conclusion I would draw from Taylor's unserious politics of recognition is that they consist more properly speaking in a combination of the politics of vanity and of grievance or complaint. So far as vanity is concerned, the subjectivity and uncertainty of cultural particularity may be regrettable, but it is also unavoidable. And second, if one seeks verification of one's subjective certainty about who one is, as may be done, for example, by pursuing the good opinions of Americans who read the *New Yorker* about one's own non-American society, then the question of competence is bound to arise: Are the Americans knowledgeable judges? And, since Canadians as well as Quebeckers already know they are not, does it not follow that recognition by the incompetent is simply vanity, which is after all a vice, not a virtue?[75] Regarding the plaintive side of mis-recognition, one is at a loss to know what to make of it. As Taylor said, Canada is hardly a threat to Quebec, and Quebec is now and has been a major beneficiary of Canadian redistributive policies. There is, finally, something unseemly in the complaint that recognition has been denied. Surely, as all the authorities attest, recognition is not something one politely asks for and then complains about if it is not granted. Recognition is a matter of pride; it is demanded. Complaining is evidence of nothing so much as a lack of seriousness, for which Brutus's rebuke of Cassius strikes just the right note (*Julius Caesar*, act 4, scene 3, lines 42–50).

Let us revisit Taylor's question, "What is the country for?" now knowing that, in Quebec, the answer is "To ensure the survival of *la nation canadienne-française*." Such a purpose makes sense only within a survivalist political myth once common to all of Laurentian Canada, both Upper and Lower, and celebrated in the literature of those parts. Other identities and other myths inform other parts, and they, each in their place, provide the substance, meaning, or purpose to the several collectivities that have constituted themselves in Canada.[76] So far as *la survivance de la nation canadienne-française* is concerned, according to Taylor, one must distinguish between "what one might call first-level diversity" from "second-level or 'deep' diversity."[77] By the former he meant differences in culture, outlook, and background in a population that, notwithstanding those differences, still shared the same idea of what it means to belong to Canada. Roughly speaking, this refers to Charter-based group rights such as are contemplated by section 27, which is devoted to Canada's "multicultural heritage." In contrast, "deep" diversity refers to a way of being Canadian that takes place by way of "a constituent element of Canada" such as *la nation québécoise* or the Mohawk Nation and every other so-called nation in the 600-plus units of the Aboriginal archipelago. For such a population, "their way of being Canadian is not accommodated by first-level diversity." But to Canadians who are keen defenders of section 27 diversity, this is very puzzling and they ask, "Why are Quebeckers and Mohawks not satisfied?"

Taylor answered with a revealing example: a Ukrainian Canadian living in Edmonton would belong to Canada in a way that did not "pass through" the Ukrainian-Canadian community, even though ethnic identity for such a person was very important. Such a person might well accept that Cree or Quebeckers "were Canadian through being members of their national communities," just as Cree or Quebeckers might accept the legitimacy of the mosaic, or of the section 27 multiculturalist identity of the Ukrainian-Canadian of Edmonton.

There are some difficulties with Taylor's suggestion. Let me approach them indirectly. One of Hegel's few jokes was that the sultan might become pope. In the same mood one might raise the possibility of deep diversity among Ukrainian-Canadians. Is this possible? What of Iranian-Canadians? Or Israeli-Canadians? Can one seriously contemplate such deep diversity expanded beyond *la nation québécoise*? The real problem indicated by these questions is that the currency of collective status and its recognition quickly gets debased for the obvious reason that it is justified not by a principle, and so by a limit, but by will, which is limitless. Certainly for a Ukrainian-Canadian in Edmonton to think of Quebeckers as the embodiment of "deep diversity," he or she would have to think of Ukrainian-Canadian diversity not as "first-level" but as shallow. Likewise, the demand by Quebec that it be recognized as a distinct society carried with it the implication that non-Quebeckers were "indistinct." That such negative implications or insults were not intended indicates only the insensitivity of Quebec nationalists – a charge that is usually hurled in the opposite direction. Then again, if the division between first- and second-order diversity is unclear, why limit it to ethnic heritage? If Ukrainian-Canadians might move from first- to second-order diversity, can lesbians do so as well?

There are other problems with Taylor's views on deep diversity or what he sometimes called "substantive liberalism" as distinct from the "procedural liberalism" supported in Canada.[78] These objections to Taylor's argument are based on his politicization of culture. For Taylor's critics, culture is essentially a non-political achievement or activity, which, if politicized, invariably entails creating an illegitimate hierarchy of cultures (which Taylor calls "thick" and "thin" cultures) and a retreat from the principles of modernity and of the UHS. The point of this last observation is to reaffirm the insight afforded by Kojève's interpretation of Hegel regarding Canada, which is, to repeat, distinct from the question of the validity of Kojève's interpretation of Hegel.

Conclusions

At the risk of illustrating the proverb "The mountain laboured to bring forth a mouse," let us nevertheless draw a few conclusions. We began from the supposition that Kojève's understanding of Hegel was politically correct so far as Grant was concerned. But Grant rejected Hegel's and Kojève's understanding of human being and Taylor never accepted it. But if our supposition was correct, and our longer justification of this supposition was sound, it provides the basis for examining the limitations of Grant's and Taylor's understanding of Canada and Canadian politics.

Grant and Taylor both look at politics from the limited perspective of Laurentian Canada and the Laurentian myth. The two major elements of it are (1) that Canada is chiefly defined by the "French fact" and the survival/*la survivance* of a bilingual country; and (2) that the chief threat to Canada comes from the south. We have argued, however, that the first element is merely parochial and the second is an error. Together they constitute a "one-sided empty ratiocination" against which Hegel warned. They are, in short, Laurentian fragments of Hegel's and, in my view, Kojève's political science.

NOTES

1 Barry Ferguson, *Remaking Liberalism: The Intellectual Legacy of Adam Shortt, O.D. Skelton, W.C. Clark and W.A. Mackintosh, 1890–1925* (Montreal and Kingston: McGill-Queen's University Press, 1993); Stefan Collini, "Hobhouse, Bosanquet and the State: Philosophical Idealism and Political

Argument in England, 1880–1918," *Past and Present* 88, no. 72 (1976): 86–111; John Irving, "The Development of Philosophy in Central Canada from 1850 to 1900," *Canadian Historical Review* 31 (1950), 252–87; T.A. Goudge, "A Century of Philosophy in English-Speaking Canada," *Dalhousie Review* 47 (1967–8): 537–49; A.B. McKillop, *A Disciplined Intelligence: Critical Inquiry and Canadian Thought in the Victorian Era* (Toronto: University of Toronto Press, 1979); S.E.D. Shortt, *The Search for an Ideal: Six Canadian Intellectuals and Their Convictions in an Age of Transition* (Toronto: University of Toronto Press, 1976); John Burbidge, "Hegel in Canada," *Owl of Minerva* 25, no. 2 (1994): 218; Leslie Armour and Elizabeth Trott, *The Faces of Reason: An Essay on Philosophy and Culture in English Canada, 1850–1950* (Waterloo, ON: Wilfrid Laurier University Press, 1981); see also David MacGregor, "Canada's Hegel," *Literary Review of Canada*, February 1994, 18–29. To these studies must be added the chapters in this volume by Elizabeth Trott and Graeme Nicholson. Mention should also be made of Robert Mynell, *Canadian Idealism and the Philosophy of Freedom: C.B. Macpherson, George Grant, and Charles Taylor* (Montreal and Kingston: McGill-Queen's University Press, 2011). See also my review, "An Invented Tradition," *Review of Politics* 74 (2012): 535–8.

2 Robert C. Sibley, *Northern Spirits: John Watson, George Grant, and Charles Taylor* (Montreal and Kingston: McGill-Queen's University Press, 2008), 1–12. Hegel's understanding of "world history," namely the process of actualization of the "world spirit" is a far cry from the commonsensical use of the term by a historian such as William H. McNeill. See his *Mythistory and Other Essays*, vol. 2, *The Need for World History* (Chicago: University of Chicago Press, 1986), 69.

3 Sibley, *Northern Spirits*, 4.

4 This means we can exclude exegetical analyses of Hegel's texts by scholars living in Canada such as H.S. Harris (1926–2007) and such undoubtedly political though not Canadian-focused disputes as the Doull-Fackenheim disagreement as to whether Hegel would today be a Hegelian, given the appearance of demonic evil in the heart of twentieth-century Europe. See chap. 7 in *Philosophy and Freedom: The Legacy of James Doull*, ed. David G. Peddle and Neil G. Robertson (Toronto: University of Toronto Press, 2003), 330. See also the contributions in this volume by Robert Sibley and David MacGregor. The discussion between James Doull and George Grant, which is ably analysed in this volume by Neil Robertson, might arguably be included in this discussion as well. From the perspective I develop, however, the Doull-Grant discussion remains largely within the Laurentian framework, notwithstanding Doull's status as a Maritimer.

5 For a justification of this term, see Barry Cooper, *It's the Regime, Stupid! A Report from the Cowboy West on Why Stephen Harper Matters* (Toronto: Key Porter, 2004), chap. 2. The term has been used in a similar fashion by Darrell Bricker and John Ibbitson in *The Big Shift: The Seismic Change in Canadian Politics, Business, and Culture and What It Means for Our Future* (Toronto: HarperCollins, 2012).

6 I should perhaps add that this use of the term *common sense* reflects the beginning of the beginning of political science in Aristotle's *Politics* (1280a7) and refers to an awareness of our participation in the common, the *xynon* as Heraclitus called it (B2), and of how we understand and interpret our common affairs. As Hannah Arendt pointed out in *The Human Condition* (Chicago: University of Chicago Press, 1958), 208–9, the only attribute of the world that allows us to judge its reality stems from its being common to us all. This is why in the pre-modern or classical tradition of political science common sense is chiefly political. It is our one sense that enables us, in contrast to the other five senses, to participate in the whole of reality and ensures that our individual sense perception discloses it. By this understanding, modern post-Cartesian common sense is, as Whitehead said, "in retreat" inasmuch as it is understood as an individual and internal capacity no different in principle from the other five senses. A.N. Whitehead, *The Concept of Nature* (Cambridge: Cambridge University Press, 1920), 32. The philosophically modern, post-Cartesian world is no longer understood as what was common to humans. Instead, for moderns, common sense has become an internal capacity of human beings "to reckon upon consequences" as Hobbes said, that happens to be common to them all. In contrast, Heraclitus said that such reliance on private experience, even if found in everyone, was akin to being asleep (B 2; 39). That is, for the modern understanding of common sense, humans are rational animals; for the older understanding, they are political animals. For our purposes, traditional or political common sense is chiefly an ability to acknowledge commonly understood political realities – facts – and to subject them to historical and theoretical analyses.

7 G.W.H. Hegel, *Grundlinien der Philosophie des Rechts* (Frankfurt: Suhrkamp, 1970), 24.

8 Ibid., 26. A thorough analysis of Hegel's apparently baffling sentence, which he repeated almost verbatim in the *Encyclopedia*, para. 6, and which he pronounced a "commonplace," can be found in Emil Fackenheim, "Hegel on the Actuality of the Rational and the Rationality of the Actual," in *The God Within: Kant, Schelling and Historicity*, ed. John Burbridge (Toronto: University of Toronto Press, 1996), 164–71.

9 Edwin R. Black, *Divided Loyalties* (Montreal and Kingston: McGill-Queen's University Press, 1975). Grant's *Lament for a Nation* is discussed in detail below.

10 See *Collected Works of George Grant*, 2:401.

11 Ibid., 402. See also Hugh Donald Forbes, *George Grant: A Guide to His Thought* (Toronto: University of Toronto Press, 2007), chap. 10.

12 The original essay by Strauss appeared in English in 1948, and Kojève's review of the French edition appeared in 1954. They are conveniently available in Strauss, *On Tyranny: Revised and Expanded Edition, Including the Strauss-Kojève Correspondence*, ed. Victor Gourevitch and Michael S. Roth (Chicago: University of Chicago Press, 2000). Grant's essay first appeared in *Social Research* 31 (1964): 45–72, and then in his 1969 collection *Technology and Empire*. See Grant, *Collected Works*, ed. Arthur Davis and Henry Roper, vol. 3, *1960–1969* (Toronto: University of Toronto Press, 2005), 532–57.

13 A more extended analysis is in Barry Cooper, *The End of History: An Essay on Modern Hegelianism* (Toronto: University of Toronto Press, 1984).

14 Hegel, *Phänomenologie des Geistes*, ed. J. Hoffmeister (Hamburg: Meiner, 1952), 12. That Hegel's claim regarding "actual knowledge" was an outrage to philosophy as love of knowledge is clear enough when read in the context of Plato's *Phaedrus*, 279d.

15 Consider Otto Pöggler, "Zur Deutung der *Phänomenologie des Geistes*," *Hegel-Studien* 1 (1961): 267; George Armstrong Kelly, *Idealism, Politics and History* (Cambridge: Cambridge University Press, 1969), 313; Charles Taylor, "Review of Kojève," *American Political Science Review* 64 (1970): 626–7.

16 For the record, it is Voegelin's interpretation of both Kojève and Hegel that, in my view, is the most satisfactory. See Cooper, *End of History*, chap. 8. See Voegelin, "On Hegel: A Study in Sorcery," *Collected Works*, ed. Ellis Sandoz, vol. 12, *Published Essays, 1966–1985* (Baton Rouge: LSU Press, 1990), 21–55; and his "Note on Hegel's 'Philosophy of World History,'" in his *Collected Works*, ed. Manfred Henningsen, vol. 5, *Modernity without Restraint* (Columbia: University of Missouri Press, 2000), 290–2.

17 Hegel, *Phänomenologie*, 59.

18 J. Hoffmeister, ed., *Dokumente zu Hegels Entwicklung* (Stuttgart: Fromann, 1936), 324.

19 See Alexandre Kojève, *Introduction à la Lecture de Hegel*, 2nd ed. (Paris: Gallimard, 1947), 485–88. This claim particularly annoyed conventional Hegel scholars. The problem of how Kojeve understood the System better than its author is discussed in Cooper, *End of History*, 230–43.

20 Gilles Lapouge, "Entretien avec Alexandre Kojève," *La Quinzaine Littéraire* 53 (1968): 19. The end of history became a trope in the English-speaking

academic world of post–Cold War international relations "theory" following the publication of Francis Fukuyama, *The End of History and the Last Man* (New York: Free, 1992).

21 They are discussed in Henri Lefebvre, *La Fin de l'Histoire* (Paris: Minuit, 1970); Kostas Axelos, "La Question de la Fin de l'Histoire," *L'Homme et la Société* 20 (1971): 193–5; Stanley Rosen, *G.W.F. Hegel: An Introduction to the Science of Wisdom* (New Haven, CT: Yale University Press, 1994), 377–83. See also Barry Cooper, "The End of History: Déjà-vu All Over Again," *History of European Ideas* 19 (1994): 377–83.

22 Kojève, *Introduction*, 145.

23 Ibid., 113–14.

24 Eric Weil, "La Fin de l'Histoire," *Revue de Métaphysique et de Morale* 75 (1970): 379–80.

25 Kojève, *Introduction*, 146.

26 Eric Weil, *Hegel et l'État* (Paris: Vrin, 1950), 71.This interpretation of *The Philosophy of Right* gives great weight to politics and accords much less significance to the political institutions of civil/bourgeois society. This problem is discussed in Cooper, *End of History*, chap. 7.

27 See Michael S. Roth, *Knowing and History: Appropriations of Hegel in Twentieth-Century France* (Ithaca, NY: Cornell University Press, 1988).

28 Hegel's account of international relations, especially the contemporary activity of religiously inspired non-governmental actors, seems to be more questionable than his account of the internal politics of "modern" states. During the war, however, Kojève wrote a lengthy essay, the *Equisse d'une Phénoménologie du Droit: Exposé provisoire* (Paris: Gallimard, 1981), that provided a more detailed account of what actual, juridical global politics would be like. See also Dominique Auffret, *Alexandre Kojève: La Philosophie, L'État, la Fin de l'Histoire* (Paris: Grasset, 1990). In any event, it is possible to reconcile the commonsensical elements of a Kojèvian interpretation of, for example, al-Qaeda, with Hegel's discussion of the "civilized" nation-state system in nineteenth-century Europe. See Barry Cooper, *Democracies and Small Wars* (Calgary: Canadian Defence and Foreign Affairs Institute, 2009). From within the Hegelian-Kojèvian "theoretical" System, which is much removed from common sense, even Fukuyama considered, long before 11 September 2001, that "Islamic fundamentalism" provided a diversion, a Pascalian *divertissement* for the ennui and boredom of post-revolutionary and post-historical life. See *End of History*, 45–6; see also Hoffmeister, *Dokumente zu Hegels Entwicklung*, 318, for a discussion of the "boredom of the world" that arises when the gods depart.

29 See Janet Ajzenstat, *The Political Thought of Lord Durham* (Montreal and Kingston: McGill-Queen's University Press, 1988).
30 Strauss, *On Tyranny*, 191–2.
31 Kojève would not disagree, though he would call it the need for commitment – Augustine's *credo ut intelligam*. Kojève would add that, by making the commitment and only by doing so, can one gain access to the System of Science. From Kojève's point of view, Strauss simply refused to acknowledge the actuality of modernity.
32 G.W.H. Hegel, *Vorlesungen über die Philosophie der Geschichte* (Stuttgart: Reclam, 1961), 134. The conventional interpretation of Hegel on this point may concede the importance of recognition in the *Phenomenology* but insists that (somehow) freedom was central in *The Philosophy of Right*. Kojève (and Strauss and Grant) all agreed that, for Hegel, freedom was, properly speaking, a consequence of recognition.
33 *Introduction à la Lecture de Hegel*, 385.
34 It was made with greater wit by Tom Darby's character Hamilton Fowler "Hambone" West in *Disorderly Notions* (Toronto: Iguana, 2011), 82–5.
35 Strauss, *On Tyranny*, 207–8.
36 This point has recently and forcefully been made by Harvey C. Mansfield, *Manliness* (New Haven, CT: Yale University Press, 2004); and Richard Avramenko, *Courage: The Politics of Life and Limb* (Notre Dame, IN: Notre Dame University Press, 2011).
37 The chief alternative to Alex and his droogs was described by Alan Bloom: "A pubescent child whose body throbs with orgasmic rhythms; whose feelings are made articulate in hymns to the joys of onanism or the killing of parents; whose ambition is to win fame and wealth in imitating the drag-queen who makes the music. In short, life is made into a nonstop, commercially prepackaged masturbational fantasy." *The Closing of the American Mind: How Education Has Failed Democracy and Impoverished the Souls of Today's Students* (New York: Simon and Schuster, 1987), 75.
38 Kojève, *Introduction*, 146.
39 Strauss, *On Tyranny*, 209.
40 There are the aforementioned philosophical objections by Voegelin noted in n16. See also Cooper, *End of History*, 328–32; and Tom Darby, *The Feast: Meditations on Politics and Time* (Toronto: University of Toronto Press, 1982), 172–5.
41 I have examined this aspect of Grant's work in Barry Cooper, "Ab Imperio Usque Ad Imperium: The Political Thought of George Grant," in *George Grant in Process*, ed. Larry Schmidt (Toronto: Anansi, 1978), 22–48; Cooper,

"George Grant as Political Philosopher," *Political Science Reviewer* 18 (1988): 1–33; Cooper, "George Grant and the Revival of Political Philosophy," in *By Loving Our Own: George Grant and the Legacy of Lament for a Nation*, ed. Peter C. Emberley, 97–121 (Ottawa: Carleton University Press, 1990); Cooper, "Did George Grant's Canada Ever Exist?" in *George Grant and the Future of Canada*, ed. Y.K. Umar, 151–64 (Calgary: University of Calgary Press, 1992).

42 The philological information regarding the revisions of the text are available in Grant's *Collected Works*, 3:271–7 and notes.

43 Dennis Lee, "Cadence, Country, Silence," *Boundary2* 3 (1974): 151–78.

44 See Janet Ajzenstat and Peter J. Smith, eds., *Canada's Origins: Liberal, Tory, or Republican* (Ottawa: Carleton University Press, 1995); Ajzenstat, Ina Gentles, and Paul Romney, eds., *Canada's Founding Debates* (Toronto: Stoddart, 1999); Ajzenstat, *The Once and Future Nation* (Montreal and Kingston: McGill-Queen's University Press). See also Cooper, *It's the Regime, Stupid*, chap. 3.

45 Clifford Orwin, "Review of Grant's 'English-Speaking Justice,'" *University of Toronto Law Review* 30 (1980): 106.

46 In this context, Grant's essay "In Defence of North America" (the title is *not* ironic) in *Technology and Empire* provides confirmation. Grant's *Collected Works*, 3:480–503.

47 See Grant, "Have We a Canadian Nation?," and "The Empire, Yes or No?," in *Collected Works of George Grant*, ed. Arthur Davis and Peter C. Emberley, vol. 1, *1933–1950* (Toronto: University of Toronto Press, 2000), 97–136.

48 Grant said nothing in *Lament* and next to nothing afterwards about the role of Dalton Camp in getting rid of Diefenbaker as leader of the Progressive Conservative Party, notwithstanding the fact that it was a very clear example of the Kojèvian themes of post-historical politics conducted in terms of a palace coup and non-lethal political "assassination."

49 Grant, *Collected Works*, 3:383.

50 I am quoting my grandfather, who knew Mr Diefenbaker, from memory.

51 Grant, *Collected Works*, 3:307, 300.

52 Ibid., 3:300, 309.

53 Ibid., 3:288–9.

54 Ibid., 3:287, 290.

55 For an extended defence of this statement, see David J. Bercuson and Barry Cooper, *Deconfederation: Canada without Quebec* (Toronto: Key Porter, 1991).

56 Grant, *Collected Works*, 3:294.

57 Ibid., 3:289.

58 Ibid., 3:311.

59 It is worth noting, however, that the fourth province of "Atlantic Canada," Newfoundland, resisted joining the capitulationist Maritime pensioners until the mid-twentieth century.
60 Charles Taylor, *Philosophical Arguments* (Cambridge, MA: Harvard University Press, 1995), x–xi. Taylor's discussion of modern self-understanding is "like additional chapters to my *Sources of the Self*," a very large book that we must also ignore along with his even larger one, *A Secular Age*.
61 Charles Taylor, "Can Canada Survive the Charter?," *Alberta Law Review* 30 (1992): 427.
62 Let me sharpen the issue with the observation that the chief beneficiaries of this solidarity of mutual help and collective provisioning happen to be residents of the province of Quebec. The major benefactors over the past generation have been the residents of the province of Alberta.
63 Taylor, "Can Canada Survive the Charter?," 430.
64 Charles Taylor, *Multiculturalism and "The Politics of Recognition"* (Princeton: Princeton University Press, 1992), 195.
65 Ibid.
66 Ibid.
67 Ibid.
68 Ibid., 26.
69 Ibid.
70 Charles Taylor, *Reconciling the Solitudes: Essays on Canadian Federalism and Nationalism*, ed. Guy Laforest (Montreal and Kingston: McGill-Queen's University Press, 1993), 190.
71 Ibid., 190.
72 See Thomas Flanagan, "Native Sovereignty: Does Anyone Really Want an Aboriginal Archipelago?," in *Contemporary Political Issues*, 2nd ed., ed. Mark Charlton and Paul Barker, 70–80 (Toronto: Nelson Canada, 1994).
73 Taylor, *Multiculturalism and "The Politics of Recognition,"* 25.
74 Taylor, *Reconciling the Solitudes*, 196.
75 This point was brought out with great clarity by Leo Strauss in his response to Kojève. See *On Tyranny*, 209 and xviii.
76 For details on the several self-interpretations of Canadian, see *It's the Regime, Stupid*, chap. 2.
77 Taylor, *Reconciling the Solitudes*, 197.
78 Taylor, *Reconciling the Solitudes*, chap. 8. See also Janet Ajzenstat, "Decline of Procedural Liberalism: The Slippery Slope to Secession," in *Is Quebec Nationalism Just? Perspectives from Anglophone Canada*, ed. Joseph H. Carens

(Montreal and Kingston: McGill-Queen's University Press, 1995), 120–2. See also Barry Cooper, "Canadian Issues and Political Science: 1970–1995," *Political Science Reviewer* 25 (1996): 100–26; and Cooper, "Taylor-Made Canada," *Literary Review of Canada* 5 (February 1996): 19–22; Rainer Knopff, "Liberal Democracy and the Challenge of Nationalism in Canadian Politics," *Canadian Review of Studies in Nationalism* 9 (1982): 23–42; and Knopff, "Democracy vs Liberal Democracy: The Nationalist Conundrum," *Dalhousie Review* 58 (1978–9): 638–46.

16 Hegel and the Possibility of Intercultural Criticism

SHANNON HOFF

In Hegel's philosophy, the concept of "ethical life" presents powerfully the way in which human beings are formed and shaped by specific sociocultural worlds around them. With the elucidation of the concept of "conscience," conversely, Hegel shows how individuals fundamentally and intractably shape these worlds, leaving the mark of their singularity upon all that forms and claims them.[1] In what follows, I will examine this two-sided account of human agency[2] for the purposes of speaking to a particular issue facing political philosophy in general and feminist theory and practice in particular: intercultural criticism, or how to identify and address problems of injustice in culturally specific contexts that are not one's own with regard to gender and sexual identity. Approaches to this issue have typically been articulated in ways that alternate between two extremes: the first is the idea that there are universal or transcultural values that are indifferent to the particularities of context and can simply be transferred to other sociocultural worlds, and the second is the idea that respect for sociocultural specificity demands the refusal of any kind of intervention in other sociocultural worlds. I will argue here that Hegel implicitly rejects these extremes: with the concept of ethical life he opposes the possibility that political mechanisms could simply be transferred from one context to another without damage or remainder, and with the concept of conscience he challenges the idea that interaction and intervention should simply be avoided.[3] Finally, through analysis of the conscientious stance of forgiveness in Hegel's philosophy, I will develop a middle road between these extremes, identifying what would be required for a just approach to political and specifically feminist action and judgment across sociocultural borders and between worlds, and what intercultural interaction and communication leading to better socio-political conditions would look like.

It is perhaps the powerful social-democratic spirit of Hegel's work, expressed in his concern both for our formation and for our autonomy, that has made it a helpful resource in the project of explaining the specific singularity of the Canadian political tradition and has caused it to speak powerfully to Canadian philosophers and scholars of Hegel such as H.S. Harris, Charles Taylor, John Burbidge, and John Russon. The tradition of Canadian scholarship on Hegel has recognized and brought to the forefront Hegel's capacity to continue to speak to contemporary issues of political, social, and economic justice, specifically the tensions between individual freedom, cultural identity, and social integration.[4] In what follows, I will continue in this trajectory, but, rather than focusing on the historical specificities of the relationship between Hegel and Canadian political and philosophical thought, I will explore how Hegel's work can speak to a political issue that faces Canada and similar political contexts now: the intersection of liberal law with cultural traditions not specifically rooted in it.[5] I will extend the traditional appreciation for the social-democratic spirit of Hegel at work in the traditions of Canadian politics and of Hegel-interpretation by bringing his work to bear on the question of how to interact justly with sociocultural worlds not one's own around issues of feminist justice, identifying in the process the resources that other Canadian scholars of Hegel have contributed, implicitly or explicitly, to this kind of discussion. In effect, I will apply the lessons of ethical life, conscience, and forgiveness to an issue that has been pressing for Canada insofar as it, like many other countries, has been shaped so essentially by immigration and globalization: developing political criticism that speaks justly with and to unfamiliar traditions and contexts. Though my argument here resonates more broadly, for the purpose of this chapter. I will focus on one specific case: the relationship between feminist analysis, Muslim women, and the practices and traditions of Islam.

Ethicality and the Specificity of Sociocultural Worlds

One significant accomplishment of Hegel's work is its elucidation of the way in which human beings are shaped by others and by the terms at work in the particular way of life they share with each other. Hegel gives the name *Sittlichkeit* or "ethical life" to these determinate ways of life that act as the formative context for human persons.[6] All individuals inhabit a particular, determinate, and shared way of life; we carry along with us a tradition; we speak, act, feel, and think in ways that reveal the operation of a specific history and culture in us. Even though we may think of our action as simply our own, as independent, self-defined, and expressive of our free and pure inner reality, we are in many ways conduits of meaning that are bigger and broader than we are; we are occasions through which a tradition or way of life makes itself real.[7] Even when we try to do things to express our unique characters, our actions speak of the reality we share with others, of our shared sense of what counts as good, and of the resources made available by our collaboration with which we accomplish such goods. We are the media of a larger reality that is sustained through us; we act in and through an inheritance. In a sense our agency fundamentally belongs to these practices and values, not merely to ourselves; our individuality is an instantiation and expression of them.[8]

This inheritance is indeed all-encompassing, since we are already involved in living in and sustaining a set of common practices and values by the time we come to develop capacities with which we can critically evaluate them. We learn how to act and what to value before we are able to reflect self-consciously on our acting and valuing, before we are able to choose the ways in which we would like to act and the phenomena that we would like to value. We become habituated to a way of life and its organizing structures, and in our very habituation we confirm and sustain their authority and efficacy; our lack of explicit consciousness of their operation testifies to how all-encompassing they are. Our identities are as if haunted by a past, a history that we cannot recover or bring to consciousness.[9]

To try to discard these terms by which we enter *into* reality, the terms through the acceptance of which we become real and human, is in a sense to give up on our own reality and to endanger our self-understanding and our sanity – and, indeed, our capacity to relate to others, the centrality of which Hegel captures with the notion of recognition.[10] People around us recognize and accept us as understandable and valuable if we show, in our action, that we are participating in the same world that they inhabit, according to terms that they share. Because the meanings that are enacted in our actions situate other human beings as well, through our enactment of these meanings we receive recognition by others and express in turn our recognition of them, as having a reality in common, as capable of supporting each other's projects, as being reliable participants in this world and not radically disruptive of it. If we abandon these terms, we jeopardize our capacity to interact with others, to be taken up by them in cooperative ways, and to have access to a world that we could not achieve by ourselves. For better or worse, the fact and promise of recognition is another powerful force behind our internalization of and habituation to the specific terms of our shared social life.

Because we rely on the operation of specific worlds or ways of life in order to become human, there will be obstacles in the way of meaningful and just interaction with others outside of these worlds. This is because, on the one hand, the specificity of our own way of life is difficult to recognize as such, since, to us who adopt them, the terms of that way of life express what it means to be human in general. To be a person is to belong to a particular world that defines itself in unique ways and thereby is ineradicably different from other worlds, but to perceive only dimly the status of that world as partial and particular, as merely one among many. Our worlds, through our adoption and internalization of their terms – through our becoming human on their basis – present themselves to us as virtually absolute. Further, since to be human is to be defined in principle in a way that is different from others who inhabit different worlds, it is exceedingly difficult to appreciate the nature of that difference and the way in which the world of others asserts itself to them as absolute. Meaningful interaction is also prevented, then, by our incapacity to understand the specificity of other sociocultural worlds and the specific relations that others have to these worlds.[11]

With this idea of ethical life in hand, we can critically assess one particular strategy for interacting with people from other sociocultural worlds on issues of feminist justice: that involved in advocating the imposition of Western political paradigms upon other individuals and states. With regard to our specific example, we can see this move especially in the direction of "West" to "East," when political paradigms typically associated with the West – such as "rights"-based paradigms of political justice and autonomy-based conceptions of agency – are imposed on or advocated for Muslim societies and communities in the name of the liberation of Muslim women. Given the reality of ethical life, however, the problems with this approach are numerous. Implicit in the ideal of individual right and the ideal of autonomy is the presumption of a separability between individual and social reality that is too severe, or that does not acknowledge the phenomenon of ethical life that we have been describing. In tying a person's significance to her individuality and not to her roles or membership in a larger group, the paradigm of rights and the ideal of autonomous agency do not reckon sufficiently with the particular processes behind human formation, their cultivation of human beings in a specific way. They imply the too facile idea that it is possible to abstract individuals from their sociocultural worlds. Further, these ideals themselves are considered to be indifferent to the specificity of context, to be neutral with regard to the values associated with specific sociocultural worlds.[12] The ways in which they are also attached to a specific world and the consequences of this attachment for how they are mobilized is under-recognized. Finally, they preclude precisely the interaction and communication that could bring to light the possible resources of liberation actually available in the "foreign" world and that could illuminate the historical specificity, and also perhaps the shortcomings, of the resources available to "our" worlds.

While to have a genuine interest in the pursuit of justice is in principle to be rendered incapable of limiting one's concern to one's own society, and, therefore, while it is understandable and right that one oppose wrong, the relation-in-principle between a person and her tradition means that the strategy of importing an established legal-political framework into a different social reality is a dishonest and failing strategy.[13] What becomes visible through the lens of Hegel's account of ethical life is that the development of feminist agency and the expression of feminist concern across borders cannot require disavowal of the situating and contextualizing tradition.[14] Individuals must recognize and acknowledge the shaping power of the worlds in which they and others are situated; they should work to discover and learn their own specificity and that of others. Saba Mahmood gives a nice analysis of the way in which worldly specificity is disavowed by the rights-based political framework that would "rescue" Muslim women, showing how this disavowal subverts Western attempts to support the agency of Muslim women. She exposes specific unexamined prejudices at work in Western feminists' characterizations of freedom and agency: that freedom is expressed through resistance to social structures, and that agency is disabled, not enabled, by religion and religious belief. She herself argues that agency is created and enabled by relations with others, identifying, further, the fact that these relations can even be "relations of *subordination*." We come into being as agents even through relations that seem on the surface to curtail our agency – indeed, it is hard to imagine the development of agency that would not be accompanied by a simultaneous curtailment of agency.[15] If agency relies on relations of subordination, Mahmood concludes, then these relations cannot simply be eliminated in the pursuit to support agency. When we operate in ignorance of the real ways in which agency is sustained and supported in specific contexts, our efforts to advance it can misfire and sabotage it instead.[16]

One specific issue that garners much political attention is that of veiling or hijab, in relation to which there seems to be a noteworthy lack of effort to understand the significance of particular practices not one's own.[17] Scholars and activists both inside and outside of the communities in which this practice is prominent have tried to increase the possibility of understanding and communication about it. Marnia Lazreg, for instance, calls attention to occasions in which the veil is used as an expression of resistance to Western domination; women may wear it, she says, as "a manner of fighting prejudice by flaunting difference."[18] Karen Armstrong observes, similarly, that many Muslim women in the United States began "wearing the hijab to distance themselves from the foreign policy of the Bush administration."[19] Leila Ahmed reflects on an interview with a woman who claims that for her the hijab "was required dress that made visible the presence of a religious minority entitled to justice and equality"; the veil, Ahmed observes, can indeed serve "as a banner and call for justice – and yes, even for women's rights."[20] Natasha Bakht discusses at length the various political contexts in which the veil takes on specific and diverse meanings, depending on the political and social issues at stake in each context.[21] While "veiling" may not simply be a site of resistance and the manifestation of political freedom, these discussions should show that it is not simply a symbol of a single belief or commitment, but complex, understandable only in reference to the religious, political, and cultural complexities of the sites in which it is operative. For those for whom its significance is not clear, coming to a better understanding of it may also be the occasion for coming to a better understanding of themselves, if in the wearing of the veil an interpretation of Western others and their worlds is also operative. Indeed, this is an occasion of how the specificity of other people can be helpful in guiding one to a clearer understanding of one's own specificity.

We can witness the significance of cultural identity in interaction with the practice of wearing the niqab in an Ontario court case that eventually reached the Supreme Court of Canada. In *N.S. v. R.*, the complainant, allegedly sexually abused from the age of six, sought to wear her niqab while testifying, to which the accused objected, asserting a right to "demeanour evidence." The ultimate decision of the Supreme Court was that such cases had to be decided case by case, and the Court developed a test by which such cases would be decided, sending *N.S. v. R.*, with the prescribed test, back to the preliminary inquiry judge.[22] According to the Women's Legal Education and Action Fund, which had been granted leave to intervene at the hearing, to order the removal of the niqab would be effectively to humiliate and degrade the complainant, thus "disenfranchising sexual assault complainants who wear the niqab from the criminal justice system," which is "inconsistent with promoting their substantive equality and respecting and protecting their s.7 *Charter* rights to life, liberty and security of the person." [23] Dissenting Justice Abella argued, similarly, that "the harmful effects of requiring a witness to remove her niqab, with the result that she will likely not testify, bring charges in the first place, or, if she is the accused, be unable to testify in her own defence, is a significantly more harmful consequence than not being able to see a witness's whole face."[24] With this case we can see the weighty reality of "ethical life": N.S. has become the human being that she is in interaction with a particular set of values, religious beliefs, and social practices that she expresses in some way by wearing the niqab; the demand that she remove it is in a sense a demand that she abandon who she is, hardly a demand that supports her agency. Even if it were a widespread view in the Canadian justice system that women who wear the niqab are oppressed in their homes and by their religion, it would not be *supportive* of their agency to require them to abandon practices that secure that agency, or to require of them a kind of intimate exposure to those who are accused of having already transgressed intimate boundaries by sexual assault.

To appreciate the significant and irreducible ways in which we are shaped by the specific worlds in which we become human would require us to engage in at least two different kinds of practices: the practice of being attentive to our own particularity and to the particular shape that our intervention in the lives of others takes, and the practice of justly perceiving the particularity of others. It would be to commit oneself, as Fred Pfeil argues, to a Gramscian "'inventory' of those historically produced discourses, practices, and institutions that have determined us, as a necessary preliminary to our engagement in a common liberation struggle."[25] It would be to explore the prejudicial character of our political ideals and ideas about others, keeping our activities of observation, judgment, and intervention under scrutiny.[26]

It would be to investigate how our intervention has reoriented the trajectory of development of the worlds in which we intervene, and has negatively and not simply positively affected the position of women in those worlds.[27] And it would be to analyse the particular trajectories that characterize different social contexts, recognizing that the narratives and accomplishments of each have an internal logic not easily translatable into others; the significance of discrete, seemingly similar events would not be the same in each, given their specific role in the narrative or logic.

We have seen why, contrary to the presumptions of a rights-based paradigm, it is essential to justice that we recognize the irreducibly specific cultural shape of agency. Now, however, we will consider a second, opposed approach to the issue of injustice across cultural borders that does take seriously the significance of sociocultural specificity, insisting that specific cultures are exclusively particular and hence uninterpretable from the outside. According to this view, to be concerned for feminist justice would be to resist and discourage most forms of judgment and action across cultural borders. To analyse this view, and to expose the *limits* of the idea that we have just explored, that individual action is an enactment of traditional practices, customs, and values, I will invoke Hegel's account of conscience. With this account, we will see the way in which individuals are irreducible to the terms presented by their tradition and hence freed for interaction beyond the kind that it makes available to them.

Conscience and the Singularity of Human Individuals

The second way in which injustice related to gender and sexuality in cross-cultural contexts is addressed can be understood as a critical response to the first. This second way asserts that to transport a specific political framework to another political location is to risk continuing to suppress the people of that location, effectively reiterating the subordination that demanded redress in the first place. This second strategy would refuse intervention in the name of the self-determination of the oppressed people with whom it identifies, at most trying to protect indirectly the capacity of the oppressed to speak and act on their own behalf. According to the terms of this model, to respect people and the exclusive particularity of sociocultural worlds is to allow them to rely on their own terms to present the meaning of that cultural specificity and enact transformation of it, since interaction across sociocultural borders is more likely to perpetuate patterns of domination than to eradicate them.

While this approach reflects the recognition that human persons are irreducibly "cultured," it fails to adequately recognize a second central aspect of human identity and agency, one that Hegel's work, again, can help us identify. While it is true that we are fundamentally shaped by our specific sociocultural worlds, such that our action is in a sense an enactment of inherited significance that extends beyond our simple individuality, it is also true that the terms of that inheritance are insufficient as guides for our action and judgment. Even in attempting to perfectly reproduce the terms of an inherited reality and a shared way of life, each person will bring with her the mark of her own individuality in discerning how to act in particular situations. Single, human individuals need to decide what *specific* action is appropriate as a response to a value or obligation that purports to be general, and what *specific* way of life would allow them to fulfil such obligations; hence they will always, inadvertently or not, identify in their action the ultimacy of their singularity. There is unavoidably and always a need for singular interpretation, discernment, and judgment in the enactment of values and the fulfilment of obligations, and a demand for decision and action in one situation that will be simultaneously a refusal to act in another.[28] Our thinking and decision-making operates, and must operate, outside the boundaries of the explicit authority and guidance of any given value or obligation, since they operate always in specific, circumscribed contexts. Thus, while any way of life persistently shapes our agency and identity, this agency and identity carry it out in a way that is irreducibly singular. Therefore, just as human individuals must recognize the shaping force of the worlds in which they are situated, so also must these worlds acknowledge the shaping force of the people who constitute them.[29]

We can see, then, that there is a problem with traditions and worlds that espouse absolute obedience and conformity. The unavoidable fact that we must always "go beyond" or interpret customary values means in a sense that we are actually required to *disobey* these values: in order to be obedient, I must interpret the value or obligation and the situation to which I think it speaks, so I disobey the demand that I simply follow it, and I obey myself. We confirm the authority and significance of traditions precisely and only by interpreting and transgressing them; specific traditions are extended into the future only by being made to speak to demands arising in unique situations. To live in and act out of such a world – which we all do, at a basic formative level, even in our opposition to it – is to be committed to its dynamism, its openness to change.[30]

It is always possible that we will not *acknowledge* that tradition always effectively demands of us its transgression (a point Hegel makes in his discussion of Sophocles's *Antigone*[31]), but Hegel gives the name "conscience" to that figure who has explicitly owned up to the fact that she must take this interpretive initiative.[32] The conscientious self has grappled with the question of how to carry out universal laws and how to act appropriately in a given context, and has resolutely come to terms with the fact that situations are singular, that actions are determinable only by her own conviction, and that guidance from elsewhere will always be incomplete. The individual truly acting from conscience takes responsibility for her interpretation, knowing that she cannot pretend that she is "simply following the law." The conscientious self may be committed in principle to doing what is right, but she knows and accepts that she is open to the world in a particular way, incapable of knowing universally and responding indifferently to all situations. She may want to carry out her tradition and obey its commands, but they never speak specifically to her unique situation, so in attempting to sustain and apply them she knows she will be creative in determining how they are relevant to her situation, and her creativity may ultimately challenge and change what others have typically understood to be the meaning of the tradition.

The phenomenon of conscience provides important lessons for intercultural criticism. First, if there is never a perfect identification between individual and world, if perfect obedience is impossible, then a tradition or culture is wrong to demand perfect obedience and expect perfect identification, and a critique of that culture in the name of the reality of conscience is possible, as is communication and understanding on the basis of the non-absoluteness of the worlds of our formation. Just as it is wrong within a culture to think that the tradition can uniformly dictate a set of specific practices for individuals, so is it wrong from outside a culture to imagine it to be monolithic and statically uniform. While we are shaped in indelible and often unthematizable ways, we also shape and must shape these worlds and specific contexts in irreducibly singular ways. Second, with the phenomenon of conscience Hegel illuminates the fact that in answering to an ideal or principle we always of necessity do something specific, something that is not identical with the ideal as such, and in this very specificity is available another lesson for those who would engage in intercultural communication and criticism. That is, specific actions and practices are enacted and engaged in so as to express a value or meaning, which means that even if the practice is unshared, the meaning could be shared, or at the very least understood. To refer to our earlier example, while some of the women Karen Armstrong observes "distance themselves from the foreign policy of the Bush administration" by wearing the hijab, a non-Muslim woman may distance herself from that same policy by marching in a demonstration. What should be recognized here is that there is a shared value operative in these different practices, a sharing that is effectively *concealed* by the differences between these practices. Here, commonality *makes itself manifest as difference*, and can be discerned only through *communication*, since the reasons we adopt certain practices or the values by which we are oriented cannot be physically manifested, or manifested to distant, disengaged, and non-communicative observation.

This means that to forgo the possibility of enacting a critical perspective on a foreign sociocultural world in the name of respecting its particularity is as inadequate an interpretive stance as the one that unilaterally insists on the application of rights. To refuse judgment and action with regard to another cultural context is to make a mistake about both oneself and the other in relation to whom one would act and judge: it is to deny implicitly the way in which all individuals, oneself and others, are never completely reducible to the specific cultural contexts that shape them, and it is to deny existent possibilities for interaction, communication, and understanding. The ideal of justice does not include an absolute respect for particularity, since particularity is never absolutely authoritative and, therefore, since the establishment of commonality across different versions of cultural particularity is never absolutely impossible. The expression of concern cannot require the disavowal of criticism, the disavowal of the imperfect authority of the worlds of our formation, and the disavowal of the possibility that a person could separate herself from the particular terms of her tradition and identify with others from other worlds.

If the particularity of a given sociocultural world is never absolutely authoritative and the establishment of commonality across borders never absolutely impossible, then specific sociocultural worlds can be held accountable to the demand to recognize the inevitable presence of conscience, similarities across traditions that would enable communication and understanding about specific issues can be identified, and, indeed, the ways in which such traditions already answer to the implicit and explicit demands for transformation at play in them can be ascertained. Uma Narayan does all of these things in relation to the place of women in Indian culture. She identifies similarities across traditions, exposing the "national agendas" that conceal these similarities and so prevent connections from being made. She herself establishes the ground for one such connection in exposing, for instance, how "forms of violence against Third-World women, such as dowry murders, get represented as instances of 'death by culture' while analogous forms of violence in Western contexts, such as domestic violence murders, often do not."[33] Narayan also identifies elements *within* traditional Indian culture that subvert it even while they sustain it, that prevent it from being perpetuated in an absolutely stable and self-identical way. She writes, and I cite at length:

> Thus my mother insists on seeing my rejection of an arranged marriage, and my general lack of enthusiasm for the institution of marriage as a whole, as a "Westernized" rejection of Indian cultural values. But, in doing so, she forgets how regularly since my childhood she and many other women have complained about the oppressiveness of their marriages in my presence; she forgets how widespread and commonplace the cultural recognition is in India that marriage subjects daughters to difficult life-situations, forgets that my childish misbehaviours were often met with the reprimand, "Wait till you get to your mother-in-law's house. Then you will learn how to behave." I would thus argue that my sense that marriage is an oppressive institution for many women ... is something I initially learned not from books but from Indian women in general, and my female relatives in particular ... [T]he mistreatments women are subjected to within their marriages ... are also staple ingredients of the "family dramas" depicted in Indian movies, and thus openly acknowledged elements of popular cultural awareness. I would argue that seeing the perspectives of feminist daughters simply as symptoms of our "Westernization" and as "rejections of our cultures," fails ... to see how often the inhabitants of a culture criticize the very institutions they endorse.[34]

In this set of observations, Narayan shows us the way in which a specific sociocultural world with a particular kind of constraint has within it compelling examples of internal resistance, internal resources for transformation, and an experiential basis upon which communication and understanding across sociocultural borders could occur.

The incoherence of the idea of an absolute respect for particularity does not demand a return to the first strategy – the imposition of a purportedly universal legal framework. What it does entail, however, is a variety of attitudes and practices that would enable better communication across differences: for instance, being suspicious of the way in which one's action is specific and enacts specific kinds of injustice that are associated with one's sociocultural world, trusting that other traditions have resources for their own critical transformation, and leaving open the possibility that there is interpretable meaning available in practices that seem alien. This suspicion, trust, and openness could be the platform for engagement in meaningful communication about our traditions and our cultural specificity, in a way that respects our mutual singularity. Let us turn now to illuminate the shape that such communication could take so as to respond to both of these ingredients of human agency – the power of tradition and the singularity of action.

Forgiveness and Intercultural Communication

Hegel's analysis of the concept of conscience reveals that individuals are rooted in, but irreducible to, their traditions, and it gives us a specific model for human interaction in the context of our cultural specificity and difference from each other. The conscientious person acts according to his conviction, in response to what he recognizes as his obligations: conscience is the simultaneous acknowledgment of the commanding weight of obligation and of individual interpretation. In thus acknowledging *the authority of* conscience in his own case, however, the conscientious person has implicitly recognized that conscience is a norm for *all*, and to make this implicit endorsement explicit is to support the conscientious action and judgment of others, even if they are different from his. Further, recognizing the legitimacy in principle of the opposing conscience goes hand-in-hand with owning up to – or, as Hegel calls it, "confessing" – the limitations inherent to his own interpretive perspective, the possibility of his own interpretive blindness and partiality.[35] The stance of conscience is thus most completely fulfilled in exposing one's interpretation to the judgment of others, in admitting their judgment is in a very basic sense legitimate, as is one's own: this is the stance Hegel calls "forgiveness," the conscientious stance that recognizes its own inability to be the "absolute" standpoint, and thus simultaneously "forgives" the opposing view and seeks forgiveness for its own limitations.[36]

This open, forgiving attitude is the ground for a kind of identity between oneself and others that is different from the one provided by the customary values and obligations of a tradition, the protective self-enclosure of culture, as well as from the one provided by the abstract universality of law, the homogenizing generality of universal rights. It is a kind of living infinite requirement, which makes itself apparent in all of our interaction with others, to respond openly, apart from the "safe" direction provided by the simple imposition of our established values and laws. Adequately responding to others whom we acknowledge to be equally legitimate to ourselves requires engaging in communication *to learn from them* what it is that requires our response, communication that could be transformative, that could change our conceptions of our own action and identity, and that could reveal things in common, such as shared values expressed in different media. Such "mutually forgiving" communication requires that we acknowledge that specific cultures and abstract laws do not give us an exhaustive account of the requirements of ethical behaviour and interaction, and that communication, learning, and transformation must extend beyond them, carefully attentive to the uniquely emergent situations that call for specific and creative kinds of responses.[37] Rather than relying upon the ultimacy of an established frame of reference, it is a matter of establishing a newly shared ground of communication upon which we can explain ourselves to and learn from each other: the ground for a future engagement.[38]

This kind of engagement can arise in various ways. It is possible, for instance, that determinate actions or practices that are radically different actually reflect similar values, and identifying such values can lead to establishment of a terrain upon which to communicate and come to greater understanding. A kind of sharing and identification can emerge also from the very fact of the difference between practices and views: available in them could be an important lesson or value that is not similarly available in our own practices and views, and through our appreciation of this lesson or value we could be brought to an appreciation of the distinctiveness of values operative in other traditions. It is possible, for instance, to see in the resurgence of Islamic virtues and practice a meaningful opposition to the political and cultural domination of the West, which in many ways demands an assertion of individuality that is incompatible with the nature of actual human experience and involves adoption of the lifestyle of a capitalist consumer. Anouar Majid identifies Islam as a site of value in the connection it makes, more forcefully than is typically made in the West, between the notion of the individual and "the spiritual and socioeconomic welfare of the community."[39] She cites Mahmood Monshipouri, who observes that "Muslim perspectives on universal human rights have traditionally revolved more around themes of social justice than of individual freedoms."[40] And she invokes Burgat's work to identify a further value available in the political reality associated with Islam: the possibility that it might be "the most authentic voice of the South in its struggle against the Western-inspired and racially informed hegemonic aims of transnational capital" and might contain therefore a "progressive and prophetic essence."[41] Majid herself enacts a kind of value-sharing between "East" and "West," identifying a similarity between Marx and Islam that is available in Marx's criticism of individual "independence" in the "slavery of civil society."[42] In her careful identification of unexpected similarities and valuable differences, she rejects a kind of recalcitrant self-certainty in favour of the possibility of better mutual understanding.[43]

An example of how to conduct this kind of conscientious communication in a cross-cultural political context is found, in implicit form, in the relatively recent political history of Ontario. Ontario's Arbitration Act, which became law in 1992, allowed for private arbitration of civil disputes, and upon its basis "Jewish and Christian groups set up arbitration boards that ruled in accordance with their religious principles."[44] All of these arbitrations were legally binding, as long as they *did not violate Canadian law*. In 2003, however, when Syed Mumtaz Ali announced that the Islamic Institute of Civil Justice would offer private arbitration in family and business disputes on the basis of the Ontario Arbitration Act and in accordance with Islamic legal principles, there occurred somewhat of an uproar in Ontario. In response, the provincial government commissioned a former attorney general of the Province, Marion Boyd, to produce a report on the use of such arbitration. Boyd's report recommended that, with the addition of new "institutionalized oversight and education on the principles of religious arbitration and Canadian family law,"[45] this arbitration "should continue to be an alternative dispute resolution option that is available in family and inheritance law cases, subject to the further recommendations of this Review," and that "the Arbitration Act should continue to allow disputes to be arbitrated using religious law, if the safeguards currently prescribed and recommended by this Review are observed."[46] The government, however, rejected the recommendation, and announced on 11 September 2005 that there would be "one law for all," introducing the Family Statute

Law Amendment Act, 2006.[47] To determine the value of this decision would require more discussion, but the option the government finally rejected could have been a powerful way of acknowledging the significance of the dual aspects of human agency, represented by ethical life and conscience, in political and social reality. It would have refused to grant absolute authority to one way of life over another, even while retaining the "last word" for Canadian law, and in so doing it could have kept the political domain open to the unanticipated significance promised by genuinely open human interaction. It would have recognized and "afforded space" for "multiple normative orders,"[48] and in so doing could have established the terrain for mutual understanding and identification. Its failure to do so marks a moment of inhospitality in Canadian history, an inhospitality not just to the Muslim immigrant but also to the future identities of those who consider themselves to be generically Canadian.

Conclusion

It is in the nature of human agency to be constituted by a tension between its capacity to be shaped by realities external to it, which thereby insinuate themselves in it, and its capacity to shape the realities external to it, which thereby find themselves vulnerable to and transformed by it. It is universally true of human beings that they are cultured, *and* that their sociocultural worlds do not carry within them the resources with which to replicate themselves on their own. Fred Pfeil eloquently captures this ambiguity – indeed, the *universal applicability* of this ambiguity to human life – when he writes, "For who among us, after all – white or nonwhite, Western or not – is not always caught precisely in the space between 'inherited traditions' and 'modernization projects'? And where else, how else, do 'cultural interpretations' come from – 'theirs' or 'ours,' local or global, resistant or complicit, as the case may be – other than from the spaces between the two, and with the ensemble of materials they provide (or, indeed, from the lack of space, the sometimes desperate need for new conceptual and material resources)?"[49]

We are all constituted by inherited traditions and moved irrevocably towards modernization projects, constituted and constituting. This means that our sociocultural worlds will always be vulnerable to singular, transformable, and unpredictable selves, and that these worlds are thus in principle committed to supporting the development of such individuals, even when that development turns out to be transgressive. It also means that to assume that one is oneself a generic instance of the species "human being," or that one need not take seriously the cultural identity of one's interlocutors, is highly dishonest and problematic. Both of these lessons could powerfully affect our interaction with those to whom we are different.

To respond correctly to the reality of the two-sided character of action and judgment – that it is specific to particular sociocultural worlds in a way that is relatively obscure to us, and that it is in principle capable of partial transcendence of this specificity in interaction with others and in self-criticism – is to develop a promising platform for the development of meaningful and effective intercultural engagement and criticism, engagement and criticism that is rightly responsive to injustice but not in a way that circuitously reiterates it. Hegel presents a particularly powerful account of this double-sided reality in what he calls "ethical life" and "conscience," and a powerful account of how to reckon with it in what he calls "confession" and "forgiveness." In his work we find a substantial platform for the development of principles for political criticism and for the pursuit of justice, one that could help us avoid the very real possibility that our pursuit of justice will reproduce the injustice it attempts to redress.

NOTES

1 I am relying for Hegel's discussion of "conscience" on §§632–71 of G.W.F. Hegel, *Phenomenology of Spirit*, trans. A.V. Miller (Oxford: Oxford University Press, 1977); Hegel, *Phänomenologie des Geistes*, ed. Eva Moldenhauer and Karl Markus Michel (Frankfurt am Main: Suhrkamp Verlag, 1970), 464–94. The notion of ethical life I have in mind is that discussed in especially §§436–83 of the *Phenomenology* and in the introduction to "Ethical Life" and the section on the family in §§142–81 of Hegel, *Philosophy of Right*, trans. Allen W. Wood (Cambridge: Cambridge University Press, 1991); Hegel, *Grundlinien der Philosophie des Rechts*, ed. Eva Moldenhauer and Karl Markus Michel (Frankfurt am Main: Suhrkamp Verlag, 1970), 292–339. "Ethical life" is described somewhat differently in each, since each treats a particular and different version of social life under the category of "ethical life." But the principle at work, which I describe in what follows, can for our purposes be treated as basically the same in each text.

2 This two-sided account of human agency, involving a focus on Hegel's notions of ethical life and conscience, defines several of the contributions

to this volume. As Charles Taylor writes, for instance, "Each life-form in history is both the effective realization of a certain pattern, and at the same time the expression of the certain self-understanding of man and hence also of Spirit. The gap between those two is the historical contradiction which moves us on." Daniel Brandes captures a similar multiplicity characterizing human agency, articulated in terms of freedom, identity, and self-making, when he writes about the possibility of "an affirmation that identity is the product, not the condition, of free action; that since freedom precedes identity and is irreducible to it, the 'making' in 'self-making' can never be reducible to the 'self' (or to say the same thing, we can never be sovereign over our actions, insulating ourselves from their unforeseeable consequences or from the new chain of actions and reactions they may provoke in others)." John Russon claims in this volume that it "is our formative cultural participation that supplies us with the terms – the means – for our own growth and development, and, inasmuch as we come from different cultures, we come at experience on different terms. Whatever universality there is in human experience is something that must be accomplished and realized on the basis of these non-universal terms … universality must emerge as the 'self-transcendence' of particularity." Further, it is conscience that is the distinctive site for grappling with this two-sided nature: "Conscience is the experience in which I experience the singularity and the particularity of [our] situation as answerable to what is absolute."

3 I discuss the way in which the tradition of feminist philosophy has contended and should contend with the different and often conflicting aspects of human life represented by ethical life and conscience in Shannon Hoff, "Inheriting Identity and Practicing Transformation: The Time of Feminist Politics," *Philosophia* 2, no. 2 (2013): 167–93.

4 In this volume, John Burbidge claims that "Hegelian thought has been mined for its ability to show how a community can be created that integrates yet respects cultural differences and individual freedom"; it has been helpful for the Canadian project of building "a consensus within a widely divergent constituency and [finding] a community that respects differences." An attentiveness to the socio-political aspects of Hegel's work is also apparent in the collective effort on the part of the Hegel Translation Group, including John Burbidge, George di Giovanni, H.S. Harris, and Kenneth L. Schmitz, in translating the "Spirit" chapter of the *Phenomenology*. See the Hegel Translation Group, *Spirit: Chapter Six of Hegel's* Phenomenology of Spirit, ed. Daniel E. Shannon (Indianapolis, IN: Hackett Publishing, 2001).

5 In this volume Neil Robertson discusses James Doull's analysis of the way in which this tension between law and culture is at play in Canadian society: "Canadians can neither agree to separate along linguistic lines … nor accept the Constitution as settled and separatism put to rest … In this incapacity of Canada to settle into one or other side of our current self-understandings, Doull suggests there is present a deeper substantiality than is anywhere given expression: the truth of Canada is both universal rights and specific community. Canadians would not feel caught in indecision, Doull argues, unless they knew implicitly that the truth is on both sides: we belong to received traditions, which we also transcend in a comprehensive universality."

6 For significant discussions of the nature and operation of ethical life, see Graeme Nicholson's contribution to this volume, "Hegel and Canada's Constitution"; John Russon, "The Ritual Basis of Self-Identity," in *Reading Hegel's* Phenomenology (Bloomington, IN: Indiana University Press, 2004), 169–83; David V. Ciavatta, *Spirit, the Family, and the Unconscious in Hegel's Philosophy* (Albany, NY: State University of New York Press, 2009), especially 55–90; and H.S. Harris, *Hegel's Ladder II: The Odyssey of Spirit* (Indianapolis, IN: Hackett Publishing, 1997), 125–230.

7 Hegel explores the thesis that our action is our own, self-defined, and expressive of who we are, in the section of the *Phenomenology* called "The Spiritual Animal Kingdom." He shows that, on the contrary, the nature of "the thing that matters" (*die Sache Selbst*) is that it "is the *action* of *single* individuals and of all individuals," and that it "is immediately *for others*, or it is a *thing that matters* [*Sache*] and is only such insofar as it is the *action of all* and *each*" (Hegel, *Phenomenology*, §418, translation modified).

8 Hegel writes, for instance, that each part can be itself only in the context of "this equilibrium with the whole" (Hegel, *Phenomenology*, §462). For discussion of this point, see John Russon, "Reading and the Body," in *Reading Hegel's* Phenomenology, 70–80.

9 George di Giovanni explains this point in a particularly powerfully way in his contribution to this volume, in the context of a discussion of the relationship between human beings and nature: "The problem, of course, is that the event that disrupts the harmony of mere nature and sets up the need for reconciliation, namely the emergence of reason, does not itself fall within the grasp of experience, for it is constitutive of the latter. It belongs to the prehistory of anyone's self-consciousness." Further, "the event that inaugurates experience is necessarily preconscious, and therefore the subject of experience *finds* itself always already engaged in a situation that it then has to justify by recovering (remembering) its origin."

10 The concept of recognition has been very influential for Charles Taylor in his development of his own philosophy; see especially Charles Taylor, "The Politics of Recognition," in *Multiculturalism: Examining the Politics of Recognition*, ed. Amy Gutmann, 25–73 (Princeton: Princeton University Press, 1994).

11 See Russon, "Ritual Basis of Self-Identity."

12 The work of Bruce Porter and Martha Jackman at the Social Rights Advocacy Centre gives a conceptual basis for fashioning rights-claims to fit specific contexts and articulating rights to substantive goods, and it enacts that conceptual framework in the context of Canadian and international politics. See especially Bruce Porter and Martha Jackman, "Socioeconomic Rights under the Canadian Charter," in *Social Rights Jurisprudence: Emerging Trends in International and Comparative Law*, ed. Malcolm Langford, 209–29 (Cambridge: Cambridge University Press, 2008); and Bruce Porter, "Justiciability of ESC Rights and the Right to Effective Remedies: Historic Challenges and New Opportunities" (paper presented at the Chinese Academy of Social Sciences, Beijing, 2008). Also helpful on this theme is James Mensch, "A Theory of Human Rights," http://cuni.academia.edu/JamesMensch/Papers.

13 Susan Moller Okin shows an oft-cited failure to appreciate this point when she says, "The female members of the culture ... *may* be much better off, from a liberal point of view, if the culture into which they were born were either gradually to become extinct (as its members became integrated into the surrounding culture)" (Susan Moller Okin, "Feminism and Multiculturalism: Some Tensions," *Ethics* 108, no. 4 [July 1998]: 680). If what I have said above is true, it is not at all clear that cultures can become extinct if their members do not, and it is also difficult to imagine a culture not having anything of value that would be unfortunate to lose, and difficult to imagine that she, determined as she is by her own such world, could make such a unilateral judgment.

14 There are many examples of political attempts to grapple with multiple forms of particularity, and it is interesting to observe where the line is drawn in such attempts. Writing about France, for instance, which passed a law in 2003 that forbids state school students from wearing conspicuous religious symbols, Caitlin Killian says that "the state has quietly negotiated with Christian and Jewish groups ... Serving fish in school cafeterias on Fridays to accommodate Catholics and not giving exams on Saturday to respect the Jewish Sabbath are areas of compromise, whereas Islamic dress is not" (Caitlin Killian, "The Other Side of the Veil: North African Women in France Respond to the Headscarf Affair," *Gender and Society* 17, no. 4 [August 2003]: 572). In 2010 France went further and passed a

law forbidding people to cover their faces in public places. Similarly, as I will discuss further, Ontario's Arbitration Act of 1991 had allowed civil disputes to be privately arbitrated, by agreed-upon principles or systems of law, which enabled Jewish and Christian groups to settle civil disputes using religious terms, but, when it became clear that Muslims intended to do so as well, the law was rescinded.

15 Saba Mahmood, *Politics of Piety* (Princeton: Princeton University Press, 2004), 18.

16 Anna C. Korteweg, pursuing the distinction Mahmood identifies between "agency as resistance" and "embedded agency," construes agency as "potentially embedded in social forces like religion, which are typically construed as limiting agentic behavior" (Anna C. Korteweg, "The Sharia Debate in Ontario: Gender, Islam, and Representations of Women's Agency," *Gender & Society* 22, no. 4 [2008]: 437). Further, Korteweg identifies how our mis-recognition of women's agency, apparent in "policy approaches to wearing the veil, arranged marriages, and honor-related violence," negatively affects women's capacity to act (450).

17 I use this general term to refer broadly to the various forms of self-covering often used by women who identify as Muslim.

18 Marnia Lazreg, *Questioning the Veil: Open Letters to Muslim Women* (Princeton: Princeton University Press, 2009), 10.

19 Karen Armstrong, "My Years in a Habit Taught Me the Paradox of Veiling," *Guardian*, 26 October 2006. She adds that "the unfolding tragedy of the Middle East has convinced some that the west is bent on the destruction of Islam. The demand that they abandon the veil will exacerbate these fears, and make some women cling more fiercely to the garment that now symbolizes their resistance to oppression."

20 Leila Ahmed, "Veil of Ignorance," *Foreign Policy*, May/June 2011, 40–3.

21 Natasha Bakht, "Veiled Objections: Facing Public Opposition to the Niqab," in *Reasonable Accommodation: Managing Religious Diversity*, ed. Lori Beaman (Vancouver: University of British Columbia Press, 2012), 2–4.

22 The test is constituted by four questions: (1) Would requiring the witness to remove the niqab while testifying interfere with her religious freedom? (2) Would permitting the witness to wear the niqab while testifying create a serious risk to trial fairness? (3) Is there a way to accommodate both rights and avoid the conflict between them? (4) If no accommodation is possible, do the salutary effects of requiring the witness to remove the niqab outweigh the deleterious effects of doing so? "N.S. v. E. (SCC) (Judgment December 20, 2012)," news release, Women's Education and Action Fund, 21 December 2012, http://www.leaf.ca/r-v-n-s-scc/.

23 Ibid. The accused in the case are the complainant's uncle and cousin. A preliminary inquiry judge in the Ontario Court of Justice initially demanded that the complainant remove her niqab, but that decision was appealed. LEAF has claimed that one must be careful not to "re-victimize sexual assault complainants and reinforce their inequality," and one must be wary of "demeanour evidence," since, while highly problematic even in most cases, it is even more so in a case that involves a woman whose demeanour is never made public. According to its self-description, LEAF works to ensure that Canadian courts provide the equality rights that Section 15 of the Canadian Charter guarantees to women and girls ("About LEAF," Women's Legal Education and Action Fund, http://www.leaf.ca/about-leaf/).

24 "N.S. v. E. (SCC)."

25 Fred Pfeil, "No Basta Teorizar: In-Difference to Solidarity in Contemporary Fiction, Theory, and Practice," in *Scattered Hegemonies: Postmodernity and Transnational Feminist Practices*, ed. Interpal Grewal and Caren Kaplan (Minneapolis, MN: Regents of the University of Minnesota, 1994), 222. As Rosi Braidotti writes, similarly, it would be to conduct "a lucid analysis of one's own national roots, of one's own inscription in the network of power and signification that makes up one's own culture" (Rosi Braidotti, "The Exile, the Nomad, and the Migrant: Reflections on International Feminism Revisited," *Women's Studies International Forum* 15 [1992]: 7–10; cited in Uma Narayan, *Dislocating Cultures: Identities, Traditions, and Third World Feminism* [New York: Routledge, 1997], 32).

26 Aihwa Ong calls the attention of Western feminists to the specific standards by which they judge non-Western women, challenging the way in which "the status of non-Western women is analyzed and gauged according to a set of legal, political and social benchmarks that Western feminists consider critical in achieving a power balance between men and women" (Aihwa Ong, "Colonialism and Modernity: Feminist Re-presentations of Women in Non-Western Societies," *Inscriptions* 3–4 [1988]: 82). Anouar Majid identifies the way in which the discourses of Western feminism have been "largely shaped by gender relations in Christian capitalist cultures and by the exhausted paradigms of Western social thought," and this particular shaping has "hindered a more subtle appreciation of women's issues under Islam" (Anouar Majid, "The Politics of Feminism in Islam," *Signs: Journal of Women in Culture and Society* 23, no. 2 [1998]: 321–2).

27 Majid argues that "European hostility and orientalism, then, fundamentalize Islam into a defensive orthodoxy and largely dictate

the cultural agenda of the Muslim peoples ... The process of Western hegemony stimulates reactionary tendencies within Islamic cultures and delays women's emancipation from the clutches of clerical Islam" (Majid, "Politics of Feminism," 338). Similarly, François Burgat claims that "the social status of women constitutes one of the terrains in which the invasion of Western reference has disturbed the dynamic of the internal normative evolution of the universe of Islam" (François Burgat, *The Islamic Movement in North Africa*, trans. William Dowell [Austin: University of North Texas, 1993], 104).

28 As Hegel writes, "Conscience knows that it has to choose between and make a decision about [a multiplicity of *duties*]" (Hegel, *Phenomenology*, §643).

29 Ludwig Siep offers an elegant analysis of the way in which the claims of ethical life and the claims of conscience can be enacted simultaneously, in "Practical Reason and Spirit in Hegel's *Phenomenology of Spirit*," in *Hegel's* Phenomenology of Spirit*: A Critical Guide*, ed. Dean Moyar and Michael Quante, 173–91 (Cambridge: Cambridge University Press, 2008).

30 To acknowledge this point is to recognize that there are resources for cultural transformation and critique internal to every tradition, available simply in their incapacity to sustain themselves without the singular action and judgment of their members. Norani Othman says, for instance, that contemporary Muslims "have attempted to demonstrate that a human rights culture comes from the *Qur'an* and the teachings of the Prophet Muhammad" (Norani Othman, "Grounding Human Rights Arguments in Non-Western Culture," in *The East Asian Challenge for Human Rights*, ed. Joanne R. Bauer and Daniel A. Bell [Cambridge: Cambridge University Press, 1999], 170–17). In another example, Janice Boddy explores how a woman's *zar* cult in northern Sudan develops a sense of agency that is consistent with their belonging to a specific tradition but also assertive of their agency. The healing cult is largely female and uses Islamic idioms, and, in a society in which the practice of Islam is largely dominated by men, it allows for a certain kind of religious and social agency for women; they have the opportunity "to assert their value both collectively, through the ceremonies they organize and stage, and individually, in the context of their marriages, so insisting on their dynamic complementarity with men" (Janice Boddy, *Wombs and Alien Spirits: Women, Men, and the Zar Cult in Northern Sudan* [Madison, WI: University of Wisconsin Press, 1989], 345).

31 See Hegel, *Phenomenology*, §§464–76.

32 As John Russon rightly identifies in his contribution to this volume, the theme of the importance of conscience in the context of Hegel's *Phenomenology* has especially defined the work of Canadian scholars

of Hegel. For excellent discussions of Hegel's concept of conscience, see George di Giovanni in this volume; H.S. Harris, *Hegel's Ladder II: The Odyssey of Spirit* (Indianapolis: Hackett Publishing, 1997), 457–520; John Russon, "Selfhood, Conscience, and Dialectic," in *Reading Hegel's* Phenomenology, 157–68; J.M. Bernstein, "Confession and Forgiveness: Hegel's Poetics of Action," in *Beyond Representation: Philosophy and Poetic Imagination*, ed. Richard Eldridge, 34–65 (Cambridge: Cambridge University Press, 1996); Bernstein, "Conscience and Transgression: The Persistence of Misrecognition," *Bulletin of the Hegel Society of Great Britain* 29 (Spring/Summer 1994): 55–70.

33 Narayan, *Dislocating Cultures*, x.

34 Ibid., 8.

35 Haideh Moghissi identifies the absence of this "owning up" when she identifies the way in which "appeals to those in Washington and elsewhere to respond coherently to Islamic regimes' human rights violations seem gravely naïve," since the issue of "the treatment of women by fundamentalist regimes ... is often used ideologically to isolate and contain adversaries of great powers. It is never raised in connection with the region's oil-producing collaborators in the Arabian Peninsula ... [G]iven the recurrent Islamophobia of media and governments in the West and the growing arsenal of racist imagery about Islam and Muslim women, targeting diasporic communities, writing critically about Islamic gendered practices and the devastating impact on women of Islamic fundamentalism forces upon one a great deal of personal and political anguish and self-doubt. The question is always whose interests are being served, and whose side one is taking" (Haideh Moghissi, *Feminism and Islamic Fundamentalism* [London: Zed Books, 1999], 3–4).

36 For a discussion of this kind of conscientious interaction, see Charles Taylor, "Ethnocentricity and Understanding," in *Philosophy and the Human Sciences: The Collected Papers of Charles Taylor*, 116–33 (Cambridge: Cambridge University Press, 1985).

37 Fred Pfeil argues that the values asserted to be universal "must be always held in a global-local tension with the cultural particularities – discursive and institutional – they encounter in any specific situation ... But the construction and continuance of that tension do require something more than a disengaged appreciation of the other's sheer, nonnegotiable difference from one's own; it requires the active *engagement with others* over and through those differences as well" (Pfeil, "No Basta Teorizar," 225).

38 In his contribution to this volume, di Giovanni emphasizes the centrality in Hegel of the situation of confession and forgiveness, and also the

authority of the humanly constituted situation as opposed to "the way things are" or, as he writes, "'History' capitalized":

> The significance in Hegel of the "beautiful soul" ... is that this fact, that violence is endemic to the human situation, is explicitly recognized. Such individuals can therefore consciously undertake (east of Eden) the task of creating a society based, not on any utopian ideal of perfect harmony, but on the reconciliation that comes from confession and forgiveness ... The beginning of reconciliation, the "melting of the hard heart," occurs only when the one recognizes the truth of the theoretical judgment and, while continuing to act, asks forgiveness for the violence that inevitably attaches to his deeds, and the other recognizes the constraints of actions and, without abdicating the privilege of theoretical judgment, reserves any moral indictment to the judgment of history. When I say "history" here, I do not mean the object of any grand theory – "History" capitalized, so to speak – but the concrete situation that given actions will immediately create.

39 Majid, "Politics of Feminism," 347.

40 Mahmood Monshipouri, "Islamic Thinking and the Internationalization of Human Rights," *Muslim World* 84, nos 3–4 (1994): 237; cited in Majid, "Politics of Feminism," 348.

41 Majid, "Politics of Feminism," 341–2, citing Burgat, *Islamic Movement in North Africa*.

42 Karl Marx and Frederick Engels, *The Holy Family*, trans. Richard Dixon and Clement Dutts (Moscow, 1956), 157; cited in Majid, "Politics of Feminism," 346.

43 Korteweg provides a concrete example of how such sharing interaction would be better pursued. She criticizes the way in which the newspapers conducted themselves in the context of the debate around sharia law in Ontario, saying that they told readers "little of what happens in the daily lives of Muslim women who do not actively participate in public debate." She adds,

> Further research needs to examine the ways devout Muslim women negotiate their lives in the intersections of Canadian (and other states') legal practices and their (communities') interpretations of religious dictates. This research should seek out these women to understand their perspectives and desires with respect to living a life in accordance with religious practice within multi-dimensional social and political contexts.

Here, understanding religion and other social forces as intersecting in dynamic ways will help us move towards a *fuller understanding of how agency is embedded in religious and other contexts*. Such research can and should occur in any immigrant-receiving nation-states that grapple with religious and other culturally informed differences. What the media could have done but did not do was try to get a sense of the experience of trying to sustain and develop a coherent sense of self in a foreign context that continually peppers Muslim women with conflicting demands, a consequence of which could have been an increase in support of these women – of their perspectives and hence their agency. (Korteweg, "Sharia Debate," 450)

44 Ibid., 436.

45 Ibid.

46 Ministry of the Attorney General of Ontario, "Dispute Resolution in Family Law: Protecting Choice, Promoting Inclusion," prepared by Marion Boyd (December 2004), 133. Boyd has held the positions of attorney general for the Province of Ontario, minister responsible for women's issues in the provincial Parliament, and executive director of the Battered Women's Advocacy Centre in London, Ontario, among others.

47 Ontario Premier Dalton McGuinty's choice of date for an announcement seems inimical to such dialogue, that date being so widely associated with the events of 2001 in New York City. This choice, whether or not it was intentional, invoked the stereotypes of a victimized West and a barbaric Muslim incapable of meaningful interaction.

48 Benjamin L. Berger, "Belonging to Law: Religious Difference and the Conditions of Civic Inclusion," *Social & Legal Studies* 24, no. 1 (2015): 47–63.

49 Pfeil, "No Basta Teorizar," 222–3.

17 Conclusion: Canada and the Unity of Opposites?

NEIL G. ROBERTSON

Reading through this collection of chapters on Hegel and Canada makes clear and compelling just how fundamental that relation is. On the face of it, such a relation seems improbable, and while recent books (many by contributors to this volume) have attested to the importance of the Canada-Hegel connection, it nevertheless remains a minority interest. It would, of course, be more natural, as scholars have done, to turn to the two founding "nations" to look for the intellectual basis of Canada: to Burke and Locke, to Montesquieu and Rousseau. While much significant work has been done – perhaps most notably by Janet Ajzenstat – in recovering such intellectual sources, especially through the debates surrounding Confederation, there remains the feeling of something being forced about such an exercise. Canada, in contrast to the United States, has been remarkably unreflective in its political culture. The American sense is that its founding was not only a political event but also an intellectual event: realizing in the New World ideals made known first through philosophical reflection of forerunners such as Locke and Montesquieu, but these in turn were innovated upon and given new significance in the context of trying to realize a federal republic and democracy. Americans look upon their founding as a primal event whose basic documents – the *Declaration of Independence* and the Constitution (perhaps especially the Bill of Rights) – remain forever true and directly inspiring. Canada's Constitution remains better lived than known; perhaps those words *Law, order, and good government* remain alone words known beyond the confines of constitutional law experts. Much of the reflection on the Canadian Constitution has been more about its plumbing than its principles.

All of this makes the Hegel-Canada connection all the more improbable. However, some of the mystery is dispelled by recalling that while it might be natural to turn to British and French intellectual traditions to explain the confederation that joined these two peoples in the common work of a new country, in fact, as a number of the authors of this collection have noted, in both Britain and France their native intellectual traditions had been substantially altered or at least inflected by the neo-idealist revival of the latter part of the nineteenth and early twentieth centuries. So when Canada was forming itself as a country and coming to determine its constitutional order, it was in the context of neo-idealism in both Britain and in North America, as well. As David MacGregor, Elizabeth Trott, and Robert Sibley have all demonstrated, Canada's intellectual and constitutional formation was shaped in very definite ways – especially through John Watson and Lord Haldane – by this neo-Idealism and, specifically, neo-Hegelianism. By this circuitous route Hegel, or at least Hegelianism, has had a surprising but still important role in shaping the country.

The Hegel-Canada connection really has two components. The first is the causal claim that Hegel or Hegelianism had a crucial role in forming the development of Canadian constitutional principles, especially through its influence upon the judicial interpretation of the Constitution. However, beyond this causal claim, there is a hermeneutical connection. While this approach can point to the causal connection as an affirmation, the hermeneutical connection is more wide-ranging. It relies on a certain resonance between Hegel's philosophy and the character of Canada as a political and ethical order. It is important to see two sides to this connection. On the one hand, there has been a disproportionate presence of extremely fine Hegel scholarship among Canadian scholars, perhaps as especially demonstrated by our five icons: Fackenheim, Doull, Grant, Harris, and Taylor. But of course the extent of Hegel scholarship is considerably greater than this, as we move into the next generation of scholars, many students of these five and a number of the contributors to this volume. In this astonishing flourishing of Hegel scholarship in Canada, not only has there been fundamental historical and translation work, but there has also been powerful readings of Hegel as a figure of still deeply contemporary interest in matters moral, social, political, and religious, as well in some of the most basic questions of philosophy. All of the five "Hegelians" this volume focuses on have done the work of bringing out what is still living in Hegel today. All of this points to the observation that the Canadian context is somehow amenable to both an interest in Hegel and a capacity to enter into his position in fruitful and significant ways.

The other aspect of the Hegel-Canada connection captured by this hermeneutical approach is that Hegel is turned to by Canadian intellectuals as a uniquely useful figure in interpreting and understanding Canada. It is this aspect of the Hegel-Canada connection that I wish to especially turn to in this conclusion. In what ways does Hegel uniquely allow us to gain insight into Canada and why? The latter question arises from the perception that the causal connection takes one only so far – it points to some important aspects of what constitutes Canada, but these are largely modifications and developments, not the fundamental being of the country. So why should Hegel of all people be particularly helpful in grasping the spirit of Canada?

As a number of the contributors of this volume have brought out, Canadian intellectuals have turned to Hegel as a uniquely valuable resource for Canada to overcome its remarkable inarticulacy about its own self-understanding: made most depressingly evident in the endlessness of the search for a Canadian identity. As a nation founded by the act of the legislature of another country, consisting of two different nationalities in the context of both a prior Aboriginal presence and a future of immigration informed by a principle of multiculturalism, it is difficult to say what this country is about at the level of nationality or self-determination. This is a country informed by a sense of new world freedom and a sense of loyalty to older and received institutions. A country where there is a federation that is complicated by both regionalism and a province bearing the substance of a "distinct society." It is a country beset not only by the "Quebec" question, but also Western alienation, Maritime resentment, and what Barry Cooper sees as the defeatism of Laurentian Canada. It is a country that has had to absorb and be transformed by substantial immigration from all over the world, while at the same time being drawn more deeply into the play of the forces of globalization. Yet it is a country with a strong sense of social solidarity. So what is most evident in Canada is the role of unfulfilled difference, but then it is hard to determine how there is to be a unity to those differences. While the parts seem to be the truth of the country, it surely it cannot exist as a country only through a certain inertia. Canada seems to be neither the enlightened society of free individuals of the United States, nor simply a European social democracy informed by a charter of social democratic rights. Yet it is all of these things. What this volume points to very effectively is the role Hegel plays, especially through the work of our five figures, in providing access to a way to think all this – not simply receive it as a set of historical givens.

It has been a tendency in Canada to see the country as held together by a certain passivity, an acceptance of it as an externally derived set of facts. Then this would be a country of situated unfreedom. But by contrast, to respond to these facts of Canada by trying to make Canada a work of self-consciously willed principles, in the spirit of the American founding, seems false and potentially self-destructive. The long history of constitutional frustration testifies to the incapacity of Canadians to give to their country the form of a willed reality. Even the Charter, while broadly accepted in Canada, has in relation to Quebec still some of the marks of Cain upon it. The claim of this volume is that it is Hegel who provides a way to think this strange combination of passive and active, of received history and willed freedom, as not simply opposed standpoints, but as belonging as aspects to the very character of a Canadian freedom. While Hegel said essentially nothing about Canada, his philosophical standpoint gives us unique access to what characterizes our state.

The readings of Hegel in this volume are not without differences in emphasis on any number of points, but perhaps especially striking is the distinction, made already in the chapter by Jim Vernon, between Hegel as a source of situated or communitarian freedom and Hegel as the source of a universal or transcendental freedom. In the thought of Charles Taylor we can see the stance of communitarian freedom in Hegel being most forcefully argued for. But such a reading is also there in this book's chapters by John Russon and Shannon Hoff. This reading of Hegel as informed by a sense of situated freedom undoubtedly gains strength from the crucial role of *Sittlichkeit* in Hegel's political thought, which, in turn, ties in with his notable critiques of contract theories of the state and Kantian morality. We find ourselves as members of an ethical institutional order that makes actual and concrete our self-activity as moderns.

However, against this reading of Hegel one can point to others that see in Hegel the standpoint of a universal and ideal revolutionary humanity, as perhaps especially found in the account of Alexandre Kojève, seen as compelling by Barry Cooper.[1] Here Hegel is seen to be the advocate of a standpoint of universal recognition that transcends and dissolves all local ethical forms. This Hegel is a radical historicist who sees in the dialectical work of history the dissolution of all situations give way to more and more complete forms of modern freedom.

What I want to suggest in this conclusion is that both of these sides are right and both belong within a Hegelian standpoint and indeed within the truth of Canada. To make this point I need to make a detour through some recent moments in political theory. The terms of this debate about how to read Hegel – situated freedom or universal humanism – parallel the terms of the debates that in many ways still inform contemporary political theory. The most obvious instance is the liberal-communitarian debate that began in the 1980s as the criticism of Rawls's *Theory of Justice* moved from the libertarian critique of Nozick to the so-called communitarian critiques of Michael Sandel, Alisdair MacIntyre, and, of course, Charles Taylor.

The original terms of that debate were apparently between two different "metaphysical" or ontological conceptions of the self. Is the self primarily a being of unsituated recognition and choice, as captured by Rawls's "veil of ignorance," or is the self ineluctably situated and possible only as constituted by a community of finite and determinate relations? Michael Sandel's *Liberalism and the Limits of Justice* was, perhaps, the most articulate exposition of the terms of the debate in this form.

What is of interest is that the debate moved beyond this form. First Rawls argued his account was not "metaphysical," but rather "political": it was not making ontological claims about the self, but rather advocating for a neutral stance from which to develop a political reason capable of constructing an "overlapping consensus." The stance invoked here was explicitly connected to that of an American Supreme Court judge. In a curious and interesting contrast, Michael Sandel responded with the claim that the privileged locus was not to be found in the American Supreme Court but in the Congress and various more local forms (state and municipal) of legislative self-governance. Sandel in *Democracy's Discontents* criticized the rise of Supreme Court activism that Rawls justified, not so much because of its corrosion of religion or an older America, but because it led to the disengagement of Americans from their legislatures as a place of communal self-governance. Sandel in more recent work continues to worry about the corrosions of the principles and virtues of self-governance as the principle of the market informs all aspects of American life. This is, of course, the trajectory of the American debate, which, even as it became more political and, indeed, institutional in its approach, remained a debate. In Canada, in figures such as Charles Taylor, coming from the communitarian side, and Will Kymlicka, from the liberal side, the movement has been to in fact argue for the unity of the two sides: Taylor presenting a communitarianism inclusive of liberal freedom; Kymlicka advocating a liberalism that supports and sustains community.

The opposition between universal revolutionary freedom and situated finite freedom has its source in the debates that took place among the young Hegelians in the 1830s and 1840s: one need think only of the opposition of Feuerbach and Marx on one side and Max Stirner and Kierkegaard on the other. Here the corpse of Hegel's thought is divided into opposed moments that came into forms of radical opposition as the basis of their unity was lost sight of throughout the nineteenth and twentieth centuries. What is noteworthy in the liberal-communitarian debate is the turn to the political and the institutional. When the liberal-communitarian debate turns to the form of privileging one or more aspects of the constitutional order, it is, I want to argue, in fact invoking that constitutional order as the ground or reality of its contrasting claims. Here we see a basis for recovering the unity of the two sides.

So I do want to suggest there is real disagreement in this book about how to interpret Hegel. These differences are present not only in the contributors, but also in our subjects: our five Canadian "Hegelians," as a number of the chapters have made compellingly clear.[2] Along with these opposed readings of Hegel are corresponding opposed readings of Canada. However, beyond these oppositions – Canada as liberal versus Canada as communitarian – I also want to suggest that the turning to Hegel to establish this very contrast points to an intuition, a Hegelian intuition, that sees these accounts not as opposed, simply, but as complementary in their very opposition – a unity of opposites, to cite our volume's subtitle.

Here I want to go on a very specific digression: in 1776 the future founder of the University of King's College, Charles Inglis, published a tract in opposition to Thomas Paine's *Common Sense*.[3] This work has only recently been republished.[4] In this short text, Inglis took up in opposition to Paine's enlightened republicanism that saw government as at best a necessary evil, the standpoint of what Inglis called "constitutional liberty." Inglis was a Loyalist, but he was not a Tory – at least not in the English sense of that term. He was a Whig: a supporter of the Glorious Revolution, an advocate of Locke and above all of Montesquieu. His argument with Paine was that Paine was betraying the principles and institutional basis of the Glorious Revolution. How so? What he argued for was the preservation of the English Constitution as a work of both history and prudence accomplished beyond the capacity of any artifice, no matter how enlightened. Paine, essentially seeing no truth in the complex history and institutional order of the English constitution, reduced political life to abstract moral individuals, and in doing so both liberty and order were dissolved, according to Inglis; the American Revolution would lead on such principles not to liberty, but to tyranny. Liberty for Inglis is inherently "constitutional." It is to this principle of "constitutional liberty" that I wish to turn as really the truth underlying the Hegel-Canada connection that this volume is dedicated to considering.

The liberal-communitarian debate taken as a whole in its history and development has pointed us to the constitutional order. When looked at as a debate, as requiring the two sides in their opposition, it reveals the totality of the constitution as the truth of the debate: not simply the legislature nor simply the Supreme Court, nor the executive. For Americans this unity remains hidden under the more explicit moments of opposition. What Inglis pointed to in 1776, in contrast to Paine and has somewhat inarticulately informed the Canadian regime, is this sense of liberty as properly constitutional. What Canada learns from Hegel is how to think unity in difference and difference in unity and that the only effective way to realize this comprehensive standpoint is constitutionally. I would argue that it is in providing his unsurpassed account of constitutional liberty and its deeper sources that Hegel is the improbable best source of Canadian self-understanding.

This is not for a second to deny that certainly Canada's Constitution bears only a partial resemblance to the one outlined in the *Philosophy of Right*. But none of our "Hegelians" – Fackenheim, Doull, Grant, Harris, or Taylor – have wanted to simply stay with the standpoint of Hegel's text in a frozen state. Rather, for each of these figures the internal demand of Hegel's thought is that it must take into itself and raise to speculative truth the movement of Spirit in history. The consequences of this cataclysmic history for Spirit since Hegel's time has been differently judged by each of our Hegelians. A number of the chapters in this book have explored just these differences, and the way they inform our capacity or incapacity to settle into institutional forms and the Canadian constitutional order in particular. Still, what I am arguing is that Hegel's thought – in seeking to unite ancient and modern, situated and unsituated freedom, religion and secularity, not in spite of, but in and through their oppositions – gives us access to a unique form of thinking in which Canada in its differences and oppositions can be known.

So I want to argue that Canada is a state that is made especially knowable through certain unique features of the Hegelian philosophy; bizarrely this German philosopher alone can explain us to ourselves. Pascal said of original sin, "Without this most incomprehensible of all mysteries we are incomprehensible to ourselves," so we might say of this strange phenomenon of Canadian Hegelianism, without it we are incomprehensible to ourselves. Yet even within this account there is something false here – so much of Canadian life fails to rise to the full promise of its Hegelian interpretation. No philosophy can guarantee the actuality of the Canadian state; only its own development can fully bring this about and so unite freedom and history to make of this country a living whole. There is still in the Canadian spirit a certain passivity and fear of activity: as if trying to settle our lived differences in a fully realized and alive constitutional order may bring that order to a crashing halt. So we tend to remain at a pragmatic level, in much of our political life, living together and yet in among real but unresolved, unreconciled differences. And thus, the question mark remains in the title: *Hegel and Canada: Unity of Opposites?*

NOTES

1 The accounts in this volume provided by Robert Sibley that argue for a connection between the Hegelian influences on Canada and a tendency towards imperialism and historicism are providing a similar universalizing reading of Hegel.

2 It is obviously problematic to use this term for the five central figures of our book. Grant would entirely repudiate it and both Taylor and Fackenheim would resist such a simple identification. Perhaps, in spite of their different readings of Hegel, only Harris and Doull would be comfortable with the term. Yet, even Grant, as a number of our contributors have argued, is still informed by Hegel, even in and through his repudiation of his thought.

3 Charles Inglis, *The True Interest of America Impartially Stated* (Philadelphia: James Humphreys, 1776).

4 See Gordon S. Wood, ed., *The American Revolution: Writings from the Pamphlet Debate, Volume II: 1773–1776* (New York: The Library of America, 2015), 707–70.

Contributors

Daniel Brandes is assistant professor of humanities at the University of King's College, the past director of the Foundation Year Programme, and the author of numerous articles on Jewish thought and the character of evil.

John Burbidge is professor emeritus in philosophy at Trent University and the author of numerous works including *Historical Dictionary of Hegelian Philosophy* (Scarecrow, 2008), *The Logic of Hegel's Logic: An Introduction* (Broadview, 2006), *Hegel's Systematic Contingency* (Palgrave Macmillan), and *Hegel on Logic and Religion* (SUNY, 1992). Professor Burbidge is a past president of the Hegel Society of America and has received Trent University's Distinguished Research Award, is a fellow of the Royal Society of Canada, and was elected honorary president of the Hegel Society of Great Britain in 2008.

Barry Cooper, FRSC, is a professor of political science at the University of Calgary and the author of over 170 articles and 30 books, including *The End of History: An Essay on Modern Hegelianism* (1984) and *Consciousness and Politics: From Analysis to Meditation in the Late Work of Eric Voegelin* (2017).

George di Giovanni is a professor of philosophy at McGill University and the author of numerous studies and collections, including *Georg Wilhelm Friedrich Hegel: The Science of Logic* (Cambridge University Press, 2010) and *Freedom and Religion in Kant and His Immediate Successors: The Vocation of Humankind, 1774–1800* (Cambridge University Press, 2005).

Susan M. Dodd is an associate professor in the Foundation Year Programme at the University of King's College and is the author of *The Ocean Ranger: Remaking the Promise of Oil* (Fernwood, 2012), and a co-editor of *Each Book a Drum: Celebrating Ten Years of Halifax Humanities* (Halifax Humanities Society, 2015).

Shannon Hoff is an assistant professor of philosophy at Memorial University of Newfoundland. She is the author of *The Laws of the Spirit: A Hegelian Theory of Justice*, as well as numerous articles on Hegel and in political and feminist thought.

Kenneth Kierans is assistant professor of humanities at the University of King's College in Halifax where he teaches in the Foundation Year Programme and the Contemporary Studies Program and is the author of numerous articles in the history of thought, including "The Concept of Ethical Life in Hegel's Philosophy," *History of Political Thought* 13, no. 3 (1992): 418–35.

David MacGregor is professor of sociology at King's University College at the University of Western Ontario and the author of numerous books on Hegel and Marx, including *Hegel, Marx and the English State* (Westview, 1992).

Graeme Nicholson is professor emeritus in the Department and Centre for the Study of Religion at the University of Toronto and the author of numerous works, and co-editor (with Louis Greenspan) of *Fackenheim: German Philosophy and Jewish Thought* (University of Toronto Press, 1992).

Neil G. Robertson is an associate professor of the humanities at the University of King's College in Halifax. Dr Robertson has served as director of the Foundation Year Programme and the Early Modern Studies Program. He is the co-editor (with David Peddle) of *Philosophy and Freedom: The Legacy of James Doull*, and (with Gordon McOuat and Tom Vinci) of *Descartes and the Modern*, an editor of the journal *Animus*, and the author of numerous articles in the history of political philosophy.

John Russon is a professor of philosophy, University of Guelph, and author of *The Self and Its Body in Hegel's Phenomenology of Spirit* (University of Toronto Press, 1997), *Reading Hegel's Phenomenology* (Indiana

University Press, 2004), and *Infinite Phenomenology* (Northwestern, 2015). He is also the author of *Human Experience: Philosophy, Neurosis and the Elements of Everyday Life* (State University of New York Press, 2003), which was awarded the 2005 Broadview Press/Canadian Philosophical Association Book Prize, and *Bearing Witness to Epiphany: Persons, Things and the Nature of Erotic Life* (State University of New York Press, 2009). His most recent book is *Sites of Exposure: AA, Politics, and the Nature of Experience* (Indiana, 2017).

Robert C. Sibley, an award-winning senior writer for the *Ottawa Citizen* and adjunct research professor at Carleton University, is the author of *Northern Spirits: John Watson, George Grant, and Charles Taylor – Appropriations of Hegelian Political Thought* (McGill-Queen's University Press, 2008) and, most recently, *A Rumour of God: Rekindling Belief in an Age of Disenchantment* (Novalis Publishing, 2010).

Charles Taylor, CC, GOQ, FBA, FRSC, is professor emeritus at McGill University. He is the recipient of numerous awards, including the Kyoto Prize and the Berggruen Prize for Philosophy. His many books include *Hegel* (Cambridge University Press, 1975), *Hegel and Modern Society* (Cambridge University Press, 1979), *Sources of the Self* (Harvard University Press, 1989), and *A Secular Age* (Harvard University Press, 2007).

Elizabeth Trott is professor in philosophy at Ryerson University and the co-author of *The Faces of Reason: An Essay on Philosophy and Literature in English Canada* (Wilfrid Laurier University Press, 1981).

Jim Vernon is associate professor of philosophy at York University and the author of *Hegel's Philosophy of Language* (Continuum Books, 2007).

Index

www.ingramcontent.com/pod-product-compliance
Lightning Source LLC
LaVergne TN
LVHW090146080826
844660LV00013B/696/J

* 9 7 8 1 4 4 2 6 4 4 4 7 2 *